INTERNATIONAL STUDIES

of the

Committee on International Relations
University of Notre Dame

INTERNATIONAL STUDIES

The Russian Revolution and Religion
Translated and Edited by BOLESLAW SZCZESNIAK

What America Stands For
Edited by STEPHEN D. KERTESZ and M. A. FITZSIMONS

Diplomacy in a Changing World
Edited by STEPHEN D. KERTESZ and M. A. FITZSIMONS

Freedom and Reform in Latin America
Edited by FREDRICK B. PIKE

Theoretical Aspects of International Relations
Edited by WILLIAM T. R. FOX

Introduction to Modern Politics
FERDINAND A. HERMENS

Soviet Policy Toward the Baltic States
ALBERT TARULIS

The Representative Republic
FERDINAND A. HERMENS

Catholicism, Nationalism, and Democracy in Argentina
JOHN J. KENNEDY

Why Democracies Fail: A Critical Evaluation of the Causes of Modern
Dictatorship
NORMAN L. STAMPS

Christian Democracy in Western Europe, 1820-1953
MICHAEL P. FOGARTY

The Fate of East Central Europe: Hopes and Failures of American Foreign
Policy
Edited by STEPHEN D. KERTESZ

German Protestants Face the Social Question
WILLIAM O. SHANAHAN

Diplomacy in a Whirlpool: Hungary Between Nazi Germany and Soviet
Russia
STEPHEN D. KERTESZ

Soviet Imperialism: Its Origins and Tactics
Edited by WALDEMAR GURIAN

Pan-Slavism: Its History and Ideology
HANS KOHN

The Foreign Policy of the British Labour Government: 1945-1951
M. A. FITZSIMONS

Bolshevism: An Introduction to Soviet Communism
WALDEMAR GURIAN

Christian Democracy in Italy and France
MARIO EINAUDI and FRANCOIS GOGUEL

The Russian Revolution and Religion

The Russian Revolution and Religion

A COLLECTION OF DOCUMENTS CONCERNING
THE SUPPRESSION OF RELIGION BY THE COMMUNISTS,
1917-1925

With Introductory Essay,
Appendices and a Selective Bibliography

Translated and Edited by

Boleslaw Szczesniak

UNIVERSITY OF NOTRE DAME PRESS • 1959

© 1959, University of Notre Dame Press

Notre Dame, Indiana

Library of Congress Catalog Card Number 58-14180

Preface

Soviet Russia constitutes the most formidable problem of the modern world, in the sphere of politics as well as in economic and cultural relationships. Thousands of books and articles have been written about the Russian Communist Revolution. Still there is a scarcity of published primary sources for the study of the suppression of religion during the revolution, 1917-1925. A collection of such documents, for the most part inaccessible to the Western reader, is one of the most needed reference books. The intention of the present author is, therefore, to publish a set of important documents pertinent to this question, selecting them from archivistic depositories and private collections of significance. In addition to these unpublished documents, the collection includes translations from official or rare Russian publications — such as laws and executive orders of the Bolshevik government and the All-Russian Communist Party; the most interesting articles from the newspapers *Pravda, Izvestiia, Krasnaia Zrezda, Bezbozhnik,* and selections from *Antireligioznik,* and other Communist Russian publications of a pertinent character. Besides such materials, the appendices provide the following: lists of anti-religious laws; lists of deported, tortured or murdered bishops of the Russian Orthodox Church; lists of desecrated relics and bodies of the Orthodox saints; short biographical sketches on some Orthodox and Catholic ecclesiastics; statistical data; and a selective, but substantial, bibliography of the subject. The author worked on the project in many libraries but principally in the Library of Congress, the Harvard Library, the University of Notre Dame Library, the New York Public Library and the University of Chicago Library.

The manuscript documents have been selected from papers of the Department of State in the National Archives, from the papers of the late Fr. Edmund Walsh, S. J., former Papal delegate to Russia, and from the papers of the last Roman Catholic Metropolitan-Administrator in Russia, the Archbishop John Cieplak, now preserved in the Polish Roman Catholic Archives and Library, Chicago. The originals of the documents are in English, French, Latin, Russian, Polish, and Italian. The English documentary translations made by the U.S. Legation in Riga, in 1921-1925, were checked against the Russian originals, corrected, and in many instances translated anew, and all the other translations as well were done by the present author.

The title of this book indicates that all religions of the Russian empire are considered for documentation of their fate during the Revolution of 1917-1925. The Russian Orthodox confession was the official religion in the tsarist empire and, therefore, the principal target of Bolshevik persecution. Other religions, before the revolution, were permitted to exist beyond the established state-church relations. Among these the Roman Catholic Church had the first place along with Protestant sects, Jewish and Mohammedan faiths, Buddhism, Shamanism and other primitive cults. The separatist sects of the Russian Orthodox Church were barely tolerated or entirely proscribed by the tsars.

The leaders of the revolution were primarily concerned with the destruction of the Christian, Jewish and Mohammedan churches. Nationally, the Russian Orthodox Church constituted the most important problem in the anti-religious fight. But the Soviet legislation concerning organized religion, called by the Communists "cults," extended its application to all religions, Christian and non-Christian. The laws were federal, but also separately promulgated by the united republics. The announcements in the official papers, like *Izvestiia* or *Pravda,* were binding upon the operations of the All-Russian Communist Party in every part of the Soviet empire.

Therefore, while the present collection of laws, documents and other materials necessarily places emphasis on the Russian Orthodox and the Roman Catholic churches, the reader will find abundant material and bibliographical items relating to all persecuted religions.

Much could be included in a publication of this nature if it were possible to expand the project into several volumes. One of the difficulties of the work was to decide what should be selected for the book. It was the author's main desire to select documents that would give a comprehensive picture of revolution and religion in Russia during the years of intensive suppression of all "cults."

The difficulty consisted also in the fact that all the documents were not of equal importance. A few are inserted here with the intention of showing the tactics of the militant Communists in the distorting of truth and to indicate the vastness as well as the character of the malice employed in the anti-religious persecutions. For this reason many of the original titles of the translated articles from the Soviet press have been retained. A selection of the official reports sent by the United States representatives abroad has been included. Some of these reports show a lack of knowledge of the canonical character of either the Roman Catholic or the Orthodox Churches [e.g. 34], or religious organizations in general. Others, transmitting erroneous or morbidly hostile accusations against the Vatican [59, 60], are inserted to show the prejudice and false information supplied to the representatives from not always reliable sources. Here are many documents from the Soviet Russian sources filled with accusations against the western nations in trying to defend their revolutionary tactics. For example, in rejecting the English intervention on behalf of the unjustly condemned Catholic priests in March of 1923, the Moscow government claimed that the intervention was designed to cover up the English atrocities supposedly perpetrated against the Irish

[79, 81] or in the colonies. The "liquidation" of the Roman Catholic Church in Russia was represented as a Polish problem [82], Russia trying already at that time to claim from Poland the Belorussian and Ukrainian minorities as Russian "national citizens" by constructing fictious and fantastically exaggerated statistics [92]. The persecution of the Jews was justified by accusing them of being international capitalistic agents [80]; the French bourgeoisie, Catholic Spain, General Smuts, English "compromisers," American capitalists, all were attacked as defenders of religion.

The documents here need no commentaries, as they are clear in their character and contents. The historian will see in the assembled material the implications of inimical ideological forces, vulgar politics, animosities, but above all the abysmal tragedy in revolutionary Russia born of the atheistic persecution of religion.

The documents — besides their value as a collection of unknown or very rare primary sources, for the first time published in English in book form — supply the student of revolution with the most interesting sociological material, pertinent not only to the Russian environment but to the typical behaviour of the Communists wherever they employ their strategy of combating traditional freedom of conscience.

The transliteration from the Russian, Belorussian or Ukranian follows the system of the Library of Congress, with a slight change in transcribing proper names, where diacritical accents denoting Slavonic pronunciation have been omitted. The first names are retained in their original form, like Sergii, Georgii, Antonii, instead of Sergius, George, Anthony, etc.

The author is grateful to the Council for Social Research for their grant-in-aid which helped to cover the expenses of his research work in the American libraries, and to the Ford Foundation whose grant to the University of Notre Dame made possible technical assistance and the acquisition of material for the Soviet and East European Study Center at Notre Dame.

Notre Dame, Indiana   B.S.
July, 1959

ACKNOWLEDGEMENTS

Special thanks are due to Mr. Paul B. Anderson for his permission of reprinting two documents (Nos. 1, 9) from his book *People, Church and State in Modern Russia* (New York, 1944); to the editor of *The Nation*, for two other documents (Nos. 4, 5) from the issue of December, 1918; to the Stanford University Press for a document (No. 24) from their book, *Soviet Russia and the East, 1920-1927* (Stanford, Cal., 1957); to the International Publishers for the Decree on the Land (No. 3), from the book by V. I. Lenin and J. Stalin, *The Russian Revolution* (New York, 1938), pp. 246-247; to the New York Herald (No. 18); to the editor of the *Osservatore Romano* (Nos. 12-17); to the editor of the *Bulletin of the National Catholic Welfare Council*, May, 1923 (No. 74); to the late Rev. Edmund Walsh, S.J., and Rev. Francis Domanski, S.J. (Nos. 53-55, 58).

TABLE OF CONTENTS

Preface

Appendices

Introduction

The Suppression of Religion in Russia, 1917 - 1925

a) THE FALL OF THE RUSSIAN EMPIRE
   AND THE PROBLEMS OF CHURCHES

In February, 1917, the Duma — a peculiar national assembly — convened in an atmosphere of dissatisfaction and popular unrest. A *coup d'état* was expected by most of the Russian people. In the beginning of March, 1917, riots broke out in Petrograd. Troops had joined the agitated street marchers. On March 8, a real revolution took hold of the city. The Duma refused the order of dissolution issued on March 12 by the emperor, remaining in session under the chairmanship of Michael Rodzianko. The radicals stayed under Alexander Kerenskii. On March 14, delegates of workers in Petrograd organized the Soviet of Workers' and Soldiers' Deputies. On March 15, Tsar Nicholas II abdicated.

The Provisional Government under Prince George Lvov assumed its turbulent reign. The energetic Kerenskii, himself a constitutional socialist, became minister of justice and vice-chairman of the executive committee of the Soviet. Other members of the government were moderate liberals.[1] The Provisional Government announced a program embodying all main principles of constitutional liberalism. The United States recognized the government on March 22, 1917.

But the liberal policy of the Provisional Government was necessarily directed against the state-protected Russian Orthodox Church, and the March revolution destroyed the traditional political and ideological structure of the Orthodox Church as well as of the other religions in the Russian empire. The March events led directly to the Communist Russian Revolution. In July, uprisings organized by the Bolsheviks burst out in Petrograd. On July 24 Kerenskii formed a coalition government, which excluded the Bolsheviks. Throughout the next weeks, until the 25th of October, the Bolsheviks grasped

---

1 Cf. Alexander F. Kerensky, *The Catastrophe: Kerensky's Own Story of the Russian Revolution* (New York, 1927), pp. 109-141, and his *The Crucifixion of Liberty* (London, 1934), 258-277. The most comprehensive account is W. H. Chamberlain's *The Russian Revolution, 1917-1921* (2 vols. New York, 1935); see his bibliography at the end of vol. II; L. Trotsky, *The History of the Russian Revolution* (3 vols. New York, 1932); Edward Hallett Carr, *The Bolshevik Revolution, 1917-1923* (2 vols. London, 1950-1952), especially vol. I; Georg Von Rauch, *A History of Soviet Russia,* Trans. by P. and A. Jacobsohn (New York, 1957), and bibliography, pp. 463-476. James Bunyan and H. H. Fisher, *The Bolshevik Revolution, 1917-1918: Documents and Materials* (Stanford, Cal., 1934), see also chronology of the revolution, pp. 687-694.

for power. They obtained it by the vote of the Second All-Russian Congress of Soviets in Petrograd. With the revolutionary tide led by the Communist inspired elements, the Military Revolutionary Committee issued on November 4 accusations against the Provisional Government, and on November 7 the Bolsheviks took the governmental powers into their hands. Thus the November revolutions brought in the Communist government headed by Vladimir Iliich Ulianov, known by his pseudonym Nicholas Lenin (1870-1924).

In this suddenly changed situation of the Russian Orthodox Church, a considerable number of the clergy showed liberal tendencies, supporting the Provisional Government against the tsarist traditionalists. Many of them signed radical resolutions. Chaos permeated the crumpling structure composed of the Orthodox clergy and laity. The prompt action of several clerical and lay members of the Duma provided a convenient organization for reform by establishing in March of 1917 the Council for Affairs of the Orthodox Church. Now, in 1918, there appeared throughout Russia liberal debates, meetings, and delegations to various authorities, all aimed at liberalization of the old church institutions and removal of disliked bishops, or demanding far reaching reforms of the church. Alexander Kerenskii and Prince Lvov, of the Provisional Government, supported the somewhat revolutionary movement of the progressive clergy against the hierarchy. Their attitude was aptly expressed by Bishop Efrem: "Raging in their gatherings and congresses, they greeted with telegrams the lay wreckers of the church (Kerenskii and Lvov) and at the same time with furious wrath threw themselves upon the bearers of church authority — the bishops."[2]

It is impossible to decide which crisis was decisive in the growth of the Russian Revolution. The country had been in a permanent crisis since 1905, with the accumulation of thousands of grievances weakening the moral and material structure of the Russian empire. Rev. E. A. Walsh, a Papal representative in Russia in 1922-1923, observed aptly that "colossal stupidity marked the closing years of the Romanov dynasty and furnished abundant provocation for the first revolution of March 1917."[3] One of the problems precipitating the series of revolutions in 1917 and 1918 was the turbulent situation of relations between the reactionary Russian Orthodox Church and the underpriviledged religions of subjugated nations and persecuted sects. And the problem of religion remained one of the most important in revolutionized Russia. To solve it on the basis of mature justice, the practice of which had existed no more in tsarist Russia than it did under the Bolsheviks,

---

2   Quoted after J. S. Curtiss, *The Russian Church and the Soviet State, 1917-1950* (Boston, 1953), pp. 16-17.
3   Edmund A. Walsh, *Total Power: A Footnote to History* (New York, 1948), p. 158; and very interesting observations on the "anatomy of revolution" in pp. 158-171.

was a task of enormous magnitude. A historian may observe that it belongs to the consistent character of revolution — whether it be the Glorious Revolution in England, the French Revolution or the Russian Revolution — to persecute religion and to suppress its organizational status. All revolutions acquire malicious aspects of religious persecution. But the Communist revolution is the most savage in these aspects.

These revolutionary changes of the old order prompted the convocation of an All Russian Church Council. The Preparatory Assembly for the Sobor of the Russian Church met in June, 1917, and between August 15, 1917, and August 18, 1918, the Sobor was held. The Preparatory Assembly demanded that the church be independent of the state; that its decisions have the force of law; that the actions of its officers be controlled by the state only so far as they bear on the state laws; that the canonical hierarchy and structure of the church be recognized by the state as legal institutions; that the clergy be exempt from military service and other civic duties; that marriage in the Orthodox Church have legal validity if one of the partners be Orthodox; that church decisions on separation or annulling of marriage be recognized as legally valid; that the registration of births by the church be recognized as legally valid; that the state guarantee freedom of conscience and religious propaganda for the Orthodox; that the Orthodox Church feasts, including Sundays, be regarded as days of rest; that the head of the state and the Minister of Confessions be Orthodox; that religious ceremonies during the state holidays be performed by the Orthodox clergy; that religious schools be granted the same rights as the state schools; that religious instruction in the state schools be compulsory; that the church have the rights of a juridical person, and the right of possessing property; that church property be tax-exempt; and that the church be supported by the state subsidies [1, 2].[4]

These demands were in their nature exactly the same as those which the privileged Russian Orthodox Church enjoyed during the tsarist regime. They were acceptable neither to the Provisional Government nor in any way to the Bolsheviks. In effect, the old "church reaction" reasserted in the new political situation its own well acquired prerogatives, rights, and privileges, even demanding now a somewhat better and stronger position in the empire by re-establishment of an independent patriarchate.

On November 5, 1917, the Sobor elected Metropolitan of Moscow Tikhon (Vasilii Ivanovich Belavin, 1865-1925), Patriarch of Moscow and All Russia.[5] The patriarchate abolished by Peter the Great in 1721 returned now in the days of Bolshevik Revolution. The new patriarchate was composed of three bodies: (1) the Patriarch, head of the Russian Church and

---

4   Cfr. Matthew Spinka, *The Church and the Russian Revolution* (New York, 1927), p. 73.

5   Cf. I. M. Adreev, *Kratkii obzor istorii Russkoi tserkvi od revolutsii do nashikh dnei* (Jordanville, N.Y., 1953), pp. 16-27, 37-47.

his chancery, combining also in his office the authority of the Metropolitan of Moscow; (2) the Sacred Synod, with the Patriarch as chairman, consisting of hierarchs elected every third year by the All-Russian Sobor—the Metropolitan of Kiev was a permanent member, while five others were elected; (3) the Highest Church Council, with the Patriarch as chairman, consisting of three hierarchs and one monk, six laymen and five lesser clerics, elected for membership every third year by the All-Russian Sobor.[6]

Two days after the setting of the new organization of the Russian Orthodox Church, still dominant, conservative and powerful, the Bolshevik government under Lenin took hold of the revolution.

The Russian empire was composed of many nationalities with distinctive historical and cultural institutions. National religion was the most important factor which preserved their separateness and constantly enhanced the spirit of independence. The dominant nation, the Russians, confessed Greek Orthodoxy Russianized by long historical development. The Belorussians and Ukrainians, forcibly attached to Russia during the Partitions (1772, 1791, 1795) of the Commonwealth of Poland, had their different independent Orthodox traditions in addition to the Uniate Catholic and Latin Roman confessions. Among them there still existed strong pro-Polish sentiment. Lithuania, and that part of Poland occupied by Russia after the Partitions, were Roman Catholic. These people had the most highly developed culture among the nations of the empire.[7] In the Asiatic lands Islam, Buddhism and Shamanism were confessed by the non-Russian subjugated peoples.

With the religious separatism, nationalistic political dissensions were often associated, directly or indirectly. The Jews, living everywhere in somewhat isolated communities, the Russian sects, the Mohammedans and Buddhists, the Protestants and the Catholics in European Russia, were perhaps the most conscious of their separateness from the Russian Orthodox Church. In the Caucasus, the small nations of ancient Oriental Christianity identified their cultural distinctions with their nationalism. When the revolution came, all these national groups tended to establish their own church organizations together with national independence.

The Provisional Government, as well as those new governments of Belorussia, Ukraine and Caucasia, took the opportunity of the disintegration of the state-supported Russian Orthodox Church to favor complete separation of the churches from the state. Even the Russian Church itself established its independence from the state by electing a patriarch. The Orthodox churches

---

6   James Z. Zatko, *The Destruction of the Catholic Church During the Bolshevik Revolution*, a doctoral dissertation, University of Notre Dame, 1958, pp. 180-200; J. S. Curtiss, *op. cit.*, pp. 15-27.

7   Cf. also M. T. Florinsky, *The End of the Russian Empire* (New Haven, 1937), p. 20. Antoni Okolo-Kulak, *Kosciol w Rosji Dawniej, Obecnie i Przyszlosci* (Cracow, 1928), pp. 6-10.

of Belorussia, Ukraine and Georgia established their autocephaly. But the Russian Church, remaining in its political program traditionally imperialistic, opposed the independence movement of other national churches. For the Bolsheviks, who represented the unity of federated Russia under the domination of Communism, all church organization, or indeed religion itself, was doctrinally inacceptable and politically dangerous. In spite of the decrees on the separation of the church from the state and of the school from the church, the executive provisions drew heavily on pre-revolutionary practices, intensifying the state control over religious organization. But this control tended to ultimate secularization and suppression of religious life, with the substitution of Communist materialistic doctrine and organized atheism.

Before the Revolution the Orthodox Church was a state organization, a large spiritual body of clergy and laymen who practiced traditional loyalty to the tsarist autocracy. The bishops and the clergy were in reality state paid civil servants. They performed their duties for God, tsar, and militant nationalism. They were a powerful force for Russification of annexed countries, the most effective organization in maintaining the control of the throne over the peasants and masses in the provinces of the whole empire where the Russian Orthodox Church was accepted or dominant.

Thus, the established church was completely dependent upon the state. No "loyal subject" of the tsar could leave the Orthodox Russian Church without being punished or persecuted. Those who relinquished their faith were treated as traitors and reconverted by force. The Russian Church was imposed also on the Orthodox faithful who lived in the provinces taken from the Commonwealth of Poland, like Lithuania, Belorussia (White Ruthenia), Ukraine, Padolia, and Volhynia. They felt until the Bolshevik Revolution that they were under an alien church.[8] The same feeling exists today, in all respects, toward the Communist-patronized Patriarch of Moscow.

When the tsar abdicated—or was dethroned—many of the people had a feeling of release from tyranny of all kinds, including the religious. The Russian Orthodox Church lived artifically, as long as the old order with the tsar supported it. But its internal weakness appeared during the revolutionary years in the collapse of the hierarchy, the lower clergy, and the spirit of the laity. As a result of the revolutionary chaos the Russian Orthodox Church suffered in the most tragic way. But the historian must ask what was its position during the last three hundred years of history. M.T. Florynsky, a well recognized authority on Russian history, observed in the most apt way

---

8 A lucid and objective comment on the subordination of the Church to State in Russia a reader may find in N. S. Timasheff's *Religion in Soviet Russia, 1917-1942* (New York, 1942), pp. 4-9, *et seq;* as for the Russian writers, next to Timasheff was P. Miliukov who treated the problem of the Orthodox Russian Church with considerable objectivity; see his "The Church During the Revolution," in the *Outlines of Russian Culture* (3 vols. Philadelphia, Pa., 1942), vol. I, pp. 151-212.

that "the Church can hardly be reckoned among the constructive factors in Russian history . . . it developed an aggressive and intolerant attitude toward other religious denominations, especially toward the Roman Catholic Church, the Reformed Churches, and the Jews. By creating innumerable vexations and futile conflicts with other denominations, the Russian Church undoubtedly made its contribution to those forces which worked for the disintegration of the Empire,"[9] and, we may add, for its own downfall.

(b) The Communist Revolution and Religion, the Revolting Masses, and the First Decrees

The Communist revolution, starting with the arrival of Lenin in St. Petersburg in April, 1917, rapidly abolished the old order and structure of imperial Russia. The Communist leaders around Lenin, hard doctrinists of Marxism, appealed to the blind masses to destroy and to "rob what was robed." The beginning of the "classless society" had to be founded with the abolition of class privileges. The old economic order had to be changed into a new one. The methods of these changes were brutal, inhuman, immoral, and bloody.

The traditional religion of the Russian people, tied to the Orthodox Church, as well as other institutional religions in the empire, Christian and non-Christian, was confronted with unanticipated horror and violence of enmity by the revolutionaries acting in the name of Marxism.

In 1905 Lenin announced that religion is "the opiate of the people. Religion is a kind of spiritual vodka in which the slaves of capital drown their human shape and their claims to any decent human life."[10] In 1909 he reasserted his view by saying that "Marxism is materialism . . . relentlessly hostile to religion. . . We must combat religion—that is the rudiment of all materialism, and consequently of Marxism. . . The fight must be linked up with the concrete practical work of the class movement, which aims at eliminating the social roots of religion."[11] Marxism demanded that the class roots of religion be destroyed together with the class system. The clergy of any established religion were to be annihilated first. In the atheistic state—it was understood— the use of forceful educational and political means can suppress religion in a short time. Then the wheels of the revolution began to roll toward that suppression.

---

9 M. T. Forinsky, *op. cit.*, p. 20 The conservative Count S. J. Witte noted in his memoirs that "the church ministry became a ministry not of the Lord but of the early gods and the Orthodoxy: orthodox paganism," see his *Vospominania* (2 vols. Berlin, 1922), vol. I, p. 116.

10 V. I. Lenin, "Socialism and Religion," *Selected Works* (New York, 1943), vol. XI, p. 658. For Lenin's anti-religious essays, see Bibliography.

11 Idem, "Attitude of Workers' Party Towards Religion," *Selected Works*, vol. XI, p. 666; see also Innocentius M. Bochenski, *Der Sowjetrussische dialektische Materialismus (Diamat)*, Bern, 1950.

The Russian peasant is an ardent Christian for whom the church and the country are identified. His faith was not "Greek Orthodoxy"; it was the "Russian Orthodox Church." Since the time of Tsar Ivan III (1462-1505), for an average Russian his faith was his national confession as well. But it was mostly a primitive blind belief without reasoning, based on the ancient tradition and the externals of liturgical practices which satisfied the religious and cultural needs of his grey life. At the same time, the submissive and obedient *krestianin* (peasant) was disturbed by recurrent reflections upon his poor existence under the tsar and the "official" clergy. What the *muzhik* (another name for peasant) might do if given a "free" choice, and with his undisciplined emotions worked upon by anti-clerical demagogues, was difficult to predict. But the leaders of the Bolshevik Revolution could depend at least upon the universal feeling among the poor masses that nothing worse could happen to them than what they already suffered, and that any change might be a change for the better. The official Russian Church was for many of them an imposed institution under which they lived with an attitude simply of hopeless resignation. It was not difficult to make the peasants see the church as merely another land owner whom they might destroy [106-108]. "Freed from their fetters, the peasants moved irresistibly toward that goal which had been so long denied to them," observed M. Florinsky, about the land hunger among the peasants.[12] Later they found how much they were deceived in their desire for privately owned land.

No other nation has been so self-destructive and self-afflicting as the Russians. And the immense tragedy of the Russian Church in the violent years of the revolution was the principal expression of this suicidal impluse. Before the cooling off time arrived the barbarous destruction was done, and in spite of a subsequent will to restore things which were in ruins, it was impossible in many ways to repair the damage. Trotskii with a terrifying pathos described the characteristics of the peasant revolution: "The movement now (1917-1918) overflows its banks, invades all districts, wipes out local peculiarities, draws in all the strata of the villages, washes away all considerations of law and prudence, becomes aggressive, fierce, furious, a raging thing, arms itself with steel and fire, revolvers and hand grenades, demolishes and burns up the manorial dwellings, drives out the landlords, cleanses the earth and in some places waters it with blood."[13] This wild avalanche invaded churches, monasteries, synagogues, mosques, houses of prayer and all religious property. There can be no doubt that the revolution had deep-rooted causes in the unrest of the Russian masses already so long oppressed, and that it became, however tragically misdirected, a spontaneous, popular movement. Former imperial Minister of the Interior, A.D. Proto-

---

12   M. T. Florinsky, *op. cit.*, p. 256.
13   L. Trotsky, *The History of the Russian Revolution*, vol. III, p. 34.

popov defined the situation in the most expressive words: "The whole of Russia appeared to me like a stormy ocean, and where were the social groups that were satisfied? There were none. Where were the social groups one could trust, that one could depend upon? There were none."[14] Still the Russian peasant remained faithful to his Christianity.

In the beginning of the revolution the Communist regime contrived a legal form for its anti-religious activities, first with the separation of the church from the state and of the school from the church by a law published on January 23, 1918 [6]. The law was particularly hurtful to the Russian Orthodox Church, which was the traditionally faithful instrument of the autocratic state. By this act the clergy lost all its traditional support from the state, economic and political, as well as the protection of functions of the church. The law for an American reader has a neutral if not favorable association with the freedom of religion. But in Russia it meant practically the ruin of the established church, which in a sense was now outlawed. Some legal repercussions were also implied against other religions, especially against the position of the Roman Catholic Church in the empire as based on the previous understandings between the imperial government and the Holy See. The act of separation, as such, was less painful for the minor Russian Orthodox sects and for Protestants, as well as for Jews, Moham- medans, Buddhists and other non-Christian denominations. They had never enjoyed the special protection of the tsarist government and often were officially persecuted or even proscribed. But the act of separation— as we see in the attached documents—opened the way for a series of laws tending to abolish not only the Orthodox Russian Church in all the lands belonging to the Bolshevized Russian empire, but finally all the religions of the realm.[15]

Hence, the revolution from the very beginning deprived the Russian Orthodox Church of all administrative prerogatives and duties in its legal relations to the state. The church was deprived of its courts and authority over marriage and divorce. Its rights pertaining to records, holidays, schools, and compulsory religious instruction were all abolished.[16]

The first serious effect on the economy of the Russian Orthodox Church as well as of other religions in all Russia was the decree on land published on November 8, 1917 [3]. It abolished land ownership.[17] Then on December 31, 1917, came laws introducing civil marriages, registration of civil status,

---

14 Cf. P. E. Shchegolev, *Padanie tsarskago rezhima* (Leningrad, 1925-1927) vol. 1, p. 149, after M. T. Florinsky, *The End of the Russian Empire*, p. 239.

15 For legal details of the church-state relations, see V. Gsovski, *Soviet Civil Law* (2 vols., Ann Arbor, 1948-1949), I, pp. 10-11, *et seq.* This work henceforth will be referred as *Soviet Civil Law*.

16 See also John Shelton Curtiss, *The Russian Church*, pp. 14-19.

17 See *Ivestiia* and *Pravda*, 1917-1918, Nov. 10, 1917.

legal equality of children born out of wedlock with those born in wedlock, divorce law, and civil registration of deaths [4,].[18]

The Orthodox Russian Church and other recognized churches lost their civic rights, privileges and duties in relation to the functions that they had previously performed, now abolished by the law. The entire significance of churches as bodies of public and state service had been abolished. On January 29, 1918, the Commissariat of War issued a decree releasing all clergymen of all denominations from the services of the War Department. At the same time the church funds and property of military units were transferred into the general budget [7].

These laws have been amended, supplemented, and restricted by later legislation of the All-Russian Central Executive Committee—especially those concerning marriage and divorce, on November 19, 1926; and those concerning religious organizations, on April 8, 1929.[19]

But the basic legal decision pertaining to the Orthodox Russian Church and all organized religions had come when the law of separation of the church and the state was passed in January, 1918. This legislation was aimed directly at destruction of the "social roots of religion."

c) THE CONSTITUTIONAL AND LEGISLATIVE MEASURES

The outburst of the Bolshevik Revolution hastened the first decrees pertaining to the relations of church and state. These decrees were issued before the whole legal system based on the new constitution could be organized. The Communist constitution in Russia, as accepted by the Fifth Congress of Soviets on July 10, 1918, is the turning point in the shaping of the anti-religious legal system which gradually like a heavy roller was intended to crush the existing Orthodox Russian Church primarily, and other institutional religions and sects or primitive cults secondarily. It also incorporated the Communist atheistic doctrine as the informing ground of its legal provisions and as the central point of departure for future legal interpretations. The constitution embodied also that most important decree issued on January 23, 1918, [6, 7] on the separation of church and state, and of the educational system from the church. Naturally, it stressed religious freedom, valid so long as it does not conflict with the law. But the subsequent laws and their official interpretations excluded that freedom, assuring freedom for the anti-religious propaganda patronized by the Bolshevik state. Freedom of religion was abolished by the very law which was acting supposedly as a guarantee for its existence.

The most important provisions of the July constitution intending to destroy religion, it should be noted, were those contained in Article 13 and Article 65. The first article recognized the decree of January 23, 1918. It was

---

18   Cf. *R.S.F.S.R. Laws*, text 160 and 153.
19   Cf. *Soviet Civil Law*, vol I, pp. 113-120, and vol. II, pp. 330-335.

promptly interpreted by the instruction [10] issued by the People's Commissariat of Justice on August 24, 1918, leaving no doubt that it refers to all the existing religions in the Soviet Union. Thus a systematic destruction dressed in constitutional and legal forms, in the midst of the revolution started the ruin of the religious institutions, their property, their laws and customs, rights and duties, privileges and traditions. This force of destruction varied in efficiency in different places, and in accordance with the home political situation moved through the years towards its tragic accomplishments [56].

The second, Article 65, was particularly concerned with the secularization of the clergy and all ministers of religion. They were eventually stripped of their rights as citizens, having no privileges of participation in local or state elections, and subsequently denied the freedom to change their religious residence, being forced to remain in the initial place of their duties. Thus, as a result of this article they were outlawed politically and socially, and ruined economically. Their congregations, according to the decisions of April 23, and of April 27, 1923, could not be less than twenty, and later adjusted to fifty, members [87].

Finally, with the liquidations of the religious administration and with the removal of the protection of law as applied to the church organization, or non-profit religious associations, the churches ceased to exist as constructive elements of society or the state.

With these follow the liquidations of all kinds of religious property [28, 32], the prohibition of the public manifestations such as processions [26], gatherings, meetings even for educational purposes; the confiscation from religious bodies of hospitals [97], schools, nurseries, houses of the poor, the closing of all the monasteries, and the denial of teaching religion in schools. What remained before 1925 as saved from these terrific clutches of "laws," "decrees," "instructions," their frequent supplementations and interpretations, was an insignificant or piteous remnant of the pre-revolutionary status. The law became 'the terror' to those who had not resigned from the organized life of religion. But, at the same time, the constitution heralded the freedom of religion in the Soviet Union under the watchword of freedom of conscience.

The perversity of the Constitution of 1918 is revealed in the commentaries of Andrei Y. Vyshinskii in his book, *The Law of the Soviet State.* He asserts that freedom of conscience is expressed in the right of the citizens of the Soviet Union to observe any religion and to "carry out the essential religious ceremonies prescribed by the cult."[20] He does not say that at the same time

---

20 For the legal commentaries and violation of law and rules concerning separation of Church and State, see *Soviet Civil Law,* vol. II, pp. 329-339; the official evasiveness of the above laws could be found in the pamphlet by P. V. Gidulianov, *Otdelenie*

the right of necessary ownership of property for religious functions and ceremonies, and the right of juridical persons [123], were denied to Soviet citizens.[21] Vyshinskii's book is a masterpiece of evasions, especially in the matter of religion, and a militant handbook of Soviet administration. The law prohibits religious propaganda and guarantees freedom of anti-religious propaganda. At the same time the All-Union Communist Party with militant atheism combats religion as inimical to Marxian materialism.[22] The executive order issued on March 23, 1919, for the party fight against religion, illustrates the methods used for the persecution of all religion in Russia [11].

d) PATRIARCH TIKHON, COUNTER-REVOLUTIONARY OPPOSITION AND RELIGIOUS DISCORD

In this strife between Communism and religion the person of Patriarch Tikhon looks most pathetic. In the beginning of his office he answered the attacks on the freedom of the church by the Epistle of January 19, 1918, in which the Communists were denounced for their crimes and solemnly excommunicated [8]. The anathema meant an open war with the leaders of Bolshevism. It tended to arouse the nation and the armed forces against the godless, to unite the Russians through the new supreme Orthodox Church authority for the defense of faith and the old order.

The uncompromising stand of Patriarch Tikhon against the new regime, perhaps, was expressed too early in the revolution. The people at that time more or less willingly accepted the anti-clerical action of the Bolsheviks, especially since the Orthodox clergy had lost ecclesiastical respect because of their old subservience to the tsar's state. The vehement enmity of the patriarch confirmed the already hostile attitude of the Bolshevik regime towards the Russian Orthodox Church and other religions. But the latter were less belligerent in public expressions of their disapproval of the Communist doctrine and practices.

Tikhon's zeal in combating militant atheism had a certain political tint of the old conservative opposition to the revolution. His anathemas appeared once and again in different forms of expression in his effort to save the Orthodox Church. The person of patriarch was a symbol of opposition in the country and abroad, especially among the large Russian political immigration. The Sobor which reconvened in February, 1918, approved Tikhon's message of condemnation of the Communists [9].

The Russian political exiles and *émigrés*, generally in their attitudes and interests conservative or aristocratic, presented an emotionally united, mon-

---

tserkvi ot gosudarstva: Polnyi sbornik dekretov RSFSR i SSSR, instruktsii, tsirkuliarov, it.d., Moscow, 1924 and 1926.

21   Andrei Y. Vyshinsky, *The Law of the Soviet State,* tr. from the Russian by H. W. Babb and J. N. Hazard (New York, 1954), pp. 605-609.

22   Cf. the important and most useful work by W. W. Kulski, *The Soviet Regime: Communism in Practice* (Syracuse, 1954), pp. 259-262.

archist front against the Bolshevik rule in their home country. With them stood the Russian clergy living abroad, among whom were fifteen bishops of importance. They all were united in an idea of overthrowing the Bolshevik regime and restoring the Romanov dynasty. These Russian *émigrés* living abroad were organized in 1921 in three ecclesiastical bodies. The first was the so-called Shremski Karlovatskii Sobor or Council, headed by the former Metropolitan of Kharkov and unsuccessful candidate for patriarch, Antonii Khrapovitskii. His seat was established in Karlovtsi, Yugoslavia, where formerly the patriarch of the Serbs in Hungary resided. The Council and the followers of it were known for their intensely nationalistic, monarchical sentiments and hatred of the Bolsheviks [29]. They organized the Supreme Administration of the Russian Eparchies and Communities Abroad, intending to unite the scattered Russians under ecclesiastical obedience to the Council of Karlovtsi. Their condemnations of the Bolshevik persecutions [21, 22] echoed in the world press throughout 1921-1928.

Next to the Karlovatskii Council, there was Metropolitan Evlogii in Paris, as Western European Eparch created by Patriarch Tikhon in January, 1922. In due time the eparchy was in discord over the question whether it should be united with the Russian Church within the Soviet Union, or outside of it. It was split into two groups headed by two quarreling bishops.

The third eparchy was that in the United States. It also was divided into political factions, those who accepted the Moscow Patriarchate and those who did not. And its influence in recent years has gradually disappeared.[23]

For the Bolshevik regime, especially in 1921-1928, the existence of the organized Russian ecclesiastical centers, having influence all over the world, created a particularly important problem of foreign relations, constantly aggravated by the skillful effort of the "White Russian" political immigrants [35, 93].

After the almost unbearable sufferings inflicted upon the Venerable Patriarch Tikhon, came the series of accusations which led to his imprisonment [92]. The vehement press incriminations of the head of the Russian Orthodox Church dated from the beginning of his elevation to the highest church office. They may be said to constitute a volume of masterpieces of venomous invective reflecting not only on the patriarch but on his church and religion in general. The main charge against Tikhon was that in his very person and office he concentrated the strength of religious opposition to the Communist regime. There were, however, several specified indictments against the patriarch when he was arrested in October, 1922. He was charged by G.P.U. (State Political Administration) as the leader of the opposition

---

23 Cf. J. S. Curtiss, *The Russian Church*, pp. 109-110; M. Spinka, *Christianity Confronts Communism*, pp. 75-77. See also an informative book edited by Guglielmo de Vries, S. J., *Il Christianesimo nell'Unione Sovietica* (Roma, 1948), esp. pp. 39-62.

in Russia to the Communist Revolution, as having treasonable cooperation with the members and Church Council abroad at Sremski Karlovtsi, as inspiring destructive action against the famine relief organized by the Soviets, as criminally responsible for the non-compliance with the laws concerning church property, religious organizations, and public observance of religious practices. The accusations had a vehemence special to the year 1923 when the summit of religious persecution was achieved. But still considerations of internal policy pursued by the young Communist regime and the pressure from various foreign governments [107, 110] forced several postponements of a formal trial of Patriarch Tikhon until at last he was released from prison on June 26, 1923 [119]. The well tried practice of Bolshevik justice made the poor patriarch supposedly voluntarily confess [112] his crimes expressing grief and promising loyalty to the Soviet state [113, 114, 116, 135].

When the patriarch was in prison, an existing deviationist faction in the Russian Church started its reformatory action with the intention to adapt the church to the Soviet rule [117]. This group is know by the name of the Living Church. The possibility of splitting the church from within was a hope of the leaders of the anti-religious war. The patriarch, while being arrested, appointed a man of virtue as his Locum Tenens [31, 36], the Metropolitan Agafangel [Appendix III]. After the deportation of the metropolitan, enormous chaos characterizes the church situation among the Orthodox Russian clergy and laymen [136]. The Soviet press gladly presented this as an additional proof of the untenability of religion, as well as the ridiculousness of its existence [98, 133, 134, 135, 146, 147]. Now the Living Church grasped the reins of the church [44] with the support of the Soviets. They established the new Supreme Church Administration which began removing from church life over one thousand of the most prominent clergymen: priests and deacons, including eighty-four bishops.[24]

Then came the political alignment of the Supreme Church administration with the Bolshevik rule of Russia [89]. Its collaboration with the Bolsheviks was expressed in the convocation of the second All Russian Church Council [90] held between April 29 and May 9, 1923, which inflicted enormous moral destruction upon the followers of the Orthodox Church in addition to the condemnation of Patriarch Tikhon and his All Russian Council [118, 126, 141]. It stripped him of his rank, his monastic status, and excommunicated the Russian clergy and faithful abroad who followed him. Of course, the patriarchal excommunication of the Bolshevik regime together with those who served it was declared null and void. With it came the abolition of the Russian patriarchate together with the declaration that there is in Communist Russia no religious persecution.[25]

---

24 See *Izvestiia*, No. 84, March 27, 1923.
25 Cf. Kirill Zaitsev, *Pravoslavnaia tserkov' v Sovetskoi Rossii* (2 pts., Shanghai, 1947), pp. 134-136.

This council met all the expectations for the time being of the Communist leaders, splitting the unity of the Russian Church at home and even abroad. The church in their view defeated its own existence, a fact most desirable in this war against religion.[26]

While the Bolshevik regime favored the deviationists from the unified patriarchal church, at the same time it ridiculed[144] the querulous groups who accused each other of political machinations and non-Orthodox or non-Christian practices. *Izvestiia* and *Pravda* carried special columns for discussion of church-affairs. The venomous E. Iaroslavskii, long known for his leadership in anti-religious activity, found much space in these and other newspapers for his humiliating sarcasm and biting satire at the expense of religion and the Orthodox in particular [133].

This ridicule was not only a weapon of the Communists in their anti-religious propaganda but also expressed their sincere intellectual attitude [103]. Leo Trotskii, the arch-master of revolution, spoke of the Orthodox religion with supreme contempt in his work, *The History of the Russian Revolution*. He quotes a saying of Prince Lvov that "idiots and scoundrels are sitting in the Holy Synod."[27] He is scandalized by the fact that the Russian ministers during the period of the retreat before the German armies in 1915 "wasted hours in those days discussing such problems as whether to remove or not to remove the bones of the saints from Kiev. The tsar submitted that it was not necessary, since the Germans would not risk touching them, and if they did touch them, so much the worse for Germany. . . This happened not in the epoch of the Crusades, but in the twentieth century when the news of the Russian defeats came over the wireless."[28] This contempt for Orthodox religion by the most brilliant Communist demagogue was shared by all Communist leaders.

e) THE REIGN OF TERROR

It is characteristic of all major revolutions that they reigned by terror, oppression and force. The Russian Communist revolution was particularly terroristic, unabating in its spread of fear constantly maintained not only to break the anti-revolutionary elements, but also to preserve its process through many years afterwards. This tended to educate a new generation of citizens who would fear the Communist practices. This is rule by intimidation. In the sphere of religion the terror possesses special significance, deep penetration to the soul, requiring particularly strong character leading in its opposition to martyrdom. And there in Russia we may count many glorious martyrs in all religions, who died for their beliefs and worship of God. With religion, which is the most noble expression of human dignity, atheistic

---

26 *Ibid.,* p. 164.
27 L. Trotsky, *The History of Russian Revolution,* vol. I, pp. 202-203.
28 *Ibid.,* p. 19.

Communism cannot find a compromise. One of them must disappear. Hence, in the deadly fight against churches or cults, all available weapons were used. Terror, rude propaganda, humiliation of man's natural dignity, unbelievable punishments of the victims of false charges, mass deportations to the Siberian punitive camps, tortures, severe imprisonments by decision of grotesque courts, cruelty and wild animalism mark the years of persecution of religion not only during the revolution but also after it through the Stalin era. There were short lulls of diminished persecution, especially in 1920 when the Bolsheviks waged wars against the remnants of the tsarist armies or during the imperialistic war against Poland.

Parallel to the reign of terror there was the work of special anti-religious propaganda. New publications were founded, in addition to the existing ones, issued by the state publisher Bezbozhnik (The Godless), which was printing such periodicals as *Bezbozhnik, Anti-religioznik (The Anti-Religious)* and others. The fighting Marxian materialism took its directions from Lenin's demand to establish such publications which would serve the purpose of combating anti-revolutionary movements, including religion:

> . . . A newspaper which wants to be an organ of militant materialism, must be a fighting organ, first in the sense of fearless unmasking and persecution of all modern "diplomaed lackeys of the Priesthood," quite regardless of these posing as representatives of the official science, or as volunteers who call themselves "leftist democratic or socialist" publicists. Such a newspaper must be, secondly, an organ of militant atheism.[29]

In this assault on religion, the main aim was to uproot religion from social life, to annihilate it among the peoples of Soviet Russia, to ruin the faith of the young generation and its moral force which opposes the atheistic Marxism.[30] Nevertheless, when in 1921 the persecution of religion came with a new vehemence, it was observed that spiritual movements appeared in several provinces of Russia among the peasants [19, 20, 22], the same peasants who at the beginning of the revolution were decidedly anti-clerical. The intensified anti-religious propaganda affected also the followers of various small religions who now manifested a conspicuous rebirth of faith, perhaps in an attempt at self-preservation. The articles, caricatures, ridicule and "poetry" of the Godless publications in the many languages of the Soviet Union did not meet sympathetic or friendly readers. Among the Orthodox, Patriarch Tikhon grew to an ecclesiastical magnitude which was unprecedented. A resolution of the Russian Church Council Abroad [21], expressing the religious renovation in Russia well declared that "the Russian people in their distress and affliction are returning to the shelter of the Church." Other national cults in the Soviet Union in a similar way united within themselves against the danger of being annihilated.[31]

---

29 Lenin, *Sochinenia* (Moscow, 1950), vol. XXXIII, pp. 203-204.
30 Cf. A. Kischkovsky, *Die sowjetische Religionspolitik*, pp. 46-47.
31 Cfr. N. T. Timasheff, *op. cit*, pp. 27-28, 61-63.

The most severe persecution of religion [40-43, 85] occurred during the years 1922-1924, a drive for annihilation of all the denominations in Soviet Russia.[32] This period is particularly known for the executions and arrests of the clergy of all religions, but especially of the Orthodox and Catholic churches. The public trials of ministers of religion, the violent anti-religious propaganda published in the daily press and in the weekly *Bezbozhnik (The Godless,* founded in 1922), the organized public manifestations against religion, the new wave of deportations of prominent members of churches, lay and clerical, the closing of all the houses of prayer, many of them converted into Communist recreation centers or theaters — all these forms of attack were employed with special vigor during these years. Many of the historical ecclesiastical buildings were destroyed, burned, left in disrepair, or abandoned. The church bells, [120], the old witnesses of the glorious Orthodox ceremonies and devotions, were silenced—the metal confiscated and converted for industrial uses. Atheism was heralded by the Komsomol (Young Communist League) in their organized carnivals before the great feasts like Christmas, Easter, and the Jewish New Year days, or the feasts of the Moslem celebrations in Central Asia.

The action of the government against religions in Soviet Russia is best revealed in the articles published in *Pravda* [98] and *Izvestiia* [95]. The articles are mostly anonymous, but they were supplied by the high officials of the Communist Party. As leaders in this anti-religious propaganda the names of N. Bukharin, E. Preobrazhenskii, P. A. Krasikov, E. E. Iaroslavskii, and A. I. Vvedenskii could be mentioned, along with many others more or less well known to the student of the Russian Revolution. Of these the most virulent was the head of the League of Militant Godless, Iaroslavskii, who with enormous energy and brilliance of demagogical eloquence combatted the "regiment of Jesus." He displayed a persistent inventiveness of method in his work of condemning weakness in anti-religious propaganda, urging children to fight religion in their families, inciting workers to violence against those who maintained religious practices, and organizing all the various activities of the infamous league which he so conspicuously served. He published several pamphlets and many articles fighting religion with atheistic arguments and the materialistic dialectics of Communism (see Bibliography). The vastness of the propaganda was such that in the bibliographies of Communist literature of the revolutionary period of 1917-1925, I found about six thousand pamphlets on anti-religious, materialistic subjects.

The drive was continued long beyond this period. Later, after 1925, the

---

32 For a documentary review of the years of intensive religious persecution, see J. S. Curtiss, *The Russian Church,* pp. 196-215; A. Valentinov, *Chernaia kniga* (Paris, 1925), vol. I, pp. 139-156. For the horror spread by State Prosecutor, N. V. Krylenko, see his *Sudebnye rechi,* 1922-1930 (Moscow, ed. of State Juridical Publications, 1931).

fight against non-Christian religions came to the crisis. But in combatting them the Soviet authorities adopted more moderate tactics. In spite of the fact that the regime realized that the religious feelings of the peasants are deep rooted, and that the Communist Party leaders cautioned the trade unions and party members, the violence against religion was conducted with greatest vigor[33] by Iaroslavskii, who was appointed by Stalin as Trotskii's deputy in the Department of Anti-Religious Propaganda. [34]

f) THE FAMINE AND THE PROBLEMS OF CHURCHES

Wars and revolutions made Russia economically disorganized. The large agrarian holdings, now disintegrated, were either left uncultivated by the new owners, who were poor peasants lacking many of the means for productive agriculture, or they were deserted by the old landlords. The industry, completely ruined, left masses of workers unoccupied. Until 1925 there was no effective organization of the national economy despite the fact that the New Economic Policy (NEP) had existed since 1921. During pre-revolutionary times in Russia there occurred sporadic local famines. But now in 1921-1922 the famine became a genuinely national calamity. Thus it was a problem for the Soviet government as well as for Patriarch Tikhon, who first acted through the church organizations in the way to alleviate the colossal tragedy of the city populace as well as that of the country. But where there was activity with the same purpose performed by the revived religious bodies and the need of official cooperation with them was clear, the situation immediately acquired political significance. In August, 1921, the patriarch desperately appealed[35] for the help of the Pope, the Eastern patriarchs, the Episcopal archbishops of Canterbury and New York, the charitable institutions and the faithful of the Orthodox Church. Later on December 9, 1921, the government's Central Committee for Aid to the Starving (Pomgol) unwillingly established some cooperation with the newly organized church institutions for the help of the famine-afflicted population [25]. On February 23, 1922, a decree was issued with vigorous provisions for confiscation of church treasures and valuables to ease the famine situation. The barbarous manner of the governmental collection of church valuables, according to vast testimony, and this type of destruction inflicted upon the church properties, [37, 38] naturally expressed the official contempt for religion in general [47, 48]. The population in various provinces rioted against the confiscations. As a result of the riots new court trials in Leningrad, Moscow, Smolensk, Kharkov, Kiev, Novgorod, Minsk,

---

33 Edward H. Carr in *The Interregnum: 1923-1924* (London, 1954), did not see religious suppression. His socialistic sympathies turned him rather to the study of political machinery of the Bolshevik government.

34 Cf. L. Trotskii, *Moia zhizn* (2 vols. Berlin, 1930), vol. II, p. 230.

35 K. Zaitsev, *op. cit.*, pp. 91-94, Patriarch Tikhon's epistle.

and other cities, sent to the gallows or jails many of the defenders of church consecrated property [95].[36]

The confiscation of church valuables horrified the faithful and the clergy. Patriarch Tikon, trying to save the consecrated vessels from seizure, agreed to use church valuables not directly involved in the divine service for famine relief. But he was afraid the church valuables would not go to the alleviation of the famine. He tried, therefore, to establish a working plan with foreign philanthropic societies and other famine relief agencies to collect money equal in value to the confiscated church valuables, and by this expedient to save from destruction many historical, artistic and religious objects in possession of the Orthodox churches.[37] The decree on confiscation of church valuables was a blow which afflicted the Catholic Church as well as other religions which possessed valuables of sacred character. The Pope, Benedict XV, cordially responded to the patriarchal request for relief[38] [39]. Prompt organization was set up and fifty train cars with clothing, medicine and food were sent to Russia by December, 1921. Pope Pius XI concluded a special agreement with the Soviet government on the problem of sending a Papal Relief Mission to Russia. The Holy See appealed to the world for help for the Russian people in a letter of April 29, 1922. The Pope was greatly disturbed by the news of the seizure of the church treasures in Russia.[39] The papal undersecretary of state, Monsignor Giuseppe Pizzardo, was authorized to negotiate with the representatives of governments, gathered in the beginning of May, 1922 to debate on the admission of Soviet Russia to the League of Nations. The Holy See proposed three points, which if accepted by the Bolshevik government through the pressure of the League, would prevent the religious tragedy in Russia: (1) freedom of conscience for all citizens or foreigners in Russia; (2) guarantee of public and private exercise of religion; (3) the guarantee of rights of property ownership by the religious confessions and the return of property which was already confiscated. The leaders of the League, Louis Barthan and Lloyd George, did not concur in the Papal efforts. At the same time, the head of the Russian delegation, George Chicherin, behaved as if he would like to negotiate with the Vatican directly[40] [50, 59, 60].

---

36   J. S. Curtiss, entitled eloquently chapter X of his *Russian Church and the Soviet State,* "The Storming of Heaven," in which he described the tragic magnitude of the Communist "drive against religion," pp. 198-216.

37   A long list of statistics of confiscated church treasures is given by A. Valentinov in his *Chernaia kniha,* pp. 269-285.

38   *Osservatore Romano,* December 19-20, 1921.

39   M. M. Sheinman, *Vatikan mezhdu dvuma mirovymi voinami* (Moscow, 1948), maliciously accuses the Holy See of having intentions to help the opposition to take over power in Russia, pp. 36-39.

40   *Osservatore Romano,* May 3, 1922.

In view of the sad status of the persecuted Christian religions during the revolutionary years, and of the difficulties imposed on the Roman Catholic church in Russia, Pope Pius XI in 1922 appointed Edmund Walsh, S.J., director general of the Papal Relief Mission to Russia and representative to treat with the Soviet Government on Catholic interests in Russia. Walsh was also a representative of American Catholics on the American Relief Administration to Russia. He stayed in Russia until the fall of 1923. During this time he worked most energetically in his important missions [152], confronting the difficult situation of the Catholic Church and trying to help the Russian people without discrimination of race or religion.[41]

g) THE SUPPRESSION OF THE ROMAN CATHOLIC CHURCH

The Roman Catholic Church in Russia has a long, respectable history, born of the relationships between Muscovite Russia and Western Europe, particularly Poland.[42] Its problems during the Russian Revolution had two main causes. First, it opposed openly and without hesitation atheistic Communism and remained loyal to the Roman See, thus uniting itself with the Catholics of the world. Secondly, its membership was composed mostly of non-Russians: the Poles, Lithuanians, Latvians, Belorussians (or Beloruthenians), Ukrainians, Germans, and Armenians. The Poles, however, were far more numerous than any other nationality among the Russian Catholics [156, 157]. The Catholics, for the most part, constituted a foreign element, included by force in the Russian empire mostly during the Partitions of Poland, with the exception of the Germans who voluntarily immigrated to the Saratov and Tiraspol Provinces on the Volga.[43] All these nationalities maintained, as much as possible, their national language, tradition and ecclesiastical peculiarities. The Russian Catholic element, which together with others belonged to the same ecclesiastical metropoly, was rather insignificant. Thus, the Catholics of Russia represented also a peculiar nationality problem which the Communists tried to solve on the basis of Marxian doctrine and Russian assimilation.[44]

---

41 Cf. Edmund A. Walsh, *Total Empire, the Roots and Progress of World Communism* (Milwaukee, 1951), pp. 6-18.

42 For the study of Russian and Polish relations concerning the Roman Catholic religion, see Paul Pierling, *La Russie et le Saint-Siege: Etudes diplomatiques,* 5 vols. Paris, 1906-1923; W. Meysztowicz. "Koscioly karolickie ob. lac na obszarach Rosji," *Millemim,* vol. II (1955), pp. 467-497.

43 Perhaps the best presentation of the Catholic problem in Russia during the revolution is that by James J. Zatko, *The Destruction of the Catholic Church During the Bolshevik Resolution* (a doctoral dissertation, University of Notre Dame, 1958), pp. 216-218; see also its bibliography.

44 L. Trotskii's inimical attitude in his *History of the Russian Revolution,* vol. III, pp. 38-61, is of particular interest for the understanding of the Catholic problem during the revolution.

In the growing rage of the revolution the Catholics strengthened their administration by the election of a new archbishop in 1917, Edward Ropp, Metropolitan of Mogilev for all Russia, and by new administrative appointments. This ecclesiastical province of colossal territorial size was administered by him with seven bishops of Latin and Slavonic rite. For the Russians of the Catholic metropoly, Rev. Leonid Fedorov was appointed exarch [Append. III]. The Metropolitan of Halicz and Uniate archbishop of Lvov, Andrew Szeptycki, who was now released from the tsarist monastery prison of Suzdal, arrived in St. Petersburg in 1917 where he presided over the first Synod of the Russian Catholic Church of Slavonic Rite, May 18-31. He worked enthusiastically for the union of the Orthodox and the Catholic Churches, planning a Catholic patriarchate in Kiev. The growing influence of Metropolitan Szeptycki extended from Ukraine to Belorussia, where several nationalists expected to reestablish a national Uniate Church to repair the Union ruined by the Muscovite russifiers ruling the Ruthenians after the Partitions.

Szeptycki's activities were tinted with some political plans which would exclude gradually from the work among the Russians all the Latin clergy of non-Russian origin. Several of the prominent Russian Catholics disagreed with this tendency. We see, therefore, a sort of split of aims among the Catholics in the Latin and the Slavic orientations. But, in spite of this the Catholics constituted a well unified bloc and disciplined church organization [Append. VI].

With the March Revolution, through the reign of the Provisional Government, the Catholics of Russia expected some relief in the life of their church, giving them equal position among other free confessions. Till this time they had been an underprivileged, persecuted church. The Catholics also felt happy, in the beginning, over the announcement of the law separating the church from the state.[45] Later came the disappointment, especially on the stipulation depriving churches of the rights of juridical persons and the right of ownership of property. At a stroke of Lenin's pen, the Catholic Church in Russia lost all its property, accumulated in many instances through long generations. It owned churches, monasteries, schools, academies, land, buildings, libraries, artistic and monetary valuables, etc.

Other disappointments came very soon. On April 29, 1919, [12, 13] Metropolitan Ropp was imprisoned by the Bolsheviks. He appointed John Ciaplak administrator and vicar general of the archdiocese of Mogilev. On November 17, 1919, Archbishop Ropp was expelled from Russia to Poland in an exchange for Karl Radek, imprisoned in Warsaw for his subversive activities there.[46] Archbishop Cieplak met with a multitude of threats against

---

45   Cf. McCullagh, pp. 204,239; J. S. Curtiss, *op. cit.*, pp. 52-53.
46   Franciszek Rutkowski, *Arcybishup Jan Cieplak* (Warsaw, 1934), p. 166.

the existence of his church created by the revolution. Three legislative difficulties first confronted the Catholics: (1) a decree demanding that twenty laymen of each parish sign an agreement with the Soviet government accepting the government's ownership of church property; (2) a decree ordering church valuables[47] to be surrendered to the Soviet relief organization, (3) a decree prohibiting religious instructions [53, 54]. The zealous Archbishop Cieplak opposed as much as possible these three legislative impositions upon the freedom of religious life, and forbade his faithful and the clergy to yield to the injustices aimed at the annihilation of the Roman Catholic Church in Russia along with the other religions [55].

In the beginning of March, 1923, all the Catholic priests in Petrograd were summoned to Moscow, to appear before the Supreme Tribunal, with Archbishop Cieplak as the principal accused [57-59]. The spectacular Bolshevik trial of the arrested Archbishop and his clergy lasted from March 21 to March 25, 1923. It is known for its malevolence, untenability of charges and severity of sentence [62-66]. The archbishop and his deputy, Monsignor Budkiewicz, were sentenced to death; the other sixteen defendants, including Exarch Leonidas Federov, were condemned to long terms of imprisonment[48] [67-69]. When the sentence of the Catholic clergymen was published, the Praesidium of the Central Executive Committee decided that the sentence of Cieplak, Budkiewicz and others was not to be executed until the Committee reached a special conclusion. This happened on March 27, 1923. On March 29, the Central Executive Committee pronounced the final sentence, imprisoning Archbishop Cieplak, and ordering execution of Monsignor Budkiewicz [83]. The Bolsheviks were satisfied with the fact that there was not too much international resentment or the threat of politically serious repercussions. The mild protests of the European governments, as well as that of the United States [70-73, 81, 82], perhaps made the Bolsheviks more audacious in their inhuman persecution of religions in Soviet Russia. The death of Budkiewicz and the subsequent suppression of the Catholic religion liquidated the great historical Roman Catholic Church in Russia. The heroic Archbishop Cieplak, released after ten months imprisonment [78], died in Passaic, N.J., during a visit to America, on February 17, 1926.

In the beginning of the Bolshevik revolution, there were 790 Catholic priests. Of these, 138 were imprisoned, 40 were murdered, and 5 died in prison. In 1933 there were in all of Soviet Russia only some two hundred priests, many of them in prison. All the churches, monasteries, schools, orphanages, houses of the poor, and other institutions were brought to a

---

47   Archb. Cieplak was ready, with the permission of the Vatican, to give the sacred vessels for famine relief; F. McCullagh, *op. cit.,* pp. 111-112.
48   F. McCullagh, *op. cit.,* pp. 106-107.

tragic end, together with the ages-old mission of Latin Christianity in that part of the world.[49]

h) THE SECTARIANS, JEWS AND MOSLEMS

The implementation of anti-religious policy varied according to the changing conditions within the Soviet empire. The official view on this problem was expressed in *Izvestiia,* April 19, 1923, that "the struggle against religion with us in Russia has already gone through several stages, each of which is determined by the concrete conditions of the time." Alexander Kischkowsky, in his excellent study on the Soviet religious policy towards the Orthodox Church, observed that the Communist government of Russia never changed its basic attitude towards religion as an evil that must be destroyed. However, in adapting policies to the existing situations, by an open persecution of some and the protection of certain other religious cults, an effective rule was pursued. This is particularly characteristic of the years of drastic revolutionary changes from 1917 to 1925 [91, 105]. In the beginning the government was compelled to follow a very liberal nationality policy; and the factor of religion was closely connected with that of the national consciousness of subjugated peoples. During the Eighth Congress of the Communist party, on February 19, 1919, Lenin said: ". . . in order to facilitate the process of the differentiation of the proletariat, it is necessary to avoid a forceful elimination of the clergy in whose power the people of Russia or Central Asia are."[50]

In the resolutions of the Thirteenth Congress of the Communist party held between May 23 and 31, 1924, there is the following paragraph concerning sectarians:

> Especially cautious must be the attitude toward the sectarians, many of whom were exposed to cruel persecutions by the tsarist government, and who display intense activity. By treating them with understanding, we can win the sectarians to cooperation with the Soviets in the utilization of their many valuable economic and cultural resources. Considering the large number of the sectarians, this work must be considered important. This task must be solved in accordance with the local conditions.[51]

Against this doctrinal background we may understand the relatively lenient policy pursued towards the vehement Russian deviationists, the heretics of the Orthodox Church. They not only enjoyed some toleration in return for their loyalty towards the Soviet rule — which in many instances gave them more freedom than the tsars did — but they also were used against the

---

49 Cf. *Index sacerdotum in Russia A.D. 1924,* MS. in the Archives of the Polish Roman Catholic Union of America (Chicago, Ill.), see vol. X; Jan Wasilewski, *W szponach Antychrysta* (Cracow, 1924), pp. 72-78.

50 V. Lenin, *Sochinienia,* vol. II, p. 423; cfr. A. Kischkowsky, *op. cit.,* p. 42.

51 *KPSS v resoliutsiiakh i resheniiakh s'ezdov, konferentsii i plenumov TK* (Moscow, 1954), vol. II p.. 52.

unity of the Orthodox faithful. This was a very cunning policy. During the years of 1921-1928, the tactics of divide and ruin did not depart from the basic, long range Soviet policy which was made sufficiently explicit when the Tenth Party Congress, held in March 1921, decided that "one of the essential tasks of the Glavpolitprosvet (Political Education Administration) is all-embracing organization, leadership, and support of anti-religious agitation and propaganda among the toilers. For this purpose, this highest propaganda center must make accessible to the broadest masses a knowledge of natural history, by publishing newspapers, books, and text-books, by a systematic series of lectures, and the utilization of all modern means of mass communication."[52]

The Jewish Zionist movement is of a particular nationalistic character, but still in its religious aspects belongs to the general problem of the suppression of religion by the revolution. After the February Revolution it had rather favorable conditions for development. The movement had about 300,000 members. In June of 1919 the Soviet government declared it capitalistic, politically dangerous and counter-revolutionary. On August 30, 1919, the National Committee for Education forbade the teaching of Yiddish and Hebrew in schools. As early as July, 1919, Zionist activities had been forbidden. And in September, 1919, the Central Committee of Zionism was suppressed in Petrograd by decision of the Cheka. In April 1920, in Moscow, 109 delegates of a Zionist meeting were arrested. In May, 1922, in a meeting of a Zionist party in Kiev, 51 members were arrested by the Cheka. These suppressive activities of the Soviet government were anxiously met by the World Zionist Executive, which attempted to negotiate with the People's Commissariat for Foreign Affairs, for legalization of Zionist activities, permission to emigrate to Palestine, the teaching of Hebrew, and public practice of the Jewish religion. But the negotiation failed and many of the Zionist leaders were imprisoned or deported to Siberia. Finally the move-ment of the organization completely collapsed and was dispersed.[53]

The persecution of Jews in Russia during the Revolution, in spite of the old anti-Semitism and anti-Jewish laws, was less severe than the persecution of other minorities and their national religions. In the well documented works of the Jewish writers it is impossible to find statistics pertaining to the looting of synagogues, martyrdom of rabbis, burning of rabbinical schools, public court trials, and other things similar to the actions of suppression

---

52 For a general summary of the Bolshevik church policy, see Alexander Kisch-kowsky, "Die Politik der Schwachung (1917-1927," *Die sowjetische Religionspolitik,* pp. 25-48, esp. p. 44; J. S. Curtiss, *op cit.,* p. 5

53 Cf. I. Margolin, "Kak bylo likvidirovano sionistskoe dvizhenie v Sovetskoi Rossi," *Vestnik Instituta,* No. 6, 1954, pp. 90-111.

applied to other religions. The violent anti-Semitism of the Bolsheviks appeared after 1930, although it existed in mild form before that date.[54]

Among the non-Christian religions in Russia Islam is the most important. The tsarist regime imposed its own laws upon the Moslems inhabiting the regions of Asiatic Russia and refused even to recognize the local languages. Islam was an underpriviledged religion confessed by the nations subdued by the Russians [109]. The freedom-loving nationalities of Central Asia identified their religious institutions as embodying traditional concepts of life and belief, in essence theistic and national. For the Bolsheviks this was dangerous philosophy opposed to Communistic materialism and Russian imperialism. Moslem sentiment stood always strong against Russia, whether tsarist or Soviet.[55] The social life of the Moslems is based to a great extent on religious customs. From the words of Lenin pronounced in 1905, that "every person should be completely free to profess whatever religion he pleases or to profess no religion at all," it seemed that the Russian state would take a neutral stand at least with regard to the Turkestan Mohammedanism. But the law of January 23, 1918, "On Freedom of Conscience and Religious Societies," [Appendix I] abolished the traditional Islamic institutions upon which the social life of the Moslems of Central Asia greatly depended.[56] It aggravated the problems of relationships between the Moslems and the central Russian government.

The Bolsheviks believed in a persistent fight against religion. A prominent Communist among the Turkestan Moslems, M. Sultan-Galiev, published a book in which he proposed a method of anti-Moslem activity [24], advocating among other things conversion of at least one Moslem to atheism in every village.[57] The Communist Party, however, adopted a legalistic method of suppression of Islamic religious customs and institutions among the Central Asian Moslems [Appendix II]. A series of legal regulations, issued between 1920 and 1925, practically suppressed the life of Islam in Central Asia, subduing at the same time the ancient freedom-loving nations [Appendix II]. "In Central Asia", observed A. G. Park, student of Bolshevism in Turkestan, "the Bolshevik determination to destroy secular prerogatives of religion collided with Moslem fanaticism almost from the outset of the revolution."[58]

---

54   For the problem of Russian anti-Semitism during the Russian Revolution, see S. M. Shvarts, *Anti-semitism v Sovetskom Soiuze* (New York, 1952), esp. pp. 1-29.

55   A very interesting account of the relations between Bolshevism and Islam of Central Asia the reader may find in the book by Alexander G. Park, *Bolshevism in Turkestan, 1917-1927* (New York, 1957), pp. 204-248.

56   Cf. Julius F. Hecker, *Religion and Communism: A Study of Religion and Atheism in Soviet Russia* (London, 1933), pp. 289-290.

57   M. Sultan-Galiev, *Metody antireligioznoi propagandy sredi Musul'man* (Moscow, 1922), p. 5.

58   A. G. Park, *op. cit.*, p. 212; see also G. Faizulin, "The Persecution of the National-Religious Traditions of the Moslems in the USSR," *Caucasian Review*, No. 3, 1956, pp. 69-76.

The same laws, decrees and administrative instructions pertained to the Islamic denomination, and to its clergy and religious educational institutions. The Moslems opposed these measures with civil war in 1919 and sporadic manifestations later. But to little avail, since by 1927 all the traditional institutions, including the customary canonical courts, had been abolished in Fergana, Samarkand, Syrdaria, Bokhara; Turkestan, Uzbek and Turkoman republics; and in several other autonomous Asiatic territories or districts.

The conservative observance of religious customs among the Asiatic nationalities remaining under Russian domination required special methods. The persistence of custom among the Bashkirs and Tartars was such that a prominent leader of atheistic propaganda, Gali Ibrahimov, advocated that the Communists work first among the women of these peoples to begin the "uprooting" of their religious beliefs.[59] It would seem that Buddhism was least molested by the militant atheists. But the Buddhists in Siberia and among the Russian controlled Mongols suffered enormously.[60]

i) THE TRAGIC LESSON

During these years of persecution the Russian Orthodox Church showed the most touching Christian virtues of charity, patience, faith and sacrifice. Many saintly martyrs witnessed most heroically their love of the church. Bishops were tortured, imprisoned, martyred and exiled to the horrible concentration camps [Appendix IV]. Monks and nuns and parish clergy as well were dispersed, persecuted and secularized, living like hunted animals.[61] Their main crime was that they believed in God and practiced their religion. The traditional mysticism and piety disappeared from the face of the Russian land. Churches were despoiled of their sacred vessels, vestments, icons, and other valuables. The great host of the new martyrs of faith is innumerable and universal. It embraces all the faiths, all rites, all those who suffered for their religion. Many monumental religious buildings of venerable antiquity and historical prominence were destroyed or left in disrepair to our days. It looked as if all the forces of darkness were gathered together to annihilate everything that had association with belief in God, whether Christian, Jewish, Mohammedan, Buddhist, or other.

---

59   Cf. Gali Ibrahimov, *Kak vesti antireligioznuiu propagandu sredi Tatarok i Bashkirok,* published by the State Publication Institute, Moscow, 1928. The booklet is a masterpiece of planned tactics for dealing with the women of Buddhist and Islamic religions or of Shamanism and other primitive cults.

60   See N. Poppe, "The Destruction of Buddhism in the USSR," *Bulletin of the Institute for the Study of the USSR,* vol. III (1956), July, pp. 14-20; *idem,* "Polozhenie buddistskoi tserkvi v SSSR," *Vestnik Instituta,* No. 5, 1954, pp. 35-46.

61   For lives of the new Russian Orthodox martyrs, see M. Polskii, *Novye mucheniki Rossiiskie, pervoe sobranie materialov.* Jordanville, N. Y., 1949. In the martyrology Tsar Nicholas II and his family are included; see for many references A. Valentinov, *Chernaia kniga.*

But those among the Orthodox clergy, and bishops especially, who could escape abroad did not properly consummate the most tragic fate of their brethren in Russia. Quixotically bound to a dream of the past, disunited and dispersed without any central organization of purpose, they continued to fight for the hopeless cause of the Tsar's return and restoration of the House of Romanov. They still associated themselves with the leaders of the Russian *émigrés* advocating the return to the old imperialism and supression of countries which tried to free themselves from the Russian yoke.

1917

1

Resolutions of the Conference of Orthodox Clergy and Laymen

June, 1917

In the Russian State, the Orthodox Church must hold, among other religious confessions, a place of priority, most favored in government and in public rights, as is fitting to her as the supreme sacred object of the people, of exceptional historic and cultural value, and also as the religion of the majority of the population. In harmony with the recognition, by the new governmental regime of Russia, of freedom of religious conscience and of confessions, the Orthodox Church must hold such freedom in all its fullness. These fundamental considerations should be expressed in the following principles: (1) The Orthodox Church in Russia, in matters concerning its structure, legislation, administration, courts, teaching of faith and morality, services of worship, internal Church discipline, and external relationships with other Churches — is independent of Government authority (autonomous). (2) Resolutions issued for itself by the Orthodox Church in accordance with order established by herself, will be recognized by the Government as the norms of law having, from the moment of their publication by the Church, obligatory meaning for all persons and institutions belonging to the Orthodox Russian Church, whether in Russia or abroad. (3) The actions of organs of the Orthodox Church are subject to supervision by the Government only in regard to their corresponding to the laws of the State: furthermore, these organs are responsible to the Government only through court procedure. . . . (10) The twelve Great Holidays, Sundays and the days especially honoured by the Orthodox Church are recognized by the Government as holidays. (11) The head of the Russian State and the Minister of Confessions must be Orthodox. (12) In all moments of State life where the Government turns to religion, the Orthodox Church shall be preferred . . . . . (17) The Orthodox Church shall receive from the State Treasury annual subventions

27

in the amount of its actual needs, under condition of accounting for amounts received in due course.

(As quoted in Paul B. Anderson, *People, Church and State in Modern Russia*, p. 41)

2
Concerning the Authorization of the Local Sobor of the All-Russian Church to Work Out a Bill on the New Order of a Free Self-Government of the Russian Church

(Translation from *Vestnik Vremennago Pravitel 'stva*, Petrograd, No. 143, Sept. 1/14, 1917)

[The Provisional Government decided:]

I. To authorize the Local Sobor of the All-Russian Church to be convened in Moscow on August 15, 1917, to work out and to submit for the consideration of the Provisional Government a Bill on the new order of a free self-government of the Russian Church.

II. To preserve, until the civil government shall recognize the new order of the supreme church administration, all affairs of the internal church administration within the jurisdiction of the holy governing synod and the institutions connected with it.

Signed: Minister-President A. KERENSKII.
Minister of Justice ZARUDNYI.

August 11th, 1917.

3
Decree on Land Nationalization, November 8, 1917

1. Landed proprietorship is abolished forthwith without compensation.

2. The landed estates, as also all appanages, the monasterial and church lands, with all their livestock, implements, farm buildings, and everything pertaining thereto, shall be placed under the control of the *volost* [village district] Land Committees and the *uezd* [district] Soviets of Peasants' Deputies pending the meeting of the Constituent Assembly.

3. All damage to confiscated property, which henceforth belongs to the whole people, is declared to be a felony, punishable by the revolutionary courts. The *uezd* Soviets of Peasants' Deputies shall take all necessary measures for the preservation of the strictest order during the confiscation of the estates of the landlords, for determining estates of which size and which particular estates shall be subject to confiscation, for drawing up inventories of all property confiscated and for the strictest revolutionary protection of all land transferred to the people and all structures, implements, cattle, supplies, etc.

4. The following peasant Instructions, compiled by the *Izvestiia* of the All-Russian Soviet of Peasants' Deputies from 242 local peasant Instructions and published in No. 88 of the *Izvestiia* (Petrograd, September 1, 1917), are everywhere to serve as a guide in carrying through the great land reforms until a final decision on the latter is taken by the Constituent Assembly.

5. The land of ordinary peasants and ordinary Cossacks shall not be confiscated.

(Published in: *Izvestiia* and *Pravda,* Nov. 10, 1917.)

4
Revolutionary Divorce Law

December 31, 1917

1. Marriage is annulled by the petition of both parties or even one of them.

2. The above petition is submitted, according to the rules of local jurisdiction, to the local court.

Note. A declaration of annulment of marriage by mutual consent may be filed directly with the department of registration of marriages in which a record of that marriage is kept, which department makes an entry of the annulment of the marriage in the record and issues a certificate.

3. On the day appointed for the examination of the petition for the annulment of marriage, the local judge summons both parties or their solicitors.

4. If the residence of the party who is to be summoned is unknown, the petitioner is allowed to file the petition for annulment of marriage in the place of residence of the absent party last known to the petitioner, or in the place of residence of the petitioner, stating to the court, however, the last known place of residence of the defendant.

5. If the place of residence of the party who is the summoned is unknown, then the day for the trial of the case is set not earlier than the expiration of

two months from the day of the publication of a notice of summons in the local Government gazette, and the summons is sent to the address of the last known place of residence of the defendant given by the petitioner.

6. Having convinced himself that the petition for the annulment of the marriage really comes from both parties or from one of them, the judge personally and singly renders the decision of the annulment of the marriage and issues a certificate thereof to the parties. At the same time, the judge transmits a copy of his decision to the department of registration of marriages where the annulled marriage was performed and where the book containing a record of this marriage is kept.

7. When annulling a marriage by mutual consent, the parties are obliged to state in their petition what surnames the divorced parties and their children are to bear in the future. But when dissolving the marriage by the petition of one of the parties, and in the absence of an understanding about this matter between the parties, the divorced parties preserve their own surnames, and the surname of the children is determined by the judge, and in case of disagreement of the parties, by the local court.

8. In case the parties are agreed on the matter, the judge, simultaneously with the decision of annulment of the marriage, determines with which of the parents the minor children begotten of the marriage shall live, and which of the parents must bear the expense of maintenance and education of the children, and to what extent and also whether and to what extent the husband is obliged to furnish food and maintenance to his divorced wife.

9. But if no understanding shall be reached, then the participation of the husband in furnishing his divorced wife with food and maintenance when she has no means of her own or has insufficient means and is unable to work, as well as the question with whom the children are to live, are decided by a regular civil suit in the local court, irrespective of the amount of the suit. The judge, having rendered the decision annulling the marriage, determines temporarily, until the settlement of the dispute, the fate of the children, and also rules on the question of the temporary maintenance of the children and the wife, if she is in need of it.

10. Suits for adjudging marriages illegal or invalid belong henceforth to the jurisdiction of the local court.

11. The operation of this law extends to all citizens of the Russian Republic irrespective of their adherence to this or that religious cult.

12. All suits for annulment of marriage which are now tried in ecclesiastical consistories of the department of Greek-Catholic and other denominations, in the governing synod and all other institutions of the Christian and non-Christian religions, and by officials in charge of ecclesiastical affairs of all denominations, and in which no decisions have been rendered or the decisions already rendered have not become legally effective, are declared by reason of this law null and void, and are subject to immediate transfer

to the local district courts for safe-keeping, with all archives in the possession of the above-enumerated institutions and persons having jurisdiction in divorce suits. The parties are given the right to file a new petition for the annulment of the marriage according to this decree, without awaiting the dismissal of the first suit, and a new summons for absent parties (paragraphs 4 and 5) is not obligatory if such a summons was published in the former order.

President of the Council of People's Commissars V. ULIANOV
(Lenin)
President of the Central Executive Committee of the Soviets
of Workmen's, Soldiers' and Peasants' Deputies I. A.
SVERDLOV
Director of the Affairs of the Council of People's Commissars
BONCH-BRUEVICH
Secretary N. GORBUNOV
R.S.F.S.R. Laws, 1917-1918, text 152.

5
Marriage, Children, and Registration of Civil Status

December 31, 1917

The Russian Republic henceforth recognizes civil marriage only.

Civil marriage is performed on the basis of the following rules:

1. Persons who wish to contract marriage declare (their intention) orally or by a written statement to the department of registration of marriages and births at the city hall (regional, district, township, Zemstvo [rural government] institutions), according to the place of their residence.

Note. Church marriage is a private affair of those contracting it, while civil marriage is obligatory.

2. Declarations of intention to contract marriage are not accepted (a) from persons of the male sex younger than eighteen years, and of the female sex, sixteen years of age; in Transcaucasia the native inhabitants may enter into marriage upon attaining the age of sixteen for the groom and thirteeen for the bride; (b) from relatives in the direct line, full and half-brothers, and sisters; consanguinity is recognized also between a child born out of wedlock and his descendants on one side and relatives on the other; (c) from married persons, and (d) from insane.

3. Those wishing to contract marriage appear at the department of registration of marriages and sign a statement concerning the absence of

the obstacles to contracting marriage enumerated in Article 2 of this decree, and also a statement that they contract marriage voluntarily.

Those guilty of deliberately making false statements about the absence of the obstacles enumerated in Article 2 are criminally prosecuted for false statements and the marriage is declared invalid.

4. Upon the signing of the above-mentioned statement, the director of the department of registration of marriages records the act of marriage in the book of marriage registries and then declares the marriage to have become legally effective.

When contracting marriage the parties are allowed to decide freely whether they will henceforth be called by the surname of the husband or wife or by a combined surname.

As proof of the act of marriage, the contracting parties immediately receive a copy of the certificate of their marriage. . .

5. Complaints against the refusal to perform marriage or incorrect registration are lodged, without limitation of time, with the local judge in the locality where the department of registration of marriage is; the ruling of the local judge on such complaint may be appealed in the usual way.

6. In case the former books of registration of marriages have been destroyed, or lost in some other way, or if for some other cause married persons cannot obtain a certificate of their marriage, those persons are given the right to submit a declaration to the respective department of registration of marriages, according to the place of residence of both parties or one of them, to the effect that they have been in the state of wedlock since such and such time. Such declaration is attested in addition to the statement stipulated by Article 3, by a further statement of the parties that the book of registration has really been lost or that for some other sufficient cause they cannot obtain a copy of the certificate.

REGISTRATION OF BIRTHS

7. The registration of the birth of a child is made by the same department of registration of marriages and births in the place of residence of the mother, and a special entry of each birth is made in the book of registration of births.

8. The birth of a child must be reported to the department either by his parents or one of them, or by the persons in whose care, because of the death of his parents, the child remained, with an indication of the name and surname adopted for the child and the presentation of two witnesses to attest the fact of birth.

9. The books of registration of marriages as well as the books of registration of births are kept in two copies, and one copy is sent at the end of the year to the proper court for preservation.

10. Children born out of wedlock are on an equality with those born in wedlock with regard to the rights and duties of parents toward children, and likewise of children toward parents.

The persons who make a declaration and give a signed statement to that effect are registered as the father and mother of the child.

Those guilty of deliberately making false statements regarding the above are criminally prosecuted for false testimony and the registration is declared invalid.

In case the father of a child born out of wedlock does not make such a declaration, the mother of the child or the guardian or the child itself has the right to prove fatherhood by legal means.

REGISTRATION OF DEATHS

11. The record of the death of a person is made in the place where the death occurred by the department which has charge of the registration of marriages and births, by entry in a special book for registration of deaths.

12. The death of a person must be reported to the department by the legal or administrative authorities or persons in whose care the deceased was.

13. Institutions in charge of cemeteries are henceforth forbidden to place obstacles in the way of burial on cemetery grounds in accordance with the ritual of civil funerals.

14. All religious and administrative institutions which hitherto have had charge of the registration of marriages, births, and deaths according to the customs of any religious cult, are ordered to transfer immediately all their registration books to the respective municipal, district, rural and *zemstvo* administrations.

> President of the Council of People's Commissaries V.
> ULIANOV (Lenin)
> President of the Central Executive Committee of the Soviets
> of Workmen's, Soldiers' and Peasants' Deputies I. A.
> SVERDLOV
> Director of the Affairs of the Council of People's Commissars
> BONCH-BRUEVICH
> Secretary N. GORBUNOV

R.S.F.S.R. Laws, 1917-1918, text 160.

1918

6

Decree of the Soviet Commissars Concerning Separation of Church and State, and of School and Church

(*Compilation of Decrees,* January 23, 1918, No. 18, Page 263.)

1. The Church is separated from the State.

2. Within the confines of the Republic it shall be prohibited to issue any local by-laws or regulations restricting or limiting freedom of conscience, or establishing privileges or preferential rights of any kind based on the religious creed of citizens.

3. Every citizen may profess any religious belief, or profess no belief at all. All restrictions of rights, involved by professing one or another religious belief, or by professing no belief at all, are cancelled and void.

Note: All reference to the professing or non-professing of religious creeds by citizens shall be expunged from all official documents.

4. State or other public functions binding in law shall not be accompanied by the performance of religious rites or ceremonies.

5. Free performance of religious rites is permissible as long as it does not disturb public order, or interfere with the rights of the citizens of the Soviet Republic. The local authorities shall be entitled in such cases to adopt all necessary measures for maintenance of public order and safety.

6. Nobody is entitled to refuse to perform his duties as a citizen on the basis of his religious belief. Exceptions to this rule, on the condition that one civic duty be replaced by another, may be granted in each individual case by the verdict of the People's Court.

7. The official taking or administering of religious oaths is cancelled. In necessary cases merely a solemn promise is given.

8. Births, marriages, and deaths are to be registered and solemnized solely by civic (secular) authorities: marriage and birth registration offices.

9. The School is separated from the Church. Instruction in any religious creed or belief shall be prohibited in all State, public, and also private educational establishments in which general instruction is given. Citizens may give or receive religious instruction in a private way.

10. All Church and religious associations are subject to the ordinary legislation concerning private associations and unions. They shall not enjoy special privileges, nor receive any subsidies from the State or from local autonomous or self-governing institutions.

11. Compulsory collection of imposts and taxes in favor of church and religious associations, also measures of compulsion or punishment adopted by such associations in respect to their members, shall not be permitted.

12. No church or religious associations have the right to own property. They do not possess the rights of juridical persons.

13. The property of all church and religious associations existing in Russia is pronounced the property of the People. Buildings and objects especially used for the purposes of worship shall be let, free of charge, to the respective religious associations, by resolution of the local, or Central State authorities.

> Signed: President of the Soviet Commissars, ULIANOV (LENIN).
> People's Commissars: PODVOISKII, ALGASOV, TRUTOVSKII, SHLIKHTER, PROSHIN, MENZHINSKII, SHLIAPNIKOV, AND PETROVSKII
> Director of Affairs of the Soviet of Commissars: VL. BONCH-BRUEVICH.

(Published in No. 15, *Gazette of the Workmen and Peasant Government*, dated January 23, 1918)

7
Abolishment of Military Chaplain Service

January 29, 1918

(The People's Commissariat on Affairs of War decrees:)

Part I

1. To release all clergymen of all denominations who are in the service of the War Department.

2. All branches of the Military clergy to be reshaped.

3. Military committees have the right, if the military units, administrations, establishments and institutions so desire, to retain the clergymen.

4. In the latter case the maintenance of retained clergymen is to be fixed not by former States but exclusively by the stipulations of the committees of the units themselves.

5. Without exception, all property and all church funds of churches of military units (are) to be handed over to the committees of the various

units and in the case of reshaping of the latter — to the committees of the higher grades.

6. For the purposes of receipt and delivery of funds and property now at the disposal of the clerical department, special commissions will be appointed.

People's Commissariat on Affairs of War
M. KEDROV, E. SKILIANSKII, V. PODVOI-
SKII, K. MEKHONOSHIN.

8
Message of the Patriarch Tikon, Anathematizing the Soviet Regime, of February 1, 1918

Humble Tikhon, by the grace of God the Patriarch of Moscow and All Russia, to Hierarchs, Clergy and all faithful children of the Russian Orthodox Church, beloved in the Lord.

The Holy Orthodox Church of Christ is now passing through hard times in the Russian land. The open and secret enemies of the Truth of Christ have begun to persecute it and are striving to destroy Christ's Cause by sowing everywhere, in place of Christian love, the seeds of malice, hatred and fratricidal strife.

The most violent persecution is begun against the Holy Church of Christ: the sacraments of grace, which sanctify the birth of man or bestow blessings upon the matrimonial union of a Christian family, are openly declared unnecessary. The holy temples are subjected to destruction or robbery and to blasphemous insults; the sacred places, venerated by the people, are being taken over by the godless lords of the darkness of this age; the schools supported by the means of the Orthodox Church and places of education preparing the pastors of the Church are being considered superfluous; the properties of the Orthodox monasteries and churches are being taken away. Where, then, are the limits to these mockeries at the Church of Christ? How and by what means is it possible to stop this attack against Her by outrageous enemies?

All this fills our hearts with a deep and bitter sorrow and compels us to address these monsters of the human race with stern words of accusation in accordance with the legacy of the Apostle: "Them that sin rebuke before all, that others also may fear" (*I Timothy* 5, 20). Bethink yourselves, ye senseless, and stop your bloody retributions. For that which you are doing is not only a cruel deed; it is in truth a Satanic deed, for which you shall suffer the fire of Gehenna in the future life beyond the grave, and the terrible curse of posterity in the present life on earth.

By the authority given us by God we forbid you to partake of the sacraments of Christ, and anathematize you, if you still bear the Christian names, although by your birth you belong to the Orthodox Church.

We exhort also all of you, the faithful children of the Orthodox Church of Christ, to refrain from communicating with these monsters of the human race in any way whatever: "put away from among yourselves that wicked person" (*I Corinthians* 5:13) . . . .

The enemies of the Church are usurping authority over Her and Her possession by the use of death-inflicting weapons; but you confront them with the strength of your faith. And if it should be necessary even to suffer for the Cause of Christ, we call you, beloved children of the Church, to bear these sufferings together with us in these words of the Apostle: "Who shall separate us from the love of Christ? Shall tribulation, or distress, or persecution, or famine, or nakedness, or peril, or the sword?" (*Romans* 8:25)

And you, Brethren Hierarchs and Clergy, without delay for an hour in your ecclesiastical action, but with a fiery zeal, call your children to defend the Orthodox Church; but call them to take their place in the ranks of spiritual fighters who will confront external force with the strength of their holy confession. And we firmly believe that the enemies of the Church will be put to shame, and will be scattered by the power of the Cross of Christ, for the promise of the Divine Bearer of the Cross Himself is immutable: "I will build My Church; and the gates of hell shall not prevail against it". (*Matthew* 16:18).

TIKHON, Patriarch of Moscow and All Russia

January 19, 1918 [Old Style]

Cf. I. M. Andreev, *Kratkii obzor istorii russkoi tserkvi ot revoliutsii do nashikh dnei* [An Outline of Russian Church History from the Revolution to Our Day], Jordanville, N. Y., Holy Trinity Monastery, 1952, pp. 21-22.

9
Instructions to the Orthodox Church Against Government Acts

February 28, 1918

The new conditions of Church life demand of Church workers, especially local ones, extraordinary care and unusual efforts, in order that requisite spiritual work may be carried on with good success, regardless of the obstacles to be met, and even of persecution. The Holy Assembly and Holy Patriarch direct the general method to be followed at the present time by the spiritual pastors. Inviting them to independent action under the present difficult conditions and cautioning against erroneous action on their part, we propose the following instructions:

Call to the Priests:

1. Priests are invited to be strictly on guard in protecting the Holy Church in the heavy years of persecution, to encourage, strengthen and unite the believers for defense against attacks on the freedom of the Orthodox Faith, and to strengthen the prayers for the enlightenment of the doubting.

2. The priests should encourage the good intentions of the believers directed towards the defense of the Church.

Organizations of the Church:

3. Parishioners and worshippers of all parish and other churches should be organized into united societies whose duty it shall be to defend all the sacred things and other church property against violation.

4. These organizations must have an educational and charitable character, as also a name, and can be presided over by a layman or priest. But they should not be called either church or religious societies, as all church and religious societies are by virtue of a decree deprived of all legal rights.

5. In extreme cases, these societies can declare themselves the owners of church property, in order to save them from seizure at the hands of the non-Orthodox or even those of another faith. Let the Church and church property remain in the hands of the Orthodox, believing in God and devoted to the Church.

6. The superiors, sister superiors and brothers of monasteries, hermitages and resting houses are to be appointed by similar united societies from among local residents and regular worshippers of the parish and all loyal parishioners.

7. The principals and teachers in church educational institutions shall establish relations with the parents of the pupils, and the employees of the united societies, for the protection of educational societies from seizure and the guarantee of their future activity for the benefit of the Church and the well-being of the Orthodox people.

8. These societies must firmly demand and endeavor by all means to ensure that the situation in the educational institutions should remain strictly intact until further orders of the church authorities.

9. Teachers of religion in the non-ecclesiastical educational institutions should by all means in their power extend their influence over the councils of educators and parents so that they may firmly defend the instruction of religion in educational institutions and co-operate with every new effort of the same for the benefit of religious training and education.

10. The removal by force of the clergy and members of the parish or monks from the monasteries should under no circumstances be permitted. In case of forceful removal, by the congregation or other persons, of the

clergy from the posts occupied by them, the diocesan authority does not fill their places and demands the reappointment to their former posts of those removed, and the re-establishment of their rights. Every interference with a priest or member of the parish should be reported to the church authorities, who alone have the authority, after investigating the matter, to remove priests and church employees from the parish congregation.

11. If it should be established that the forceful removal was due to the request of any member of the clergy, the guilty person is subject to an episcopal tribunal and strict punishment, denied the right of clerical duties, and expelled from the clergy.

12. Church vessels and other appurtenances of the church service should be protected by all possible means against desecration and destruction, and for this reason should not be removed from safe depositories. And the latter should be constructed in such a manner that they could not be easily opened by robbers.

13. In case of attempted seizure of church vessels, appurtenances of the church service, church registers and other church property, the same should not be surrendered voluntarily, inasmuch as (a) church vessels and other appurtenances of church service are blessed for church use and the congregation should not even touch them; (b) church registers are indispensable for church uses, and the secular authorities, if in need of same, should see to the preparation of them themselves; (c) church property belongs to the Holy Church, and the clergy and all Orthodox people are merely their guardians.

14. In cases of attack by despoilers or looters of church property, the church people should be called to the defense of the church, sound the alarm and send out for help.

15. Should seizure nevertheless take place, it is absolutely necessary to make a report thereof to the diocese, signed by witnesses, with an accurate description of the articles seized, and indicating by name those guilty of the seizure.

* * * * *

(Articles 16-27 deal with excommunication of guilty persons; Articles 28-31 with Church marriages.)

32. Until further notice of the church authorities, it is obligatory to enter promptly in the books of record the births, certificates of baptism, marriages and deaths in the usual manner.

33. The collecting by the clergy of statistical data and the forwarding of the same to the civil authorities is not compulsory on the clergy. However, the representatives of the civil authorities must have access to the church records, for the copying of information required by them, under the supervision of members of the diocese.

(From Anderson, *People, Church and State in Modern Russia*, pp. 55-57.)

10
Resolution of the Commissariat of Justice Concerning Execution of the Decree of Separation of Church and State, and of School from Church.

(Compilation of Decrees, 1918, No. 62, page 685)

1. The decree concerning "Separation of Church and State, and of School from Church" (*Compilation of Decrees*, No. 18, Article 263) applies to: a) The following churches: The Orthodox, The Old Believers' Church, the Roman Catholic Church of all Rites, the Armenian-Gregorian, and the Protestant Church, and the following Creeds: the Jewish, the Mohammedan, the Buddhist-Lamaite; b) all other private religious associations formed for the purpose of religious worship according to any religious cult, prior to as well as after the promulgation of the decree concerning the "Separation of Church and State, etc.," and also c) all associations membership in which is limited solely to persons of one and the same creed, and which, be it even under the guise of charity, education, or other aims, serve the purpose of rendering direct support and assistance to any religious cult whatsoever (in the shape of maintaining the ministers of such cult, or institutions of the cult, etc.).

2. All associations mentioned in Article I under the Decree concerning the "Separation of Church and State, etc.," are deprived of the rights of a juridical person. Individual members of such associations shall have the right to arrange only collections for the purpose of acquiring property for religious purposes, and for satisfying other religious needs.

3. Charitable, educational, and other similar associations mentioned in clause "c" of Article I, as well as those of them which, although veiling their religious aims under the guise of charity or education, etc., spend money for religious purposes, shall be closed, all their property being turned over by the Soviet of Workmen-Peasant Deputies to the corresponding Commissariats or Departments.

PROPERTY INTENDED FOR THE OBSERVANCE OF RELIGIOUS RITES

4. All property which, at the time the Decree concerning the "Separation of Church and State, etc." was promulgated, was under the management of the Orthodox Ecclesiastical Department and other religious and ecclesiastic institutions and associations, shall under the Decree be transferred to the direct management of the local Soviets of Workmen-Peasant Deputies, on conditions laid down in the following articles.

5. The local Soviet of Workmen-Peasant Deputies shall make it incumbent upon the representatives of the former ecclesiastical departments or other persons belonging to the given religious creed, in whose actual posses-

sion and management is the church and all other property for purposes of religious worship, to compile in triplicate, a specification of all property intended specially for the performance of divine service and religious rites. According to such specification the Soviet of Workmen-Peasant Deputies takes over the property from the representatives of the said religious cult, and hands it over, together with the specification, for use free of charge, to such local inhabitants of the same religious creed who want to use such property; the second copy of the specification, with the signatures of those who have taken the property over, shall be kept in the local Soviet of Workmen-Peasant Deputies, while the third copy is to be sent to the Commissariat of Education.

6. The number of local inhabitants required for obtaining the use of such ritual property shall be fixed by the local Soviet of Workmen-Peasant Deputies, but cannot be less than 20 persons.

7. If the representatives of the abolished Ecclesiastical Department, or those persons in whose actual possession the given property is, refuse to produce the required specification, as mentioned in Article 5, the representative of the local Soviet of Workmen-Peasant Deputies shall check such property and compile a list of it in the presence of the group of persons to whom such property is to be handed over, or their representatives, before witnesses summoned from the number of local inhabitants, and shall turn it over to the group of persons of the respective creed who have stated their wish to receive such ritual property for use for purposes of religious worship.

8. Those who have taken over the property for use shall undertake: (I.) to keep it carefully, as property of the people entrusted to them; (II.) to keep the said property in good repair, and cover all expenditure connected with the possession of the property, such as: expenses for heating, insurance, protection, payment of debts, local taxes and dues, etc.; (III.) to make use of such property solely for the purpose of meeting religious requirements; (IV.) to make good all losses during the use of such property, bearing joint responsibility for the integrity of the property entrusted to them; (V.) to keep a detailed specification of all ritual property and to enter in this specification all subsequently added articles and objects used for religious worship (presented as gifts, transferred from other churches, etc.), provided they are not the private property of individual citizens; (VI.) to admit freely and unrestrictedly, at times when divine service is not going on, persons authorized by the Soviet of Workmen-Peasant Deputies to make periodical revisions and inspections of the property; and (VII.) in case the Soviet of Workmen-Peasant Deputies should disclose pilferings and malpractices, to immediately surrender such property to the said Soviet, whenever requested to do so. All the above conditions are to be introduced into the agreement which is to be concluded by the aforesaid group of citizens with the local Soviet of Workmen-Peasant Deputies (Appendix).

9. Churches and houses of prayer of historic, artistic, and archeological value shall be transferred in accordance with a special instruction elaborated by the Museum Section of the Commissariat of Education.

10. All local inhabitants of the corresponding religion shall have the right to sign the agreement mentioned in Articles 5 to 8 also after the transfer of the said property, and they shall thus acquire the right to participate in the administration of the ritual property, on the same level as the group of people which originally received this right.

11. In case there is nobody desirous to take over on the above mentioned conditions the ritual property, the local Soviet of Workmen-Peasants Deputies shall make a public offer three times through the agency of the local press, and exhibit a notice to that effect on the doors of the houses of prayer.

12. If after the expiration of one week after the last publication there is no application for taking over the property on the conditions mentioned above, the local Soviet of Workmen-Peasant Deputies shall notify the Commissariat of Education of this. In its communication the Soviet of Workmen-Peasants Deputies shall state the time at which the given house of prayer was built, pointing out its merits from an economic, historic, and artistic point of view, and mentioning for what purpose it is proposed to utilize the building, with further comments, if any, on this subject.

13. On receipt of a reply from the Commissariat of Education, the Soviet of Workmen-Peasant Deputies will carry out the suggestion of the Commissariat of Education, or, if there are none, its own notions on this point.

14. So-called sacred objects contained or kept in buildings not utilized for religious purposes may be handed over either to a group of persons belonging to the corresponding religious creed in accordance with the rules laid down in Articles 5 to 8, or else be turned over to the corresponding institutions of the Soviet Republic.

15. The erection of new churches and houses of prayer shall be permitted unrestrictedly on the condition that general technical rules applying to building work are observed. Estimates and plans of the construction are subject to approval of the Architectural Commission of the local Soviet of Workmen-Peasant Deputies. Completion of such building work shall be guaranteed by the builders by depositing with the State Treasury a certain sum to be fixed by the Soviet of Workmen-Peasant Deputies, which sum shall be paid back in installments to cover building expenses in the measure as the work progresses. Possession of the thus constructed church is to be given in conformity with Articles 5 to 8 of the present Instruction.

OTHER PROPERTY

16. All other property of Church and religious associations which does not serve special religious or ritual purposes, also property of the abolished departments, such as: buildings, landed property, country estates, works, candle

factories and other factories, fishing grounds, hospices, hotels, funds, and generally speaking, all property yielding profit, irrespective of the character of such property, which has up to the present not yet been taken over by the Soviet institutions, shall immediately be confiscated and taken away from the said associations and (abolished) departments.

17. The local Soviets of Workmen-Peasant Deputies shall request the representatives of the (abolished) religious departments, Sections of the People's Bank, Savings Banks, and persons, in whose actual possession such property subject to nationalization may be, to furnish within a fortnight, under penalty of the law, information concerning all property belonging to local religious organizations, or to the former (abolished) religious departments.

18. Information thus received shall be actually verified and checked by persons specially authorized for this purpose by the Soviet of Workmen-Peasant Deputies, and the results of such verification shall be recorded in writing, which record, together with the specification of articles of property, shall then be attached to the other documents relating to the property of the abolished religious departments and of Church or religious associations. The same is to be done with all other documents and records relating to such property. One copy of the specification submitted to the Soviet of Workmen-Peasant Deputies, and verified by the latter, the said Soviet shall forward to the Commissariat of Education and the State Audit Commissariat.

19. All capital in money belonging to the abolished religious departments, and churches or other religious associations, whatever the description of such capital and wherever they may be deposited, shall, when found, be taken over by the Soviets of Workmen-Peasant Deputies within a fortnight. (Appendix)

Note: If the contingency arises, the local Soviet of Workmen-Peasants Deties shall have the right to leave, at its discretion, to the group of persons who have entered into the agreement referred to in Articles 5 to 8, a certain amount of money required for the performance of religious rites to the end of the year.

20. All capital belonging to the abolished religious departments and Church or other religious associations, which may be in the hands of private persons or organizations, shall be claimed and called in from then within a fortnight. The holders of such monies, if they fail to comply with this regulation and omit to surrender such monies in their possession, shall be held criminally and civily liable for embezzlement of such sums.

21. All monies thus collected must be deposited by the Soviet of Workmen-Peasant Deputies with the local Treasury Branch not later than within three days after the receipt of such monies, and shall be placed to the credit of the Republic's name and revenue account, the receipts relating to the paying-in of such monies to be attached to the corresponding records. The Soviet of Workmen-Peasant Deputies shall be held to notify the Commissariat of

Education and the State Audit Commissariat without delay of the receipt of such monies.

22. If the Church or religious associations have monies in savings banks or in branches of the People's Bank, the bank books and banking documents and vouchers must be surrendered by the holders at the first request on the part of the Soviet of Workmen-Peasant Deputies. Such documents, after being endorsed to the effect that they are null and void, shall be attached to the other documents recorded, but the respective savings banks and branches of the People's Bank shall be notified by the Soviet of Workmen and Peasant Deputies that the respective monies must without delay be credited to the treasury. Of this too the Commissariat of Education and the State Audit Commissariat must be informed.

23. For illicit use of property belonging to the Republic, or for intentional damage to such property, the guilty shall be held criminally responsible.

24. All measures in connection with the confiscation of Church or religious property must be completed not later than within two months after the present Instruction has been published, and information regarding execution of the Instruction must be given to the Commissariat of Education and to Section VIII. of the Commissariat of Justice.

25. All law suits that might be filed subsequently concerning the rights of private persons to any property of the abolished religious departments or religious and Church associations, nationalized in accordance with the Decree concerning "Separation of Church and State, etc." and the present Instruction, shall be tried and settled in the way of ordinary civil procedure.

BIRTH, MARRIAGE AND DEATH REGISTRATION BOOKS

26. All registration books of all religious creeds and covering all previous years, which for one reason or another have until now not been taken away from the ecclesiastical authorities and consistories, Church administration, municipal councils (Jewish registration books), and all other provincial institutions where such books hitherto were kept, shall without delay be turned over to the Provincial (Oblast) Birth, Marriage and Death Registries.

27. Registration books covering all previous years from all urban and rural churches of any creed are subject to immediate seizure by the Soviet of the Workmen-Peasant Deputies, one copy to be turned over either to the local (urban or volost) Registration Sections, or to the corresponding notarial offices (in places where the notarial sections attend to such registration) while the other copy (the clean copy numbered and filed) shall be sent to the Provincial Birth, Marriage and Death Registration Section. After the books have been seized, servants of the cult shall have the right to take copies from such registration books, if they need them and desire to do so.

28. In conformity with the prohibition to make on passports, or other official documents establishing personal identity, endorsements relating to

the religious creed of citizens, it shall likewise be prohibited to make on passports inscriptions or endorsements concerning the performance of certain religious rites (such as baptism, confirmation, circumcision, marriage, burial, etc.), as well as divorces pronounced by servants of religious cults, or religious institutions of any creed whatever.

RELIGIOUS CEREMONIES AND RITES

29. In state and other public premises intended for the performance of legal acts, it shall be absolutely prohibited:

a) To conduct religious rites and ceremonies (divine services, memorial services, etc.).

b) To exhibit religious images of any description (sacred images, pictures, religious stationery of any character, etc.).

30. The local Soviet authorities shall adopt every suitable measure to eradicate such practices as mentioned in the previous article, as being contradictory to the Decree concerning freedom of conscience.

Note: The removal of religious images of artistic or historic value, as well as decisions concerning their further fate, shall be attended to with the consent of the Commissariat of Education.

31. Religious processions, and the performance of religious rites in streets and public places, shall be permitted only by written permission of the local Soviet authorities, which permission the arrangers of such procession shall be held to obtain in good time, and at any rate not later than two days previous to the proposed performance of the religious ceremony. In the matter of issuing such permission the Soviet of Workmen-Peasant Deputies shall be guided by Article 5 of the Decree concerning "Separation of Church and State, etc."

32. The local Soviet authorities shall remove, or cause the competent or concerned persons to remove, from churches and other houses of prayer constituting national property all articles offending the religious feelings of the labor masses, such as: marble or other boards, inscriptions on the walls and on objects used for divine service, in memory of any persons who were members of the dynasty overthrown by the People, or its supporters.

RELIGIOUS INSTRUCTION AND TEACHING

33. In view of the separation of School and Church, instruction in any creed must not in any case be permitted in state, public, and private educational establishments, with the exception of purely theological establishments.

34. All credits voted for religious instruction in schools shall be immediately stopped, and leaders of religious creeds shall be deprived of all rations and supplies hitherto issued to them. No state or other public institution shall have the right to issue the instructors of religion any monies for the present time or due to them since the month of January 1918.

35. The buildings of spiritual, educational and training establishments of any creed, as well as of the parish church schools, shall, as national property, be turned over to the local Soviets of Workmen-Peasant Deputies, or to the Commissariat of Education.

Note: The Soviets of Workmen-Peasant Deputies may lease or let such buildings for the purpose of establishing in them special training establishments of any religious creed, on general conditions applicable to all citizens, and with the knowledge of the Commissariat of Education.

Signed: The Commissar of Justice: D. KURSKII
August 24, 1918.

(Published in No. 186 of the *Izvestiia,* dated August 30, 1918.)

APPENDIX

Agreement

We, the undersigned citizens (of such and such a locality or town), residing in such locality, have concluded the present agreement with the . . . (such and such) Soviet of Workmen-Peasant Deputies, represented by its plenipotentiary (office, name and surname) to the effect that on this . . . . day of the month of . . . . in the year . . . . we have taken over for use, for an indefinite period and free of charge, the (description of the Church or religious building) situated (. . . .), with property required for ritual purposes in accordance with a special list, signed by ourselves, on the following conditions:

1. We, the undersigned citizens, undertake to maintain and keep the national property entrusted to us, and to use it solely for the purpose it is intended for, assuming all responsibility for the integrity and safety of such property entrusted to us, and also for the fulfilment of other obligations devolving on us under this Agreement.

2. We undertake to use, and to permit our co-religionists to use, the churches and ritual articles in them solely for the purpose of satisfying religious needs.

3. We undertake to make sure that the property entrusted to us is made no other use of than for purposes mentioned in Articles 1 and 2 of this Agreement.

More particularly we undertake to prohibit in religious buildings and premises taken over by ourselves:

A) Political meetings hostile to the Soviet regime.

B) The spreading or selling of books, pamphlets, and other literature hostile to the Soviet regime or its individual representatives, and,

C) Delivering sermons and speeches hostile to the Soviet regime or its individual representatives.

D) The ringing of alarm bells for the purpose of calling up the population and inciting it against the Soviet regime; in view of which we undertake to fulfill all regulations and orders of the local Soviet of Workmen and Peasant Deputies in regard to the rules for using belfries and belltowers.

4. We undertake to cover from our own sources all current expenses in connection with the maintenance of the Church (or other building for religious purposes) and articles or objects in it, such as: keeping it in a proper state of repair, heating, insurance, guarding, payment of debts, taxes, local imposts, etc.

5. We undertake to keep an inventory of the entire ritual property in which we shall enter all articles newly acquired (by way of gifts, offerings, or transfer from other churches) for ritual purposes, unless they are the private property of individual citizens.

6. We undertake to admit without restriction, at times when no divine service is going on, persons authorized by the Soviet of Workmen-Peasant Deputies to inspect and check the property.

7. For loss of, or damage to, articles entrusted to us we assume civil liability conjointly, to the extent of the actual loss or damage sustained.

8. In case of return of property entrusted to us, we undertake to return it in the same shape and condition in which we received it for use and for keeping.

9. In cemetery churches and in grave yards we undertake to bury co-religionists, in case persons interested desire it, with observance of religious rites which in all cases must be at equal fees for all citizens, the amount of such fee to be brought by ourselves to public notice every year.

10. In the event we fail to adopt all measures in our power in order to fulfill all our obligations under this agreement, or for direct infractions of the provisions of this Agreement, we shall be criminally liable and shall be dealt with with all severity of revolutionary law; and in such contingencies the Soviet of Workmen-Peasant Deputies shall have the right to cancel this Agreement.

11. In case we desire to terminate this Agreement, we undertake to give notice in writing to the Soviet of Workmen-Peasant Deputies, and for the space of one week after such notice has been given by us to the Soviet of Workmen-Peasant Deputies, the provisions of this Agreement shall continue binding on us, and we shall continue to be responsible for its execution; we also undertake to return within this space of time the property taken over by us.

12. Every one of us who has signed this Agreement shall have the right to withdraw from it, giving notice in writing to the Soviet of Workmen-Peasant Deputies; this, however, shall not relieve the given person of liability for losses and damage sustained by the respective national property during the time the given person participated in the use and administration

of such property, prior to giving the Soviet of Workmen-Peasant Deputies notice of his intention to withdraw.

13. None of us, nor all of us taken together, shall have the right to refuse any citizen, who is our co-religionist and not disqualified by verdict of court, to sign after this date the present Agreement, and to participate in the adminisration and management of the property mentioned in this Agreement, on identical conditions with all other persons who have signed it.

The original of this Agreement shall be kept by the . . . . Soviet of Workmen-Peasant Deputies, and a duly certified copy shall be issued to the group of citizens who have signed the Agreement, and who have taken over for religious uses the Church and the ritual articles in it, as specified in the inventory.

1919

11
On Religion

From the Program of the All-Russian Communist Party
Adopted at the Eighth Congress, March 18-23, 1919

13. With reference to religion, the All-Russian Communist Party does not content itself with the already decreed separation of church from state — i.e., with measures which are a part of the program of bourgeois democracies, but never fulfilled in those democracies because of the many various ties binding capital with religious propaganda.

The All-Russian Communist Party is guided by the conviction that only the realization of conscious and systematic social and economic activity of the masses will lead to the disappearance of religious prejudices. The aim of the Party is finally to destroy the ties between the exploiting classes and the organization of religious propaganda, at the same time helping the toiling masses actually to liberate their minds from religious superstitions, and organizing on a wide scale scientific-educational and anti-religious propaganda. It is, however, necessary carefully to avoid offending the religious suscepti-bilities of believers, which leads only to the strengthening of religious fanati-cism. (Moscow, 1920, Communist Library, No. 6.)

12
Telegram of Cardinal Gasparri to Lenin

April 2, 1919

Lenin
Moscow

Pope Benedict XV has learned with boundless grief that Monseigneur Ropp, Archbishop of Mogilev, has been taken as a hostage in Petrograd by the Bolsheviks. He earnestly asks Mr. Lenin to give orders which will set him free at once.

Cardinal Gasparri

49

13
Telegram of Lenin to Cardinal Gasparri

Cardinal Gasparri:
After receiving your telegram I requested an explanation from Petrograd. The reply was that Archbishop Ropp had never been arrested; it is his nephew Evgenii Vasilevich Ropp, a young man, 22 years old, who was arrested for speculation and who is a confederate of Lamnsen Gobaget.

Lenin

[Archb. Edward Ropp was arrested; see *Osservatore Romano,* Dec. 28, 1919, Mar. 22, 1920]

14
Letter of Archbishop Silvestr to Pope Benedict XV

Omsk, February 7, 1919
To His Holiness:
"The supreme authorities of the Orthodox Church in the parts of Russia liberated from the Bolshevik power address you, Venerable Father, with a humble entreaty of obtaining your attention in the following matter. Having seized in 1917 the supreme power in Russia, the Bolsheviks began to destroy not only the higher social classes and objects of art but also the monuments of religious cults, and the representatives of all the religions which are highly respected by all the people. The churches of the Kremlin in Moscow and of the towns of Iaroslavl and Simferopol were ransacked, many temples sacrilegiously stained, and historical sacristies as well as the libraries of the Patriarchs in Moscow and Petrograd looted. The Metropolitan Vladimir of Kiev, nearly twenty Bishops, and hundreds of priests, were assassinated. Before the executions, the Bolsheviks bind the legs and arms of their victims; some are buried alive. Religious processions attended by great crowds of people in Petrograd, Tula, Kharkov and Soligalich were dispersed with the use of arms. In areas where Bolshevik authorities rule, the Christian Church is persecuted with more ferocity than in the first three centuries of Christianity. In violation of the religion, they proclaim the socialization of women and licentiousness in the most disorderly passions. Death, cold and famine are seen everywhere. The population is depressed, submissive to outrages. Some come out of it purified, others only yield to it. It is only in the southern and Ural region of Siberia that, after the expulsion of the Bolsheviks, it is possible to regulate civil and religious life under the aegis of law.

It is with a feeling of profound sorrow that we inform you, Venerable
Father, of the woes suffered by millions of Russians in Russia proper. On
the strength of human solidarity, and in the feeling of Christian fraternity,
Venerable Father, we count on your compassion as the Representative of the
Christian Church and hope your flock will be informed of the things going
on here. We hope and trust that to Him Who keeps in His Hands life and
death you and your people will send up ardent prayers for those who in this
part of Europe have become, through love for Christ, martyrs of their faith
in the 20th century".

Archbishop Silvestr
President of the Supreme Church
Administration

15
Telegram of Pope Benedict XV to Archbishop Silvestr

April 2, 1919

Archbishop Silvestr
President of the Supreme Church Authority, Omsk

We thank Your Worship for the telegram which he sent to us and we
wholeheartedly participate in the anguishes and preoccupations there manifested. Vicar on earth of Him who is the Prince of Peace, we raise to Heaven
our earnest prayers that peace and tranquillity return soon in Russia and that
the consolations and implored heavenly succours are granted to all.

BENEDICTUS PP. XV

16
Telegram of Cardinal Gasparri to Lenin

April 2, 1919

Lenin
Moscow

It is reported by reliable sources that your partisans persecute ministers of
God, particularly those who belong to the Russian religion called Orthodox.
The Holy Father Benedict XV implores you to issue strict orders that ministers of all religions be respected. Humanity and religion will be thankful to
you for this.

Cardinal Gasparri

17
Telegram of Chicherin to Cardinal Gasparri

April 2, 1919

Cardinal Gasparri

Rome

Having received your telegram of March 12, I have to assure you that the reliable source mentioned in this radio-telegram has misled you. The separation of Church and State having been accomplished in Russia, religion is treated there as a private matter. Thus, it is absolutely erroneous to talk about the persecution of clergymen. In our country nothing has happened to the Orthodox similar to the regular mistreatment of them in areas dominated by the Roman Catholic Church. Regarding the special interest which you reveal concerning the religion which was previously condemned by the Roman Catholic Church as schismatic and heretic, and which you call Orthodox, I can guarantee you that no clergyman of this religion has suffered on account of his religious convictions. As for those among them who participated in conspiracies against the Soviet Government and the authority of the workers and peasants, we are going to continue with the treatment which we have inflicted on them because they have to be subject to the same laws as the other citizens, and because no privileged situation, in comparison with laymen, should belong to them. With regard to the spirit of solidarity shown by you in respect of the Orthodox clergy I can inform you that, in the midst of general scarcity, immense wealth which had been gathered by the Orthodox clergy has been discovered in the cloisters. Some of those clergymen, instigated by the measures directed against us by allied and associated Powers against whom you have not as yet made any protests, had secretly amassed enormous stocks of provisions, thus depriving of them the masses of our people.

You inform us that the Supreme Head of the Roman Catholic Church implores us to change our attitude towards the Orthodox clergy. This sign of solicitude for them, however, arrives at the moment when an open and determined action of our popular authorities has nullified the frauds through which the clergy deceived the masses and on which they based their ascendancy. Golden sepulchres glittering with precious stones, containing what the clergy called incorruptible saintly relics, were opened, and in the place where supposedly should be present the relics of Tikhon of Zadonsk, St. Mitrofan of Voronezh, Prince Konstantin of Murom and his children Mihhail and Feodor, Makarii of Kaliazin, Bishops Ioann and Feodor of Suzdal, and others, there were discovered some rotting bones crumbling into dust, a lot of cotton wool, cushions, dresses, and even women's stockings. It seems to me necessary to point out that it is just at this moment that our actions in respect of the clergy have had the misfortune of displeasing you. It is also unfortunate that innumerable atrocities were committed by the enemies of the Russian people, by the Czecho-Slovaks, by the Governments of Kolchak, Denikin, Petlura, and among others by the parties actually in power in Poland, which include Catholic Archbishops among their leaders. The agents of these Polish organizations — who use atrocious tortures against the champions of the people's cause who fall into their hands, and who have even assassinated the members of our Red Cross mission in Poland — have not become the object of protets from you. The voice of humanity for which our popular revolution fights is not respected by those who consider themselves to be your partisans, and not a word from your mouth has been issued in its favor.

People's Commissar for Foreign Affairs
Chicherin

(Nos. 12-17, *Osservatore Romano*, April 2, 1919)

1921

18

The New York Herald on Soviet Church Policy

The New York Herald, Sunday, June 9, 1921

BOLSHEVIKS BEGIN ATTACKING CHURCH
START NEW PAPER CARICATURING
ORTHODOXY AND RELIGION IN RUSSIA

Closing Monasteries — Their Lands, Money, Factories,
Hospitals and Asylums Sequestered.
Ban Set on All Worship.

Those Refusing to Carry Out Programme to Be Dealt With Severely.

Special Correspondent to the NEW YORK HERALD

Revel, June 1. — The Bolsheviks are beginning their long delayed attack on religion, and have consequently started in Moscow a new paper called "Revolution and the Church", filled with articles, caricatures and poetry designed to turn the Russian Church into ridicule. The first number of this paper contains the following account of Church and monastic property sequestered by the Bolsheviks since the suppression of the monasteries: Three hundred and twenty-seven thousand, three hundred and forty *desiatinas* of land, 4,247,664,520 rubles, 84 factories, 1,112 leased houses bringing in a good income, 706 hotels, 227 hospitals and asylums, 435 milk farms, 602 cattle sheds and 311 beehives.

The Extraordinary Commission has also in a circular to all the members of the Bolshevist party, drawn attention to the deplorable fact that many of those members still remain "in the zone of orthodoxy," sing psalms occasionally, and attend sometimes to their religious duties. All this the Extraordinary Commission denounces as "'improper."

MUST BAR RELIGION

"In almost every lodge of our organization" it says, "there are to be found individual members who do not adhere to our rules regarding religion. Point thirteen of our programme makes it obligatory on all members of our party to carry on anti-religious propaganda, but while the party as a whole is carrying on this struggle with religious tendencies there are to be found individual members who not only refrain from carrying it on but actually strengthen the religious sentiment among the people with whom they live and to whom they are bound by material, economic and family ties. Apparently they lack the strength of mind to oppose this tendency.

"In the struggle with this evil the various lodges of our party must take whatever measures seem most suitable to meet the necessities of each individual case. The Central Committee appeals to all the organizations and to all members of the party to send it concrete proposals in this connection and to bring out the most striking facts known to them touching these breaches of our rules. All communications to be sent to the Anti-Propaganda Department, Central Committee, Russian Communist Party, Iaroslavskii, Head of the Anti-Propaganda Section, Katanian."

PARVUS ON WAGE REDUCTION

The German master spy, Parvus, writes as follows about Bolshevism in his newspaper the *Kolokolo:*

"Russia is the only country in the world which can dare to reduce the salaries of her workmen. Consequently, Russia will become the greatest centre in the whole world for industry and trade. Russia will create millionaires in comparison with whose colossal wealth all the other millionaires whom the world has yet seen will only be beggars. And, in addition to this, Russia, thanks to her peasantry, is the only country in the world which can mobilize an army. England could not carry out a general mobilization again: it would cause a revolution, so unpopular has military service become among the workmen; and it is doubtful if France could do so either. But the Russian peasants will be passive weapons in the hands of the Government, against opposition inside Russia and from without."

The same writer divides the Bolsheviks into two categories — the seekers after adventure and the idealists. The first class is, he thinks, the more numerous. They are more energetic and active than the idealists. They have got rich through "plunder and confiscation and speculation, but now that there is a danger of all their riches being useless to them, because of Russia's tendency to collapse, they are trying to establish trade with the outer world. If they do good business these desperate adventurers will change completely and become merchant princes. With the growth of trade they will utilize their strength so that their vast wealth will be placed on a solid basis and in absolute security."

EVOLUTION OF IDEALISTS

Of the Bolshevist idealists, Parvus says that they are now going through "an amazing and terrible evolution. The Bolshevist idealists, or at least those among them who understand that it is impossible really to unite themselves with Western European Socialism, now wish to establish an enormous business republic in order to realize Socialism by means of an adaptation of economic methods. This plan will lead them finally to hold down all Russia by armed force.

"In the Communist *Red Flag* there has already been printed a letter from Moscow about the triumphs of the Second Red Army in Gruzia. That letter tells how the Soviet Government has now in its hands all the oil of the Caucasus, but it never seems to strike the writer that this is naked imperialism.

"In order that State trading on the gigantic scale that the Bolsheviks contemplate may give the desired result, it will be necessary to crush the opposition of the working classes. The Bolsheviks have already begun to do so, and they will continue on that path until it leads them to a period of colossal capitalism with intellectual Bolshevist leaders in charge."

Before condemning this prophecy one should call to mind the fact that the Germans have shown an almost uncanny insight into the capabilities of Bolshevism. When not one Russian in a million knew who Lenin was, and when the Russian secret police and the British and French governments were almost equally in the dark, Germany knew exactly what Lenin would do if he was sent to Russia — and he did it.

19

Letter of the U.S. Commissioner in Riga to the Secretary of State

August 30, 1921

CONFIDENTIAL
The Secretary of State,
    Washington, D.C.
Sir:

I have the honor to forward, in quintuplicate, a confidential memorandum in regard to the religious movement in Russia.

I have the honor to be, Sir,

Your obedient servant
Evan E. Young
Commissioner

Enclosure: As stated.

Confidential — From J. S.

August 24, 1921

RELIGIOUS MOVEMENT IN RUSSIA

After the Bolshevik revolution in Russia, the new rulers were not slow to realize the danger which the church might constitute, and consequently set to work to oppress all faith and to combat religion.

In spite of the great influence of the Church, it was obviously impossible, in the existing state of feeling in the country, to attempt to resist the new rulers by force, and thus the only aim of the clergy was to try and preserve their influence over the masses, and to save what remained of their authority until such time as conditions had changed.

This passive role has now been adhered to for three years, and during this period the personality of the Patriarch Tikhon has been of the utmost value. He is neither vain nor ambitious, and has only aimed at reestablishing the authority of the church over the people, and winning them back to religion. As a result of his wise policy the Church in Russia is once again winning back her influence. This has been brought about by many causes, among which are the persecution and acts of sacrilege committed by the Bolsheviks, the narrow materialism they preach, and the disasters which have overtaken Russia, and which the peasants ascribe to the visitation of God. For some time past attendance at churches has been increasing, and now in the larger centers they are always crowded. Renewed interest is being taken in religious questions, and the Church is regaining all her old influence. Popular clergymen are reappearing, and not only hold together large congregations, but also form the centers of tendencies and movements which influence the minds of people.

The religious revival now taking place is in no way due to any special ability on the part of the clergy, — for reforms in the Russian Church are still essential. It rather indicates that the masses of the people are regaining their lost ideals. It is also of interest to note that, in the centers, active propaganda is being carried on for a union between the Greek Church and Catholicism.

How far the revival of religion in Russia will affect the future it is difficult to foresee. In connection with the famine relief, it became clear that the Church was the only organization outside the Government which had the power and means of assisting, and this was recognized by the Soviet leaders themselves.

It is not in the direction of organizing any movement against the present regime that the influence of the Church will be felt, but rather in moderating the tendencies of the population in any future upheavals which may occur, and of eventually uniting them under a moderate Government, and in assisting in the regeneration of Russia.

20
Soviet Russia (Religious Movement)

Riga U.S. Commissioner, (From J. S.)
November 21, 1921

Information has been received in the small Kremlin to the effect that, among the peasants of the Vetluga, Iaransk, and Kotelnich districts of the

Kostroma and Viatka governorships, there has been a religious movement on foot since the autumn, which has followers and workers among the clergy and non-communist village teachers. The principal objects of this movement are the protection and restoration of the Orthodox Church, and the fight against anti-religious propaganda. Simultaneously, the promoters of this movement, who are secretly and energetically spreading their doctrines, are pushing the idea of finding a new government which would be in a position to protect the Church and its flock from persecution at the hands of the Communists. The movement is most successful among women and old believers. In view of its development in adjacent governorships, i.e. Kazan, Nizhni-Novgorod, Iaroslavl and Vologda, the governorship Chekas have been instructed to keep a special watch on the activities of the clergy, and to report on any of the priests who are suspected of taking part in meetings, with a view to transferring them to other governorships. The Soviet Government fears to use stronger measures because of the enormous influence of the Church among the people, which might bring about results highly undesirable for the Bolsheviks. This is referred to in the special memorandum from the All-Russian Cheka sent to its local branches about the end of October last.

Simultaneously, the circular instructions to party Communists issued in July last, regarding the intensification of anti-religious propaganda, were confirmed.

It would appear that the Patriarch Tikhon is not connected with the movement.

21
Resolution Taken by the Russian Church Council Abroad at Sremski Karlovtsi, Nov. 21/Dec. 3, 1921

Kingdom of the Serbs, Croats and Slovenes

To the scattered and exiled Children of the Russian Church.

Beloved in Jesus Christ!

The avenging hand of God is held over us. Russia is suffering for grievous sins and the Russian people are scattered over the whole world.

There is no limit or measure to the crimes perpetrated on Russian land. Temples have been defiled, sacred relics defamed. There is a struggle against God, and blood flows.

The blood even of the Sovereign anointed by God has been spilled and he has ended his life as a martyr.

The land is impoverished, people are perishing, those in power are godless and the Church is persecuted.

The Russian Land is in darkness and men look in vain for the path to salvation.

But God in his mercy has left to the horror-struck people an unquenchable light — the Orthodox Church.

The Patriarch has been placed at the head of the Russian Church by Providence, so that in the unity of the Church there may live a hope of Russian unity.

The Russian people in their distress and affliction are returning to the shelter of the Church.

The Temples are filled to overflowing, unceasing are the cries of penitence, the prayers for mercy, and for a power which will defend life and work and guard the Christian soul. The measure of God's wrath is not yet full, grief is not yet over.

Our duty in foreign lands — that duty of the scattered ones who have saved their lives and who do not know such distress as is destroying our native country and its people — is to be united in a Christian spirit, gathered under the sign of the Cross of God, under the shelter of the Orthodox Church and Faith.

Let our unceasing prayer to God the Merciful be that He should pardon us and our country our grievous sins and crimes and enlighten our minds with the light of truth, our hearts with the flame of love, and strengthen our will in the path of righteousness.

Russia has always been preserved from evil and built up during centuries by the prayers of Saints and ascetic men and by the toils of its anointed Tsars.

Therefore, now also let our unceasing prayer be that the Lord shall show us the way to save and build up our native country; that He shall give protection to Faith and Church and our entire country and that He shall enlighten the heart of the Nation; that He shall return to the Throne of All-Russia His anointed, strong in the love of the people, the lawful Orthodox Tsar of the House of Romanov.

Praying for the forgiveness of our sins, asking for light in the future, let each one take on himself the sins of his brother — so that joined by faith and love we shall all enter into our House when the Lord opens the way, like the united flock of one shepherd, ready to bring sacrifice for the service of our Country and for the welfare of the Nation.

Metropolitan Antonii,
President of the Russian Church Abroad.

22

Epistle to All Orthodox Russian Refugees Abroad from the Russian Church Council at Sremski Karlovtsi, Nov. 21/ Dec. 3, 1921, Kingdom of the Serbs, Croats and Slovenes.

*By the rivers of Babylon, there we sat down,
yea, we wept, when we remembered Zion* [Ps. 137:1]

Deep sorrow at the loss of our fatherland and especially that our country has fallen under the power of godless men — Jews and Chinese — brings horror to your hearts, and the ruin that has befallen you, the pressing need of earning a piece of bread, even if it be stale, torments your souls.

It is true that most of our refugees, young as well as old, have learned much through their misfortune, but even for them the long duration of the trial that has befallen us may cause hopelessness and bring them to repining. To prevent such a sin, the Russian Church Council, having representatives of all refugees abroad, meeting at Sremski Karlovtsi on the day of St. Michael, deems it its duty to turn to you, Russian refugees, with some words of consolation.

Our first consolation is of course the idea that we are not forgotten by God, but punished by Him for forgetting Him and His Commandments. The punishment of God is nothing but a proof of His love, as is certified by St. Paul the Apostle.

However, it is not of the sins of the Russian society that we shall write to you but of the good that has appeared in the life of Russian refugees abroad. There has been more good than could have been expected. The first thing is that they have remembered their God; many who did not before know the strength of prayer have now learned to pray; others who used to pray in their youth and ceased to do this under the influence of sinful passions and false teachings, have again returned to prayer. Many in these difficult years of their life have turned to the reading of the Gospel; many are reading books on philosophy and theology wishing to be rationally guided in their beliefs, while before they were religious by habit and by chance. Many fashionable delusions, such as theosophy, spiritism, and all kinds of falsely-liberal ravings in which they believed before, have been entirely laid aside. Not only this, but they openly and frankly admit how wrong they have been in their former theories, or rather prejudices. Further, although not of their free will but through necessity, men and women — young as well as old, accustomed to luxury — have undertaken heavy work, showing an exemplary endurance, laboriousness and humility of spirit. When one sees these people at their work of making shoes, washing clothes or loading coal, when one sees them happy and unrepining, submitting to the privations that have fallen to their lot — then one is convinced that our nation, not only in the peasants but also in its intellectual class, has a glorious future, as it shows its fine soul and Christian patience, a great capacity for life and a great adaptability to the changes of fortune.

We must not shut our eyes also on the dark side, on the fact that many Russians in exile, giving in to the voice of hunger and privation, have lost the conception of honesty and honor, that the men sell their conscience and the women their honor. These sorrowful facts among the million refugees are, it is sad to say, inevitable, but not by this but rather by the consolatory signs should we judge of the present state of mind of Russian refugees and guess at the future fate of Russian society. To fall is natural in any society thrown into misery and exile, but the greater moral rise that we see on the other hand can only appear in a nation or society whose soul is much better than its exterior and than it is considered to be by casual observers. Now it is made clear that our intelligent class had a Christian soul under a worldly exterior; that at the bottom of their souls they kept, perhaps not knowing it themselves, the high evangelical rules of humility, submission to God's will, and the readiness to redeem their former sins by suffering.

If only they will keep the lessons learned in this hard school of exile. If only on their return to Russia, surrounded again by wealth, power and the possibility of influence, they will not lose the treasures of the spirit which they have earned by their suffering. What an amount of good they would then bring into the resurrected life of Russia, how much love they would show their younger brothers, how well they would understand the suffering of others and how this would bridge the gulf between the classes of society.

Everyone, beginning from the Russian Tsar, without whom of course there can be no question of the resurrection of Russia, and ending with the last citizen who is richer or more talented than at least one of his brothers, all will turn their hearts to those weaker than they and then there will be left no room for jealousy of those stronger — that devil's jealousy through which in the first place death entered the world of God and which according to the Gospel brought our Lord Jesus Christ to the Cross. (*Mark* 10: 15).

It is not in vain that we have spoken of the Tsar as such a spirit of mutual yielding. Not a struggle for one's own success and the downfall of one's neighbor, a struggle of classes, races and professions — but the spirit of moral order in national life, is possible only during a monarchic and Christian order, when at the head of the State there stands an individual conscience, a conscience which solemnly proclaims itself in submission to the Gospel and to the Church of Orthodox Faith, a conscience, rather than a group of temporarily chosen men, struggling with each other for power.

Russian people, let not this great visitation of God remain fruitless, this great lesson which can only be learned by heavy suffering. Let us thank God as the righteous Job — and we will receive his reward. Not in luxury, not in the search of power, but in obedience and patience let us look for the aim of life — individual and general.

God Himself has helped us in the first, and in the second let us seek help in our general longing to rebuild a Christian state of things, a theocratic order of life, and one moreover with a greater brotherly care of the weaker by the stronger than there was before the unhappy revolution.

Let our involuntary exile serve us as the captivity of Babylon served ancient Israel. Until this captivity the Jews, worse than the Russian society of the last half century, had forgotten their God and listened to false teachings; but after captivity the care of the whole nation was the guarding of the true faith and the love of their country, and no one even dared to think of worshipping idols.

Our exile is not 70 years, but only three or four in duration, but this is enough to acknowledge our former mistakes and to turn our hearts to God, the Church, the Tsar and our Nation.

Until this takes place we cannot return Russia to God, nor can we return to Russia. Upon you, Russian people, upon your internal resurrection, depends the duration of our trials and the time when the Lord shall pardon us.

Prepare yourself a path to our blessed Country, unite into patriotic groups, learn mutually from each other to know God and your Country, your past history and the right organization of our country in the future.

"Pour into our hearts, O Lord, Thy Divine Light."

The President of the Council
Antonii
Metropolitan of Kiev and Halich

23
Revival of Religion in Russia

[Rome, December 9, 1921]

(Report of the U. S. Ambassador in Rome)

The religious instinct, which in Russia can never be suppressed for long, has been finding its outlet by devious channels. The revival is in fact approaching a culmination. As regards the Orthodox Church, it is strongest in the cities and along the railways; wherever, in fact, Bolshevik control is strongest, religious feeling, necessarily opposed to that control, has been growing.

Its growth synchronizes with the return to their villages of demobilized army soldiers, who, with astonishing rapidity, lose their army veneer to become peasants. In a few weeks, their change from a Communist to a peasant small owner is complete. On the land, ex-zealots of Communism have developed into ardent enemies of communal ownership and fight the higher organs of authority to the death.

With these changes has come the religious revival. Women and men, old and young, have become something like religious enthusiasts. The first days of the revolution undermined and shook the prestige of the clergy. Now that these work on the land as hard as their own parishioners, the dividing wall between priest and peasant has fallen and priests are no longer open to the old taunt that they battened upon their people.

In the country districts of the Volga region, where the priests were driven out or murdered, there have been curious reversions to primitive pagan forms of worship, among which various kinds of fetishism have largely figured. The peasants' idol in these districts is generally a bull's head, which they hoist up into a tree and worship from below. But such idolatry belongs to the outlying country. In the towns, the Christian revival is gaining strength and generally there is a feeling that religion is the only common bond left to the Russian people. The Bolshevik authorities are becoming genuinely alarmed at the processions which they feel themselves powerless to prevent, especially as these processions consist of the very people who, from time to time, constitute the unwilling audience to harangues by Trotskii, Zinovev, Bukharin and other "enlightened" leaders. The masses are, in fact, regaining their lost ideals.

The revival is not due to any special ability or virtue on the part of the clergy, who generally and excusably contented themselves at first with leaving ill alone. It was futile from the beginning to attempt to resist the Bolsheviks by force, and passivity was the better part. Religion survived the flood, and the Soviet leaders themselves now recognize that the Church is the only organization outside the Government which has the power, the will and the means to assist in famine relief.

When the Tsar was deposed, the Patriarch Tikhon wisely accepted the position of head of the Russian Church and kept his Synod about him. The Orthodox Church was thus kept intact under its former headship despite the elimination of the Tsar, its theoretical head. The Patriarch remains in constant communication with his Bishops and the latter with their clergy. The Synod sits regularly in Moscow and the Bolsheviks have for some time past ceased to interefere with its activities.

In July the Patriarch and Church Synod decided to appeal to the heads of the Christian Churches to relieve the famine, and telegrams to the Pope, the Archbishop of Canterbury and the Evangelical Archbishop of New York were actually drafted. It has not been the least of the crimes of the Bolsheviks that they, who are at present screaming for the relief of the hunger-stricken, for months were assiduous in concealing the need for such relief. They suppressed the appeals. But not for long. Presently Lenin, by and with the consent of the Council of People's Commissars, sent Maxim Gorkii to request that the Patriarch should appeal not only to the heads of Churches, but also to the heads of all Christian States. Tikhon replied that he had already done his best to do the former. Gorkii said the suppression of the appeals was a mistake. Gorkii begged the Patriarch, as all material means had failed, to order prayers for the salvation of Russia.

He might have based his request on spiritual failure as well. The rulers of Russia, after their wont, were not without *arrière penser*. It has since been ascertained that, in enlisting the Patriarch's services, the Government, guided by Lenin, hoped not only to obtain famine relief, but regarded the appeals as a subsidiary means for entering into diplomatic relations with the Western States.

An upright man in his plain dealing is often a match for the astutest contriver. Tikhon refused. Negotiations with the heads of foreign governments, he said, were not for him. He consented to approach the heads of Christian Churches, with results which have been made public. It was the Patriarch's wish that foreign promoters of famine relief should conduct their activities through the church, whose power and influence, he is convinced, would suffice to direct relief into the proper channels. An emissary of his sent abroad at the end of July had instructions to suggest to the heads of Christian Churches that if the church were able to relieve the Russian people, the Russian people would look to it as their saviour. He pointed out also that control of distribution by the government would mean that the army, its own officials, and supporters would be given priority. Tikhon ended by saying that he was no politician and that he spoke merely as the head of the national church.

Meanwhile, the religious revival as a whole is not confined to the Orthodox Church. In addition to the curious lapses into paganism previously noticed, strong bodies of Catholics, Uniates, Methodists and even Theosophists have been formed during the past eight months in all big cities, dissonant in doctrine among themselves, but united in their opposition to Bolshevik theory. The Uniate Church, with the ritual of the Greek and the dogma of the Latin, has been gaining ground in Moscow, where it previously has had small scope, its main stronghold having been in the South. The growing strength of this Church, which recognizes the Pope as its Supreme Head, may not be without influence upon any negotiations which may be pending between the Roman and Orthodox Churches.

1922

24
Methods of Anti-Religious Propaganda Among the Moslems

The question of the methods of anti-religious propaganda among the Moslems is complicated on the one hand by the position which Islam occupies in the lives of the Moslem peoples, and on the other hand by the social and political conditions of the Moslem peoples in general.

The question of the necessity of anti-religious propaganda among the Moslems, not only in Russia but far beyond Russia's borders, arouses, of course, no disputes or disagreements among us, the Communists. For us, all religions are alike. . . . What concerns us is choosing the methods by which to carry through this task painlessly and successfully. . . .

We must acknowledge that there are a number of reasons for adopting methods absolutely different from those used among other peoples. . . . Among the "great" religions of the world, Islam is of comparatively recent origin, and therefore it possesses particular strength and vigor. . . . In addition it provides — more than any other faith — rules of political and civil behavior, and in that way it differs from other religions, in which spiritual and ethical motives predominate. *Shariat,* or the Moslem law, represents a code of laws and legal norms which regulate the entire life of a Moslem. . .

The second important fact which complicates anti-religious propaganda is the social and economic position of the Moslem people during recent centuries. The defeat dealt to the Arab culture on one hand, and to the Turko-Tatar culture on the other (the expulsion of Arabs from Spain and the Turko-Tatars from southeastern Europe, the conquest by the Europeans of North Africa and Near Eastern Moslem possessions, and the subjugation by the Russians of the Tatars, the Bashkirs, the Mountaineers of the Caucasus, and the Turkic peoples of Central Asia) resulted in the political, social, and economic enslavement of almost the entire Moslem world of 300 million people. . . .

The above fact bound to have a repercussion on the Moslem people's faith. The first encroachments of Western European imperialism on the Moslem countries took the form of Crusades, but in recent years the struggle has become purely economic. Nevertheless, in the view of the Moslems, or at least the majority of them, this struggle is still interpreted as a political struggle, i.e., the struggle against Islam as a whole. Such an attitude can be easily explained because, according to the Moslems, the entire Moslem world, without distinction of nationality and tribe, represents one undivided whole.

Consequently, Islam is even today, in the eyes of the Moslem peoples, a religion which is oppressed and which must be defended. Hence the difficulty of anti-religious propaganda among the Moslems. . . .

Speaking of obstacles to anti-religious propaganda among the Moslems, we must also mention that these peoples are very backward. . .

What, then, are the methods that should be used?

First, a very careful and dexterous approach. . . . Our program should be of the nature of anti-religious propaganda, and not of anti-religious struggle. We must knock from the hands of our enemies the weapon they use against us: We must openly say to those concerned that we do not conduct any struggle against any religion, but only propagandize our own atheistic views — which we have an absolute right to do.

Second, we must clearly indicate that we have no connections whatsoever with the former missionary groups, and we must have only Communists of Moslem origin to carry on anti-religious propaganda. . . .

Third, we must conduct effective propaganda, and make our own conduct an example of it. . . . It is necessary for every Moslem to get well acquainted with an atheist and to form a good opinion of him. It is desirable to carry on discussions on religious subjects among the Moslem workers in towns and in factories, and gradually pass the information on to the villages.

But when we conduct anti-religious propaganda among the Moslems, we must not forget for a moment that their cultural backwardness and their position as a politically and morally downtrodden people are their main evil. . . . Even since the formation of the autonomous republics, the Moslems have very often stayed away from participation in the political life of their republics. As long as we do not break these chains [of political backwardness], as long as we do not make these peoples truly free and equal citizens of the Soviet republic, no anti-religious propaganda can be successful. The improvement in the education of the Moslem peoples; the extensive drawing of these people into economic and administrative, and also political, organs of the government, whenever that is possible; the widening of party work among them — these are the tasks of the day in the work among the Moslem peoples. . . .

(Reprinted from M. Sultan-Galiev's *Metody anti-religioznoi propagandy sredi mus-ul'man* [*Methods of Anti-Religious Propaganda Among the Moslems*], Moscow, 1922, pp. 3-7; in *Soviet Russia and the East, 1920-1927*, Stanford, Calif., Stanford University Press, 1957, 46-47.)

25
Epistle of Patriarch Tikhon To All the Faithful
of the Russian Church

[February 15, 1922]

By the Grace of God, Humble Tikhon, Patriarch of Moscow and all Russia, to all the faithful of the Russian Church.

The grace of our Lord Jesus Christ be with you. Among all the severe trials and calamities which have befallen our country for our impurities, the greatest and most awful one is famine, reigning over a vast space with many millions of inhabitants. In August 1921, when we first heard about the horrid calamity, we considered it our duty to come to the rescue of our spiritual children, and addressed to the heads of the independent Christian churches, Orthodox Patriarchs, the Pope, the Bishop of Canterbury and the Bishop of New York, an appeal to collect money and provision and send it to the starving people of Volga for the sake of Christian love.

At the same time, the Russian Church Committee for help to the starving was founded and money collected in all churches and among the faithful for that purpose. But this church organization was disapproved by the Soviet Government and all the collected money ordered to be handed to the Committee of the Government.

But in December it was ordered to begin collecting money and foodstuffs for the starving through the Ecclesiastical Administration, Holy Synod, High Church Council, the Council of the Diocese and of every parish.

In order to help the starving people more, we found it possible to allow the parish committees to give for that purpose ornamental jewels from the churches and such things as were not used for the holy rites — and this was proclaimed by a special epistle to the faithful, which was approved by the Government.

But soon after that, when the official press harshly spoke against those who were spiritually guiding the church, 13/26th February, the All Russian Central Executive Committee ordered for the benefit of the starving the seizure from the churches of all valuable things, the sacred objects needed for the holy rites included.

From the point of view of the Church, such an act is a sacrilege, and we considered it our duty to inform all the faithful about it.

Considering the painful circumstances, we allowed the possibility of giving up such things as are not sacred and not used for the holy service, and we compel the faithful even now to do it, heartily wishing that it might help our suffering brethren. But we cannot approve even a voluntary sacrifice of the sacred things, the use of which for any other purpose but that of the holy rites is forbidden by the laws of the church and is punished by her as a sacrilege — common people by excommunication, clergy by taking their holy orders from them. (*Can. Ap.* 73; *Con. Can.* 10.)

Given in Moscow.

The Humble Tikhon, Patriarch of Moscow and all Russia

26
The *Atheist* Attacks Public Religious Processions and Teaching

"THE CLERGY"

(Summary from the Monthly *Ateist*, No. 2, March 1922)

The Decree of January 23, 1918, about the separtion of the church from the government, was not enforced. The following are some of the paragraphs of Chapter III of this penal code regarding the clergy.

No. 103. Those avoiding the fulfilment of their civil duties on account of their religious belief are subject to punishment.

We consider that persons subject to this paragraph should publicly prove their sincerity in the People's Courts. Certainly, exceptions from the general rule for the anarcho-religious people cannot go further than excusing liability to military service and even this should be of a temporary character, and cannot be interpreted in favor of bourgeois capitalistic interests.

No. 104. Religious teaching of all beliefs is prohibited in the schools for juniors and children, and is punishable by one year of hard labor.

We suggest that all local departments of the Commissariat for People's Education should see to it that no schools where religion is taught to people under 18 years of age be permitted to operate.

Organization of monarchistic religious schools of any belief is an organization for attack on the workmen-peasant revolution.

Entire prohibition — at the present moment — of the opening of similar monarchistic religious schools, is but the self-defence of the laborers against the attacks of parasite classes.

Therefore, we insist that religious teaching in the schools for all ages shall be punished by imprisonment for a period of not less than one year. No counter-revolutionary propaganda will be countenanced.

No. 237 of the Code prescribes the punishment for religious demonstrations. It reads: Infringement of freedom of movement of citizens on account of religious demonstrations or ceremonies against the law or the orders of local authorities is punishable by 6 months at hard labor.

We are definitely opposed to the wording of this point. It permits the demonstrators, clad in wild dresses, with flags and rags, with their idols, with pieces of the rotten bodies of some old "saints" who were usually merchants or landlords, to walk about and sing their counter-revolutionary hymns. We therefore hold that paragraph 237 should read: "Those guilty of organizing religious demonstrations outside the walls of churches or temples, are to be punished by 6 months of hard labor."

27

Memorandum of Conversation with Mr. Colton of the American Y.M.C.A.

April 18, 1922

Mr. Colton has been in Russia for several months in connection with the relief work among the Russian students. He expressed the opinion that despite the appalling economic conditions which now unquestionably prevail throughout Soviet Russia there is little likelihood of the early downfall of the present regime. Interesting information was procured from Mr. Colton with reference to the seizure of the Church valuables. He gives the following summary of events which culminated in the issuance of the decree providing for the seizure of the jewels and valuables: Mr. Colton's information was apparently procured from a personal conversation with Tikhon.

In the very early days of the famine, Tikhon informed the Soviet authorities of his willingness to join in an appeal to the world for assistance. This suggestion was immediately turned down by the Soviet authorities. Later, when he received information regarding the proposed issuance of the decree, he notified the Soviet authorities that the Church as an institution was willing and able to raise a sum of money approximating the worth of the valuables which would be seized under the decree, this money to be used by the Church or expended under its direction for famine relief. The money was to be raised through subscription on the part of the members of the Church and through the sale of a portion of these valuables. This proposal was also refused. Mr. Colton left Moscow on April 7 and on that date Tikhon was called before the Soviet authorities for the third time in regard to this matter and was informed that he was allowed a period of one week within which to bring the Church into line with the Soviet policy regarding the seizure of the valuables. Prior to this date Tikhon made confidential inquiry of Colonel Haskell as to whether the American Relief Administration would, if requested, assist the Church in effecting the sale of the valuables in America and whether the A.R.A. would take over the funds so realized and use them for famine relief purposes. To this inquiry Colonel Haskell sent a confidential reply to the effect that such action on the part of the American Relief Administration would at once be construed by the Soviet authorities as an interference on the part of their organization with political internal affairs and he was therefore unable to send an affirmative reply to the Patriarch. Colonel Haskell added that he regretted the more his inability to comply with the request in view of the fact that it was certain that the valuables would not be applied by the Soviet authorities to relief work, since the A.R.A. already had more food and supplies at all ports and on all lines leading into Russia than the Soviet transportation could handle. During the progress of the negotiations between Tikhon and the Soviet authorities he was asked whether he would be willing to proceed to the United States for the purpose of raising funds for relief work. Tikhon replied in the negative, feeling certain that if he started on the journey he would undoubtedly "disappear" enroute. Mr. Colton informs me that the Church is firmly of the opinion that the proceeds from the sale of the Church valuables will immediately be placed in the "war chest."

(E. E. Young, U. S. Commissioner, Riga)

28
The Confiscation of Church Property in Russia

(A Report of the U.S. Commissioner in Riga)

April 21, 1922

The opposition to the confiscation of Church property is increasing and is causing anti-Jewish feeling, as the Jews are held to be responsible for the Decree.

At Smolensk a pogrom occured on March 28th and 29th, and disturbances occured in the Vologda and Viatka Governments. In Petrograd Jews have been beaten in the streets, while the churches in the Vyborg district, and the church of the Appearance of Our Lady of Great Novgorod were closed, and large crowds assembled around them. As a result the Commission returned without taking anything. At other churches only one fourth of the scheduled valuables was collected.

At Ivanovo-Voznesensk, Iaroslavl, and other centers, the removal of the goods proceeded quietly, but has caused high feeling. When the valuables from the churches in Tverskaia Street, Moscow, were being removed, a large crowd assembled, and cavalry were called out and fired volleys in the air. Reports are received daily by the Central Executive Committee urging the cancellation of the Decree, as the results are dangerous, and may lead to an outburst of religious fanaticism.

In order to prove that valuables are not being confiscated only from the Orthodox churches, the Central Executive Committee has issued urgent instructions to all Government representatives either to take over or at least to make an inventory of valuables, at churches of other Faiths, and especially synagogues. Both in the capitals and elsewhere, a number of clergy have been arrested for "anti-soviet agitation." The situation of the Patriarch Tikhon and the other important clergy is very difficult, since on the one hand they are blamed by the people for maintaining a neutral attitude, and on the other hand the Soviet authorities suspect them of agitation. The Patriarch is said to have received anonymous letters threatening his death, if he makes no decided protest, or does not take steps to ensure that the proceeds from the sale of the valuables are devoted to the famine sufferers. The Soviet Government has filled up all the Patriarch's house, except 2 rooms, with children from the famine area, and this is regarded as a reprisal for his supposed resistance to the Decree.

29
Epistle of the Holy Synod of the Russian Church to Metropolitan Antonii

May 5, 1922

To the President of the Supreme Administration of the Russian Church Abroad, His Eminence Antonii, Metropolitan of Kiev and Halich: With the benediction of the Holy Patriarch, the Holy Synod and the High Church Council in a united meeting (28th March/10th April of this year) examined the following proposal of the Holy Patriarch:

"I enclose herewith copies of the newspaper Novoe Vremia of 3 and 4 December, 1921 and of 1 March, 1922. Therein are published the proclamation of the Council of [Sremski] Karlovtsi and its application to the world conference. These acts bear a political character and as such are contradictory to my proclamation of 25 September, 1919.

Therefore,

1. I consider the Council of Karlovtsi, consisting of Russian clergy and laymen abroad, as having no canonical importance, and its epistle concerning the restitution of the dynasty of Romanov and its application to the Genoa Conference as not expressing the official opinion of the Russian Orthodox Church.

2. In view of the fact that the Russian Church Administration Abroad is preoccupied with programs of political enterprise, and since the Russian parishes abroad are already entrusted to the care of the most reverend Metropolitan Evlogii, residing in Germany, the Supreme Church Administration is to be abolished.

3. The Holy Synod is to examine the responsibility of certain clerical persons abroad for their political actions taken in the name of the Church."

After the examination of the above-mentioned proposal of the Holy Patriarch *it was decided:*

1. To consider the epistle of the Church Council Abroad addressed to the Children of the Russian Orthodox Church in exile, concerning the restitution of Monarchy in Russia with a Tsar of the House of Romanov, published in the *Novoe Vremia* of the 3 December, 1921, No. 184, and the Epistle to the World Conference in the name of the Russian Church Council Abroad, published in the same *Novoe Vremia* of the 1 March, 1922, No. 25, signed by Your Eminence, — as being acts not expressing the official opinion of the Russian Orthodox Church, and in view of their purely political character having no canonical significance.

2. In view of the fact that the Supreme Church Administration Abroad has taken part in politics in the name of the Church and taking into consideration the fact that, by the nomination by the same Administration of the Metropolitan Evlogii as Head of the Russian Orthodox Churches Abroad, no place for action remains for the Supreme Church Administration Abroad — the above-mentioned Supreme Church Administration is to be abolished, temporarily leaving the administration of Russian Churches abroad in the hands of Metropolitan Evlogii and asking him to submit his opinion concerning the administration of the mentioned Churches.

3. For the examination of the clerical responsibility of certain clergy abroad for their political acts in the name of the Church, measures are to be taken for gathering all the necessary information. The examination itself, in view of the fact that several of the mentioned persons have the rank of Bishop, is to be postponed until the Holy Synod can be convened with the complete number of members fixed by the clerical council rules.

Your Eminence is informed of the above so that the necessary orders may be given.

April 22/May 5, 1922, No. 348.

Signed: Archbishop Faddei,
Member of the Holy Synod
Secretary: Numerov

30
Mr. Richard Child to the Secretary of State Concerning the Roman and Russian Church

Received From Genoa, dated May 5, 1922.
Secretary of State
Washington, D.C.

Don Sturzo here has indicated to me strong preferability of coalition Roman and Russian Church. Negotiations have been going on all this winter. This accounts for interest of Rome in successful conclusion of attempt at bargain between Russia and allies and for Pope's message to Lloyd George. I consider this has become important element in all considerations of Russian question.

Child

31
Izvestiia on the Supposed Resignation of Patriarch Tikhon

"PATRIARCH TIKHON HAS OF HIS OWN ACCORD TEMPORARILY RESIGNED"

(Translation from the *Izvestiia*, No. 108, May 17, 1922)

On May 12th a group of clergymen, consisting of the priests Vvedenskii, Krasnitskii, Kalinovskii, Belkov, and Stadnik, visited Patriarch Tikhon at his residence, and had a lengthy interview with him. In the course of the interview they called the attention of the Patriarch to the trial which had just been brought to an end at the Moscow Governorship Tribunal, and in which eleven sentences of death had been passed for resistance to the confiscation of church valuables. The above clergymen held Patriarch Tikhon responsible for such bloodshed, because of his proclamation of February 28th. In the opinion of the above mentioned clergymen the spreading of that proclamation in the provincial churches gave the signal for a new outbreak of civil war waged by the Church hierarchy against the Soviet regime.

The priest Krasnitskii pointed out that the name of the Patriarch had been generally connected with a counter-revolutionary church policy, which had materialized in the following concrete instances: (a) in an anathema demonstratively pronounced by the Patriarch on the Bolsheviks on January 19,1918; (b) in a proclamation issued by the Patriarch on February 15/28 1918, enjoining believers to hide the church valuables, to ring alarm bells, and to organize the laity for the purpose of resisting the Soviet power (according to Krasnitskii this proclamation had caused 1,414 sanguinary excesses and conflicts); (c) in that the Patriarch's sending through the medium of Bishop Germogen, his blessing and a wafer to Nikolai Romanov at Ekaterinburg; (d) in his ordaining to the priesthood, and raising to high places in the Church hierarchy, persons who had clearly shown themselves to be adherents of the old monarchistic regime; (e) in his generally converting the Church into a political organization which under priestly robes and in its parish councils gave refuge to irresponsible elements which in the name of the Church, and under the flag of the Church, endeavor to subvert the Soviet power.

Pointing out that under the guidance of Patriarch Tikhon the Church has fallen into a state of complete anarchy, that by its counter-revolutionary policy in general, and its opposition to the confiscation of valuables in particular, the Church has forfeited its authority, and lost every influence on the masses at large — the group of clergymen demanded that the Patriarch call immediately a Church Council for regulating the affairs of the Church, and that pending the decision of the Church Council the Patriarch should withdraw from all Church affairs.

As a result of this interview, and after some consideration, the Patriarch tendered his resignation, appointing as his substitute, pending convocation of the Church Council, one of the higher Church dignitaries.

32
Situation of Russian Church and Confiscation of Church Property

(Report of the U.S. Commissioner in Riga)

May 26, 1922

A year ago even the most extreme Communist leaders hesitated to interfere with the Church, fearing an outburst of religious feeling. Now, by clever maneuvering, aided by the vacillating policy of the higher church officials, they have attained a notable success, and the results may be far reaching. The policy of openly attacking the Church was soon recognized as unwise and the press was ordered to stop this, but instead to depict the sufferings of the starving populace and the help the Church could give by surrendering some of its property. The self-seeking attitude adopted recently by some of the minor clergy and the general disorganization of the population made the campaign easier, so that the Patriarch's second message, calling on the people to resist, and referring to the confiscation as sacrilege, failed to create much impression. Early in April, the Gospolitupravlenie (State Political Administration) learned of a secret meeting called by Patriarch Tikhon and his assistant, Archbishop Nikandr, in February, at which it was recommended that all possible measures be taken to resist confiscation. Subsequently, at a meeting of the Commissariat of Justice, on April 23rd, it was decided to destroy this "nest of reaction."

Meanwhile, instructions were issued to conduct the confiscation of the Church valuables in the most orderly way possible, and to act on the advice of the Moderates and devote the proceeds to the starving. As already reported, inventories of valuables at Churches of other faiths have also been made, and especially at synagogues, so as to put an end to anti-Jewish agitation.

The results of this maneuvering have been very successful and after the arrest of the Patriarch the employees at some works, notably the Gorkoma and Dinamo, expressed satisfaction that the last of the bourgeoisie were being dealt with and passed a resolution to try all Bishops and confiscate all Church property.

It is characteristic of the change of feeling in Russia, induced by misery and want, that even Dobroliubov and Zaozerskii and other Vicars of Moscow churches warned the Archbishop Nikandr last April that they did not believe their parishioners would offer any resistance to the confiscation; that the Patriarch's second appeal would only involve the higher clergy, and give the Soviet Government the opportunity it was awaiting.

The Patriarch Tikhon is now confined in the Monastery of Our Lady of the Don near Moscow.

The members of the clergy who have been condemned to death will be reprieved. Not even Trotskii and the Extremists opposed this proposal by Kalinin on the 5th of May, as they were more than satisfied with their victory.

The question of the elimination of the higher prelates of the Church and the establishment of an Administration for the Russian Church on democratic lines is now being considered. But Sorev's proposal, which Trotskii supported, to abolish the canonical orders of Patriarch, Metropolitan, and all Archbishops, was considered premature. Many of the minor clergy are, however, agitating for the summoning of a Church Congress, to carry out reforms, and in this case the religious office of Patriarch will disappear. There is also a movement to grant complete autonomy to certain groups of Parishes and to form separate Church unions, which is attributed to Lunacharskii.

The Communists are now aiming at destroying the unity of the Church and creating independent groups, being convinced that disputes regarding questions of the ritual will soon arise and tend to destroy the influence of the Church as a whole.

Even now there is a dispute between the Moscow and Ukrainian churches regarding services being held in the Ukrainian language and the Communists are fostering the desires of Ukraine to be independent of Moscow.

33
Report of the U.S. Commissioner in Riga to the Secretary of State Concerning Peasants and the Russian Church

No. 2122   May 31, 1922
Sir:
I have the honor to forward therewith a translation from the *Izvestiia,* No.

108, May 17, 1922, with reference to the resignation of Patriarch Tikhon.

The mission is endeavoring carefully to follow the developments in connection with the attitude of the Soviet authorities toward the Church. It is, of course, a well known fact that the Soviet Government has, up to the present, failed in its efforts to obtain the sympathy and support of the Russian peasants. There is little question that the Soviet leaders believe that this failure on their part is in no small measure due to the strong hold of the Church on the peasants and its conservative influence. Some observers here are of the opinion that the confiscation of Church valuables, and the deposing of Tikhon, are but steps in a carefully prepared program and line of action aimed at the breaking of the hold of the Church on the peasants.

I have the honor to be, Sir,

Your obedient servant,

E. E. Young, Commissioner

34

Report of the U.S. Commissioner in Riga to the Secretary of State Concerning the Vatican and the Orthodox

CHURCH IN RUSSIA

No. 2148   June 5, 1922

Sir:

Supplementing previous reports from this mission with reference to the status of the Church in Russia, I have the honor to forward herewith an interesting report (J.S.-2) in regard to the matter.

I have the honor to be, Sir,

Your obedient servant,

E. E. Young

Commissioner

May 29, 1922

THE VATICAN AND THE ORTHODOX CHURCH IN RUSSIA

The Soviet Government has for some time past been unable to stem the increasing influence of the Church headed by Patriarch Tikhon among the populace. The Orthodox Church today is the only large and well-preserved organization remaining which reflects and retains the traditions of the old regime and is possessed of sufficient influence to be a source of danger to the Soviet authorities. It was found that the influence of Iliodor and the "Red Clergy" and the support lent to the latter came to nothing.

A blow is now to be made at Orthodoxy by an agreement with the Vatican. If Roman Catholicism can be introduced into Russia the last mainstay of the old regime will have been uprooted, and further, the Soviet Government will be in agreement with the Church rather than antagonistic to it.

The Communists, however, go further, as they consider that Catholic propaganda will result eventually in causing the whole structure of the Church to crumble. While it is true that the majority of the peasants will not be able to make a distinction between the two religions, it is exactly here that the movement is insidious, since new ideas clothed practically in old beliefs will create a sense of bewilderment in the peasant mind. This is the wedge that the Communists believe is destined to break the superstitious grip that the Church holds on the country.

> (Source: Archbishop Joan [Ioann] of the Orthodox Church in Latvia. Very reliable informant being in direct touch with Patriarch Tikhon and with the Orthodox Metropolitan of Western Europe, Antony, formerly Bishop of Penza.)

The Bolsheviks have realized that without assistance from the outside, it will be impossible to paralyse the influence of the Church, since Orthodoxy and the Russian people are fundamentally one. To effect their purpose the Soviet Government has adopted a course calculated to give the most promising results; that is, an alliance, through the Vatican, with the hereditary enemies of the Orthodox Church — the Jesuits.

Through this alliance the Bolsheviks are looking forward to a disintegration of the Church, since they expect that it will cause not only a split among the clergy, but will mislead and confuse the peasant class of the Church followers.

The moment has been very well chosen, since, owing to the present absence of morale and the existing hardships, the work of the Catholic missionaries will be easier, as Catholicism can be presented to the ignorant class as a way out of a difficult situation.

There are, and have been for some time past, a large number of representatives of the Jesuit Order in Moscow (among them Baron Ropp) who have been quietly at work, engaged on the question, and the agreement between the Vatican and the Soviet Government is the result of their efforts. The Pope (though he left the Jesuit Order before he was elected) when concluding the agreement with Chicherin acted entirely on the instructions of Count Ledukhovski [Ledóchowski], the Chief of the Order. The Vatican hopes, by means of the pulpit, to split the Orthodox Church in Russia and thereby bring it under the domination of Rome, but for this purpose it was indispensable in the first place to remove the head of the Orthodox Church (i.e. to get rid of Patriarch Tikhon) which, in the opinion of the Bolsheviks, has now been done. (This, however, is not the opinion of informant.)

The Jesuits and the Vatican have promised the Soviet Government that after the conclusion of the Concordat they will do all in their power to put pressure on the governments of Italy, France, and Belgium, but mainly on the latter two, to hasten the recognition of the Soviet Government in Russia. The Bolsheviks consider Patriarch Tikhon as having deliberately abdicated the title of Patriarch. Actually, however, the Patriarch has not done this and the whole of the Orthodox Church continues to recognize him as Patriarch.

Owing to the fact that the Patriarch Tikhon was called up for interrogation and arrested, he was forced to appoint a deputy — Veniamin — for the time being. This act is now being interpreted by the Bolsheviks as voluntary abdication on the part of the Patriarch. The Soviet Government, therefore, has not recognized Veniamin as head of the Church and has appointed several of its own men — for instance, Soviet bishops Antonin and Leonid and several priests — men with unenviable pasts, particularly the two bishops mentioned.

The Patriarch of Constantinople, the Metropolitan Antonii, and all the Orthodox Bishops abroad, while still recognizing the Patriarch Tikhon, consider that to protest against his arrest is unwise and that the appeal published by Russian organizations in Germany can only do him harm, since the Bolsheviks will affirm that it is the work of counter-revolution.

The fight has begun and will be long and persistent, and will doubtless claim a large number of victims. The struggle against the Communists will not be so hard as that against the Jesuits, but here the Orthodox Church has the benefit of experience and is confident of the ultimate result from a religious point of view, although politically she may lose much of her present significance.

Bishop Joan [Ioann] is now forced to carry on the struggle with the Jesuits in Latvia, who have openly threatened him and have tried to get him out of Latvia, but so far have not met with any success although the head of the Order is a Frenchman and under the patronage of Count Martel, the French Minister.

Influential Bishops are in communication with the heads of the Anglican Church, and it is possible that a rapprochement between these two churches may be a result of the struggle that is going on today.

35
Letter of the Supreme Russian Church Administration Abroad
To President Warren G. Harding

[June 5, 1922]

Sir:

The High Russian Ecclesiastical Administration Abroad, consisting of

Bishops, clergy and laity, elected by the Assembly of the members of the Russian Ecclesiastical Council 17/30th May this year, decided to address you, together with the Heads of all other Churches, with the following:

You are, of course, already informed that Patriarch Tikhon of Moscow and of all Russia is arrested and brought before the tribunal by the Soviet authorities. He has been accused of rebellion against the said authorities in connection with the implementation of their decree about the confiscation of the Church valuables for the benefit of the starving.

The epistle of the Holy Patriarch about it, herewith enclosed, shows the falsehood of this calumny.

The Holy Patriarch suffered more than anybody else for his starving flock and he was the first who ever cared about the people and endeavoured to help them by publishing his well-known appeal to all the world. He blessed and allowed also the offerings of the Church valuables for the benefit of the starving, in the limits determined by the Holy Canons which he had no right to overthrow, being the first keeper of the Church Laws.

Moreover, a deep conviction of all the Russian people was such, that the confiscated valuables would not serve for the help of the starving people, but rather give more strength to and prolong the rule of Communism, which is hostile to all religions, especially to Christianity. Moreover, it is evident to every unprejudiced mind, that the first stimulus and the reason of the awful proportions of the famine is due to Communism, which is systematically killing during the last five years every personal enterprise, the source of fruitful labour, and destroying all social life in Russia.

It explains the common disbelief and manifold protests of the Russian population which took place almost everywhere when implementing the aforesaid decree, in spite of the evident usefulness of this extraordinary measure, having neither limits, nor consideration for the religious convictions and feelings of the religious Russian people, and such are in great majority in Russia, now religiously regenerated.

Now the government of the Communists, who are, as is well known in all the world, only in small quantity among the Russians, the Government which forcibly and criminally reigns still over the Russian people, shall bring before its tribunal the Head of the Russian Church! And as their baseness is well known the worst may be expected. Without any law-suit they tortured and destroyed almost every member of the Russian Imperial Family; they spilt the blood of millions of Russian patriots who would not have accepted the fantastical and pernicious International; they allow themselves everything; every means is approved, if serving for their purposes.

The Russian people, defenceless, downcast and tortured, hardly can defend their Holy Father. He will not even be allowed to ask for help.

That is why the High Russian Ecclesiastical Administration Abroad, in searching for salvation of the Father of All Russia, considers it a filial duty and an urgent necessity to address you also with the most serious prayer, by all means which are in your power and in your heart's desire, to help to save the Patriarch Tikhon from this lawless tribunal.

Almost all the world was indifferent when the torturers of the Russian people killed the guiltless Russian Tsar and his family and destroyed almost all the Imeprial House. Do save now for the Russian people their High Priest.

We hope that even your bold protest will have a good influence for the safety of the Patriarch and for all the Russian people. The voice of the Socialists in defence of their comrades in Moscow stopped their execution. The intercession of the American representatives of A.R.A. saved many priests from death. But the voice of the Governments in the Patriarch's defence shall have much more influence.

And Our Lord and Saviour, Who told in the Gospel: "In everything as you want men to do unto you do ye likewise unto them" (*Matthew, 7:12*) will repay you in due time by his merciful defense. And the Russian people, risen from their deep humiliation, will always remember this your deed of Christian charity and truth with the feelings of deep thankful love.

> President of the High Russian Ecclesiastical
> Administration Abroad, METROPOLITAN ANTHONY
> Secretary E. MACHAROBLIDZE

N1076
"2/15"th June 1922
Serbia, Srem. Karlovci.-

(This poor translation was apparently made from the French, and attached to the original text which was not found in the National Archives. Editor)

36
Epistle of the Locum Tenens of the Holy Patriarch of Moscow and of All Russia, Metropolitan of Iaroslavl, Agafangel, to the Priests and All the Children of the Russian Orthodox Church

Grace to you, and peace, from God our Father and the Lord Jesus Christ. [*Romans* 1:7].

Our Holy Patriarch and Father — Tikhon, sent the following letter to me dated 3/16 May 1922.

"In consequence of the great difficulty in the administration of the Church which has arisen as the result of my summons before the civil court, I consider it necessary for the good of the Church to authorize you to rule the Church until the meeting of a Church Council. The consent of the civil authorities to this is obtained. Therefore, be so good as to come to Moscow at once. Patriarch Tikhon."

In the name of obedience and in conformity with my episcopal oath, I intended immediately to begin the service for the Church entrusted to me, and to go as soon as possible to Moscow. But, against my will, and under circumstances for which I am not responsible, I have been unable up to the present time to go to the place of my service. At the same time, as is officially known to me, other people have arrived at Moscow and have taken over the administration of the Russian Church. I have no knowledge of what authority they have received, or from whom, and therefore I regard the powers they have assumed, and their acts as unlawful. They have declared their intention to revise the dogmas and the moral teachings of our Orthodox Church, the canons of the Holy Ecumenical Councils, the Orthodox Church discipline given to us by holy men and champions of Christian piety, and to organize in this manner a "New" [Church], called by them the "Living" Church.

We do not deny the necessity of some modifications and changes in the practice and customs. Some of these questions were submitted to the All Russian Church Council of 1918, but no decision was reached because of its premature dispersal under the circumstances of that time. But in any case, all modifications and Church reforms can be made only by the authority of a Church Council. Therefore, I consider it my duty, assuming rule over the Church, to call an All Russian Council — which lawfully, in conformity to the Word of God and within the limits of the rules of the Ecumenical Holy Council, those first and fundamental sources of our Church organization, will decide what is necessary and good for our spiritual welfare. Otherwise, all innovations may bring disturbances in the conscience of believers, a pernicious dissent among them, and the increase of impiety and of deep sorrow. With great concern we already see the beginning of this.

Beloved in God Reverend Bishops,

Bereaved temporarily of supreme administration, govern your dioceses now in independence according to the Holy Scriptures, the Holy Canons; in future, until the restoration of the Supreme Church Administration, decide definitively the questions which before you referred to the Holy Synod; and in doubtful cases apply to our humility.

Honest Priests and all servants in Christ of the Altar and the Church,

You are closely connected with the life of the people. Their progress in the spirit of the Orthodox Doctrines must be dear to you. Increase your holy zeal. When the believers will see in you the blessed burning of the Spirit they will not turn away from their holy altars.

Brothers and Sisters in God,

Preserve the unity of the holy faith in the union of brotherly peace. Do not submit to doubt, which the new people send to bring into your hearts concerning the doctrines of our Orthodox Faith. Do not be enticed by the temptations with which, acting not by lawful decisions of the Councils but according to their own intellect and understanding, they try to seduce you to make changes in the Orthodox service. Do not be tempted by the unlawful ways by which new people want to lead you to some new church; search for lawful means and paths with which to remove Church discord. Hold to and do not turn away from your spiritual leaders and priests. Obey with good conscience, enlightened by Christ's light, the Government authorities, execute in a spirit of love and peace your citizen's duties, remembering the teaching of Christ: "Render to Caesar the things that are Caesar's, and to God the things that are God's." Especially increase your prayers, defending yourself from the spirit of evil who is the enemy of our salvation.

Thus, beloved Children in Christ, keep the teachings, the rules and the canons of our faith, keep all that was transmitted to us, keep to the Church of God, remember that those who turn away from the Holy Church leave their Saviour. (The words of the Apostle [Paul], The Second Epistle to the Thessalonians, 2:15.)

Signed: Locum Tenens of the Holy Patriarch,

AGAFANGEL, By God's Will

Metropolitan of Iaroslavl

5/18 June 1922, No. 214, Iaroslavl.

(From the National Archives, Washington D.C.)

37

Requisition of Church Valuables

(Translation from the Moscow *Izvestiia*, No. 136, June 22, 1922)

According to information supplied by the Central Famine Relief Committee, the following quantities of confiscated church valuables were received in the district financial divisions between June 10 and 17.

Gold — 2 poods, 22 pounds, 31 zolotniks; silver — 1260 poods, 12 pounds, 80 zolotniks; others metals — 1 pood, 4 pounds, 36 zolotniks; brilliants and diamonds — 3,555; pearls — 2 poods, 33 pounds, 25 zolotniks; other stones — 2,139; silver coins — 6,033 roubles worth; sundry articles set with diamonds, pearls and other stones — 13 pounds, 38 zolotniks and 2 pieces.

Of all the church property which up to June 8 has been handed over from Finance Departments in the various localities to the State treasury, the fol-

lowing quantities have been overhauled in detail, and sorted out: silver —
1,892 poods, 9 pounds, 25 zolotniks; precious stones — 1 pood, 9 pounds,
76 zolotniks. Besides, 980 articles of value as antiques, weighing in all 48
poods, 22 pounds, and 92 zolotniks, have been separated from the lot.
Confiscation of church valuables will shortly be closed everywhere.

38
Results of the Confiscation of Church Valuables

(Translation from Moscow *Pravda*, No. 147, July 5, 1922)

According to telegraphic information from the district Finance Departments there had been confiscated throughout the R.S.F.S.R. by July 1st the
following quantities of Church valuables: gold, 26 poods, 38 pounds, 8 zolotinks; silver, 21,137 poods, 11 pounds, 85 zolotinks; other metals, 84 poods,
10 pounds, 39 zolotinks; diamonds, 33,456 stones weighing 10 zolotinks and
1,313 karats; pearls, 5,486 pieces, 27 strings, weighing 10 pounds, 76 zolotinks and 100 karats; other precious stones, 72,383 pieces weighing 1 pood,
29 pounds, 59 zolotinks, or 344 karats; silver coin, 19,064 roubles; gold coin,
1,595 roubles; articles with precious stones, 49 poods, 24 pounds, 39 zolotinks.

39
Apostolic Letter to the Patriarchs, Primates, Archbishops and
Bishops of the Catholic Universe, Ordaining a General
Subscription in Favour of the Population of Russia

Pius XI, Pope
Venerable Brothers, greetings and Apostolic Benediction.
You will recall that about a year ago Our lamented predecessor — with a
heart seized by paternal compassion at the sight of the extreme misery of the
Russian population, who, having been the victims of the greatest calamity in
history, were decimated by epidemics and famine — had solicited in their
favour, in the most urgent terms, the mercy and charity of the whole world.
At the same time, he made representations to all the chiefs of state how
important it was, in the interests of civilization, to bring about common understanding and the marshalling of resources to support with effectual promp-
titude so many people in such a bitter necessity.

For Our part, you recollect that, by virtue of the same mission of love which Jesus Christ has entrusted to Us, We also addressed not long ago an urgent message to the delegates of the powers assembled in Geneva, requesting them to work through concerted action on the re-establishing of order among these peoples. To them — although the adversity of former times had separated them from the Apostolic See — We have sent words of consolation and affection and Our ardent hope for their return to the unity of the Church.

Indeed, in spite of the difficulties which face the nations and individuals of almost all the world, the appeals of the Soverign Pontiff were answered with generosity. Our dear Sons from thriving America — it pleases Us to declare it here — have taken the first place through the scope of their munificence, the unanimity of their assistance, and their talent for organization. Moreover, it is not only distressed Russia but the whole of mankind that shares the debt of gratitude to them. We should not pass over in silence the important credits voted for the same purpose by the Senate of the United States.

But what are these subsidies or any future subsidies when compared with the immensity of the scourge to be combatted!

Each day We receive more terrifying information and entreaties constantly more anguished from the hard pressed unfortunates. It is impossible to enumerate those who cannot do without assistance: little children, adolescents, women, the aged. If they do not obtain succour without delay they are condemned to a horrible death, or at least to a continuance of life in the most poignant distress.

Moreover, pressed by the duty of universal charity which is imposed on Us by Our sacred office of Supreme Shepherd and common Father to all the believers, We must once again implore, Venerable Brothers, from the bottom of our heart, your compassion, and through you, the compassion of all those who are animated by Christian, or even simply human, sentiments. We implore you to come to the aid of those in so much want; the field for charitable action must expand to the same extent that the misery itself multiplies.

It will not escape you that the charity, to be effectual and fruitful, calls for a wise method in the organization of collections as much as in the distribution of the offerings. It will be the concern of your solicitude, Venerable Brothers, to put into operation the best means of raising alms. The delegates chosen by Us will carry the sums thus collected to the places where the need will require them; they themselves will distribute them to the most destitute, without distinction as to religion or nationality.

With the purpose of giving others, in similar circumstances, a practical encouragement by Our appropriate example, as it befits Us and to the extent allowed by the resources at the disposal of the Holy See, We devote to this deed of charity two and a half million liras.

But above all, We resort to prayer, humble and fervent, so as to draw the divine mercy on the almost infinite number of Russians who die of starvation, and who become dearer to Us the more they suffer.

As a proof of the eternal reward and in testimony of Our paternal kindness We accord very affectionately the Apostolic Benediction to you, Venerable Brothers, and to all those who will come to the aid of Our brothers in distress.

Given in Rome, at Saint Peter's, July 10, 1922, in the first year of Our Pontificate.

Pius XI PP.

40
Report of the U.S. Commissioner in Riga Concerning the Situation of the Church in Russia

July 17, 1922

FR/3 gives the following information:

In May Patriarch Tikhon was handed over to the tribunal and placed under domiciliary arrest. In view of the subsequent inquiry and trial it has been decided to hand over the management of the Church to the Metropolitan Agafangel; the latter, however, refused, whereupon the Patriarch nominated the Metropolitan Veniamin to the management of the Church. He was arrested almost immediately by the Bolsheviks and handed over to the tribunal, ostensibly for offering resistance to confiscation of Church property in Petrograd. At the same time a certain group of clergy, under the title of the "Living Church," headed by Bishop Antonin, a pro-Bolshevik and an extremely eccentric individual, visited the Patriarch and tried to persuade him to renounce the Patriarchate completely. Tikhon did not do this, but stated that he would take no further part in the management of the Church.

The "Living Church" ("Zhivaia Tserkov") group then formed a supreme administration including the following: Bishop Antonin; priests — Vvendenskii, Sergii Kalinovskii, Krasnitskii, Belkov, Stadnik, Rusanov, Ledovskii, Borisov, Bykov, and Filevskii.

This Supreme Administration declared a policy of loyalty to the Bolsheviks, and its individual members are supporters of the idea that the Church must use its authority to assist the coming social revolution in the world.

The Supreme Church Administration have convened a "Predsoborny" Conference [i.e. Conference of representatives of the Clergy and People] to prepare the election of an All-Russian Ecclesiastical Congress to meet in the autumn of this year.

The new Church Administration has already begun to bring its programme into force. All bishops and priests who, for one reason or another, are undesirable in the eyes of the Soviet Government have been dismissed, several married priests have been raised to bishoprics (which is contrary to the canons of the Church), and the Supreme Administration has stated in one of its circulars to the Church that it intends to delete certain forms from the Church service, which is to be simplified.

Both sides are anxiously awaiting the elections to the All-Russian Ecclesiastical Congress at which the basic questions of Church management are to be decided. However, the new Church Administration will have realized a number of its reforms before this Congress meets. Incidentally, Bishop Antonin and his supporters are endeavoring to prevent "counter-revolutionaries" from being elected to the Congress.

This new "Living Church" is practically the re-appearance of the "New National Church" formed in Penza in 1919 under a certain Prince Vladimir Putiatin, an unfrocked priest, who died a natural death in 1921.

At the present time, besides those under the direct instructions and orders of the Supreme Church Administration, in all the towns of Russia groups of the "Living Church" are busily at work, agitating in favor of complete recognition by the Church of the Soviet Government.

Previous to the signing of the Concordat with the Vatican, Bishop Dalibor [Dalbor] stated in Poland that over 1,000 Catholic missionaries had left for Russia. The Concordat provides for the work of three Catholic orders: "Redemptorists" — Northern Russia; "Jesuits" — Central Russia; and "Brothers of the Word of God" — South Russia. They all come to Russia in the capacity of employees of the Catholic Organizations for Famine Relief.

Patriarch Tikhon is at present at the Monastery of Our Lady of the Don in Moscow, which has been transformed by the Bolsheviks into a concentration camp for isolating political and criminal offenders. The Patriarch is allowed a special cell, but is not allowed to perform the Church services in the Church of the Monastery, entry into which is prohibited, as is also entry into the monastery. The treatment of the Patriarch by his guards is good; he has been permitted to get his own food, but is not allowed to hold any communication with the outside world, is not allowed any visitors, and may not write to anyone.

The clergy abroad have, however, received a communication from the Patriarch in which he warns them against any papers or documents which might make their appearance under his name, as these might be forgeries.

FR/50, Moscow, states that now that the Bolshevik campaign against the Orthodox Church has met with a considerable amount of success their eagerness to keep on the best relationships with the Vatican has considerably cooled off.

41
Report of the U.S. Commissioner in Riga Concerning the
Divisions in the Russian Orthodox Church

July 17, 1922

Until some six months ago it appeared that the Orthodox Russian Church would be able to maintain her authority in Soviet Russia, and there were many signs that events had in no way impaired her influence, but rather had intensified it. The churches have always been well attended; church processions have always defied the efforts of the Communists to interfere, and members of the Communist party have even resigned membership on religious grounds. The superstitious and primitive religious tendencies of the peasants have always made the influence of the Church very great in agricultural areas.

On the other hand, the Soviet authorities have always aimed at getting the Church under their influence, realising its great hold over the people, and it now seems that they have secured a fairly complete victory. This is the result of their very astute diplomacy, and affords a remarkable object-lesson of their methods.

Their campaign, which was assisted by the weak and vacillating policy of the Patriarch, on which they probably reckoned, began by taking action against various persons who were alleged to be encouraging "Pogroms" and counter-revolutionary schemes. The Church disclaimed all political activity; the Soviet Government strove to prove the contrary. At first only lay members were dealt with, but subsequently minor clergy, and finally those holding higher offices.

Simultaneously, an intensive propaganda campaign was carried on in the press and by agitators, which at first was atheistic in tendency, but when this failed to produce the desired effect, was changed to accusing the Church of refusing to assist the starving population in the famine area. At the same time the invariable Soviet policy of trying to sow discord among its opponents was adopted, and every effort made to encourage dissension and to confuse the people as to the real issues.

Considerable use has been made of unfrocked priests, and renegade clergy and the Russian Orthodox Church is now split into two main groups, "Right" and "Left," the latter comprising Vvedenskii, Krasnitskii, Kalinovskii, Belkov and others, who are undoubtedly working under the instructions of the Soviet authorities.

At Petrograd the Clergy, headed by the Metropolitan Veniamin, have been combatting the new tendency to the best of their ability. The statements that the Patriarch had voluntarily resigned, and had agreed to the formation of the new "Higher Church Directorate," incensed the clergy, and both Veniamin and his Chaplain, Nikolai Petergovskii, refused to recognize this new authority. On the 28th and 29th of May they issued letters declaring it illegal and excommunicating Vvedenskii and others. The Supreme Church Administration is a temporary institution to replace the Patriarch until a "General Church Council" is formed, which will be very shortly.

Vvedenskii, however, arrived at Petrograd two days later, with full powers from the Supreme Church Administration to organize a "Collegiate [Kollegialnoe] Administration," and to dismiss Veniamin.

On the 30th of May he presided at a Conference of Clergy at Petrograd, and on the 4th of June gave a lecture. This was attended by special delegates from Communist organizations and germ-cells who applauded vigorously, while any persons who dissented were removed.

Bishop Aleksii of Jamburg, who foresaw the course of events and supports the new order of things, was promised Veniamin's post by Vvedenskii on the 18th of May and has been appointed Head of the Petrograd Council from the 30th of May by a decree of the Supreme Church Administration. He is, however, subordinate to the North and North-Western District Council, of which Vvedenskii is President.

One of the first decrees of this new body was to declare Veniamin's excommunication of Vvedenskii illegal.

Meanwhile the newly-appointed Supreme Church Administration decided to appoint two priests, Ioann Albinskii, and A. Pokrovskii, as Bishops, ignoring all the usual precepts (regarding celibacy and the normal methods of preferment). Antonin, the Head of this body, supported by Leonid and the moderates, protested at first, but ultimately gave way and agreed to their being consecrated.

Albinskii, now Bishop Ioann, will succeed the Podolsk Bishop, Nikandr, one of the Patriarch's staunchest supporters.

A conflict is now going on between the "Right" and "Left" groups regarding the clergy abroad. The latter group demand their removal from the Church, acting under the influence of the Soviet Government, who, in return, promise their assistance in the reorganization of the Church.

The Moderate Group are urging that the Metropolitan Antonii of Volinia, and the Archbishop Evlogii be consulted, and also the clergy abroad generally, as some may be ready to accept the new conditions.

The "Left" group will not assent to this and threaten to publish a special proclamation to the people. As they now have the support of the two new bishops (Albinskii and Petrovskii) their position is much stronger. The question is not yet definitely decided, but it is probable that the clergy abroad will be dismissed from their posts.

At the instance of Albinskii and Belkov the "left" group are also demanding the issue of a letter calling on both clergy and laity to unite in unconditional recognition of the Soviet authority.

Bishop Antonin said it was quite clear that the Soviet Government was already recognized, as everything was being done at their instigation and with their permission, but the letter will probably be issued.

The opposition to the Supreme Church Administration at Moscow is increasing, the main form being that the churches of the "left" clergy are being avoided.

In the provinces an increasing number of the clergy are in favor of recognizing and submitting to the new institution, but so far Church Administrations have been formed only at Rostov, Tsaritsyn, and Minsk.

The confiscation of church valuables in the Petrograd Government is nearly completed, and preliminary data show that the proceeds from the St. Isaakii's Cathedral head the list, and include 140 poods of silver and four of gold. The Cathedral of Our Lady of Kazan furnished 125 poods of silver and one of gold.

There were 14 cases of resistance with bloodshed, in which six communists and eleven militiamen were killed.

The largest protest gathering occurred at the Church of the Appearance of Our Lady of Great Novgorod on the 19th of May, at St. Vladimir's Cathedral on the 18th of May, and at the Cathedral of Our Lady of Kazan on the 23rd.

After Veniamin's trial the Soviet authorities intend to break down all resistance.

The Soviet Government is taking all possible steps to secure a decisive majority in the "Church Council" which is shortly to be formed and in which both clergy and laity will be represented.

The majority of the "right" clergy are only striving now to preserve the ritual and traditions of the Church so far as is possible under the new regime.

The ease with which the Soviet Government has so far secured its ends is all the more striking, since it seems clear that at the beginning of the "confiscation" campaign the Patriarch had a large majority of the population with him. This is borne out by the fact that, as a result of his letter of the 28th of February, 1,414 cases of resistance leading to bloodshed occurred.

It now remains to be seen how far the Russian Church will succeed in maintaining its principles under the new system, and whether it will survive the reformation or become merely an instrument in the hand of the Communist party.

42
Report of the U.S. Commissioner in Riga to the Secretary of State Concerning the Persecution of the Russian Orthodox Church

No. 2432   August 1, 1922
Sir:
    In connection with my former despatches concerning the situation of the

Russian Church, I have the honor to forward herewith a confidential report
(J.S.) giving the summary of an interview with Archbishop Aleksandr of
Revel.

The Archbishop states that he has information to the effect that the persecution of the Church continues; that the Higher Church Council is not introducing any wide reforms at present, as the attitude of the Soviet Government
towards that body has become less enthusiastic of late; that the continued
persecution of certain of the clergy has roused hostility towards the Government and the so-called "Progressive Clergy"; that there is now talk of "cleaning out" the monasteries, where valuables are believed to be hidden.

Fear is expressed that the Archbishop Tikhon will suffer the same fate
as the Czar. The Bolsheviks are making great efforts to connect him with
the Council of [Sremski] Karlovtsi, a monarchist organization.

The Archbishop Aleksandr states that while strong efforts are being made
to increase the influence of the Roman Catholic Church in Russia, it is
doubtful whether it will ever gain deep influence in Russia, though it may
cause further weakness in the Orthodox Church.

I have the honor to be, Sir,

Your obedient servant,

Evan E. Young

Consul in Charge

43
Interview with Archbishop Aleksandr of Revel Concerning the Persecution of the Russian Orthodox Church

The following is compiled from reports received and from an interview
with Archbishop Aleksandr of Revel.

The persecution of the Church and religion continues, but the Supreme
Church Council is not introducing any wide reforms at present, since the
attitude of the Soviet authorities to this body has become less enthusiastic
of late.

The number of partisans of the "Progressive Clergy" is increasing very
slowly and there is some doubt as to how far the Church Congress will support the Government. Hence its convocation is being delayed.

The treatment accorded to Veniamin has caused indignation at Petrograd,
and the numerous trials of the clergy (37 between the 15th of June and 15th
of July) have evoked hostility to the Government, and more especially to the
"Progressive Clergy."

Bishop Filipp of Smolensk was compelled to sign a declaration that the Church was wrong in opposing the Soviet authorities, and that wide reforms were necessary, while attempts are being made to force others of the higher clergy to sign similar documents. Most of these have so far failed.

Arsenii, Archbishop of Rostov, was thrice approached and threatened by apostate clergy (Serov, Znamenskii, and Kruchinin), and eventually said that if any further attempts were made he would "hunger-strike."

So far, besides the Bishops in the Supreme Church Council, only five have joined the "Progressive Clergy," among them being Bishop Ioann of Voronezh, and Bishop Melkhisedek of Minsk.

There is now talk in Communist circles of "cleaning out" the monasteries, where a lot of valuables are believed to be hidden. The Supreme Church Council are being urged to order this. It is probable, however, that this will be postponed owing to fear of opposition.

Archbishop Aleksandr fears that the Patriarch Tikhon will suffer the same fate as the Tsar and his family.

Bishop Aleksii is now regarded as the head of the Russian Church, and his supporters are Vvedenskii, Krasnitskii, Kalinovskii, Belkov and others. These act under the instructions of the Soviet authorities from whom they receive funds, but are not recognized by the general masses. It is unlikely that the Soviet Government will try to abolish religion at once, but they will insist that capitalism is not to be preached, and will do their utmost to destroy the unity and influence of the Church.

Although the new regime is not popular with the general masses, they are now so downtrodden that little resistance can be looked for.

The Orthodox Church in Estonia and Finland is entirely independent of Moscow, and no negotiations will be carried on.

Bishop Aleksandr states that great efforts are being made to increase the influence of the Roman Catholics in Russia, and that several priests have lately arrived in Russia who speak the language.

Despair and trouble are causing some to change their religion but it is doubtful whether the Roman Catholic faith will ever gain deep influence in Russia, though it may cause further weakness to the Orthodox Church.

The former Rector of the Church Seminary — Martinson — who arrived last week from Petrograd, informed Archbishop Aleksandr that the Soviet authorities are making great efforts to connect the Patriarch with the Council of [Sremski] Karlovtsi (a monarchist organization) and, if this succeeds, the fate of the Patriarch is sealed.

He also states that the silver taken from the Churches is being made into Persian and Indian coins, which are then despatched to those countries. (I am making further inquiries regarding this, as apparently this is for propaganda purposes.)

The clergy in Russia are afraid to write abroad, as there are now over 5000 persons employed in censoring letters, many of whom are Germans.

Archbishop Aleksandr states that he has information that 25 bishops and higher clergy, and 185 priests, have been shot.

44
Message of the Living Church "Sobor" of August 6, 1922

The Holy Sobor urges all churchmen to abandon all attempts to use the Church for temporal political schemes, for the Church belongs to God and must serve Him only. There must be no place in the Church for counter-revolution. The Soviet Government is not a persecutor of the Church. In accordance with the constitution of the Soviet Government, all citizens are granted genuine religious freedom of conscience. The decree regarding the separation of the Church from the State guarantees such freedom. The freedom of religions, equally with anti-religious propaganda, affords the believers an opportunity to defend by argument the merits of their purely religious convictions. Hence, churchmen must not see in the Soviet authority the antichrist; on the contrary, the Sobor calls attention to the fact that the Soviet authority is the only one throughout the world which will realize, by governmental methods, the ideals of the Kingdom of God. Therefore, every faithful churchman must not only be an honorable citizen, but also fight with all his might, together with the Soviet authority, for the realization of the Kingdom of God upon earth.

(Quoted in Anderson, *People, Church and State in Modern Russia*, pp. 80-81.)

45
Memorandum of the U.S. Commissioner in Riga to the Secretary of State Concerning the Vatican and the Russian Orthodox Church

No. 2488   August 14, 1922
Sir:

I have the honor to forward herewith, for the confidential information of the Department, a memorandum regarding the Vatican and the Russian Orthodox Church.

I have the honor to be, Sir,
Your obedient servant,
Evan E. Young
Commissioner

Enclosure: Memorandum.

THE VATICAN AND THE RUSSIAN ORTHODOX CHURCH

I have just been able to ascertain from an absolutely reliable source the following information concerning the Vatican and the Russian Orthodox Church. My informant is a personal friend of Father Walsh and enjoys his confidence.

As early as November 1921, the Soviet Government sent an emissary to Rome with a proposal that the Vatican send a mission to Moscow to investigate the possibilities of the religious exploitation of Russia by the Roman Catholic Church. The proposal created wide interest in Roman Catholic circles and since that time many conferences have taken place between Soviet representatives and the Vatican.

Father Edmund Walsh was sent into Russia, ostensibly in connection with relief work, but really for the purpose of investigating the situation. He submitted a report to Rome last April and went personally to Rome just before his recent return to Russia.

Father Walsh is a Jesuit priest; a native of Boston, Massachusetts. For a number of years he was an instructor in Georgetown University, Washington, D.C. When that institution established its "School for Foreign Commerce" he was placed at its head. During the war he was appointed by President Wilson as a member of a board of educators, whose duty it was to coordinate military training in the various educational institutions of America.

On his last trip to Russia, Father Walsh took with him the sum of $300,000. He will expend this sum in relief work at the rate of $100,000 per month. This will give him an opportunity to travel about the country, study the sentiment of the people and the general religious situation. He will then submit a further report to the Vatican.

Father Walsh informed my informant that, in the event the American Relief Administration withdraws from Russia, the Pope contemplates calling upon Catholics to contribute $1,000,000 for relief work in Russia. If this is done, Father Walsh will be placed in charge of the distribution of the relief.

There is a wide difference of opinion among prominent Catholics concerning the feasibility or the advisability of attempting to establish the Roman Catholic Church in Russia at this time. Many of them believe that, because the teachings of the Catholic Church are in direct opposition to at least two of the fundamental tenets of Bolshevism (regarding family ties and private property), the Bolsheviks would encumber them with so many restrictions that the attempt would end in flat failure.

The other group of Catholics believes that the Bolsheviks, realizing the immense power of the Catholic Church throughout the world, are so anxious to incur the good will of Catholics, thereby gaining their tremendous influence in international affairs, that they would grant concessions to the Vatican which would insure the success of the movement.

46
Church Valuables Delivered to the State Fund

(Translated from Moscow *Bednota,* No. 1308, September 2, 1922)

In view of the fact that the campaign of requisition of church valuables has been terminated, the People's Commissariat of Finance has instructed all finance organs to deliver all church valuables immediately to the State Fund (Goskhran) in Moscow, notwithstanding any reasons for which they have so far been withheld.

47
"Collection of Church Valuables"

(Translation from Moscow *Izvestiia,* No. 197, September 3, 1922)

From the beginning of the campaign until August 10th there have been collected by the State Fund (GOSKHRAN): 8 poods, 2 pounds, 84 zolotinks, 61 dolias of gold; 16,904 poods, 37 pounds, 78 zolotinks, 81 dolias of silver; 84 poods, 38 pounds, 93 zolotinks, 73 dolias of copper; 1 pood, 20 pounds, 65½ dolias of pearls; 170 diamonds and 1,163 other precious stones weighing 166 karats. There were also collected 3,265 rubles in gold coin and 19,586 rubles in silver coin, as well as 41 gold watches. These figures do not include the valuables collected in Petrograd and Siberia.

48
Letter of the U.S. High Commissioner in Constantinople
to the Secretary of State Concerning the Situation
of the Russian Church

No. 453   September 14, 1922
Sir:

I have the honor to enclose herewith in translation copies of an epistle addressed by the Metropolitan of Iaroslavl to the Orthodox Russian Church. This document, the original of which was received by the Russian Diplomatic Mission at Constantinople from the Russian Embassy at Paris, throws a certain amount of light on the extraordinarily complex and obscure situation of the Russian Church at the present time. Anything like an accurate estimate of that situation, however, is next to impossible. I have been entirely unsuccessful, for instance, in my efforts to gauge the importance of the so-called Progressive or Living Church which under the leadership of Bishop Antonin has separated from Patriarch Tikhon's party and indeed from the Russian Church itself. The Bolshevik radio, as the Department has undoubtedly observed, contains frequent references to the so-called Progressive clergy, their sympathy with the Bolsheviks, and their intentions to reform the Church along radical lines. Apparently this movement has the approval and the support of the Bolshevik authorities who have used with great skill the Church property confiscation of last winter to discredit the Russian Church and to foster the "Progressive" movement. Whether in this work the authorities have been able to appeal to any rivalry between the Black or higher and monastic clergy and the White or lower clergy, I am unable to say, although such an appeal appears entirely possible and indeed probable.

Of course, the Russian Church is a serious obstacle in the way of the Bolsheviks and, outside of Russia at least, the ecclesiastical authorities have often taken a marked counter-revolutionary and imperial attitude. In this connection the translations of the two resolutions of the Council of the Russian Church outside of Russia held at [Sremski] Karlovtsi in December, 1921, enclosed herewith, are of importance. Many of the delegates, including Bishop Veniamin, now residing in Constantinople, and said to be the connecting link between Patriarch Tikhon and the thirteen Russian Bishops outside of Russia, strongly opposed this alliance between the Church and the Romanovs. However, the resolutions stand and have doubtless been used by the Bolsheviks to justify their campaign of de-Christianization and demoralization of Russia and especially of Russian youth.

I have been told by reliable observers who have recently come out of Russia that the conditions prevailing in such schools as exist are unspeakably bad from the moral as well as from the intellectual point of view. I am assured that the teachers are not allowed to bring any books into the school buildings and that discipline of any kind is proscribed. I have even heard of one Russian school where this anarchical state of things ended by wearying even the pupils, who accordingly organized themselves along Soviet lines and petitioned the teacher to give them some instruction— with what result is not recorded. An American who has been in Russia for some time told me that in his judgment the worst state of things in Russia would come when the present generation of demoralized and debilitated children grows up and endeavors to participate in the political and economic life of the country. Doubtless such a possibility has not escaped the Department's attention. The present religious and moral situation of Russia in my judgment deserves the

most searching examination by those who are seeking to forecast the future
with any degree of accuracy.

> I have the honor to be, Sir,
> Your obedient servant,
> Mark L. Bristol
> Rear-Admiral, U.S. Navy, United
> States High Commissioner

49

Letter of the U.S. High Commissioner in Constantinople
to the Secretary of State Concerning the
Russian Church Abroad

No. 498   October 10, 1922

Sir:

   With reference to my dispatch No. 453, of September 14, 1922, I now
have the honor to enclose herewith in translation copies of an epistle addressed by the Patriarch Tikhon to [Metropolitan] Antonii, formerly of Kiev
and Halich, but now in charge of the Russian Church in Serbia. This document is of capital importance in judging of the present situation of the
Russian Church. The Congress [Sobor] which met at [Shremski] Karlovtsi in
December 1921, and which is mentioned in my dispatch No. 453, took two
important decisions [29] — (1) it publicly identified the cause of the
Russian Church with the cause of the Romanovs, and (2) it established an
organization for the Russian Church outside of Russia and with this object
in view certain Archbishops and Bishops were appointed to have jurisdiction
over the Russians in the several countries of Europe and in the United States.
The Patriarch, however, in his latest Epistle has emphatically repudiated the
first of these acts and has disapproved the second. While I have no doubt
that the extreme Monarchists are greatly chagrined at the Patriarch's stand —
some have gone so far as to doubt the authenticity of the Epistle — the more
moderate elements and notably certain of the prominent Russians at Constantinople, are greatly relieved at this nullification of the political action
taken at [Shremski] Karlovtsi against which they fought and in which they
finally acquiesced with greatest reluctance. With reference to the Patriarch's
disapproval of the organization of the Russian Church outside Russia and
his emphasis upon the powers already exercised by Archbishop Evlogii, it is
felt that the Patriarch does not fully realize the ecclesiastical situation and
the number of the Russians at present outside of their country. A new con-

gress [Sobor] will assemble shortly and will formulate for communication to the Patriarch certain observations on this subject which may lead to a modification of his views with respect to organization as expressed in the Epistle.

From a high Russian Ecclesiastic I have secured the following information regarding the present situation of the Church in Russia. The Metropolitan of Iaroslavl who was delegated to rule over the Russian Church during the Patriarch's imprisonment, and translations of whose Epistle [36] were transmitted as enclosure No. 1 to my despatch No. 453, has been exiled by the Bolsheviks to Siberia. It is not known, therefore, who is actually at the head of the Russian Church at the present time. The so-called Progressive Church was brought into existence by the Bolsheviks in connection with the controversy over the confiscation of Church property. They found an effective ally for this work in the person of Bishop [Archbishop] Antonin, who is the leading ecclesiastic in the new organization. Recently, however, there has been dissension in the Progressive Church itself and a group of clerics has actually broken away over the question of the marriage of the clergy and the promotion of the lower clergy, who are always married, to the episcopacy, heretofore restricted to the monastic clergy. Bishop [Archbishop] Antonin believes that this question should be settled by a Church Council, but certain of the Progressive clergy have become unduly impatient for marriage and the highest ecclesiastical preferment at the same time, and this disagreement has carried to the point of inaugurating still another Church organization.

With reference to the status of Church property in present-day Russia, my informant stated that the Bolsheviks had adopted many features of the Combes legislation in France and that the title of Church property was vested in the State, but the use for purposes of worship was and is granted to the ecclesiastical authorities. I was somewhat surprised to learn that many of the monastic establishments have not been molested This remark, however, applies chiefly to such establishments in rural districts. The larger monastic buildings in the cities have doubtless been put to secular use. The Ecclesiastical Academies and Seminaries have pretty generally been closed, but the education of candidates for the priesthood still goes on, the funds being furnished by private subscription. During the earlier stages of the Revolution there was no interference with the appointment of Bishops by the Patriarch. More recently, however, such interference has been constant and notorious. In fact, at least a quarter of the Bishops are now in prison. I questioned my informant as to the attitude of the Bolsheviks towards the Raskolniks or Old-Believers. He said that at first the Bolshevik authorities had made a distinction between the Raskolniks and the Orthodox Church, very much to the benefit of the former. When, however, it was discovered that from the Bolshevik point of view the Old-Believers were about as bad as the members of the Orthodox Church, a more uniform course of treatment was adopted and has been followed with a consistency which would be worthy of praise in other circumstances.

I have the honor to be, Sir,
Your obedient servant,
(-) Mark L. Bristol
Rear-Admiral, U.S. Navy, United
States High Commissioner

50

Letter of the U.S. Ambassador in Rome to the Secretary of State Concerning Conversations with the Russian Minister to the Vatican on the Relations between the Russian Orthodox and the Roman Catholic Churches

No. 478 — Confidential   October 21, 1922
Sir:

On the receipt by the Embassy of a copy of Mr. Young's despatch No. 2488 to the Department, dated August 14, 1922, from Riga, transmitting a Memorandum regarding the Vatican and the Russian Orthodox Church, a member of my staff talked with the Russian Minister to the Vatican on this general subject.

The Minister, Mr. Aleksandr Lyssakowsky, a layman, and a member of the Orthodox Church, was accredited to the Holy See by the Russian Provisional Government in the Spring of 1917. He is a keen, intelligent and agreeable man, who enjoys the hearty respect of his colleagues, and fills a difficult and somewhat anomalous position with skill and dignity.

In general, Mr. Lyssakawsky said, the Vatican at present is pursuing a policy of watchful waiting in regard to Russia. Its attitude is opportunist. Therefore it is exceedingly difficult to foretell what positive program, if any, it will adopt.

Mr. Lyssakowsky began his remarks by giving a brief historical account of the relationship between the two Churches. He mentioned the attempt at union at Florence shortly before the Turkish conquest of Constantinople, and the subsequent attempt in Poland in the sixteenth century. Both were cases where the weaker church sought the stronger. Neither arrangement endured. He pointed out there were eight million Catholics in Russia in 1914, the great majority of whom were Polish. The Catholics elsewhere in Russia were included in one diocese.

On the occasion of the separation of Church and State by the Kerensky

Government in 1917, Mr. Lyssakowsky was sent to Rome with the text of these laws, which were drafted in collaboration with Polish and Russian Catholics. He spoke of the original hostility of the Vatican to the Bolsheviks and of its conversations with them in 1920. The futility of these discussions as a basis for carrying out a program of positive action became finally apparent to the Vatican at the Genoa Conference.

During the past year the Bolsheviks have despoiled Catholic churches as well as Orthodox, but the cautious and diplomatic attitude of the Vatican has not allowed this action to result in a discontinuance of its conversations with them. It was also pointed out that Bolshevist tenets in conflict with the Catholic Church are no conclusive obstacle to a rapproachment from the Vatican's point of view, for the Vatican, as in similar instances in the past, by recognizing the Bolshevists as head of the State, could wink at their tenets. The "New Living Church," established in August of this year by the Bolshevists, under the Orthodox Bishop, Antonin, Mr. Lyssakovsky believes will continue to be no more than a nominal and artificial organization.

He summarized the actual situation as follows: The present Pope, who has lived in Poland and has studied Russian conditions at first hand, felt, after the Genoa Conference, that the Vatican did not possess sufficiently accurate information about current conditions in Soviet Russia. Purely for the purpose of improving this information, emissaries were sent. At present there are twelve in Russia, who are there merely for intelligence purposes, and who have orders not to attempt to proselyte. Lyssakowsky appeared to regard this situation with perfect equanimity. Comprehensive attempts by the Catholic Church to proselytize would develop a widespread and stubborn hostility. He emphasized at the same time the faith which the Vatican has in Russia's eventual rehabilitation under a non-Communist regime. "That," he said, "is the reason why I am still here." To the question as to what the Vatican intends or hopes to do when Russia re-enters the family of nations, he replied that it does not know. It will depend on the contemporary situation and not least on the Pope in power. The training and personality of the Pope has much to do with the shaping of such policies. The present Pope, he thought, would be comparatively transigeant on such a matter; more so, for instance, than his predecessor would have been.

A possible accord between the two Churches would involve primarily the question of the recognition of papal supremacy. Matters of dogma and ritual would be of secondary importance, on which Rome would not be so insistent and which could be comparatively easily settled from the point of view of the Orthodox Church.

In discussing the current events in the Near East, Mr. Lyssakowsky expressed the opinion that religious factors did not influence the attitude of his country toward Turkey. He stated that he had no fear of the present Bolshevist-Turkish Entente, for the reason that as soon as Turkish success exceeds certain limits it will conflict with Russia in two ways: (1) The question of the Straits for Russia is an economic matter and therefore an enduring issue, for it is Russia's only all-the-year-round outlet, and in immediate proximity to Russia's most productive region. (2) The Turk will clash with the Bolshevists in the Caucasus, where there are large communities of Mussulmen within the limits of the old Russian Empire, and now within Bolshevik territory. Finally, Lyssakowsky said, Kemal's success will react in a purely political way on the Mohammedan world. He feels that except for the obvious way in which Kemal forced England's hand, recent events in Egypt have had as great an effect on English prestige among Mohammedans as the present Turkish success is having.

I have the honor to be, Sir,

Your obedient servant,

Richard Child

51

Status of Religion in Russia: Report of the Department of State

November 22, 1922

STATUS OF RELIGION IN RUSSIA

In accordance with the teaching of Communism, the first activities of the Soviet Government were directed to the complete extermination of all religion. During the first months of the Soviet domination, the Church was separated from the State, its property nationalized, the clergy and lay officers of the Church disfranchised, — the restriction is still in force — and all adherents of any religion whatsoever generally classified as "counter-revolutionary."

These regulations had only a small effect on religion and as a consequence the Soviets resorted to anti-religious and atheistic propaganda. In character and intensity this propaganda took the form of a "drive," similar to an American Liberty Loan drive. By speeches, movies and posters, atheism was promulgated in an official way by the Government. A sample poster is attached. The teaching of religion in public and private schools was forbidden by law. Although considerable headway was made in the Communist schools, this anti-religious teaching made no impression on the peasants and only partially undermined the faith of the city proletariat.

The third and present stage, i.e., the disorganization of the established Russian Church, has been the most effective. Flattery proving ineffective, the

Soviet authorities then threatened the Church hierarchy, and succeeded in creating an opposition within the ranks. The Metropolitan, Archbishop [Patriarch] Tikhon, was finally removed by the Soviet authorities on the grounds that he opposed the distribution of Church treasures for the famine relief. This is a misstatement of fact. He agreed to the distribution of the Church treasures with the exception of the consecrated vessels used in the communion service. The Soviets were enabled to establish the "Living Church," composed of a small group of bishops and other ecclesiastics who are sympathetic to the Soviet Government. The rest of the hierarchy steadfastly opposed the Living Church, and as a consequence many of Russia's enlightened clergy were executed by the Soviet authorities. The underlying motive of the Soviets is the breakup of all large religious organizations, substituting for them innumerable sects. At present there are three principal divisions: (1) the "Living Church," under Soviet domination; (2) the old group; and (3) the so-called "Protestant" faction. The first and third are not only not opposed to the government, but to a large extent receive its support. The last mentioned is apparently the group with which Bishop Nuelson, referred to in the *New York Times* of November 21, 1922, was in conference while in Moscow. This group desires cooperation with the Protestant groups of Europe and the United States. The second group limits its cooperation to that with the Angelican Church of Great Britain, and is also wooed at present by the Vatican at Rome.

It may therefore be said that the Soviet has failed to uproot religion not because it is tolerant, but in spite of its energetic endeavors.

THE CONDITION OF SCHOOLS AND PUBLIC BUILDINGS IN MOSCOW

The *Izvestiia,* the leading official newspaper of the Soviets, in its issue of August 18, 1922, questions whether any schools will exist during the coming school year, in view of the "extreme state of disorganization, destruction and neglect." Teachers in Moscow, according to the same source, "are drawing 12th class pay — 25 million rubles per month, and that only 2 or 3 months after it has become due. A messenger boy cannot be employed for 30 or 40 million per month. In the provinces it is much worse. . . Under such conditions, the educational level is sinking, and illiteracy grows." The conditions of school buildings appear to be no different. The same newspaper (*Izvestiia,* May 12, 1922) reports that "The number of decaying houses in Moscow which are occupied by various institutions, establishments, and organizations, is growing on account of the terrible mistreatment of these houses by the above institutions, and their gross neglect in regard to this nationalized property." *Kommunisticheskii Trud,* another Soviet newspaper, in describing Moscow says that 15,698 apartments in Moscow are entirely unfit for occupation — although occupied — and that 75% of the remaining apartments are dangerous to health, that walls and ceilings are defective, that most houses have no window panes, no water, and that the fireplaces are more or less destroyed.

Reports by Americans and foreigners who have visited Russia in 1921 and 1922 appear to agree that an improvement in the outward appearance of Petrograd and Moscow is visible and progressing slowly, but do not agree with the statements made by Bishop Nuelson.

Colonel Groves, a member of the ARA, reports that "with respect to the schools and the educational system, while in theory it was impressive enough, it hardly existed at all in practice. Parents were unwilling to send their children to the schools, and the impossibility of procuring fuel for the schools during the winter, and the fear of cholera and typhus, militated against any effective educational system."

Foreigners visiting Petrograd and Moscow are impressed by the "model" buildings, especially renovated and kept in order for the "guests" of Russia. There are also a number of similar model schools in both Petrograd and Moscow.

AWK:EBS.

52

Decision No. 4 of the Far Eastern Revolutionary Committee
November 26, 1922, Chita

The Far Eastern Revolutionary Committee passed the following resolution:

1. To put into effect, in the entire territory of the former Far Eastern Republic, the Decree of the Council of People's Commissars concerning "the separation of the Church from the State" (Code of Laws of 1918 No. 18 Cl. 268) *263*, and the Resolution of the People's Commissariat of Justice which was passed on August 24, 1918 regarding the "realization of the decree concerning the separation of the Church from the State, and of Schools from the Church." (*Code of Laws of 1918*, No. 6 Cl. 685 *62*.)

2. Pending the election of Councils of Workmen's and Peasants' Deputies throughout the territory, the execution of the duties of the Councils, resulting from the above mentioned decree and resolution, shall be entrusted to the local Revolutionary Committees. The execution of the duties, conferred by the same regulations upon Offices for Registration of Marriages and Births, shall be entrusted to the local Registration Offices.

3. Copies of data concerning the execution of the decree and of the resolution (Cl. 24 of the Resolution), inventory lists of properties (Cl. 8),

schedules of capital (Cl. 19), must be presented, within an established time at the Justice Department of the Far Eastern Revolutionary Committee, and the originals must, at the same time, be sent to the proper People's Commissariats.

4. This order shall take effect upon its receipt by the local Provincial Revolutionary Committee.

Original signed by
KOBOZEV
President of the Far Eastern
Revolutionary Committee
STEPANOV
Secretary
No. 819, National Archives, Washington, D.C.

53
Letter of Archbishop Jan Cieplak to Rev. Edmund Walsh, S.J., Director of the Papal Relief Mission in Russia

Pontifical Aid In Russia /P.X.I./

[December 6, 1922]

"CATHFUND" — Moscow
My Reverend Father,
You undoubtedly know that the Soviet Government ceased to demand from us — probably as a result of an intervention by the Holy See — the signature on formal contracts for the use of our churches, and that it was replaced by receipts (raspiska) through which those who accept the churches become responsible to the government for guarding the churches and the objects of worship.

Because those receipts are in reality nothing but the same contracts, only masked, the Catholics refused to sign them.

As a punishment for these refusals they had threatened us with reprisals and now are going to put them into effect.

Yesterday, December 5, in Petrograd the agents of the government, accompanied by armed militia, came to our churches and, having used brutal force, closed and sealed them all, taking the keys with them.

We are threatened with reprisals if we organize the Divine services in private houses. Some priests have had verbal warnings.

The same thing had taken place last Sunday in Gatchina (near Petrograd) where the agents disturbed the Divine service and the Communion of 150 children, and also brutally closed the premises on which, after the closing of the church, for four months the faithful had gathered to pray to our Merciful God. As a result we are left in Petrograd without a house of God. We have no place to pray, to deposit our tears and our sorrows! The Catholic population is in mourning.

Naturally, we are doing everything possible to have this great and cruel injustice rectified soon, our rights respected and our churches reopened. To this end we organize delegations to the central government in Moscow, and here to local authorities — but there are so few of us and we are so weak — our only refuge and our hope is the Holy See. I want to ask you earnestly, My Reverend Father, to notify the Holy See as soon as possible about all these facts and to apply to the Holy Father for enlightenment and counsel which we might follow in a situation so critical and so dangerous to the Holy Church and Catholic interests.

Please accept my best regards,

Your devoted,
Jan Cieplak,
Archbishop

December 6 — 1922 — Petrograd
(Translation from the French)

54

Letter of Archbishop Jan Cieplak to Rev. Edmund Walsh, S.J., Director of the Papal Relief Mission in Russia

December 19, 1922

Very Reverend Father,

I have learned with great satisfaction that the Holy Father intends to assign you to negotiations with the Soviets to settle our religious problems. Your high intelligence and the fact that you know the conditions in which we live and the milieu with which you will have to deal give us a guarantee that your work will be successful and that you will bring some comfort to our Church.

Your first task, My Reverend Father, will be to have our churches in Petrograd reopened as soon as possible; this is necessary for the following reasons:

(a) The faithful become weary of the existing situation. There is no place to pray, to participate in the Mass or to receive the Sacraments. Although up to now we have not refrained from holding the divine services in private houses, it is very inconvenient; only a small number of the faithful can assemble there, and the rest, left behind, do not come any more to the services.

(b) All the pastors are summoned before the examining magistrate for their attitude in the affair of church closures. If the churches are reopened the reason for summonses might thus disappear.

(c) There is danger that the Bolsheviks, exasperated by our opposition, might seize the churches and the objects of worship (the keys to the churches are in their possession).

But if the credentials which you expect from the Sovereign Pontiff do not come in time, what are we to do? Could we in such a case sign the declaration whose text was presented by our deputation to Mr. Krasikov and which he changed according to his will (you certainly have the copy of it)?

Here are some reasons which seem (only in the case that the reply from Rome fails to come) to justify the signing:

(a) It is not a *dogovor* [Contract] nor a *raspiska* [receipt] but a simple declaration of what the parishioners will do with their churches (that they will take care of their upkeep and maintenance).

(b) In this declaration the church and the objects of worship are not called the property of the state or of the people.

(c) The pastor, although he is not named in the declaration, would not be prevented from signing it. He can sign the declaration with his parishioners.

(d) The most important thing is that this document is but a temporary measure. In case some agreement between the Holy See and the Soviets comes into existence the declaration might be replaced with another one or be left off completely.

Nevertheless I do not dare to decide upon such a serious matter without your opinion and I do ask you for the assistance of your advice. Please reply to this as soon as possible (maybe by cable).

Please accept, My Reverend Father, my deep regards.

Your devoted,

Jan Cieplak, Archbishop

(Translation from the French)

55
Letter of Archbishop Jan Cieplak to Rev. Edmund Walsh, S.J., Director of the Papal Relief Mission in Russia

December 31, 1922

My Reverend Father,

I hasten to let you know that we have been assured again that the place to which our affair has to proceed is Moscow (Mr. Krasikov!) and that the case could be adjourned or totally put aside if an intervention of some authority took place. It was added that haste is necessary and that next Tuesday (January 2) will be the last effective day for proceedings, since by Wednesday (January 3) all the dossiers have to be in the hands of the Prosecutor General, who will deliver them personally to the Revolutionary Tribunal. It is determined, apparently, that the case is to begin without delay.

I have received today a letter from Mgr. Ropp (our Archbishop) from Warsaw. He writes that, since the events have become so serious and the Bolsheviks are closing the churches, and since it is impossible to receive in time the necessary instructions from Rome, we may on our own give the permission to our parishioners to sign the formula called for (Mgr. Ropp not knowing the last formula with which Mr. Krasikov has presented us). Everybody, Mgr. Ropp adds, will excuse us once they are acquainted with our position. He talked it over with the Nuncio in Warsaw, who did not oppose it.

But, on the other hand, we are already pledged (as you know, My Father) not to sign any formula which would be opposed to the Canon Law, even the last formula of Mr. Krasikov.

I had sent yesterday to the Smolnyi a request demanding that the seals be taken off the churches so they could be opened. A special deputation of parishioners confirmed my request. We rely on the letter which you wrote me on December 23. We were told that up to now (it was December 29) no order or instruction from the central authorities in Moscow had reached the Smolnyi.

The good will of those Messrs! . . .

The best solution in this situation would be:

(1) That the case might be at least adjourned;

(2) That I might personally go to Moscow one of these days.

If you can, My Father, try to obtain this and please cable me the reply.

Your devoted,

Jan Cieplak, Archbishop

(Translation from the French)

1923

56
Violation of the Rules on the Separation of the Church and the State

(Translation from the Criminal Code of the R.S.F.S.R., Official Edition, Moscow, 1923.)

119. Utilizing the religious prejudices of the masses with the object of overthrowing the Workman-Peasant government or of rousing opposition to its laws and orders, is punishable by the penalty prescribed in paragraph 69 of the Criminal Code.

120. Fraudulent actions performed for the purpose of rousing superstition among the masses of the population, and also for the purpose of thereby securing any kind of advantages, is punishable by privation of liberty up to one year or forced labor up to one year.

121. Imparting religious instruction in State or private educational institutions to children or minors, is punishable by forced labor up to one year.

122. Any employment of compulsion in making collections in favor of religious organizations and groups, is punishable by forced labor up to six months, by privation up to two years of the right of concluding contracts with local Soviets for the use of ritual property and religious edifices, and by confiscation of the property of the organizations.

123. Assumption by religious or Church organizations of administrative, Court or other functions of a public-legal character and of the rights of juridical persons, is punishable by forced labor up to six months, by liquidation of the above mentioned organizations and by confiscation of their property.

124. The performance in Government buildings and institutions of religious ceremonies and also the placing in these buildings of any sort of religious symbols, is punishable by forced labor up to three months or a fine up to 300 gold rubles.

125. Hindering the performance of religious rites, in so far as they do not disturb the public peace and are not accompanied by infractions of the rights of citizens, is punishable by forced labor up to six months.

69. Propaganda and agitation, in the form of instigation of the overthrow of the government of the Soviets by forcible or treasonable actions or
by active and passive resistance to the Workmen-Peasant Government, or by
mass non-compliance with military and tax obligations imposed on citizens,
is punishable by privation of liberty for not less than three years with strict
isolation.

For the same crimes, committeed in circumstances of war or during
popular disturbances, the penalty is increased to the extreme limit of the
law [the death penalty].

Instigation of non-compliance with, or of opposition to, orders of the
central or the local authorities, where counter-revolutionary aims are not
proven, is punishable by the penalties prescribed in paragraph 83 of the
Criminal Code.

---

83. Agitation and propaganda of any kind, including the instigation of
the crimes defined in paragraph 75-81d, and also the rousing of national
hatred and dissension, is punishable by privation of liberty for not less than
one year, with strict isolation.

If the agitation and propaganda take place in time of war and are directed
toward non-compliance by citizens with military obligations or obligations
connected with military operations which have been imposed on them, the
penalty may be increased up to the supreme penalty of the law.

[The paragraphs referred to, 75 to 81d, deal with crimes against the
administrative order.]

57
Letter of the Pastor of the Church of Our Lady of France,
Rev. M. Amoudru, O.P., to Dr. E. Walsh, S.J.

Petrograd, January 17, 1923

Doctor,

Monsignor Archbishop asked me to inform you that even my church has
been closed today, the only one left open in Petrograd, and I was told that
it is absolutely forbidden to arrange any meeting at my place for the purpose
of praying.

The commissar then disclosed that Mr. Chicherin had sent a telegram to
Rome yesterday in which he asked the Holy Father in the name of twenty
thousand Poles for authorization to sign the *dogovor* [contract] so that the
churches would be reopened. The falsehood is evident, but it is possible that
such a telegram actually was sent, in a maneuver of which it is well we should

be aware. After all that has been told me, I have an impression that their aim is to wear out the people so as to stir them up against their clergy and thus separate them. They pretend to have already obtained some successes in this respect. I do not believe this, but it is good to understand their game.

Please accept, Doctor, the compliments and respectful sentiments of your humble servant.

M. Amoudru, O.P.

Pastor, Notre Dame de France

(Translation from the French)

58

Letter of Archbishop Jan Cieplak to Rev. Edmund Walsh, S.J.,
Director of the Papal Relief Mission in Russia

January 20, 1923

My Reverend and very dear Father,

I wish to thank you from the bottom of my heart for all that you have done for us; I hope that our Merciful God will continue to bless your efforts. The case is never going to start and it cannot but be the result of your measures.

All our churches are closed now and they are beginning to obstruct meetings in private houses.

We intend to send a delegation to the Smolnyi next week demanding the reopening of the churches, but without much hope. The people also want to send a delegation to Moscow but I am going to ask them, if they do go there, not to do anything without first seeing you.

Lastly, in the strictest confidence, I have to tell you in order that you may be forewarned that in the next few days serious trouble will be made for the Franciscans. Their farm has been seized and under the pretext of thefts, non-existent on this estate, five were imprisoned and the Abbess and a dozen of the nun teachers have been expelled, to the great detriment of the children. Their chapel is going to be closed. One of the commissars told them that they plan to turn the people against the clergy, close the churches, and disperse their organizations.

This news, however, is for you only — the time has not yet arrived when it can be used without causing any inconveniences.

Please accept, my dear Father, my deep respect.

Devotedly yours,

Jan Cieplak, Archbishop

(Translation from the French)

59

Letter from the U. S. Legation in Riga to the Secretary of State Concerning the Catholics and the Russian Church

No. 412.

February 16, 1923

Sir:

I have the honor to forward herewith two confidential reports (J.S.) as follows:

(1) The Russian Church

This report states that seventy-six representatives of the Roman Catholic Church have arrived in Soviet Russia, fifty per cent of whom belong to the Jesuit order. It would appear that their movements are being carefully observed by the State Political Administration and that the Communists are inaugurating additional anti-religious movements with the idea of counteracting the work of the Catholic missionaries.

(2) The Vatican and the Russian Church

It is stated that the "Living Church" is sending five priests to Berlin for the purpose of organizing a "Supreme Church Administration Abroad."

The report contains certain information given by Dr. Rafalovskii, formerly of the Orthodox faith, but now working in the Baltic States for the American Methodist Church. He claims that the Vatican is assisting the Bolsheviks in their efforts to disintegrate the Russian Orthodox Church and is likewise turning its attention to Russian emigrés in Europe and America. As evidence of this he states that fifty thousand Orthodox children in France, Poland, Czecho-Slovakia and Switzerland, whose parents are unable to educate them, have been taken into schools and colleges at the expense of the Vatican and that several thousand adult Russians have been accepted as students in Jesuit seminaries in Germany, France, Czecho-Slovakia and Poland. Reference is made to the existence of certain religious sects in Europe which are being used to assist in the disintegration of the Orthodox Church.

According to Dr. Rafalovskii, the Vatican is seeking to prevent any rapprochment between the Russian Orthodox and the Anglican Churches.

I have the honor to be, Sir,

Your obedient servant,

F. W. B. Coleman

Enclosures: 1) The Russian Church; 2) The Vatican and the Russian Church [61, 60].

60
The Vatican and the Russian Church
(Report from the U.S. Legation in Riga)

January 29, 1923

THE VATICAN AND THE RUSSIAN CHURCH

1) "The Living Church" is sending 5 priests to Berlin for the purpose of organizing a "Supreme Church Administration Abroad." This Administration is to include representatives of the "Smenoverkhovsty" [Russian emigrés] who turned pro-Soviet].

2) (The following is from Dr. Rafalovskii, who is now in Riga. Formerly of the Orthodox faith, he is now working in the Baltic States for the American Methodist Church.)

The "Living Church" is now trying to transfer its work abroad among the Russian emigration. The Chapel at the Berlin Soviet Mission is being repaired and a group of priests from the "Living Church" is being sent to Berlin, but Vedenskii is not with them.

The Vatican is giving the Bolsheviks all the assistance it can in the work of disintegrating Orthodoxy. Documentary proof of this is in the hands of the Orthodox clergy abroad. At the present moment the activity of the Vatican and the Jesuits is limited to "Relief" work, but a plan for further internal work in Russia has been drawn up by the Vatican on a wide scale for the execution of which the Vatican will have to expend large sums. While limiting its activities for the present to "Relief" in Russia, the Vatican has turned its attention also to the Russian emigrés scattered over Europe and America, being of the opinion that this is the most cultured and intelligent class of Russian Orthodoxy. So far the results of this work are as follows:

(A) 50,000 Orthodox children in France, Poland, Czecho-Slovakia and Switzerland, whose parents are not in a position financially to educate them, have been taken into schools and colleges at the expense of the Vatican.

(B) A large number of adult persons, to a total of several thousands, some of them former prisoners of war, others simply emigrants, have been accepted as students in Jesuit seminaries in Germany, France, Czecho-Slovakia, and Poland where they will complete their education at the cost of the Roman Catholic Church. There are about 40 such schools in all, similar to those in Marienfeld (Germany), and Elisavetgrad (Czecho-Slovakia).

(C) Special Jesuit agents in all countries are getting needy Russians, unable to continue their education, to enter Catholic schools, and inducing Russians with well-known names, or who formerly occupied prominent positions in Russia, to enter the Catholic faith or other sects. Of these sects, one of the most prominent at present is the so-called "Licht im Osten," ["Light in the East"] whose headquarters are at Vernihorod. Its pastors are Jacques and Kruker. It has branches at Riga (2), Reval (1), Helsingfors (2), and Kovno (1). This sect is neither purely Lutheran nor Catholic, but the aim of the Jesuits is to disintegrate the Orthodox Church, and for this reason they welcome the work of the organization. General Palen recently joined this sect and is now one of its most active workers.

(D) The results of last year's visit to Revel of the Papal Legate Sazzini are noticeable. Many Russians there have gone over to the Catholic Church. Mons. Sazzini has been appointed Legate for the whole of the Baltic States, with headquarters at Riga. His work will, however, only touch the Baltic States indirectly, being mainly directed to Soviet Russia, whither he will send Papal workers.

The work in Russia of the Catholic Church directed from Poland will be carried out by Bishop Ropp, brother of the Ropp formerly in Russia. The Vatican has already bestowed upon Ropp the right to consecrate priests of the Uniate faith and to give permission for Catholics to hold mass on an Orthodox altar and vice versa.

(E) The Vatican is disturbed by the efforts of the Orthodox Church to seek help and reapprochmement with the Anglican Church. It has been decided to carry on decisive work against this tendency and to devote particular attention to observation over the work of the Orthodox Church in America, as it is thought that a rapprochement between the Greco-Roman and Anglican Churches is most likely to be attained by this road.

61

The Russian Church (Report from the U.S. Legation in Riga)

February 2, 1923

THE RUSSIAN CHURCH

Some 76 representatives of the Roman Catholic Church have arrived in Soviet Russia, fifty per cent of whom belong to the Jesuit order. A large number of these have gone to the provinces, while the following important members — Father Karnitskii [Karnicki] (Polish), Father Nossini (Italian) and Father Norten (German) — are in the Western Area. Their work is closely watched by the State Political Department, whose agents report that they are trying to convert more influential persons and clergy who are losing faith in the restoration of the Russian Orthodox Church. The follow-

ing have already gone over to the Roman Catholic Faith.
  1. Monsignor Butkevich [Budkiewicz] (a Pole).
  2. Zharov.
  3. Polodetskii.
  4. Zabotin.
  5. Rylskii.
(Note: The agent does not specify who these persons are, but presumably they are well-known locally.)

The State Political Department does not regard such conversion to Roman Catholicism as dangerous, except in certain localities where anti-religious propaganda, carried on by Communists, has been checked by the work of the Catholic Missionaries, such as Zhyobin, and in parts of the Smolensk Government.

As a counter measure some of the best atheist propaganda workers including Sarabianov, Tregubov and Mikhail Okunev have been sent for a circular tour in the Smolensk governorship to give anti-religious lectures.

Medved, the well-known Chekist, who is the chief of the Moscow Branch of the State Political Department, is urging strong measures against the work of the Roman Catholic clergy.

62
"Christian Exploits"
Trial of Roman Catholic Priests

(Translation from Moscow *Izvestiia*, No. 63, March 23, 1923)

The trial of Archbishop Cieplak and a number of other representatives of the Roman Catholic clergy began yesterday in the Supreme Court.

One present at the trail becomes convinced that the Soviet authorities were right to include in the Criminal Code of the R.S.F.S.R. Article 119 which provides the punishment for "taking advantage of religious prejudice with the aim to overthrow the Soviet régime or to resist its orders and instructions."

The hearing of the case begins with the activities of the accused after the promulgation of the decree concerning the separation of the Church from the State [Decree of January 23, 1918]. At a number of secret conferences which took place in Petrograd between the end of 1918 and March 1920, the Roman Catholic clergy has worked out ways and means in connection with the enforcement of the said decree. Originals of the minutes of these conferences are among the materials collected by the preliminary investigation concerning the case of Cieplak and others. It was resolved that every way and means could be adopted: direct and indirect. All sorts of circulars and instructions have been worked out which called the agreements between the groups of believers and the Soviet institutions "profanation of the privileges of the Church." Believing Catholics have been forbidden to participate in these "transactions."

Naive and simple, and especially "religious," persons could probably think that a struggle is being carried on by the clergy only in the "formal religious sphere." But the holy fathers have very carelessly disclosed their plans. They have passed a resolution concerning the "struggle from the altar against the Bolshevist infection," which threatened the excommunication from the Church of all persons who joined the Communist Party. A blind man can see that the case is purely political and has nothing to do with religion. God's name is being used by the "fathers" only as means of psychological influence. Even Patriarch Tikhon did not dare to inaugurate such methods of unconcealed "pure politics."

The Roman Catholic clergy has not limited its activities to thorough utilization of every kind of religious propaganda and agitation against the Soviet power. It has established a formally religious but actually political organization with numerous branches, the object of which is to resist the enforcement of the Decree concerning the separation of Church and State. This organization consists of local committees of believers and a central committee at the Archbishop's "which should exist during the revolutionary time until a strong legal order is established in Russia." Any politically educated person will understand the last words as "until the overthrow of the Soviet power."

At one of the secret conferences in the beginning of 1920 Archbishop Cieplak proposed to inaugurate an "aggressive policy instead of a defensive one."

Thereafter the Roman Catholic clergy began to carry on open resistance to the orders and actions of the Petrograd Soviet in connection with the enforcement of the decree separating Church and State and the decree of February 23, 1922, concerning the confiscation of Church valuables. The disclosure of various details concerning the criminal activities of the accused will constitute the substance of the judicial investigation.

63
"Christian Exploits"
Trial of Roman Catholic Priests

(Translation from Moscow *Izvestiia*, No. 64, March 23, 1923)

The Petrograd governorship Executive Committee resolved sometime last year to conclude a contract again with the Roman Catholics concerning the lease of churches and church property for temporary use, because the former contracts of 1918 were signed by the Roman Catholics with certain amendments: "Temporarily until the receipt of an instruction from the Head of the Catholic Church, the Pope" and also because of the absence of some members of the Church Committees, who signed these contracts. The priests now being tried have not only refused to sign the new contracts but have even been trying to agitate among the belivers against the Soviet power and its demands. The witnesses, Smirnov, Kodik, Nemchenko, and Kolesnikov, representatives of the local administrative departments of the Petrograd Soviet, have been forced to seal the Catholic churches after all attempts to come to an agreement with the Catholics failed. In spite of their continual proposals the Catholic priests refused to call general conferences of believers in order to settle the question peacefully, refused to negotiate with the authorities, and explained their attitude by their teaching and non-receipt of instructions from the Pope. They also took every possible step to collect in the church, on the day when the sealing of the church was to take place, the largest possible number of believers; in some cases the believers would not leave the church, but knelt and prayed the whole day; in other cases they cursed and threatened and sometimes even threw stones. The priests of the Church of the Assumption of the Holy Virgin, Rutkovski and Pronsketis, knelt and began to pray as soon as the authorities entered the church. They were of course, followed by the believers. The same thing usually happened in other churches. The priests and believers refused to make any agreements with the Soviet power and when the latter tried to enforce its decrees they showed every possible concealed and unconcealed resistance. The priests would not speak politely to the authorities. The priest Eismond said to the witness Kodik that he would not tolerate "hooligans" in his church. The priest Iunevich [Juniewicz] simply told the authorities "to go away."

The accused do not deny the facts related by the witnesses but only try to explain them by the requirements of their religion.

Comrade Krylenko who acts as prosecutor at the trial disclosed by his clever examination all the secret plans of the accused and their counter-revolutionary attitude.

64
Concerning the Trial of Catholic Priests

(Translation from Moscow *Izvestiia*, No. 64, March 23, 1923)

At the discussion conference of the Polish population in Moscow a resolution has been passed by a majority of 240 votes against 8 concerning the criminal activities of the Catholic clergy who now are being tried by the Supreme Court:

"We non-partisan citizens express our profound contempt of Archbishop Cieplak and his adherents and demand that they be severely punished. Let the proletarian court punish those who are in the churches and around them and let the priests remember that "there is no power but it is from God" and submit to the verdict which they have deserved by their crimes.

We also express our thanks to the Communist Party for its struggle against the black army of priests, who deceive the proletariat. We demand that this resolution be read in the Court and that its echo be heard by the Polish working masses."

65
"Christian Exploits"
Trial of Roman Catholic Priests

(Translation from Moscow *Izvestiia,* No. 65, March 24, 1923)

In the course of the examination of the accused, which has already lasted three days, it became clear that all the priests without exception continued to conduct Divine services in different places which had not been registered, contrary to the decree concerning the sealing of churches; consequently this conduct was the result of the refusal on their part to come to an agreement with the Soviet power. At these "private" services, sometimes from 100 to 150 persons participated, as stated by the accused themselves. The accused do not regard these actions as a violation of the decree concerning the separation of Church and State, explaining them as Divine services of "private, family" character. It has been established also that even from a formal standpoint these services have not been of "private" character, since they often took place in rooms adjacent to the churches. It is interesting to point out the following fact: the investigation disclosed at these services all the necessaries of Church rites. The President Comrade Galkin and Prosecutor Krylenko are very much interested to discover where these necessaries have been obtained since the churches were closed. All accused answered that the articles were their own property. It must be also pointed out that the "holy fathers" understood what a powerful weapon in their hands the teaching of Gospel to the youths was. They have been very stubborn in disregarding the decrees of the Soviet government concerning the separation of Church and State and continued during all the years of the revolution to teach the Gospel privately to groups of youths. The accused stated that they taught the Gospel in a private manner. Some of them declared that they were going to teach the Gospel in the future.

Certainly all the priests declared that they did not pursue any political aims in their activities, and still less counter-revolutionary aims, and that they could not possibly comply with the demands of the Soviet power, since these demands contradicted the teaching of their Church. All their actions must be explained by devotion to the Church. The struggle was purely ideological and not for uncontrolled possession of Church valuables. The real thoughts of the "holy fathers" have been disclosed by a document of "private character" which the Prosecutor Krylenko attached to the case. That is a letter written by the priest Iunevich [Juniewicz] (who told the Soviet officials "to go away" from the church)) addressed to his brother, living in Moscow. In this letter the priest Iunevich [Juniewicz], in addition to such phrases as "we emphasize our discontent now and then" and "our positions are strong and we hope that the Lord will help us to hold on," says the following: "Our living conditions as before are not very bad, the people care for our welfare now even more than they did before." These are certainly important words. The letter was read in the court.

The Supreme Court paid its attention to a fact which concerns the charge brought against one of the chief accused, Archbishop Cieplak. At the time of the confiscation of church valuables the Iaroslavl priest, Rutkovski, made an inquiry of Archbishop Cieplak after he had received an order from the authorities to submit the list of valuables in his church. The letter sent a very explicit answer to Rutkovski: "The demand is illegal. Submit no information." That means that Cieplak gives an order to disobey the orders of the Soviet power.

"Does Cieplak understand his words the same way?" asked Krylenko. Cieplak explains that the word 'illegal' must be understood thus: the demand of the Soviet authorities is illegal from the point of view of the Catholic Church. He certainly did not mean to say that the demand of the Soviet authorities is illegal. "Why in such case did you add the words: 'Submit no information'?" asked Krylenko. The Archbishop was compelled to admit that the last words of his telegram contain practical instructions to the priest Rutkovski and that they did order the latter not to submit any information concerning the valuables present in the Church. Krylenko asked the Court to read the verdict passed by the Iaroslavl Revolutionary Tribunal concerning the case of the priest Rutkovski, who refused to submit the list of Church valuables.

The Court also read a circular sent by Cieplak on January 3, 1922, even prior to the promulgation of the decree concerning the confiscation of Church valuables (February 23, 1923). Foreseeing the "Church" questions which the priests would have to face after the promulgation of this decree, Cieplak "finds it necessary to give certain instructions to the Roman-Catholic clergy:"

"First of all it is necessary strictly to observe the rules of the Church," reads the circular.

And the rules of the Church certainly say that the Church property and especially the necessaries of the Church rites constitute the indisputable property of the churches, that they are sacred, and so forth. These articles cannot be handed over either to the groups of believers or to the State and therefore cannot be included in any lists or inventories or still less be confiscated without the special permission of the Church. In this circular Cieplak tried to justify, not only from religious but also from the judicial standpoint, the practical instructions which he gave to his subordinates. He also emphasized that in case "unauthorized institutions" made any demands in this sphere, there must be pointed out to them the decree separating Church and State, according to which the State has no right to interfere with the internal affairs of the Church, and also the Riga treaty, which guaranteed immunity to the Roman Catholic Church.

Not denying the right of Cieplak to give instructions to the Roman Catholic clergy, Krylenko reminds Cieplak that the decree separating Church and State says the Church buildings and the Church property are declared the property of the State and of the people, and that they can be handed to the groups of believers for temporary use only and according to special treaties. Krylenko called Cieplak's attention also to paragraph 7 of the Riga treaty, to which Cieplak himself referred as one guaranteeing the immunity of the Church in the R.S.F.S.R. This paragraph clearly says: "Within the limits of the internal legislation of the R.S.F.S.R." And, therefore, as long as there is the above amendment in the Riga treaty the Soviet power was right to confiscate the Church valuables, not only from the standpoint of the internal constitution of the R.S.F.S.R., but also from the standpoint of the obligations which the Republic assumed in the treaty with Poland.

Cieplak found nothing better for reply than to state that the amendment "within the limits of the internal legislation of the R.S.F.S.R." was understood by the Roman Catholics as a "pure formality." Cieplak stated also that such interpretation was accepted not only by him but also by Russian and Polish lawyers.

"Why in such a case did you not inquire at the People's Commissariat of Justice for a definite explanation?" asked Krylenko.

"I considered that this matter is of an international character," replied Cieplak.

"But, nevertheless, you made an inquiry of the Polish Government?"

"N-no . . ."

Krylenko then asked to attach to the case a document which proved that Cieplak had communicated with the Pope in connection with the contract concerning the use of the churches. Cieplak stated that he is subordinate directly to the Vatican and has received an answer from the Pope's representative in Poland, Archbishop Lawrence. The answer says that "the Holy Father wants to inform him that he rejects a treaty of such a kind and that if the above mentioned (Soviet) government intends to close the churches, he, Cieplak, has to inform the Vatican directly."

From explanations given by Cieplak in regard to this document, which was read in the Court, it became obvious that in addition to the maintenance of communications with the Vatican and Poland through official channels (People's Commissariat of Foreign Affairs) Cieplak had also private channels, which fact he was compelled to admit.

Then the judiciary investigation tried to disclose all the details of the underground work of the Roman Catholic clergy during the period 1918-1922. During this period a number of secret conferences took place at the Archbishop's, at which methods of resistance to the decree separating the Church from the State were discussed, as well as the "struggle from the Altar against the Bolshevist infection." This part of the investigation has particular interest (a number of interesting documents have been read in Court) and a special report ocncerning it will be given in the next issue.

[Signed by] L. N.

66
"Christian Exploits"
Trial of Roman Catholic Priests

(Translation from Moscow *Izvestiia*, No. 66, March 25, 1923)

After the examination of Cieplak, Krylenko asked the Court to put down the most important points of his evidence: the fact, which he admitted, of his sending a telegram to the Iaroslavl priest Rutkovski forbidding the latter to submit the list or inventory of church valuables; the fact that the refusal on the part of Rutkovski to submit the inventory of Church valuables was a direct consequence of this telegram; and the fact that the circular sent by Cieplak on January 3, 1922, was a direct practical instruction to the Roman Catholic clergy as to what attitude they should take in order to resist the enforcement of the decree separating the Church from the State. Krylenko points also to the fact that Cieplak maintained communication with the Vatican and Poland through private channels, in other words illegally, and upon the receipt of an answer from the Pope's representative in Poland, forbidding the Roman Catholics to enter into any agreement with the Soviet power concerning the right to use the churches, Cieplak informed all Roman Catholic priests of this answer, not considering it necessary to inform the Soviet government of the same. Cieplak declared also that as far as the disposal of Church property is concerned the decisive word in this sphere belongs to the Archbishop.

It has already been pointed out that the accused explain all their criminal activities by the canons of their religion. Several canons of the Roman Catholic Church have been referred to during the legal proceedings. Cieplak stated that the canons are just as old as the Church itself and during many centuries no alteration has ever been made in them. These canons have been compiled in a Code by Pope Pius X. It is interesting to point to the fact that Cieplak himself admitted that these canons reflect to a certain extent the period of struggle of Pope against Emperor.

Cieplak gives the following answer in regard to the confiscation of Church valuables:

There could be no talk about sanctioning the confiscation of articles from the Roman Catholic churches. But, on the other hand, there was no definite and direct prohibition.

Next to Archbishop Cieplak in the dock sits the priest Butkevich [Budkiewicz], Superintendent of St. Catherine's church in Petrograd, the property of which has been valued prior to the war at 7,000,000 rubles, and brought in about 300,000 rubles of yearly income. He is also one of the most active initiators of the counter-revolutionary movement among the Roman Catholic clergy. Butkevich [Budkiewicz] is not talkative; his answers are short, careful and indefinite. As he says, he has a poor memory. Fortunately, a few cases which Butkevich [Budkiewicz] happened to forget have been established by the documents. And documents are numerous: originals of minutes of the secret conferences which took place in the Archbishop's apartment, originals in Butkevich's [Budkiewicz's] handwriting. The accused Cieplak, Butkevich [Budkiewicz], Iunevich [Juniewicz], Vasilevski [Wasilewski], Fedorov, Eismond, Khodnevich [Chodniewicz], Ianukovich [Janukowicz], Matulianis, Khvetsko [Chwiecko], Maletski [Malecki], and Ivanov admit that they participated in these conferences. The priests Troigo [Trojgo], Rutkovski, and Pronsketis deny their participation.

Butkevich [Budkiewicz] confirmed that at these conferences have been discussed all questions which arose in connection with the decree separating Church and State and the School from the Church, as well as the methods which the clergy should adopt in compliance with the canons of the Church — in other words, the question of non-conclusion of agreements concerning the use of churches, questions of the attitude of the Roman Catholic Church towards the Communist Party, and a number of other similar questions.

Krylenko asked the Court to read two documents personally written by Butkevich [Budkiewicz]: "Concerning the signing of an agreement under present conditions" and "Historical note concerning separation of the

Church and State in Bolshevist Russia." Butkevich [Budkiewicz] writes that if the Archbishop permitted in 1918 the signing of contracts with the Soviet authorities concerning the use of churches, with certain amendments showing the temporary character of these contracts, it was because the downfall of the Soviet regime had been expected in the near future. But "since Bolshevism still exists and it is quite indefinite how long it is going to last we have no legal reasons to conclude any contracts without the permission of the Vatican." Budkiewicz further adds: "The signing of such contracts contradicts the canons of our Church, and those who sign them will be excommunicated." Budkiewicz further writes: "The non-signing of the contracts has an advantage — we shall not be bound by any obligations and the Bolsheviks will have to pay more attention to the protesting Roman Catholics than to the yielding ones. "Butkevich [Budkiewicz] recommends the policy of delays, protests, etc. He cynically admits that such policy is the most "practical one."

[Budkiewicz's] letters to Archbishop Cieplak and to a certain "Dear Sir" (private person) have been read in the Court. These documents show that Budkiewicz, who has always been and still is a Russian citizen, addressed the Polish Government with a request to take steps towards the return of the confiscated houses, churches, and confiscated church property generally. On July 18, 1918, he, together with Archbishop Ropp, took part in the solemn opening of the Polish Mission in Moscow. After a solemn Divine service and a dinner, the assembled Polish patriots sent a telegram to the Polish Government expressing their patriotic feelings, which telegram was also signed by Budkiewicz, who, as has been already stated, has been and is a Russian citizen.

It is interesting to point to the explanations given by Budkiewicz after he was requested to Krylenko to make them.

"I think that everything is so clearly stated in the documents that I find it unless to give any explanations," says Budkiewicz.

The Supreme Court and Krylenko fully agree with Budkiewicz that no explanations are necessary.

The rest of the fourth day of the trial was devoted to the ascertaining a number of details, which supplement the general picture of the criminal activities of the accused. It is also interesting to point out that at the very end of the examination, Cieplak stated that just before the trial began the Vatican gave permission to conclude contracts with the Soviet power in regard to the use of churches but the accused had no time to carry out this instruction . . .

SPEECH OF KRYLENKO

The debates have been opened by the speech of the Prosecutor, Krylenko. In his last explanations the accused, Cieplak, stated that the central question in the case might now be dropped, since the Vatican had sent new instructions just before the beginning of the trial permitting the signing of contracts with the Soviet authorities in regard to the use of churches. From the standpoint of the accused, this fact certainly settles the question, since they explain their resistance to the policy of the government by the canons of their Church. But the object of the prosecution is not to study the canons of the Church, but to examine the activities of the accused under the conditions of actual life in Russia. Our Court is an institution which has to protect the revolution and the existing order. In this case the problem of the Court is to examine the question whether the laws of the Republic have been violated; to determine who of the accused has violated them; and finally, to decide whether these crimes appear to be socially dangerous for us. No canons, no doctrines which have not been confirmed or accepted by us, can be considered.

Krylenko further analyses the social, historical role of the Church. Reminding the Court that the Church has always been a definite reactionary force, Krylenko emphasizes that the Soviet power was right to include in its constitution an article depriving the clergy and the monks of all political rights, as has been done with other non-laboring and exploiting elements. The whole past of the Church shows us that the Church is our worst enemy. That is what the constitution of the Soviet power says.

Krylenko then emphasizes that the Church is a powerful means for enslaving the masses. That is why the decree of the Soviet power has strictly prohibited the teaching of Scripture to the youths under 18 years of age. On the other hand, the accused admit that up to the last moment they continued to teach Scripture to children from 7 years old.

The accused carried on during five years a desperate struggle for uncontrolled influence upon the minds of the masses and for uncontrolled disposal of Church valuables.

Krylenko further tries to ascertain the general line of counter-revolutionary activities of the accused. These activities consisted of the utilization of religious prejudices with the object of rousing the masses against the Soviet power and showing resistance to the enforcement of the laws of the Soviet government. And what about the preaching in the churches, when the priests called on the Catholic parents to struggle in favor of teaching Scripture to their children, contrary to the decrees of the Soviet power? That is a political war against the Soviet power! By agitating among the population against certain laws of the Soviet power, the priests agitated against the Soviet power as a whole. And after all that, the accused dare to say that they have not been carrying on a political struggle against us, but an "ideoligical" one!

Emphasizing certain points incriminating each of the accused separately, Krylenko proves that all the accused have been united into an *organization*.

Krylenko urges that the case of the accused comes under Articles 63 and 119 of the Criminal Code, which provides the death penalty for such crimes. Krylenko demands capital punishment for the chief criminals, Archbishop Cieplak and the Priest Butkevich [Budkiewicz], as the initiators and organizers of the counter-revolutionary movement. The other priests should be sentenced to various terms, from 3 to 10 years. He also thinks that the case of the accused Sharnas [Sarnas], a Roman Catholic 17 years old, the charge against whom was participation in disorders, must be examined separately. Krylenko proposes that he be sentenced to 6 months' imprisonment on account of his youthful age.

The speech of Krylenko lasted two hours.

[signed] L. N.

[March 26, 1923]

THE VERDICT

[March 26, 1923]

The Supreme Court finds that the Roman Catholic Clergy of Petrograd, led by Archbishop Cieplak and Metropolitan Ropp, understood the decree separating the Church from the State as one granting to all Roman Catholics as to all other citizens complete freedom of religious feelings and absolute immunity of the believers while performing their religious services and, therefore, did not comply with Paragraphs 8, 9, 12, and 13 of the said decree; which established the right of the civil authorities to keep inventories and register the property; separated the School and the Church; deprived religious societies of property rights and the rights of a "juridical person"; and declared the Church property the property of the Russian Soviet Socialistic Republic. However, this law was issued in the early days of the revolution, and it was not enforced completely. The clergy then remained quiet. But in the course of time, when nationalization of properties (in compliance with the above decree) was commenced, with the confiscation of such enormous properties as that in possession of St. Catherine's Church in Petrograd, the Roman Catholic clergy began to work out practical measures of struggle against the Soviet power for the lost property and rights.

Being, however, quite convinced of the instability of the Soviet power and expecting its downfall any moment, the leaders of the Roman Catholic clergy in Russia have been inclined to permit the believers to conclude contracts with the Soviet authorities concerning the use of churches and property, considering these contracts unimportant and of a temporary character only, and still regarding the property as really belonging to the Church. The Priest Budkiewicz has even, with permission of Archbishop Ropp, pawned the property of the St. Catherine's Church to private persons for 600,000 rubles, with the understanding that this debt would be paid after the overthrow of the Soviet power and the return of property to the Church.

When Cieplak, Budkiewicz, Ropp and others lost their hope for the overthrow of the Soviet power, they began to organize mass resistance to the enforcement of the decree of January 23, 1918, separating the Church and the State, and have arranged a number of preliminary conferences for working out methods and combined action, deliberately and with the object of securing the return of the Church property, of undermining the dictatorship of the working class and the achievements of the October revolution, Their efforts in this struggle included the following:

The Archbishop Cieplak, who replaced Ropp, considered (as he admitted in the Court) that the Church [councils] soviets, which have been established on the initiative of the government for handling the Church property, are dangerous for the Church hierarchy, because they undermine the discipline among the believers and put an end to the uncontrolled handling of the property by the Church leaders. He issued an instruction to the subordinate clergy to resist by all means the establishment of soviets at the churches, and not to sign any contracts with the authorities concerning Church property. As the result of an energetic campaign against the Soviet power on the priests Maletski [Malecki] Butkevich [Budkiewicz], Ianukovich [Janukowicz], Vasilevski [Wasilewski], Eismond, Iunevich [Juniewicz], Matulianis, Khvetsko [Chwiecko], Troigo [Trojgo], Khodnevich [Chodniewicz], Ivanov and Fedorov, the Roman Catholics refused to sign the above contracts, this resulted in the closing of the Roman Catholic churches in Petrograd as having nobody to answer for their property. The measure was enforced in December, 1922, causing indignation on the part of the Roman Catholic masses; and such indignation has been deliberately provoked by the above enumerated persons. When, before the Christmas holidays, a delegation of Roman Catholics went from Petrograd to Moscow and asked the permission of the People's Commissariat of Justice to open their churches, a corresponding permit was granted by the said Commissariat, on condition that instead of contracts the believers would sign a simplified receipt. Archbishop Cieplak, who received these documents, concealed them from the belivers and from the Soviet authorities in Petrograd and declared that the Soviet government refused to permit him to open the churches on Christmas holidays. Cieplak by so doing provoked open insurrection against the Soviet power.

Furthermore, Cieplak, foreseeing the promulgation of the decree concerning the confiscation of Church valuables for the relief of the starving, issued in January 1922 a circular to all Roman Catholic priests in Russia, stating that such confiscation was illegal and in the telegram to the Iaroslavl priest, Butkovski, he simply prohibited him to deliver the valuables and to submit an inventory of the Church property.

Simultaneously, a group of priests headed by Cieplak organized in Petrograd numerous conferences at which questions of a purely practical character were discussed, such as: the substance of Communism, the program of the

Communist Party, and others. Ways and means have also been worked out for further resistance to the Soviet authorities with mass participation of the believers. They have published a counter-revolutionary magazine "Mogilëvskaia Khronika" in the Polish language, which was a purely anti-Bolshevist publication.

One of the chief initiators of these conferences was the Priest Butkevich [Budkiewicz], who submitted at the conferences written reports on political matters and drafts of practical measures of struggle against the Soviet power. Thus, in anticipation of help from Warsaw and in expectation of instructions from the Vatican, Butkevich [Budkiewicz] proposed a policy of delays in negotiation with the Soviet power, which policy had to be changed later on into an offensive attitude with participation of the believers. This policy resulted in open resistance on the part of the believers, led by the same priests, and in the closing of the Petrograd Church of the Assumption of the Holy Virgin on Pervaia Rota street. The believers, led by the priests Khvetsko, Rutkovski and Pronsketis, showed resistance to the closing of the church, during which citizen Sharnas [Sarnas] insulted the authorities who tried to make up a list of valuables. A similar crime was committed by the believers of the St. Kazimir Church on Vshakovskaia street, under the leadership of the priest Eismond, in July 1922, and by the believers of the St. Stanislaus Church under the leadership of the priest Juniewicz. Resistance to the authorities was shown also in the St. Catherine Church, the mob being led by the priest Khodnevich [Chodniewicz]; in the Churches of the Immaculate Conception, of St. Francis, of the Sacred Heart of Jesus, of the Sacred Heart of Maria, and of St. Bonifacius, the mob being led by the priests Vasilevski [Wasilewski], Ianukovich [Janukowicz], Matulianis, [Maletski] Malecki and Butkevich [Budkiewicz].

Furthermore the Priest Butkevich [Budkiewicz], being present in Moscow at the solemn opening of the first Polish Mission, sent together with other persons a telegram to the Polish Government, expressing his devotion to that government, despite the fact that he has been and still is a Russian citizen.

In addition to all that, the accused priests have declared in the Court that they consider obligatory for them only the orders of the Pope, not only in regard to religion itself but also in regard to the confiscation and nationalized Church property, in spite of the Pope's instructions being contradictory to the decrees of the Soviet government. The priests have also declared in the court that, disregarding the Article 121 of the Criminal Code they have been teaching and will continue to teach the so-called Gospel and have not and will not recognize the above mentioned Article prohibiting the teaching of the Gospel.

In connection with the above stated the Supreme Court found guilty:

1. Ian [Jan] Giatsintovich [sic!] Cieplak and Konstantin Iulianovich

Butkevich [Bukiewicz], of deliberate supervision of the above counter-revolutionary activities of an organization of the Petrograd Roman Catholic priests, which activities consisted in resistance to the Soviet power, undermining the dictatorship of the proletariat, attempted restitution of the former property rights of the Church, and provoking uprisings of the masses against the Soviet regime. These provocative actions resulted in uprisings which were due to the fact that the masses have been still under the influence of religious prejudice and also in refusals to obey the laws, which crimes come under Articles 62, 119, and 121 of the Criminal Code.

2. S. F. Eismond, E. S. Iunevich [Juniewicz], L. A. Khvetsko [Chwiecko], P. V. Khodnevich [Chodniewicz], L. I. Fedorov — of active participation in the counter-revolutionary organization, established by Cieplak and Butkevich [Budkiewicz], which participation has been displayed by acts enumerated in the descriptive part of the verdict, and also by refusal to obey the Soviet laws, which crimes come under Articles 62, 119, and 121 of the Criminal Code.

3. A. I. Maletski [Malecki], A. M. Vasilevski [Wasilewski], P. I. Ianukovich [Janukowicz], T. I. Matulianis, I. I. Troigo [Trojgo], D. A. Ivanov, F. F. Rutkovski, and A. P. Pronsketis — of assisting the priests Cieplak and Butkievich [Budkiewicz] in their crimes, and of refusing to comply with the Soviet laws as well as of agitating against the Soviet regime, which actions have been described in the first part of the verdict and come under Articles 68, 69, Part I of Article 119 and 121 of the Criminal Code.

4. I. I. Sharnas [Sarnas] — of insulting the Soviet government at the time of the confiscation of Church valuables in the Assumption [of the Holy Virgin's] Church, which crime comes under article 78 of the Criminal Code.

The Court sentenced:

Cieplak and Butkevich [Budkiewicz] — to capital punishment — death.

Eismond, Iunevich [Juniewicz], Khvetsko [Chwiecko], Khodnevich [Chodniewicz] and Fedorov — to 10 years' imprisonment with strict isolation and with the loss of rights for the period of five years in accordance with Article 40 of the Criminal Code.

Maletski [Malecki], Vasilevski [Wasilewski], Matulianis, Troigo [Trojgo], Ivanov, Rutkovski, and Pronsketis — to 3 years' imprisonment, without strict isolation and with the loss of rights for the period of three years.

Sharnas [Sarnas] — to be imprisoned conditionally for 6 months and without the loss of rights.

In view of the fact that the accused continued to commit their crimes even after the declaration of the amnesty on November 7, 1922, the said amnesty must be applied in their cases. All the property of the accused Cieplak, Butkevich [Budkiewicz], Eismond, Iunevich [Juniewicz], Khvetsko [Chwiecko], Khodnevich [Chodniewicz], and Fedorov must be confiscated and included in the Treasury of the Republic. Sharnas [Sarnas] must be released from arrest.

67
Execution of the Verdict Concerning Cieplak and Budkiewicz is Postponed

(Translation from Moscow Izvestiia, No. 67, March 27, 1923)

The Presidium of the Central Executive Committee resolved:
To postpone the execution of verdict concerning Cieplak, Butkevich [Budkiewicz] and others until the special order of the Presidium of the Central Executive Committee.

68
Speech of Mr. Sikorski, President of the Council of Ministers, Delivered Before the Polish Senate on March 27th [1923]

In response to the questions addressed to the President of the Council of Ministers and to the Minister for Foreign Affairs, on the subject of the Archbishop Cieplak affair and the verdict recently pronounced against the high dignitaries of the Catholic Church in Russia, I have the honor to present to the High Chamber the following account of this affair:

The Polish Government, from the moment that the affair of Archbishop Cieplak was raised in connection with the requisitioning of precious religious objects in the Catholic churches in Russia, that is to say, more than a year ago, has not only declared its concern, but in every particular phase of this action has adopted an attitude corresponding to that phase. The trial in the first place interested all the civilized world, considering that the question is the liberty of religion, as well as the liberty of the Catholic Church in Russia — which, since the new system of government was inaugurated in Russia, has been exposed to innumerable persecutions directed in a methodical fashion and with one object. It is for this reason that the Polish Government, at the beginning of this trial, appealed in the first place to the Holy See, presenting this affair in a consistent manner, and awaiting an indispensable intervention on the part of the Holy See. At the same time we commenced a counteraction in opposition to the Bolshevik violence which had the support of the entire civilized world. But since, at the same time, the Chief of the Catholic Church in Russia is a Pole, beloved by the entire Polish nation, and since in this case the question relates to Polish national minorities in Russia, that is to say about two million of our nationals living in Russian territories, it is understandable that the Polish

Government and the Nation are interested to the highest degree in the course of this trial. That is the reason why the Polish Minister Plenipotentiary at Moscow received each time instructions which recommended that on the one hand he inform the Polish Government of the course of the trial, and on the other hand, that he inform the Russian Government of the firm and clear attitude adopted by our Government in regard to this question. During a year the Russian Government gave us explanations absolutely reasuring, informing our representatives that the intended trial of Archbishop Cieplak was of a purely formal character, without serious consequenses. However, the Polish Government did not lose sight of this question and the suspicions which, in common with all the civilized world, it had in connection with the case —suspicions which, were shown, alas, to be justified. In the course of the last month — after the judicial investigations had been dragging along for nearly a year, and Archbishop Cieplak and his fellow prisoners had been set free, not threatening, it appears to me, the state of affairs existing in Russia nor conducting any political activity — the trial took an unexpected turn. The Archbishop Cieplak was arrested unexpectedly, the investigation was conducted and terminated very quickly, and, to the great surprise of the entire world, a verdict of death was passed on the supreme dignitary of the Catholic church and against the priest Budkiewicz.

I could, in speaking to Mr. Obolenskii, representative of Soviet Russia, only define this verdict as one having nothing in common with the application of justice.

I also wish to declare here, in this High Chamber, and speaking not only in the name of the Polish people but at this moment in the name of the civilized world, that any man who thinks in a reasonable and objective manner must feel a justifiable suspicion that this affair has motives other than religious, that the question in the present case is a purely practical one, the court's actions dictated by a policy known all over the world, a policy applied constantly and without any consideration by the Soviet Government. The Government, therefore, and not its docile instrument the Revolutionary Tribunal at Moscow, continues to be entirely responsible for the execution of this barbarous verdict.

The situation being grave, this Government did not confine itself to communicating its categorical opinion to the representative of the Russian Bolsheviks at Warsaw, but also addressed itself to the Vatican and to the Western Powers in order to express a common protest against this verdict, which violates all the rights which the national minorities enjoy in every country, and especially in a state desiring to pass as the most progressive. Mr. Obolenskii, representative of Soviet Russia in Warsaw, has kindly told me that the verdict would not be executed, at least in the immediate future, and that the affair will be the object of future diplomatic negotiations.

Official news came today from Moscow confirming the attitude of the Russian Government. Nevertheless, I do not wish in communicating this news to de-emphasize the gravity of the situation. On the contrary, I want to underline with particular force that we have had in the past too many experiences which prove to us that similar or other declarations of the Soviet Government are afterwards modified for various political reasons. And, in any case, I desire to state publicly that this affair — which I think, will also interest equally all the Western Powers and especially the Holy See — must not become in any sense the object of political bargaining.

(Translated text from the *Polish Diet Debates,* March 27, 1923)

69

"Christian Exploits"
Trial of Roman Catholic Priests

(Translation from Moscow *Izvestiia,* No. 67, March 27, 1923)

The Counsel of the defendants, Barristers Bobrishchev-Pushkin and Kommodov, maintained that there are no formal reasons to indict the accused of counter-revolution, which involves an intention to overthrow the Soviet regime. Another fact they tried to establish was that the accused did not belong to an *organization,* as such. The actions of the accused are separate actions of separate persons against certain laws of the government (offenses against the administrative order). That is how the defending counsel regards the crimes from the standpoint of a judiciary qualification of the activities of the accused. Defending counsel tried also to describe the psychology of the clergy in general and of the Roman Catholic clergy particularly, for whom the Pope is not only the "Holy Father" in an internal-religious sense but also the supreme manager of the whole property of the Roman Catholic Church, which in compliance with the decrees of the Soviet power should have been handed over to the State. The Roman Catholic Clergy had therefore to choose between obedience to the Soviet power and obedience to the Vatican.

Krylenko gave the defending counsels a most brilliant answer. Referring again to a large number of secret conferences and resolutions passed by them dealing with the question of the struggle against the Soviet power and the resistance against the enforcement of the decree separating the Church and the State, illegal printed matter of clearly counter-revolutionary character, and a large number of other documents, Krylenko, reading the most interesting parts of them, proved even more definitely than in his first speech that the accused have been connected with each other. He proved that they have established a definite counter-revolutionary organization, which has been acting against the Soviet power and showing desperate resistance to its acts and laws for a period of five years, which has deliberately and systematically ignored the orders of the Soviet institutions, and which has taken advantage of religious prejudices of the Catholic population to arouse it against the Soviet power. Krylenko said also that the activities of the Roman Catholic priests contain the formal features of counter-revolution, the absence of which has been claimed by the defense. Even if no formal features had been disclosed in the activities of the accused, if only the fact of actual counter-revolutionary actions had been established, the Court could still be guided by Article 10 of the Criminal Code, which deals with the qualification of crimes, and could bring the defendants to account under certain articles of the Criminal Code which deal with crimes "similar to and most resembling the given case."

The debates finished at 2 a.m. on March 24. The accused said their last word on Sunday, at 12 noon. First spoke Archbishop Cieplak, who stated that neither he nor any other representative of the Roman Catholic Church pursued any counter-revolutionary aims. The crimes which have been charged against them must be explained only by their obedience to the canons of the Church and the Pope, who forbade them to comply with the demands of the Soviet power in connection with the separation of the Church and the State. Cieplak expressed the hope that the "Judgment of Men" will be just and merciful for him. The last words of the Priest Butkevich [Budkiewicz] were almost the same. He admitted that they, the clergymen, had no right to carry on a political struggle. But then all of a sudden he declared:

"What do we care about the social order, we are busy with religion."

The other accused declare their solidarity with what was said by Archbishop Cieplak and almost exactly repeated his words, emphasizing only a few practical details of various facts.

The Supreme Court retired to deliberate its judgment at 4 p.m. The discussion lasted 8 hours, and only at 1 a.m. was the verdict passed.

[Signed] L. M.

70

Memorandum of Conversation with the Belgian Ambassador

(Department of State,
The Undersecretary)

March 27th, 1923

The Belgian Ambassador advised me this morning that he was in receipt of a telegram from Cardinal Mercier, in which the Cardinal asked whether this Government would take any action in behalf of Archbishop Zepliak [Cieplak], head of the Roman Catholic Church in Russia, who has been condemned to death by the Soviets. This request, it appears, comes directly from Cardinal Mercier, and not through the Belgian Foreign Office.

I told the Ambassador that it was very doubtful whether we could do anything; that we had no representative near the Soviets, and that the members of the A.R.A. were in Russia on the understanding that they would not engage in politics; but that even if we had some medium of approach, it would probably do more harm than good to make any official gesture on behalf of the Archbishop.

The Ambassador said he quite appreciated that this was the situation, and he agreed that any step of this kind would merely encourage the Soviets to make further arrests.

W. P.

71

Telegram from the Secretary of State, Charles E. Hughes, to President Warren G. Harding

Washington, March 28, 1923

The President,
St. Augustine, Florida.

The Department is receiving appeals from various Catholic societies in this country to protest against the sentence of death reported by the press to have been passed by the Russian Soviet authorities on Archbishop Cieplak and other ecclesiastics. The Belgian Ambassador has presented a similar appeal from Cardinal Mercier and our Legation at Brussels has telegraphed an urgent message from the Cardinal for you expressing the earnest hope that something can be done to save these persons. It is understood that the governments of Great Britain and Poland have already entered protests. There is a press despatch this morning that execution of sentence has been postponed and this is probably correct. It is doubtful whether any representations which we might make would have any effect. It is possible nevertheless that in view of the appeals which are being made you may care to have me instruct Houghton to make known to the Soviet representative in Berlin how deeply the action which has been taken against these ecclesiastics has stirred public opinion in the United States. I shall be very grateful for an expression of your views. Our Embassy in Berlin would probably be the best medium of approach.

Charles E. Hughes

72

Telegram from President Warren G. Harding
to the Secretary of State, Charles E. Hughes

St. Augustine, Florida, March 28, 1923

Hon. Charles E. Hughes,
Secretary of State, Washington, D.C.

I know nothing of the merits of the cases of Russian ecclesiastics but it can do no harm and may be helpful to convey through Houghton an expression of American sentiment in opposition to death sentence. You may instruct Houghton accordingly.

Warren G. Harding

73

Telegram from the Secretary of State, Charles E. Hughes
to the U.S. Ambassador in Berlin [Houghton]

Washington, March 28, 1923

Amembassy, Berlin
URGENT!!

Public opinion is aroused in this country by the report of the death sentence passed on Archbishop Cieplak and other Roman Catholic ecclesiastics in Russia, and there are many appeals for intercession on their behalf. It is fitting that the humanitarian sentiment of the American people should find expression and it is thought that the advisable course is to have you communicate informally on the subject with the Soviet representative in Berlin. You may say that the public mind in this country has been much stirred by reports of the sentence passed and that execution of the sentence against these ecclesiastics cannot fail to have a most unfortunate effect. You may say that it would seem to be only the part of friendliness to let him know the extent and intensity of the feeling which has been aroused and to express the earnest hope in the interest of humanity that the lives of these ecclesiastics may be spared. The Department must leave it to you to determine the form and manner of communication taking account of the absence of recognition and official intercourse, and you of course will avoid a formal official representation.

Hughes

74
Protests from Archbishop Edward A. Hanna
Chairman, National Catholic Welfare Council

Washington, March 28, 1923

To The President:

The National Catholic Welfare Council urgently requests that the Government of our country protest to the Soviet Government of Russia against the sentence of death which it has so unjustly imposed on Archbishop Cieplak and Monsignor Budkiewicz. We ask this in the name of our country and of civilization.

Edward A. Hanna,
Archbishop of San Francisco
Chairman, Administrative Committee
National Catholic Welfare Council
Washington, March 28, 1923

To M. Chicherin,
People's Commissar for Foreign Affairs,
Moscow, Russia.

Sentence of death passed on Archbishop Cieplak and Msgr. Budkiewicz has shocked Christian world. It is being interpreted as a denial of all religious liberty. The National Catholic Welfare Council of the United States has been sympathetic with the woes and sufferings of the Russian people. Its representatives are now in Russia and have been there for nearly a year distributing to the starving peasants the aid so generously contributed by American Catholics. What will these charitable people of America think if in return for their charity the Soviet Government executes a high Ecclesiastic of their faith on the sole reported ground that he objected to governmental denial of free religious expression and to the spoliation of churches under his jurisdiction?

We respectfully, but vigorously, urge the Soviet authorities to prevent the carrying out of a sentence which will outrage not only the charitable and generous Catholics of America, but the entire Christian world.

Archbishop Edward A. Hanna
Chairman, Administrative Committee
National Catholic Welfare Council

75

Protest from the President, Robert E. Speer, and the Chairman, John M. Moore, of the Administrative Committee of the Federal Council of Churches of Christ in America to the People's Commissar for Foreign Affairs of the U.S.S.R., Chicherin

March 29, 1923

Minister of Foreign Affairs
Moscow

Federal Council of Churches of Christ in America including constituency twenty million Protestant Christians who have shown friendship for Russian people by generous contributions for famine relief respectfully urge Russian Government that in interest of humanity and religious liberty it reconsider reported decision to execute Roman Catholic and Eastern Catholic Church officials.

John E. Speer, President
John M. Moore, Chairman, Administrative Committee

76

Telegram of the Protestant Episcopal Bishop William T. Manning of New York to President Warren G. Harding

New York, March 29, 1923

The President

I trust that our government will feel it right to use every effort possible to prevent carrying out of barbarous sentence of death by the Russian Soviet against Archbishop Cieplak and his vicar general. Signed

William T. Manning,
Bishop of New York

77

Report of the U.S. Ambassador in Warsaw, Hugh Gibson, to the Secretary of State, Charles E. Hughes

No. 1582   Warsaw, March 29, 1923

CONFIDENTIAL WEEKLY POLITICAL REPORT

Sir:

Public attention this week has been chiefly centered upon the trial and sentence of Monseigneur Cieplak and various other prelates by the Soviet tribunals. The news of the death sentence produced an outburst of indignation from the entire press regardless of party and there was a general clamor for action by the Government.

On the 26th instant the Prime Minister sent for Prince Obolenskii, Minister of the Soviet Government, and impressed upon him forcefully the indignation of the Polish Government and people at the manner in which Monseigneur Cieplak and Father Butkevich [Budkiewicz] had been condemned to death. These representations were confirmed in a note which was apparently strong enough in its terms to satisfy Polish opinion.

On the 27th the Prime Minister made a speech in the Diet in reply to an interpellation as to what steps the Government had taken to prevent the execution of Monseigneur Cieplak and Father Butkevich [Budkiewicz]. I transmit herewith enclosed copy and translation of this speech.

While I was lunching with the Prime Minister yesterday he excused himself and went down to receive a large number of delegations which presented petitions urging the Government to exhaust all possible efforts to prevent the execution of the two prelates. General Sikorski told me confidentially that he had received an intimation from the Soviet representative that it would be possible to prevent the imposition of the extreme penalty if the Polish Government would consent to surrender a common criminal, the murderer of Archbishop George, as well as several Bolsheviks held in prison here. General Sikorski said that while it was difficult to take any decision which would entail the execution of Archbishop Cieplak he felt that he could not yield to a blackmailing offer of this sort; that acceptance of the Bolshevik suggestion would open the way to an unending series of similar incidents and that whenever the Bolsheviks wished to force Poland to do anything it would be possible to do so by seizing a few prominent Poles and stirring up public sentiment in Poland. General Sikorski said that it was very difficult to estimate exactly the mentality of the Soviet Government at present but that he was inclined to believe that the sentence would not be carried out.

My German colleague yesterday afternoon called upon Prince Obolenskii and discussed with him the advisability of carrying out the sentence. He gave me an account of his conversation in confidence immediately afterward. He told him that there was a distinct German interest in avoiding any action that would still further prejudice the civilized world against Russia and that the proposed execution was a gross act of stupidity without any possible compensation or advantage. In this connection Mr. Rauscher drew the attention of Prince Obolenskii to the statement made by the Secretary of State on March 21st in regard to our attitude toward the Soviet Government, and said that an execution of this character was the one thing best calculated to bring home to the American people the soundness of everything the Secretary had said and convince those who were the advocates of recognition that they were in the wrong. I had furnished my German colleague with a copy of the Secretary's statement at his request, and he gave it to Prince Obolenskii, who read it and said that he realized the great importance of doing nothing to antagonize feeling in the United States. Prince Obolenskii told my German colleague that the representations of the Polish Prime Minister had been so emphatic and offensive as to produce a very harmful impression in Moscow. He said that the Soviet Government was now in a very difficult position as it could not very well yield under a direct threat from the Polish Prime Minister. If it were to do so it would suffer humiliation in the eyes of the whole world and that was one thing it was not prepared to do. Prince Obolenskii stated that the execution had been deferred and that it was possible that some means might be found of securing an amnesty. He intimated that while the Soviet Government was not prepared to yield to Poland it would be less difficult to comply with a direct request from the Vatican and that representations from that quarter would not be unwelcome. I am informed by the Papal Nuncio that the Vatican has already taken the question up through various channels and that it is hoped to prevent the execution of the sentence.

This morning's Warsaw papers announced that the execution of the sentence had been deferred and among other steps that had been taken to save Monseigneur Cieplak it is prominently mentioned that I called upon Prince Obolenskii and delivered to him a note in behalf of the Diplomatic Corps to refrain from executing the decision of the court. I need hardly say that there is no truth in this statement as I have never seen Prince Obolenskii and there has been no discussion of the subject by the Diplomatic Corps.

I have the honor to be, Sir,

Your obedient servant,

Hugh Gibson

78

Resolution of the Presidium of the Central Executive Committee: Archbishop J. B. Cieplak's Death Sentence Suspended

(Translation from Moscow *Izvestiia*, No. 70, March 30, 1923)

The Presidium of the Central Execution Committee, having examined the appeal of citizens Cieplak and Budkiewicz who have been sentenced to capital punishment by the Supreme Court, resolved:

1. The activities of citizen Cieplak, which have been established by the Supreme Court and which have been deliberately directed against the interests of the working class and the fundamental achievements of the Proletarian Revolution, have been committed by means of ill-intentioned misinterpretation of the religious freedom which has been guaranteed by the law to all citizens of the Republic. This must be regarded as one of the greatest crimes, for which in the revolutionary Republic, which continues to be surrounded by numerous enemies, there can be no other punishment but that ordered by the Supreme Court.

Taking into consideration, however, that citizen Cieplak is the representative of a religious teaching which in the times of Tsarism and the Bourgeois Republic suffered from opression, and the execution of the deserved sentence against citizen Cieplak could probably be interpreted by the unenlightened of the Roman Catholic citizens of Russia, whose religious prejudice has been exploited by Cieplak and his followers, as directed especially against a priest of their religion —

To commute the Supreme Court's sentence of capital punishment against citizen Cieplak to 10 years' imprisonment with strict isolation.

2. In regard to the accused citizen Budkiewicz, who combined his criminal activities on a religious basis with open counter-revolutionary activities in contact with a foreign bourgeois government which is hostile towards the Soviet Republic, and by so doing used his post of priest for open treason to the state —

To reject the appeal for pardon.

President of the Central Executive Committee: M. KALININ
Secretary of the Central Executive Committee: T. SAPRANOV
Moscow, Kremlin, March 29, 1923

79
"Artificial Indignation"

(Extracts Translated from Moscow *Izvestiia*, No. 70, March 30, 1923)

The sentence which has been passed on the Roman Catholic priests for their counter-revolutionary activities has alarmed the reactionary circles of the bourgeois countries . . .

The Church in general, and the Roman Catholic Church in particular, is one of the main buttresses of the world's reaction and the bourgeois rule. And if the reactionaries in general and the Archbishop of Canterbury started a row at the time of the arrest of Patriarch Tikhon, then we must not be surprised at all that around the trial of such an important personage as the Roman Catholic Archbishop in Russia this row became still wilder. The hooligans and pogrom-makers of the entire world have certainly not missed their chance . . .

Supposing there are even two million Poles living in the territory of Soviet Russia (the majority of whom, by the way, simply hate "Pan" Sikorski and his government), how many citizens of Russia nationally live on the territory of the Polish State? . . .

We would recommend, therefore, to "Pan" Sikorski that he watch his step in making demands, because the consequences of these demands might not please him at all . . .

There is no persecution of religion, but only struggle against the counter-revolution.

The gracious lords and the workmen deputies who feed at the King's table understand very well that their talk about the persecution of religion in Soviet Russia is nothing but a dirty lie. They know very well that Archbishop Cieplak, as well as a number of clergymen of other religions who have been tried in the court, have been tried not for their religious beliefs, about which nobody cares and which do not interest any statesman in Russia, but for definite political acts, for resistance to the decrees of the Soviet power, for violation of the laws of the Republic, and so forth . . .

THE VERDICT WAS MITIGATED AFTER ALL!

The Archbishop and his followers in active counter-revolution, in resistance to the Soviet power and in violation of its decrees, deserved their fate and the verdict has been passed in strict compliance with the existing Soviet the verdict has been passed in strict compliance with the existing Soviet legislation. Nevertheless, the Soviet power found it possible to mitigate the verdict for Archbishop Cieplak, not because it paid attention to the hypocritical cries of its enemies, who took advantage of the present extraordinary cases in order to aim new blows at the working masses, but because it pays attention to the feelings among the national minorities in the name of whom and in favor of whom various Sikorskis attempt to speak. Under the tsar's rule these minorities have certainly suffered religious persecution. They might be misled (especially with the generous assistance of Soviet enemies) and think that the trial of Cieplak was nothing but a continuation of the old tsarist policy. Their national and religious feelings are hypersensitive on account of the former persecutions, and they are inclined to all sorts of misinterpretations. Considering the prejudices and abnormal state of mind of these minorities the Soviet power resolved to mitigate the verdict.

HANDS OFF!

But this kindness on the part of the Soviet power must not be misinterpreted. Let everybody know that no matter under which flag the counter-revolution might try to hide its face, it will always meet with the most energetic counterattack of the Soviet power. And also let everybody know that the Soviet power will not tolerate any interference in its own affairs, regardless of the form which such intervention might assume. There is no doubt that the recent occurences in the British and Polish parliaments bear the character of an open intervention in our internal affairs. We would like to see what face Lord Curzon would make if our Central Executive Committee should raise the question of the really savage massacres committed by the British "Kulturtraeger" in South Africa, India and other colonies. No doubt both Lord Curzon and the American Minister Hughes would regard such an act as an "intrigue of Moscow" in the interest of Communism and world revolution. But when these gentlemen interfere in a most impudent manner in our internal affairs they think that they do exactly the right thing.

But we shall never permit that! We shall tell them: "hands off!"

80
"International Capital and the Verdict Passed on the Catholic Priests"

(Extracts and Summary from Moscow *Pravda*, No. 70, March 30, 1923)

"A terrible thing has happened in that land of horrors, Soviet Russia. A Catholic Archbishop — who has tried to save the valuables accumulated by the Catholic clergy in the course of centuriess by all sorts of scoundrelly tricks, and keep them from being used for feeding the masses of famine-stricken people — has by the Revolutionary Tribunal of the Soviet Republic been sentenced to death. Prior to the revolution, the courts were working hand in hand with the priests, for the priest as well as the court always encouraged exploitation of the masses by the squire and the capitalist alike. In terrible Soviet Russia everything is the other way about. The tribunal upholds the cause of the toilers, protects the famine-stricken, while the Catholic as well as the Greek Orthodox priests are sticking to their old positions, remaining the defenders of capitalism and the defenders of the manorial landlords. There is nothing surprising in the fact that the entire "civilized world" has raised a shout against the Tribunal's betrayal of the "traditional task of administration of justice." There is nothing surprising in the fact that the whole so-called "civilized world" has got to its feet to defend the Catholic Archbishop who has played the glorious role of defender of stolen valuables against the attacks of the hungry."

The author then proceeds to narrate how the news of the verdict was accepted in the various countries: how Catholic Spain "raised a howl," notwithstanding the fact that it was the country where many a person had been burned at the stake for opposing the "regime of the squires." The "friend" of Soviet Russia, M. Herriot, the representative of the "radical liberal French bourgeoisie," has also raised a protest. In this connection, the author looks back upon the French Revolution and states that at that time the revolutionary bourgeoisie was dealing in a similar way with recalcitrant ecclesiastics, sending them "by the fastest route to Kingdom Come" — the same Kingdom of which they used to hold out hopes to the hungry and the suffering. But now the French bourgeoisie is in its turn exploiting the laborers, and has made peace with the Church. Therefore, it is not surprising that the "liberal Mister Herriot, the enemy of every Church, who at the Lyons Fair is offering up prayers to the god of profit," is horrified by the verdict. The article turns also on the "Jewish Bankers" who "rule the world," together with the "un-circumcized rabbis of all creeds," and states that Soviet Russia would not "stop at hanging even the spiritual representative of the firm of bankers 'Kuhn and Loeb' or 'Rothschild Brothers'", if this were necessary to the revolution. "The world bourgeoisie is advancing in closed ranks, teaching the proletariat a lesson of unanimity and energy in the defense of one of the strongholds of their class supremacy." In passing the author deals with "old, honest Lansbury" and "old man Ben-Turner," the leaders of the English "compromisers." In the forties of the last century the representatives of labor were opposed to any religion, but now the leaders of the Reformist laborers in England "go to Church of a Sunday, putting on a black coat and top hat in order to look like other 'respectable' people." "Old man Ben-Turner" has sent a wire: "Don't hang the Archbishop." In this connection, the author points out that the English Labor Party sent no telegrams of protest when General Smuts, the "idol of English Liberalism," was shooting the strikers in South Africa. This gives the author occasion to say that world capitalism is supported not only by bayonets, clergy, bourgeois press and bourgeois science, but that its last, and "perhaps its most powerful stronghold, is the servility, the mental flunkeydom, of the reformist leaders of the proletariat."

Much the same is said of Poland, the Polish gentry, and the "Polish-Jewish" capitalists and industrial magnates. General Sikorski's speech in the Polish Diet is referred to as an "impertinent attempt to meddle with internal affairs of Soviet Russia, and to place responsibility for the verdict with the Soviet Government." In this connection, it is pointed out that the Poles are oppressing the Russian Orthodox population in Poland, and an instance is cited in which they were alleged to have turned a Russian Orthodox church into a police station.

"In reply to Mister Sikorski's threats and the howl set up by the bourgeois

Polish press, we can utter only a curt 'Hands off! . . . Don't hope, Gentlemen, that your shouting will create the slightest impression upon the Soviet
Government." The Central Executive Committee has confirmed the sentences
passed on the Archbishop and other priests, "having consulted solely their
revolutionary conscience, and being guided only by considerations of revolutionary expediency." The verdict is entirely in keeping with the "conception of justice prevailing in the proletarian masses". . . "But at the same
time the Central Executive Committee had to bear in mind the fact that
the Catholic poor had lived under the yoke of tsarism, and that the persecutions characterizing that regime had created a deep impression on the
minds of those masses. Lest these masses should understand the verdict
passed on Archbishop Cieplak as a continuance of the tsarist policy of
persecution and oppression directed against the Catholic Church, the Central Executive Committee has commuted the capital sentence passed on
Cieplak to ten years imprisonment. As regards the priest Butkevich [Bud-
kiewicz], his sentence cannot be commuted, because he acted not merely from
religious fanaticism, but as a spy in the interests of a foreign bourgeois
power."

"The resolution of the supreme Soviet authority, the Central Executive
Committee of the Soviets, will be carried into effect. Let international
counter-revolution shout as much as it likes: that resolution will not be
altered. No shouting will be of any avail. Soviet Russia never permitted her
policy to be influenced by capitalistic powers while she was weak. Much
less will she brook any interference with her internal affairs now."

81
Concerning the British Intervention on Behalf of
Mgr. Budkiewicz

(Translation from Moscow *Izvestiia*, No. 72, April 1, 1923)

The People's Commissariat for Foreign Affairs is in receipt of the following declaration from the British Trade Mission in Moscow:

George Chicherin, People's Commissar for Foreign Affairs.

Sir:

In compliance with the instruction of His Majesty's Secretary for Foreign
Affairs, I have the honor to address to you in connection with the death
sentence upon Monsignior Butkevich [Budkiewicz], which has been confirmed by the Presidium of the Central Executive Committee, an earnest

and final appeal to postpone the execution of his sentence. I have to point out that execution of the sentence will cause in the entire civilized world feelings of horror and indignation, which fact would be undesirable for the Russian government even from the standpoint of economic interests, to say nothing of other considerations.

Taking the opportunity to express again my highest esteem,

I remain, Sir,

R. M. Hodgeson

March 30, 1923

In reply to this declaration the People's Commissariat for Foreign Affairs addressed the following note to the British Trade Mission in Moscow:

Sir,

The People's Commissar for Foreign Affairs has authorized me to point out, in reply to your note of March 30, that Russia, being an independent country and a sovereign State, has an indisputable right to pass verdicts in accordance with its own legislation upon persons who violate the laws of the country, and that every attempt to interfere from outside and to protect spies and traitors to Russia is regarded as an unfriendly act and the resumption of intervention, which has been successfully repulsed by the Russian people.

It is also necessary to point out that, simultaneously with your note, Comrade Chicherin received a telegram from the representative of the Irish republic in France concerning the same matter, in which note the undersigned, asking that the sentence of Cieplak be commuted, states that he does it in spite of a hypocritical interference on the part of the government of Great Britain, which is responsible for the cold blooded murder of political prisoners in Ireland. The note asserts that 14,000 persons in Ireland, including women and girls, have been barbarously and inhumanly treated with the acquiescence of Great Britain, and that the control of British authorities over the telegraph connection prevents the civilized world from becoming acquainted with the horrible details of these massacres.

If similar events which took place in India and Egypt under British rule are taken into consideration, it will be difficult to consider sufficiently convincing the appeal of the British government in the name of humanity and the sacredness of human life.

I beg permission to assure you, Sir, of my highest esteem,

G. Veinshtein

In Charge of the Sub-Department of Allied Countries.

March 31, 1923, Moscow

82

Answer of the Soviet Government to the Declaration of the Polish Premier Sikorski

(Translation from Moscow *Izvestiia*, No. 73, April 3, 1923)

From the People's Commissariat of Foreign Affairs.

In connection with the declarations of the Polish Premier Sikorski, in the Senate and in an interview with the Minister of the R.S.F.S.R. in Poland, Comrade Obolenskii, with reference to the trial of the Catholic clergy in Moscow, the Commissariat of Foreign Affairs has instructed Comrade Obolenskii to hand the Polish Government the folowing verbal note:

"By instruction of the Russian Government, the Legation brings the following to the attention of the Polish Government:

"The Russian Government finds a plain contradiction between the repeated peaceful assurance of the Polish Government and the declarations of the President of the Council of Ministers with respect to the Cieplak affair. In view of the fact that every government has the indisputable right to punish criminals in accordance with its own laws in its own country, the attempt to interfere with that right and the attempt to hinder the execution of a legal sentence pronounced against a number of Russian citizens, convicted of crimes against the People and the State, (an attempt) accompanied moreover with threats and unparalleled insults addressed to the Russian Government, is unquestionably an unfriendly act, and displays an aggressive policy towards Russia. The Russian Government finds it superfluous to consider the inadmissible expressions of which the declarations of the President of the Council of Ministers consist, and indignantly repels his unparalleled claim. The Russian Government in particular repels the claim of the Polish Government to play in Russia the role of protector of Russian citizens of Polish origin, and reminds the Polish Government that there are living in the bounds of Poland ten million Ukrainians and Belorussians with respect to which the Polish Government violates the most elementary principles guaranteeing the existence of national minorities. Categorically denying that the representatives of the Soviet Government told the Polish Minister in Moscow, or anyone whatsoever, that this trial had merely formal importance and would not have any serious results, the Russian Government refuses to enter upon a discussion of the inadmissible and unfounded accusations against the Russian Court and the Russian authorities. The Russian Government declares that responsibility for the consequences of such a step, unexampled in international relations, rests exclusively with the Polish Government."

March 30, 1923

83
The Shooting of Mgr. Budkiewicz

(Translation from Moscow *Izvestiia*, No. 73, April 3, 1923)

The sentence of the Supreme Court of the republic with respect to Butkevich [Budkiewicz], that he be shot, has been executed, his plea for pardon having been denied by the All-Russian Central Executive Committee.

84
Letter of the Secretary of State, Charles E. Hughes, to the Right Reverend William T. Manning, the Protestant Episcopal Bishop of New York

April 9, 1923

My dear Bishop Manning:

I acknowledge for the President the receipt of your telegram of March 29, 1923, asking that this Government use every effort to prevent the carry- ing out of the death sentence passed on Archbishop Cieplak and other ec- clesiastics in Russia.

As you may have seen in the press statements, the Department took steps, immediately after the situation became known, to give expression to the humanitarian interest of the American people and their earnest hope that the lives of these ecclesiastics would be spared.

With high regard, I remain,
Very sincerely yours,
Charles E. Hughes

85
Letter of Christian A. Herter to Dewitt Clinton Poole, Department of State; and a Report on the Religious Situation in Russia

Dear Dewitt:

I am enclosing herewith copy of extracts of a letter from one of our men in Moscow, who is a very good reporter.

The description in connection with some of the details of Butkevitch's [Budkiewicz's] death will, I know, interest you and may be of interest to your Secretary as giving local color to a phase of the present Russian regime.

Sincerely yours,
Christian A. Herter
Assistant to Mr. Hoover

Moscow, Russia
April 12, 1923

Dr. Walsh is pretty jumpy. I had him and Duranty to dinner the other night along with Quinn and Burland and he talked for three hours on his opinion of the whole Russian situation and on the murder of the Catholic priest. This which I shall now recount to you is confidential for the time being so handle it carefully.

Apparantly Duranty's dope was wrong about the priest Butkevich [Budkiewicz]. The charges against him were entirely trumped up, particularly those which said that he had conspired to oppose the Russian Government's seizure of church treasures for famine funds. Dr. Walsh told us, and the fact came out in the trial though it was immediately hushed up, that last spring the Pope had sent two messages — officially through Chicherin — to Russia offering to pay for all Catholic church treasures according to the evaluation of the Soviet Government, no matter what that sum might be. To neither did they receive an answer and the Bolos seized the treasures. That obviously completely exonerates Butkevich [Budkiewicz] on that charge. As to his having dealings with the Polish Government, it appears that the foundation for this charge was a telegram signed by some fifteen Poles in Russia to Papal Nuncio at Warsaw giving thanks on the establishment a Polish mission in Moscow.

Then you will remember Duranty's idea was that the Bolos first planned clemency and were driven into executing the priest by the protests (rather undiplomatically worded) of the Poles and British. Walsh said that wasn't true — and this is the reason: The British message was received on Friday morning at 2:30 (this was the time set for the execution originally remember). Dr. Walsh was awakened by the ringing of his phone. He answered it to hear a coarse Russian voice asking "Kuda or Ku-da" ["Kto tam?"] — the general sense of this remark being "are you there?" Dr. W. answered "Da" — whereupon the voice at the other end of the phone burst into a roar of coarse laughter and appeared to turn to talk to other men in the room, for there was a general sound of laughter and turmoil and some shouting. Dr. Walsh then asked in German and French with whom he was speaking and was answered each time by the same rather coarse laugh. Then the voice began a long tale in Russian, frequently interrupted by laughter and by comments from the other men in the room. After about five minutes of this Dr. Walsh hung up.

Half an hour later — at 3:00 — his phone rang again, and exactly the same story was repeated. Again at 3:30 and finally at 4:00, at which time Dr. Walsh refused to answer the phone.

In the morning Dr. W. learned from Russians to whom he told the story, that this was the common procedure of the Cheka after executing a prisoner. Generally they called up a mother, wife or father to tell them what had been done. Can you imagine anything more brutal? It struck us who heard the story that this was conclusive proof that at that hour Friday morning Butkevich [Budkiewicz] had been executed — and not Saturday morning as the Bolos later declared. (Friday was Good Friday, remember.)

Dr. Walsh's idea is that this attack on the Catholics is a deliberate step on the part of the fanatical left wing group as a sort of test to see if they can do the same thing to foreign religions in this way: The Bolos had roughly five fronts which they meant to attack to put their ideas across: (1) political, (2) economic, (3) religious, (4) social, (5) intellectual. They have had to back down on the first two, the shipping out of the professors last fall — which they very much regret now — was the last, the shooting of the Catholic priest was No. 3

Duranty has asked a lot of his sources of info. Communistic and other what they think of this idea, and has come to the conclusion that it is not the correct explanation, except for perhaps a few of the heads such as Krilenko [Krylenko].

Dr. W. is very jumpy and somewhat bitter. He said he didn't know where he would get supplies after the A.R.A. pulls out, and I suggested that he buy rye flour in Russia as the Swedes had done at Samara. At that he went off the deep end and declared that he considered buying Russian supplies to feed Russians betraying the donors of relief funds and that he would never do it. As for grain export he condemned it unequivocally, saying that while it might have a perfectly logical justification if one started from certain premises, the people who suggested it failed to see the main issues. He says that though this may be one means of rehabilitating Russian agriculture, it is not the only one, and it is one which will cost Russian lives. The Soviets need money. Very well, let them get on a business basis, establish confidence in their good will, and they can get it from abroad on loans, concession, etc. It is only because they refuse to give up their ideas which have failed and which are therefore wrong that they have to export grain to get money. Then he says that, if they do export grain, no one has any assurance that they will use the profits thereof for machinery and manufactured necessities — which is true. He says further that he has definite proof that large sums of money are still being spent on foreign propaganda for the world revolution. He cites the case of an English newspaper which has received money to his knowledge within the last few months.

My impression is that the Dr. is a bit too irritated to be sound at present. Trotsky's report on heavy industry which began appearing serially in the papers yesterday would indicate that the leaders, even those considered "Left" and in spite of Lenin's being out of it, are fully in accord with the return to the principles of capitalistic business. Trotsky says that the Professional Unions have got to stop butting in in the running of industry and mind their own business; that factories and industry must be put under competent managers, who though they are to look after the interests of the workers are to remember that their first duty is to speed up production. Then he also indicates that contrary to its policy up to the present, the Government is willing to turn over heavy industry to private and foreign capital. That is a tremendous step — as Duranty said today at lunch — almost as tremendous as the announcement of New Economic Policy itself.

Dr. W. also told me about an attempt on the part of the Bolos to steal 50,000 dollars worth of medical supplies sent to him through the Russian Red Cross from the Vatican. They arrived in February and have not yet been turned over to him. He, however, has them by the short hair in writing, fortunately, and can prove that they are crooks when he wishes. They thought they could put something over, apparently, but after two months find they can't. Now it appears they would like to get rid of the whole damn thing but can't because they have sold some of the medical supplies and don't know how to replace them. They appear to be very uncomfortable.

I am writing this so damn fast that my fingers ache, so it may be illegible.

Duranty says that the big guns are most extremely sorry about the shooting of the priest. They feel that they are in hot water and don't know what to do about it. Please note that Tikon's case has again been postponed (trial thereof, I mean) probably indefinitely, which means that they have grown afraid to shoot him, as a trial would certainly have rendered inevitable. I think this highly significant.

The reason they didn't shoot the Archbishop Cepliak (Catholic) was, so Dr. W. says, that they were afraid to shoot so important an official — being afraid of the word "Archbishop shot" in foreign print.

Dined last week also with Hodgeson of the British Mission, who had little to say. However, he was pretty worried, apparently. The amusing reason for the fact that little Weinstein signed the English note came out. Apparantly the Soviet Trade Delegation in London keeps insisting that it should be allowed to deal with the Foreign Secretary. England says, no, deal with the Chief of the Northern Department, he's good enough for you. Which arouses the ire of the Bolos. In retaliation they refuse to let Hodgeson see or deal directly with Tchitcherin. About the British note, Hodgeson said that "its matter was Radek's, its style Tchitcherin's, and its signature Weinstein's."

Hodgeson refused to accept the first note, because of its tone; Weinstein then sent another which was less insulting.

86
Trial of Tikhon's Followers

(Translation from Moscow *Izvestiia,* No. 91, April 26, 1923)

Krasnodar, April 24. The trial of 18 of Tikhon's followers has come to an end. They have been indicted for resisting the confiscation of Church valuables, for maintaining contact with Tikhon, for spreading counter-revolutionary pamphlets and for agitation against the Soviet power. The majority of the accused are the organizers of a rebellion in Eisk City on the day of the confiscation of the valuables. The Head of the Tikhon movement, Priest Rozhdestyenskii, has been sentenced to 7 years' imprisonment; his active assistant, Priest Sosko, to 5 years; Agriculturist Gatesov and Teacher Zaitsev, to 3 years; others to shorter terms; and several persons were acquitted.

AGAINST TIKHON

Ekaterinoslav, April 24. The Diocesan Committee of the "Living Church," together with the parish, have declared Tikhon guilty of a number of crimes against the Soviet power, as well as of violation of the Church canons. The Diocesan Committee thinks that Tikhon deserves severe punishment for his criminal political activities.

Minsk, April 24. The meetings of the Red Army soldiers have passed resolutions demanding severe punishment of Tikhon.

87
Instruction Concerning the Registration of Religious Societies and Issue of Permits for Convocation of Their Congresses

(Translation from Moscow *Izvestiia,* No. 92, April 27, 1923)

(1) The citizens of the R.S.F.S.R. can have at their disposal places of religious worship and the necessary property for carrying on religious serv-

ices either by means of organizing groups of persons belonging to a certain religion, registered in accordance with the order established by the instruction of the People's Commissariat of Justice of August 24, 1918 (Compilation of Decrees, 1918, No. 62, page 685), or by organizing religious societies in compliance with the Decree of the Central Executive Committee of August 3, 1922 (Compilation of Decrees, 1922, No. 49, page 622.) and registered in accordance with the present instruction.

(2) According to the Decree of the Central Executive Committee of August 3, 1922, no religious society of any religion whatsoever can begin its activities without being previously registered in the administrative department of a Provincial or Regional Executive Committee.

(3) Citizens desiring to establish a religious society must submit to the administrative department of a Provincial or Regional Executive Committee together with a declaration concerning registration, the following documents in three copies: (a) minutes of the conference of the founders of the society (three copies); (b) articles of incorporation of the society (three copies); (c) the list of founders (three copies), attaching also the following information concerning their personalities (three copies) — (1) name, surname and father's name, (2) residence and address, (3) social standing, (4) social and official position since 1914, (5) class to which they belonged prior to the revolution, (6) financial standing, (7) date on which they joined the given religion; (d) the necessary stamp duty must also be provided.

(4) The societies existing at the time of the promulgation of the present instruction have to submit to the administrative department of a Provincial or Regional Committee, together with a declaration concerning registration (three copies), the following documents: (a) articles of incorporation of the society (three copies); (b) list of members of the society and membership of the executive committee at the present time (three copies), in a form indicated in Paragraph "c" of Article 3 of the present instruction; (c) list of priests, bishops and preachers and other responsible workers according to the form established by Paragraph "c" of Article 3.

(5) The administration department of a Provincial or Oblast Executive Committee will refuse registration of an existing society, or one being established, in the event that: (a) the number of members or founders of the religious society is less than 50 local inhabitants enjoying full rights; (b) articles of incorporation of the given society, its object or methods of preaching, violate the Constitution or laws of the R.S.F.S.R.

(6) In case there are no reasons to refuse the registration of a religious society, the administrative department will return a copy of the articles of incorporation of the society with an endorsement and seal concerning the registration of the society, which copy must be kept in the files of the society.

(7) Religious societies which are not registered within the period of three months from the date of the promulgation of the present instruction in the *Izvestiia* will be closed.

(8) Religious societies of the same religion are permitted to convoke provincial or All-Russian congresses on the basis of and in accordance with, the decree of the Central Executive Committee of June 12, 1922 (*Compilation of Decrees, 1922, No. 40, Page 477*) and instruction concerning its enforcement of August 10, 1922 (Compilation of Decrees, 1922, No. 49, Page 624).

(9) Provincial and All-Russian Congresses of religious societies are permitted to elect executive bodies. The lists of members of these executive bodies must be submitted to the People's Commissariat of Internal Affairs or to the administrative departments of a Provincial or Regional Executive Committee in compliance with a form established by Paragraph "c" of Article 3.

(10) The congresses of religious societies and executive bodies elected by these congresses cannot (1) establish obligatory money collections; (2) possess religious property or receive it against contracts; (3) conclude any kind of transactions or contracts.

(11) The People's Commissariat of Internal Affairs and its local departments are instructed to exercise control over the activities of religious societies, unions or congregations.

(12) All religious societies are subject to the general rules concerning private societies and organizations, but are deprived of the rights of a juridical person and (of holding) property.

(13) All religious societies of any religion have equal rights, as concerns their rights and duties, and enjoy no privileges or subsidies, either from the government or from its local autonomous administrations.

(14) Members of religious societies or their representatives are permitted to collect voluntary donations for covering the expenditures connected with the possession of common religious property, such as heating, protection and cleaning and repairs of places of religious worship.

(15) Possessing no rights of a juridical person or of property, religious societies are permitted to conclude contracts of a private legal character connected with the exploitation of religious property, such as contracts concerning the hiring of a chorus, repairs of books, etc.

NOTE: Such transactions cannot assume the character of a commercial or industrial contract, even when connected with religion, such as the lease of candle factories, printing establishments for printing religious books, etc.

(16) The citizens belonging to a religious society are permitted, for the execution of resolutions of their general conferences as well as for representation, to appoint, if need be, their religious officials and to appoint from

ᵐong themselves the necessary number of representatives who will act within the limits of the rights granted to them.

NOTE: The lists of officials and other responsible persons must be submitted to the administration departments, together with information required by Paragraph "c", Article 3 of the present instruction.

(17) The order of the closing of religious societies is established by Articles 6 and 11 of the decree of the Central Executive Committee of August 3, 1922.

People's Commissar of Justice:
Kurskii
Assistant People's Commissar of Internal Affairs:
Beloborodov

88
Results of Anti-Religious Campaign

(Summary from Moscow *Pravda*, No. 102, May 10, 1923)

The results of the anti-Easter propaganda are already to be seen. This campaign, carried on in all villages of the Uman district, governorship of Kiev, had an enormous success and provoked in the rural districts unusual interest. Ordinarily, only about 100 to 200 people used to attend the village meetings. On the first Easterday, the meetings were frequented in some places by up to 500 people, among them a large percentage of women. Some meetings made important and effective decisions. At the meeting of the village Mankorka, about 400 people, among them about 60 women, decided after having heard the origin of religion and religious feeling to ignore the Easter ceremonies in the future.

After the meeting at Nesterovka, it was decided to ask the Soviet government to pursue energetically the enlightenment of the large working classes, and to show them the absurdity of religious teachings. Another meeting, in the village Sokolovka, decided to collect at once the icons in their homes and to bring them to the committee, sitting near the church, and to burn them solemnly.

In some *volosts* [village districts] the teachers, for the first time since the revolution, kept the boys busy on the first Easter holiday, cleaning the school and planting trees.

The peasants have already changed very much. They no longer believe much in the different saints, who, as has been supposed, preserve people from hardship and illness. They no longer apply, in case their cattle are ill, to a certain saint, but they go to the *volost* veterinarian to get help. And it is the same in cases of diseases in the family.

The schism of the church is progressing and deepening. Many new churches already exist in Russia: the Tikhon Church, the Autocephalous Church, the Progressive Church, the Living Church, the Apostolic Church, etc., and innumerable new sects are being created. Our anti-religious propaganda is doing good work. But we must pay still more attention to this propaganda, because we have had many failures in this respect. It is absolutely necessary to base our anti-religious campaign entirely on science. It is absolutely necessary to create committees for the examination the different districts, and besides, it is necessary to provide the rural districts with popular literature concerning the actual religious situation.

But the reaction is already being produced in peasant circles and the authority of the church is vanishing, little by little.

89

Membership of the Plenum of the Supreme Church Administration Elected by the All-Russian Council of the Russian Orthodox Church

(Translation from Moscow *Izvestiia*, No. 103, May 11, 1923)

Priest S. Kanarskii; Archpresbyter V. D. Krasnitskii; Metropolitan of All Siberia, Petr; Moscow Metropolitan Antonin; Archbishop Petr Sergeev; Priest A. Diakonov; Deacon S. Dobrov; Priest B. Dikarev; Priest P. Krasotin; Priest A. Boiarskii; Layman A. Novikov; Priest D. M. Soloviev; Priest D. Adamov; Professor A. Pokrovskii.

90

The Supreme Church Council of the Russian Orthodox Church

(Translation from Moscow *Pravda*, No. 106, May 15, 1923)

President: Metropolitan of Moscow, ANTONIN.
Vice President: Archpresbyter of the Orthodox Church VLADIMIR KRASNITSKII.
Metropolitan of the whole of Siberia: PETR.
Archbishop of Krutitsk: ALEKSANDR VVEDENSKII.

Archbishop LEONID.
Metropolitan of Odessa: EVDOKIM.
Archpriests: P. KRASOTIN, G. DOBRONRAVOV, DIKAREV, DIA-
KONOV.
Archdeacon: DOBROV.
Manager of the Supreme Church Council of Laymen: A. NOVIKOV.
Moscow, The Campus of the Holy Trinity Monastery.

91
Anti-Religious Propaganda in Ivanovo-Vosnesensk Governorship

(Translation from Moscow *Pravda,* No. 106, May 15, 1923)

The Ivanovo-Voznesensk Governorship Committee of the Russian Communist Party is giving sufficient attention to anti-religious propaganda.
During the last period a large anti-religious campaign was carried on, disputes and lectures were held, reports and references given, in which the
Governorship Administration of Political Education took an active part.

But the results were not always the same: the disputes which were held in
the industrial districts and among the workmen yielded splendid results, but
among the peasants and the small bourgeoisie the results were not always
positive, and even in some cases negative. The Russian clergymen, profiting
by the simplicity of the audience, used all sorts of demagogic devices to very
good effect.

At Boniahkal, for instance, during the dispute, where peasants, old
women and men were present, a clergyman moved the assembly to tears,
when complaing of the present and past persecution of the Church. The
impression and effect of this touching discourse was enormous.

It is obvious to say, the disputes among the simple peasants will provoke
feeling in favor of the church and the popes. There were cases when the
speaker could not finish his conclusions. But such disputes made quite a
different impression among the workmen and especially among the youth.
The audience was entirely on the side of the Communists and the disputes
had a real success in all factories and in the town.

Lectures had more success among the peasants, not to speak of the population of the town. It is true, you can hear sometimes from an old peasant:
"However, let us have our God, don't touch this." But that is all. The attitude towards the clergy is becoming definitely unfavorable.

The anti-religious circles of the Governorship Committee took into consideration these experiences, and decided to stick to the following methods:

Each lecturer must first of all take into consideration his audience and the manner and matter of the report or lecture must conform to the respective audience. There is one manner and matter for red-guardists, for the youth; other methods are to be used with peasants and with workmen. Disputes should no longer be held among the simple peasants and the uneducated classes of the population, but serious reports and lectures, not hurting the religious feeling of the audience.

Splendid results are obtained by anti-religious evening meetings, devoted to Bruno, Galileo and Copernicus. Such meetings were arranged by the Committee of Union of Youth, and thousands of members of workmen-peasants youth circles and of red-guardists attended these meetings.

There is no more doubt that youth has escaped the sphere of religious and clerical mystification.

The agitation committee of the Governorship Committee is paying great attention now to the choice of the agitators and lecturers to be sent to the different districts. Anti-religious circles are formed by the Governorship and District Committees and in the larger areas.

92
The Case Against Patriarch Tikhon

[For the purposes of propaganda the Soviet Government issued a booklet in 5000 copies for distribution among the population, giving details of the case of Patriarch Tikhon. It is entitled, *Act of Accusation in the Case of Citizens: Vasilii Ivanovich Belavin, Nikandr Grigorevich Fenomenov, Arsennii Grigorevich Stadnitskii, Petr Viktorovich Gurev*. Moscow, Glavlit, 1923, printed by the Typography of State Political Department. The pamphlet is signed by: A. Vishinskii, Prosecutor of Judicial Collegia of Supreme Tribunal of R. S. F. S. R.]

RESUMÉ OF CONCLUSION OF ACCUSATION IN CASE
OF PATRIARCH TIKHON

1. The "Accusatory Conclusion" commences by giving a description of the Church Convocation [referred to as Sobor, held in Moscow on the 15th August, 1917] at which Patriarch Tikhon was President. The Sobor is stated to have been a collection of delegates representing the political aspect of Orthodox Russia. Statistics regarding the membership of the Sobor are incorrect. For instance, Kerenskii and Avksentiev are stated to have been present as members — besides a well known figure in Moscow, Princess Trubetskaia, a former agent of the Cheka, and later mad. The two first named were never members of the Sobor; and the last named, as a woman, could not have been. Other persons (Count Tristov, for example) are also mentioned as having been members who did not attend although they were elected.

2. In order to prove that the Sobor did not represent the Russian people but a certain group of persons, chiefly belonging to the Church, the statistics concerning the number of members taking part are also incorrect; for instance the total number of clergy taking part is given as 277, whereas the actual number who did take part was 239. All other figures given are distorted in some way.

3. In recording the speeches, only those are menitoned which can be with advantage for the aims of the "accusatory Conclusion," all others being left out.

4. The final characterization of the Sobor is based not upon the resolutions and decisions of the Sobor, but upon some speeches actually made by members and other speeches by members who were not even present.

5. The actual speeches and conclusion of the Patriarch himself are left out, these clearly not being suited to the purpose of the "Conclusion."

6. The persons drawing up the "Conclusions" have not hesitated to include in it a direct lie, stating that the Patriarch himself renounced his post in favor of the Supreme Church Council, whereas it was known to the Soviet Government and the public generally (on the basis of documents) that the Patriarch had merely handed over authority temporarily to the Senior Metropolitan, Agafangel.

7. In reading the act of accusation it becomes clear that the actions of the church authorities and the Patriarch were known to the Soviet government in all details throughout the years 1917 to 1922. Since no action had been taken and all persons implicated in former cases in this connection had been released, it is clear that the present case is actuated by political considerations only. Concerning their own motives the Bolsheviks themselves write in the "Act of Accusation": "It is necessary to prove to everyone that the Soviet Government of 1923 is not that of the earlier years." Thus the accused are victims not of their own political activities but of the Bolsheviks who now considered themselves strong enough to deal with them.

93

Documents Presented to the U.S. Government by the Former Representative of the Russian Provisional Government in Bern Concerning the Status and Persecution of the Russian Church (1923)

To All Governments, Churches and the Faithful of All Confessions:

For several years liberty of conscience, a right recognized as inalienable and sacred throughout the world, has been denied to the Russian people.

Today, the persecution of religion undertaken by the Soviet authorities is reaching its utmost limits.

The sufferings inflicted on the faithful, the punishment and murder of priests of all cults, are not enough for the Soviets. An unheard of crime is being openly prepared, in the sight of all the world, against the Orthodox Church and against its highest dignitary, the Most Holy Patriarch Tikhon, legitimately elected at the All Russian Council of 1917.

A pseudo-council lately held in Moscow, respondent to the voices of the mercenaries of power, and acting on a list of entirely fictitious accusations, has announced the deposition of Patriarch Tikhon. The civilized world will not allow itself to be deceived by this parody of a council, nor will the conscience of humanity be blind to the true meaning of the condemnation dictated in advance to those who will judge the Patriarch.

The Committee of the Russian Zemstvos and Cities unites in a common spirit with all the Russians in foreign lands, and raises its voice of indignant protest in the hope that the civilized world will be able to prevent the attempt prepared against the Patriarch, who personifies the religious conscience of the Russian people.

Committee of the Russian Zemstvos and Cities

MEMORANDUM

A bloody persecution has been taking place in Russia during the last five years. Up to the present time thirty bishops and more than twelve-hundred Russian Orthodox priests have been put to death "Here are some names which I know," writes Monsignor Evlogii, the Metropolitan of All the Russian Orthodox Churches of Western Europe:

1. Metropolitan of Kiev, Vladimir, murdered in Kiev in 1918
2. Metropolitan of Petrograd, Veniamin, shot in 1922
3. Archbishop of Perm, Andronik, tortured to death in Perm (in 1922)
4. Archbishop of Chernigov, Vasilii, killed in Chernigov in 1918
5. Archbishop of Revel, Platon, murdered in Dorpat in 1919
6. Archbishop of Astrakhan, Mitrofan, killed in Astrakhan in 1918
7. Archbishop of Irkutsk, Anatolii, shot in 1922
8. Archbishop of Nizhnii-Novgorod, Ioakim, killed in Crimea in 1920
9. Bishop of Orel, Makarii, tortured to death in Smolensk
10. Bishop of Tobolsk, Germogen, tortured to death in 1918 in Tobolsk
11. Bishop Lavrentii, Vicar of Nizhnii-Novgorod, killed in 1919 in Nizhnii-Novgorod
12. Bishop of Kirilov, Varsofonii, Vicar of Novgorod, killed in 1919 in Kirilov

13. Bishop Amvrosii killed in 1919, in Sviazhsk, governorship of Kazan
14. Bishop of Selenginsk, Efrem, killed in 1918 in Moscow
15. Bishop Isidor, Vicar of the diocese of Riazan, killed in 1918
16. Bishop of Semipalatinsk, Kiprian, killed in 1919
17. Bishop Leontii, Vicar of Astrakhan, killed in 1918 in Astrakhan
18. Bishop Pimen, Vicar of Perm, killed in 1918

"There were other bishops murdered by the Bolsheviks," Metropolitan Evliogii, told us "but there is no exact information about them." The following bishops were imprisoned or deported:

1. Agapit, Archbishop of Ekaterinodar, died in prison
2. Andrei, Bishop of Ufa, deported and was shot in prison
3. Averkii, Bishop of Zhitomir, in prison
4. Arsenii, Metroplitan of Novgorod, in prison
5. Anatolii of Samara, in prison
6. Arsenii of Rostov on the Don, in prison
7. Illarion, Vicar of Moscow, deported
8. Iosif, Vicar of Iaroslavl, deported
9. Iuvenalii of Tula, in prison
10. Konstantin, Archbishop of Mogilev, in prison
11. Nikanor, Archbishop of Krutitsk, in prison
12. Nikodim, Archbishop of Taurida, in prison
13. Prokopii, Bishop of Kherson, exiled
14. Aleksei, Vicar of Petrograd, deported
15. Kirill, Metropolitan of Kazan, in prison; actually deported to some concentration camp in Siberia
16. Serafim of Tver, deported
17. Serafim of Orel, in prison
18. Sergii of Ekaterinodar, deported
19. Nikhail of Grodno, deported
20. Innokentii, Bishop of Ladoga, deported
21. Venedikt, Bishop of Kronstadt, in strict confinement
22. Mikhail, Metropolitan of Kiev, after being tortured is imprisoned in Moscow
    etc., etc., etc........

"These data are not complete," says Metropolitan Evlogii, "but we are able to affirm with full conviction that not one of those who remain faithful to patriarch Tikhon has kept his post. More than a thousand priests perished because they remained faithful to the Church. At the head of all these martyrs is Patriarch Tikhon. After having endured all the sufferings of imprisonment he was handed over to a Soviet tribunal, and now, an ill and aged man, is detained in a damp subterranean cell."

The atheistic government of the Soviets, without right and against the laws of the Church, proclaimed Antonin, the head of the Living Church and a bishop interdicted by the patriarch, as the Metropolitan of Moscow, and granted the right of administering the Orthodox Church to the Sobor convened by Antonin. This Supreme Administration of the Church undertook to nominate some archbishops and priests who were loyal to it so as to have the authority to organize an impressive All-Russian Sobor. The purpose of the Sobor was fixed in advance: (1) the deposition of the Patriarch; (2) the legitimization of the authority of the Supreme Administration of the Church; and (3) the subordination of the Church to the civil authority. This purpose was not indicated openly, but there was talk of "reconciling the ends of the Church with those of Communism and the Soviet authority," which without having the faith tries to realize the "Kingdom of God."

There is no doubt that the Sobor of Moscow cannot be considered as a regular Sobor; on the contrary, this meeting is completely illegal as the folowing considerations prove: (1) Since Patriarch Tikhon was the legal head of the Russian Church according to the canons, the civil authority had no right to depose him without a decision by an ecclesiastical tribunal. (2) In the absence of the Patriarch, his canonically appointed Locum Tenens, Metropolitan Agafangel, had the sole right to convoke a council. This right did not belong to the Administration of the Church arbitrarily created by the civil authority and against the canonical laws. (3) The canonical laws do not recognize the right of the civil authority to interfere with the affairs of the Church, and consequently they are not able to recognize any power which is openly anti-Christian and anti-religious. (4) The elections were organized in such a manner that the council could be formed only according to the views and desires of the civil power and not according to the interests of the Church. (5) On the agenda of the council were several dogmatic questions; these do not fall within the competence of a local council and can be discussed only at an ecumenical council.

This illegal and wicked meeting began its activities with an act plainly contrary to justice. In the absence of the imprisoned Patriarch Tikhon, fictitious charges were presented to the assembly. Without hearing the accused, but in order to please the atheistic civil authority, this council decided to inflict on the Patriarch the most humiliating punishment, the loss of his post and of his rank of patriarch, "for having used all the force of his authority to overthrow the existing regime." One could not more grossly outrage the holy truth and the Russian Orthodox Church. In the districts of Orel, Saraisk, Spassk, Tambov, Riazhsk, etc., the Orthodox faithful held public meetings, and by way of protest demanded that their priests celebrate a *Te Deum* for the health and welfare of the patriarch. But the Soviet authorities sent Red detachments immediately to suppress the protests.

Finally, the Bolsheviks have confiscated many churches, which they have sometimes changed into museums, but more often into theaters or meeting places. They have collected from these churches the sacred objects of cult—

holy icons, crucifixes and banners, and priestly vestments—and brought them to one place in the city. Or, as in Kharkov and Odessa, they have put them in a shed and burned them. The newspaper *Times* for June 3 reports that during May twenty-seven churches were closed in Moscow and seventeen priests shot.

One may ask how the Bolsheviks, enemies of all religion, are able to tolerate the Living Church and to patronize it. The answer is easy. The Living Church is in the service of the Bolsheviks, being allowed to show a concern for the religious sentiment of the Russian people, and at the same time serving to establish in the life of the people Bolshevik principles which are contrary to those of Christianity—principles of hatred and violence opposed to the principles of the love and sweetness of Christ. The rulers of the Living Church do not offer a single reproach or one word of blame against the Soviets. On the contrary, they not only proclaim their praises but justify all their violence and their murders; and they chant prayers for the prolongation of their days.

Does not the complacency with which these rulers turn the churches over to the Bolsheviks, who make them places of blasphemy and orgy, reveal the secret work of the Living Church as tending to the destruction of the true Church of Christ in Russia? The Living Church is not a Church of Christ. It still bears His name but it has already denied the spirit and the grace of Christ. It is for this reason that it is dear to the Bolshevik authority.

94
The Liquidation of the Monastery of the Nativity of Our Lord

(Translation from Moscow *Izvestiia*, No. 107, May 16, 1923)

The People's Court of the Sokolnik region has examined the claim of the All-Russian Sick and Wounded Red Army Committee of the Central Executive Committee regarding the expulsion of 96 nuns from the Monastery of the Nativity of Our Lord.

The All-Russian Sick and Wounded Red Army Committee closed a contract with the Moscow Administration of Nationalized Property regarding the lease of the Monastery of the Nativity of Our Lord with all its buildings. Part of the buildings were used as workshops for the invalids, but in other buildings the nuns remained, who did not want to quit their old premises, although they did not have any contracts and, besides, paid the rent rather irregularly. Their houses were intended for living houses for the invalids, who were working there in the workshops.

The plaintiff withdrew at the court his demand to turn out 18 nuns of advanced age, but insisted on turning out the remaining ones. The court gave satisfaction to the demands of the plaintiff.

95

Anti-Religious Propaganda

(Translation from Moscow *Izvestiia*, No. 110, May 20, 1923)

In the middle of April a conference was held at the propaganda department of the Moscow Committee concerning the results of the Easter campaign, in which it was established that the great defect of the campaign was the lack of scientific knowledge on the part of the agitators and the absence of scientific literature, etc. The conference proposed to the Moscow Committee and Central Committee to take the necessary steps for education and study and collection of materials for such campaigns; to draw the attention of other regions to the necessity of carrying out the campaign; to begin systematically to drive out religious life by scientific, cultural and revolutionary civil means; to give to the anti-religious propaganda in the clubs of the youth a more artistic and impressive character; to divide the serious part of the propaganda from the recreative and amusing, and to strengthen the latter.

The general work of the anti-religious propanganda in April was much handicapped by the Easter campaign. The Party Congress has also diverted attention from it.

96

"Denial of False Information."

(Translation from Moscow *Izvestiia*, No. 113, May 24, 1923)

The London *Times* on May 8 published a report from Moscow stating that the sessions of the Church Council, which had been opened in the church of Christ the Saviour, were later transferred to the III House of Unions and that about 100 delegates, disgusted with the speech of Antonin, had left the Council immediately after the end of the speech.

The special Berlin correspondent of the above newspaper adds on May 10 a few similar details concerning insulting shouts with which Antonin was met, about a stone thrown at him, about dispersion with armed force of the mob which gathered in the street, etc.

The Press Bureau of the People's Commissariat of Foreign Affairs denies categorically both communications of the said newspaper, which represent a base lie.

[Press Bureau of the People's Commissariat of Foreign Affairs.]

97
Closing of the Hospital Chapels

(Translation from Moscow *Izvestiia*, No. 113, May 24, 1923)

In view of the fact that no places of religious worship are permitted to be attached to State institutions, the Administrative Department is liquidating all the chapels in the hospital buildings. The chapels of Medvedin, the First and the Second Municipal hospitals and the nurse school on Sobachia Ploshchadka have been already closed. In the near future 20 more similar chapels will be closed.

98
"The Religious Foolishness"

(Translation from Moscow *Pravda*, No. 114, May 25, 1923)

The Baptists had come to the village not long before the Revolution. Aunt Afinia had sent her three maiden daughters to the big town for service in the houses of rich Baptists, and three years later they had come back to the village as "believers." Nor was that all. The three sisters succeeded in converting to the Baptist religion their mother, brother, uncle and other members of the family. There were three such "believers' homes" in the village.

Soon, preachers of the Gospel began to come to the village, arranging meetings, propagating their faith among the peasants, and trying to persuade them to "acknowledge faith in Christ." The conditions were favorable, with the church crumbling on its foundations and the authorities not desiring to mix in religious matters, and the preachers made the most of the opportunity.

"Repent and come to Jesus: Faith alone will save you! Faith alone will redeem you, brothers and sisters."

They were well fed, well and even fashionably clothed, young, wearing on their hands gold and diamonds. They used to come to the village only when the three sisters happened to be at home.

The country women began to mock at it.

"By all the Saints, it's not for the old that they come; it's the young girls."

Even the old women began to be discontented.

"It's nice work, however, they are doing in our village, these rascals."

The village youths, also, frequented these religious meetings, indulging in disputes with the preachers, who, however, always proved to be stronger in their arguments, owing to an ever ready flow of expressions and their ability to turn the questions. But the youths did not much mind being vanquished. They knew their turn would come when a certain Zarubin, a native of the village, and now working in a factory, came back to the village.

The village knew him well, this Zarubin; the whole village felt obligated to him. He had done very much for the peasants, and whenever trouble arose, the peasants were sure to have his support. He had interfered in quarrels about the distribution of land, school matters were promptly decided by him, and even the church had had to feel his authority. Popes and the so-called "kulaki" of the village [rich people] had seen a thing or two. His good turns to the village were immunerable, and no wonder his authority was universally recognized and his opinion respected.

At the time of the emperor Nicholas he had worked in more than one factory, had been put into prison for striking, and been brought many times back to his home under escort. Working now in a neighborhood factory, he often comes home to see his old father, in summer. He knows absolutely everything, foreign countries, the food-tax regulations, why the Soviet regime is better than all other forms of governments; he is versed in religious matters as well, and the popes did not like him much. Briefly, he knows all, explains and promptly settles all matters.

Those who did not like him used to call him: "Whirl, Gavrila" [Kruti, Gavrila].

And Zarubin came to visit his sick father, again, and by chance, he arrived the day when our preachers from the big town were present in the village and had just arranged a meeting, for the same evening. They had chosen that day the largest room in the village, the schoolhouse, in order to have more comfort.

Youth came in masses to the assembly. Every one instinctively felt that the decisive moment had come. Long rows of peasants, women, children, girls were to be seen coming slowly, as peasants do, to the school, and even the worn out and disabled old Sema left his hot corner on the stove bunk. No room at all in the school, nowhere to sit down, to stand up, even the windows did not give fresh air. A throng in the room, near the window, in the streets, a throng everywhere. Well seen by everybody, and ranged according to rank, our Gospel messengers were seated at a large table, where an imposing heap of books was lying. A polished young man, with black moustache and careful part of the hair, making large gestures, was talking with a thin, shrill, noisy voice. He was repeating again and again the same thing, Faith in Christ.

Having finished, he invited the audience, his brothers and sisters in God, to ask questions.

"With your permission!" said Zarubin, stepping forward.

The crowd gave way and he came to the table.

Zarubin talked clearly, putting the stress where necessary, underlining cleverly the significance of certain phrases, pausing at moments.

"You come to tell us that all the wrong in this world, all the vices, everything is to be corrected through Faith. You have blamed the non-believers in your faith for rudeness, ignorance. You pretend to make the world happy only through your faith. But, culture, knowledge, do they mean nothing to you, have they lost all significance? Do they not correct, do they not improve the life of mankind?"

The preacher realized immediately with whom he had to do, and tried to interrupt him.

"We are talking in different languages, brother," he said.

"I have understood you very well, and you have me," Zarubin, and continued:

"I know, you do not believe in your teaching yourself. Nonsense, all that. Cultured mankind will know without your faith that it has not to do wrong. All that heap of books on the table is not worth a single scientific treatise. You have been saying a lot about humility and love. We know what these phrases mean. Look how the capitalists, belonging to your own faith, exploit us workmen. Big houses are built with the profits they get from our work, high walls surround their mansions, and cruel dogs watch them. They watch their property. Humility is only asked of us. Your faith is only to hide the sharp teeth of these ever hungry wolves."

The crowd was listening, holding its breath. Somebody said: "Bravo, Alekha! Go on!"

And Zarubin continued to talk at some length. He mentioned the behavior of the Baptists during the Civil War when they came to the authorities to entreat them to exempt them from military service and from participation in the civil war.

"Is it not however only owing to our victory that the Baptists can exercise their religious rites and profess their faith unmolested?"

Red as a turkey, our preacher, excited and gesticulating, cried:

"We will never understand each other, our discussion is absolutely useless."

But Zarubin, turning to the peasants, continued and said:

"Peasants! How many hundreds of years have people used their brains and their energy to study the bibles, psalters and ancient books! How many faiths there are! Each of them tries to seduce and to attract people to come to their little church shops, each of them praises its produce, as the Baptists here in our village are now doing. But this produce is rotten, it putrefies. For us workmen, religion, whatever it may be, is nonsense and useless. "Drive them away, rather; they prevent us from living sensibly. Let them work, these preachers, these popes and all that sort of people. Close up the chapels, the churches, the synagogues! It was time long ago."

The peasants did not disperse for a long time. They discussed the meeting at some length, this day being a very important one in their lives. And even the religious peasants approved Alekha, wondering how easy it was for Zarubin to settle matters.

After this memorable day our preachers have never come back to the village! They disappeared entirely. They are frightened.

99
After the Church Council

(Summary from Moscow *Izvestiia*, No. 117, May 30, 1923)

The account states that the representatives of the "Free Labor Church" as well as of other "extreme" groups were admitted to the Council only as "guests," without a voice. The results of the new elections in the various groups are also given: thus to the Central Committee of the "Living Church" was elected among others Archprebyter Krasnitskii. To the Central Committee of the Union of Congregations of the Ancient Apostolic Church was elected, among others, Archbishop Aleksandr Vvedenskii. The Central Committee of the third group, the League of Church Revival, was not elected anew. To this group belongs the Metropolitan Antonin. The Siberian group, at the head of which stands the Metropolitan Petr, made a declaration in which it is pointed out that there was no difference in principle between the two predominant groups [the Living Church, and the Ancient Apostolic Church] but merely a difference in regard to tactics. The Siberian Church claims that it, i.e. the Siberian Church, occupies the middle between those currents and may therefore be regarded as the resultant of these two forces, and as their reconciliation. The Siberian Church (1) recognizes the social revolution in Russia, and the principles proclaimed by it — namely: "social equality, general obligation to labor, and . . . equality in the use of land; (2) it rejects and denounces all counter-revolution, and (3) it adheres to the resolutions of the Council concerning the status of monks, marriage of bishops, and re-marriages of clergymen. Besides, the Siberian Church wants to reform "dogma, ethics, and the canons."

The Free Labor Church with Bishop Ioannikii at its head, celebrates Divine Service according to a "somewhat simplified ritual"; it purports to embrace all "free-minded Christians," including sectarians, and wants to abolish all formalism and "image-worship." The Council has been trying to infuse new life into the "senile organism" of the Church by merely freshening it up outwardly.

100

"Eighty Four Churches"

(Translation from Moscow *Pravda*, No. 122, June 5, 1923)

Tiflis, June 3. Eighty four chapels of various religions have been closed in the Gori District. Sixty clergymen have voluntarily discarded their robes.

101

"Among the Clergy"

(Translation from Moscow *Izvestiia*, No. 123, June 6, 1923)

CONFERENCE IN THE MOSCOW DIOCESE

Clergy of the Moscow Diocese, members of the diocesan administration, district representatives, and members of the district administration of the Moscow Diocese, 75 persons in all, held a conference on May 30 at Moscow, with the participation of the Metropolitan Antonin, Archbishop Leonid, Ioannikii and Bishop Georgii under the presidency of the plenipotentiary of the Supreme Church Council, Archpresbyter Krasnitskii.

After hearing the report of Krasnitskii on Church problems the conference unanimously adopted the following resolution:

1. Considering that, under the present conditions of Church life, it is not enough to abandon the previous counter-revolutionary activity of the Church organizations — to summon all the clergy of the diocese and the elected representatives of the Church councils to active support of the con-

solidation in Russia of the revolutionary regime of the workmen and peasants' government.

2. As necessary for that purpose — to explain to the believers, by means of sermons and pastoral teachings, the moral aims of the revolutionary movement.

3. To establish the justice of the main revolutionary claim — the equal rights of labor and life of all classes on the free, native soil.

4. To defend the justice of Russia's struggle against foreign capital to free our country from systematic secular bondage to the imperialistic governments and to establish the national and long cherished principles of the Russian social revolution.

5. To defend the justice of world social revolution, as a great deed for the freeing of humanity.

6. To consider it the duty of the clergy to participate in practical government measures for the benefit of the Soviet regime.

7. To consider it necessary to convoke a conference of all the believers of the city for the decision of practical questions in connection with the participation of the Church in revolutionary construction work, on the basis of the instructions published by the People's Commissariat of Justice on April 27, regarding the registration of religious associations.

8. To elect a special commission to handle the registration of the parish associations, and to instruct it: a) to work out normal regulations about Orthodox religious associations; b) to work out a normal application form for the members, and c) to settle all technical and financial questions in connection with the above work.

9. To the commission are elected: from the Living Church protopresbyter V. D. Krasnitskii; clergymen S. N. Orlov, Porfirii Smirnov, I. I. Skvortsov, and V. A. Iuvalov; and layman I. K. Oparnikov; and from the Union of Parishes of the Old Apostolic Church, clergyman Ternovskii-Riazanov.

It was decided to introduce the new calender June 12.

102

Report from the U.S. Legation in Riga on Anti-Religious Propaganda in Soviet Russia

Riga, Latvia, June 8, 1923

Sir:

Supplementing previous reports on anti-religious propaganda in Soviet Russia. I have the honor to report that three additional copies of *Bezbozhnik* (*Atheist*) have been placed at the disposal of the Legation for perusal.

No. 4 displays little artistic merit. The frontpiece represents the Jewish, Christian and Mohammedan Deities seated idly together. The former has one Cyclopean eye in the middle of the forehead and, instead of a nose, a vulgar combination of three fingers. Below, the infant Jesus is reading *Bezbozhnik*. In another picture entitled "The Miracle at Cana of Galilee", Jesus is making home-brew with a Samovar still. The last page represents angels stealing the peasants' eggs, chickens, pigs, milk, grain, etc., and carrying them to the priests.

Nos. 19 and 21, of May 1 and 13, are on cheap newsprint paper and are without color illustrations. The few woodcuts accompanying the text are of subordinate importance. But the text displays an astonishing change; *Bezbozhnik* now combines the functions of a semi-official religious organ with anti-religious propaganda. The Church Council is treated seriously and its political resolutions are quoted with approval. In conclusion, the editor declares that the course of the Council shows that "nobody can now say that the Soviet power is persecuting the Church and religion." Nevertheless, the same editorial declares the Church Reformation announced at the Council is a bluff and says the priests are merely trying to save their sinking ship by jettisoning part of the cargo.

Radek contributes a polemical history of the Archbishops of Canterbury. There are alleged anonymous letters from unnamed villages about the progress of atheism among the peasants.

In general these later issues leave the impression that the editor has received orders to moderate his tone in view of the doubts of the Communist leaders whether the anti-religious propaganda to date has not done harm to their cause both abroad and at home.

Pravda continues to encourage and guide the anti-religious zealots. The information is vouchsafed that "the schism of the Church is progressing and deepening . . . and innumerable new sects are being created." But it creeps out that the priests have had the best of some joint debates, and that the effort to discredit religion has strengthened it in many places, especially in the villages.

The matter has been taken in hand seriously by the Moscow Committee of the Russian Communist Party, which is trying to train and equip anti-religious lecturers. The object is stated to be "systematically to suppress religious life by scientific, cultural and revolutionary civil means."

A Moscow court gave judgment for eviction of 78 nuns from the Monastery of the Nativity of Our Lord to make room for the sick and wounded Red Army men. Eighteen nuns of advanced age were allowed to remain.

It has been found necessary to piece out the previous accounts of the Church Council with further bits of information. The principal addition is that the "Free Labor Church," with Bishop Ionannikii its head, celebrates Divine service with a "somewhat simplified ritual."

The press bureau at the Commissariat of Foreign Affairs has entered a general denial of stories that have appeared in the London *Times* and other foreign newspapers in regard to manifestations against President Antonin of the Church Council, connected with the meetings of the Council. The lack of sufficient specifications in the report detracts from its value.

I have the honor to be, Sir,

Your obedient servant,

F. W. B. Coleman

103

Reformatory Church and the Arrest of Patriarch Tikhon

(Translation from Moscow *Pravda*, No. 126, June 8, 1923)

"CHURCH QUESTION"

Referring to the information of the foreign newspaper *DNI* of May 26, 1923, No. 171, concerning alleged steps taken by me with regard to the former Patriarch Tikhon, I must say that I have not made any application either to the Council of People's Commissars or to the Central Committee of the Russian Comunist Party, aiming at interference in the fate of the above mentioned persons, nor have I any reason to do this. The Church Council has in principle pronounced its decision and also settled the matter of Church and public opinion as to the civil process. But its action cannot pass beyond the limits of the Church reformatory movement, and therefore agitation against the former Patriarch Tikhon especially in the famine districts cannot be a task of the reformatory Church. Having condemned the former Patriarch Tikhon, the reformatory Church considers it superfluous to agitate in favor of, or against, his condemnation.

Metropolitan Antonin

June 6, 1923

104

Anti-Religious Propaganda

(Translation from Moscow *Izvestiia,* No. 125, June 8, 1923)

In view of the fact that certain labor unions have begun to conduct anti-religious propaganda in a rather inconsiderate manner, such as passing resolutions concerning the closing of all the chapels, replacing the usual days of rest by other days (there were even a number of cases of expulsions from unions for getting married in church or for belonging to a sect), the Central Soviet of Trade Unions has sent a circular to all trade unions signed by Comrades Tomskii and Seniushkin which contains the following instructions concerning this question:

The revolutionary trade union movement sees its final aim in freeing the working class from the yoke of capitalism and economic exploitation, poverty, ignorance and slavery, uniting for this purpose all hired labor and defending their economic interest, regardless of their nationality, religion and political platform.

In order to develop the revolutionary class conscience of the workmen and continually raise their cultural level the trade unions are struggling and must struggle in the future against the consequences of mental slavery, darkness, ignorance and superstition, as obstacles to the mental liberation and ideal development of the proletariat. But this struggle should be carried on in the form of conviction, and of stubborn, systematic, cultural educational work, which would inculcate in the masses the materialistic interpretation of history and nature. The question of anti-religious propaganda must be handled very carefully and cautiously so that no negative results shall be attained. The trade unions, adopting a Marxist point of view in their work, must display complete tolerance towards the religious feelings of their members and not expel them from unions or hurt their feelings by inconsiderate and tactless actions.

With regard to the question of anti-religious propaganda, the trade union organizations and the separate trade union workers must know how to connect the propaganda of materialism with the general problem of the trade union movement and the final ideals of the working class. Only by so doing will the trade unions be able to accomplish one of their fundamental tasks, to be a school of Communism without weakening and disorganizing the ranks of trade unions.

105
Peasants Close the Churches

(Translation from Moscow *Pravda,* No. 127, June 10, 1923)

Tiflis, June 8 — Rural meetings in the Sumurzakansk, District of Atkhazun, decided unanimously to close 9 churches.

Kustanai, June 8 — Different associations decided to close 10 churches. The buildings were turned over to schools.

106

Letter of Cardinal Mercier to Mr. Harding, President of the United States, on behalf of Patriarch Tikhon

(Translation)

Archeveché de Malines,
June 12, 1923

Mr. President:

I presume to beg of Your Excellency a humanitarian intervention. I am addressing the same message to His Majesty the King of England.

It appears that Soviets are preparing a new outrage. A council, which is not qualified to speak in the name of the Orthodox Church, has pronounced the deposition of the Venerable Patriarch Tikhon, whose crime is his constancy in duty, and his fidelity to his religious mission at the head of the Orthodox Church of Russia.

The aim of this impious verdict is transparent; the members of the Council have wished to make it easy for the Soviets to condemn to death a leader whom the people venerate.

Out of respect for civilization, out of gratitude to the unhappy people, who were our allies, out of pity for their distress, prevent, we entreat you, this new assassination.

If, unfortunately, your intervention should not save the life of the Patriarch, it would nonetheless be an authorized, public reprobation of the hypocrisy, of the injustice, of the cruelty — a powerful consolation for the moral and religious conscience of humanity.

Your very humble and very devoted servant
Card. Mercier, Arch. de Malines

107

Peasants Against the Clergy

(Translation from Moscow Izvestiia, No. 128, June 12, 1923)

Kustanai, June 9 — The population of the village Kopiginskaia has changed the church into a school, and the priest was ordered to quit the village in five days. In the village Aleksandrovskoie the money received from the sale of the church objects was used for the repair of the school and for the fund of mutual aid.

Zlatoust, June 10 — In many villages the peasants are taking off the church bells and selling them, using the money for the improvement of agriculture and the support of schools.

108
Proclamation to All Moslems in the World

(Condensed translation from Moscow *Izvestiia*, No. 128, June 12, 1923)

The Russian Administration for Religious Affairs of Russian Moslems declared to all the Moslems of the world:

The British Government, the oppressor of Islam, has started nefarious work against the Soviet Government, the protector of the oppressed, including Turkey. England is making preparations for armed intervention against the Soviets. The Russian Moslems have read with great agitation the British note to the Soviet Government. The oppressor of Islam, the British Government, is accusing the Soviet Government of persecuting religion because of the trial of the Orthodox clergy and Patriarch Tikhon for resisting the confiscation of church valuables for the needs of the starving people.

The Administration of Religious Affairrs considers the action taken by the Soviet Government correct. The Administration also considers the separation of the Church from the State to be just because the Orthodox Church during the old regime was the ruling one, and the others were oppressed. All religions, except the Greek Orthodox, were very much oppressed. With the institution of the Soviet Government the support of one religion to the detriment of another disappeared. The faith of Islam received freedom. The Administration of Religious Affairs announces to the whole Moslem world that it considers the accusation of the Soviets by the British Government false. The Soviet Government has always shown its care for the needy Moslem people. The representatives of the Famine Relief Commission, whom the Administration of Religious Affairs has been sending to different places, has never had any difficulties with the Soviet Authorities. Turkey, which wanted to lend a helping hand to the starving Moslems, was prevented from doing so by England, because it hates the Moslems. Tagir Iliasov, who was to travel to Cairo, was not let through. The representative of the Famine Relief Committee, who was to go to Turkey, was maltreated and returned. The rapacious government of England, having robbed Turkey of its holy places, has taken them under its control and supervision, and after having armed the hangmen of Greece, it instigated them to attack Turkey in order to deprive the later of its territories. But by the grace of God and by the assistance of the Soviet Government the heroic Turks have repulsed their enemies. At present our co-religionists in India and Arabia are oppressed by England and many of them are suffering in prisons. We Moslems have been sending our prayers to God to give the victory to Turkey and to drive out the Greeks from Turkish territories. Turkey gained the victory. One of the reasons was the support of Turkey by the Soviet Government. The Moslems of the whole world must not forget this and must thank the Soviet Government.

We, the Moslems of Russia, consider the Soviet Government the protector of the oppressed and declare to the 400 million Moslems of the world the necessity of full support of the Soviet regime.

President of the Central Administration of Religious Affairs of Moslems in European Russia and Siberia "Kazi" Riasaidin Rakhertdinov.

Members: "Kazi" Kashafutdin Tarzhimanov, "Kazi" M. Sabir Khasanov, "Kazi" Mukhliss Bubi.

May 23, 1923

109
Memorandum of Conversation with Belgian Ambassador Concerning the Letter of Protest from Cardinal Mercier on Behalf of Patriarch Tikhon

(Department of State: The Undersecretary)

June 13, 1923

The Belgian Ambassador called with a message from Cardinal Mercier to the Secretary of State and to the President, asking whether the United States Government would not protest against the reported execution of Tikhon, Patriarch of the Russian Church. In reply to my inquiry, he did not know whether the Belgian Government had taken any such step. I said that our information was that the execution was being postponed continually, and the time, therefore, did not seem ripe for any such protest. I gave him the impression that I was not particularly favorably inclined towards such action on our part.

The Ambassador said that he would call upon the Secretary of State tomorrow (Thursday) and hoped that he might receive a reply.

W.P.

110
Commentaries of the U.S. Legation in Riga on the
Legal Status of Religion in Russia

Riga, Latvia, June 14, 1923

No. 952

The Secretary of State, Washington.

Sir:

I have the honor to report that there has been important recent Soviet Russian legislation in regard to the legal position of religious bodies in Russia. It would seem to be opportune therefore to review the entire subject.

The decree on the separation of Church and State and Church and School, published in the official *Izvestiia*, No. 15, January 23, 1918, is doubtless known to the Department in its main provisions, but a careful translation is attached. In addition to secularizing birth, marriage and death registers, and all ecclesiastical real property, this decree forbade any collections of money or property for religious purposes except voluntary contributions, but guaranteed the free exercise of religious rites as long as the public order was not endangered.

This decree was interpreted by an instruction of the Commissariat of Justice, published in *Izvestiia*, No. 186, of August 30, 1918.

All bodies pursuing religious aims, whether openly or under the guise of charity or otherwise, were declared subject to the decree. They were deprived of the rights of juridical persons, but collections for the payment of current expenses and the acquisition of ritual requirements were permitted. Provision was made for the immediate transfer of all ecclesiastical property, but Church edifices and ritual requirements could be loaned free of charge for religious use, under an agreement to be signed by adherents of a religious cult and the Soviet authorities.

The erection of new Church edifices was permitted under the general building regulations, but the new edifices must be State property and manged in the same way as previously existing edifices. Religious processions and ceremonies in public streets were tolerated only when special permission was obtained.

Religious instruction in schools of any kind, except purely theological establishments, was forbidden.

This instruction had a form of agreement as annex.

There followed the publication in the *Izvestiia*, No. 180 of August 12, 1922, of a decree in regard to the registration of association not for profit, including all religious bodies, after confirmation of the articles of incorporation submitted by them.

The Criminal Code contained a chapter directly applicable to offenses against the decrees and instructions on the separation of Church and State. Paragraph 121, forbidding religious instruction to children and minors in schools of any kind, was cited in the trial of the Roman Catholic prelates. Paragraph 123 is interesting, forbidding the assumption of the rights of a juridical person or any administrative, judicial or other official functions by religious bodies. Paragraph 125 forbids the hindering of the performance of religious rites which do not disturb the public peace.

Certain other offenses of a graver, political, nature, were however brought under the provisions of other parts of the Criminal Code. Among these, though it does not directly allude to ecclesiastical matters, was paragraph 57, which imposes the death penalty in certain cases. This paragraph also was cited against the Roman Catholic prelates.

We have now reached the most recent ecclesiastical legislation, following the Church Council at Moscow. This is a revision of registration legislation applicable to religious bodies. It is provided that houses of worship may be secured either under the instruction of the Commissariat of Justice, already cited, or under the general registration provision, and [the legislation] proceeds to define the mode of registration in the latter case.

In the application for registration information must be given *inter alia* as to the social standing of the applicants, their social and official position since 1914, the class to which they belonged before the revolution, their financial standing and the date of their adhesion to the cult. A list of members of the association and of the executive committee is also required, as well as a list of priests, preachers and bishops and other responsible workers. Registration will be refused to less than 50 local inhabitants of good standing. Religious societies which are not registered within three months will be closed.

Provincial and All-Russian congresses of religious societies are permitted to elect executive organs, but they are subjected to the same restrictions as the individual societies.

The legislation in regard to the convocation of congresses and conferences, including religious congresses, is found in Paragraph 477, No. 40, of the Collection of Decrees and Orders of the Workmen-Peasant Government, of June 15, 1922. The permission in each case of the secular authorities is required. The Commissariat of Internal Affairs was directed at the same time to take steps looking to the registration of all organizations, including religious bodies, to dissolve those not properly registered, and not to permit the formation of new organizations without registration. Paragraph 624 of the same issue contained detailed instructions in regard to the enforcement of paragraph 477.

The form of articles of incorporation annexed to enclosure 5 was replaced by an instruction of the Commissariat of Justice, published in *Izvestiia*, No.

102 of May 10, 1923. This instruction introduces important changes, which substantially affect the right previously accorded to religious bodies. Admission to membership shall be by a majority of votes of the members in open ballot. Expulsion shall be by a two-thirds majority of actually enrolled members. The list of members is submitted to the secular authorities annually. All questions raised shall be settled by simple majority in open ballot, and meetings shall be open, with specified exceptions. The articles may be changed by general meeting when proposed by two-thirds of its members, or on proposal of the secular authorities.

The religious associations so registered are thus placed under rules similar to those of a social or political club. There is no provision for the exercise of disciplinary functions by the heads of the association, which indeed seems to be directly forbidden by the Criminal Code.

On the other hand, the Russian Communist Party carefully restricts admission to its membership, and expulsions are ordered by the Central Control Commission, which, with the Central Executive Committee, possesses plenary disciplinary power.

It remains to be seen whether the Soviet authorities will not go farther in the future and make this mode of incorporation, registration and management of religious bodies exclusive. In this case all religious bodies would have the most democratic character, and, in the present state of Russia, they would be exposed to innovations at any moment.

As matters stand, the Soviets are dealing mainly with the newly established machinery of control of the Russian Orthodox Church, and I have been unable to discover in the Soviet press any traces of the recognition of more democratic religious bodies, except the so-called Labor Church and the various new branches of the Orthodox Church; and so far it has not appeared whether any of them, or any of the non-conformist sects have been registered or have made contracts with the Soviet authorities for the use of Church edifices and ritual property. As long as the control of the Orthodox Church machinery gives satisfactory results, its hierarchy may be encouraged and strengthened. If the contrary should at any time appear, the Soviets would be free to consider the thorough democratization or sovietization of the Orthodox Church by depriving the hierarchy of all influence on the parishes and by securing control of the parishes through pretended believers, whose admission they could enforce with the police power.

The legislation in regard to the registration and management of religious bodies is not free from obscurity and confusion, and possibly inconsistency. The authority con ferred on the Commissariat of Internal Affairs by Paragraph 477, No. 40, of Collection of Decrees and Orders of June 15, 1922, would appear to be in part conferred on the Commissariat of Justice by the other legislation, as well as by the decree on the organization and competency of the Commissariat of Justice, which was fully summarized in my despatch

No. 455 of February 27, 1923. As was stated in that despatch, this Commissariat has a department or section of religious cults which is authorized to draft instructions and measures of Soviet policy toward religious bodies, and to supervise the execution of decrees in relation to the separation of Church and State and the management of all matters pertaining to religious cults of every description.

Possibly the solution will be found in joint action by the two Commissariats, particularly as respects the convocation of religious congresses and the use of police, including CHEKA, agents in the supervision of religious bodies and in the enforcement of administrative measures.

The directing personnel of the Russian Orthodox Church has been published in the *Izvestiia*.

Further references to Patriarch Tikhon and his adherents among the Orthodox clergy are enclosed.

Hospital chapels are being closed by general order.

Traces of anti-religious propaganda have become less noticeable in the press, but it is known that large numbers of Communist Youth have been sent to the provinces to see what can be done under the propaganda rules of the Moscow Committee of the Russian Communist Party, recently transmitted to the Department. For quite a long time there have been no notices dated from specific villages and signed by a real name. It is believed that anti-religious propagandists and chroniclers have been maltreated and threatened in many places. It is reported by a recent visitor to Russia that at least one has been killed. An example of an obviously anonymous effort in regard to alleged successful propaganda in an unnamed village is attached as a curiosity. It is of course pure fiction. It is interesting to note, however, that the atheistic champion is quoted as inciting the peasants to drive off the preachers that he had just defeated in an impromptu joint debate. This would have been against the provisions of the Criminal Code, and punishable by imprisonment, but it is hardly probable that the Soviet authorities are exercising much vigilance against infractions of that paragraph of the Code.

I have the honor to be, Sir,
Your obedient servant,
F. W. B. Coleman

111
"Union of Church Regeneration"

(Summary from Moscow *Izvestiia*, No. 133, June 17, 1923)

The All-Russian Union of Church Regeneration has compiled an A.B.C. of Church reforms. The following are some extracts from it:

"The Union aims to put Church life on the basis of Soviet reality."

"The Union sincerely accepts the Soviet system, believing that religious liberty is promoted when the government is not religious, seeing that the non-religious Soviet government has no reason to sovietize the Church, or to exploit religious feelings to establish and confirm its own power; nor is it in the Soviet interest to take an aggressive stand toward the religion actually professed by the majority of the population. The Union accepts the resolution of the Second Church Council concerning its attitude towards the Soviet government, recognizes the latter as the legal authority because it is the government of the laboring masses, bases its activities on the moral dignity of labor, aims at the improvement of the condition of the laboring masses, and the equality of all in the obligation to work and in the right to enjoy average conditions of living. The Union accepts the object of the Revolution, to create not only Platonic but practical fraternity, and regards Socialism as a practical way of attaining such fraternity. Considering, however, that there is a danger of the ocncentration of all forces on one side, i.e., compulsion, oppression, exploitation, the Union believes the preservation of social balance also requires the religious factor.

"The Union approves the decree separating the Church and the State, since it releases the clergy from police duties. The Union will exist on terms equal for all religious societies, permitted by the government. The Union regards it as its duty to accept and execute all the ordinances and decrees of the Soviet government which do not reject religious principles. The Union welcomes the permission of free propaganda. The Union will establish a Committee of Action to increase the moral influence of religion and will combat anti-religious propaganda."

112

"Declaration of Vasilii Belavin (Former Patriarch Tikhon)"

(Translation from Moscow *Rabochaia Moskva*, No. 139, June 27, 1923)

Tikhon confesses his counter-revolutionary activities. He recognizes the just decision of the Supreme Court to try him. Tikhon regrets his activities against the State regime.

On June 16 the former Patriarch Tikhon addressed the following declaration to the Supreme Court:

"I address the following declaration to the Supreme Court of the R.S.F.S.R. and find that it is my pastoral duty to declare the following:

"Having been brought up in a Monarchistic society and being up to my arrest under the influence of anti-Soviet persons, I had indeed *hostile feelings towards the Soviet power,* and those hostile feelings sometimes changed from a passive state into overt acts, such as the declaration in connection with the Brest treaty in 1918, the anathematizing of the authorities in the same year and finally an appeal against the decree ordering the requisition of Church valuables in 1922.

"All my anti-Soviet activities are formulated, with the exeception of a few inaccuracies, in the indictment of the Supreme Court. *Recognizing the correctness of the decision of the Court to bring me to trial,* according to the articles of the Criminal Code enumerated in the indictment, for my anti-Soviet activities, *I regret my actions against the State regime* and request the Court to do away with my detention, i.e., to release me from arrest.

I also declare to the Supreme Court that *I am no longer an enemy of the Soviet power. I am finally and positively breaking all relations with the Monarchistic Whiteguardist counter-revolution at home and abroad.*"
June 16, 1923

Patriarch Tikhon (Vasilii Belavin)

113

Resolution of the Supreme Court Concerning the Release from Custody of Patriarch Tikhon

(Translation from Moscow *Pravda,* No. 141, June 27, 1923)

The Collegium of the Supreme Court for Criminal Cases, consisting of Comrade Karklin, as President, and Comrades Galkin and Chalyshev, as members, has on June 25, 1923, resolved as follows: To accede to the request of citizen Belavin, and, in accordance with Articles 161 and 242 of the Code of Criminal Procedure, to discontinue the measure of dentention applied in respect of him, and to release him from custody.

114

Court Trials of Shipkov, Chernikov and Korostelev

(Summary from Moscow *Pravda,* No. 142, June 28, 1923)

There was a hearing on June 26 of the case of the pastor of the Church of Nikita the Martyr, Peter Shipkov; the warden of the same church, Chernikov; and an employee of the Moscow Provincial Court, William Korostelev. This case, however, has lost its interest after the publication of the last letter of Ex-Patriarch Tikhon, now Vasilii Belavin, in which he renounced his errors and has taken the part of the Soviet Government.

Nevertheless, in view of some very characteristic facts, this case must be mentioned. Shipkov is the son of a shopkeeper, was several years at the university, but entered into business before finishing it. Four years ago, at the time when the Soviet Government restricted most energetically private business, Shipkov left his business and embraced the clerical profession. Having finished a short-term clerical course, he soon received a post as pastor.

As for Chernikov he was a workman in the timber trade, but had entered already in 1904 into the Moscow police, where he reached the rank of inspector. After a few years of "faithful service to the tsar and to the country," he was nominated commissionary of rural police, where he distinguished himself in prosecution of the criminal element and was rewarded with the order of Stanislav and pensioned shortly before the outbreak of the revolution as Collegiate Councillor.

The defendants are accused of having decided at a church meeting soon after February 26 of last year, i.e., after the publication of the decree concerning the confiscation of church valuables, not to submit to this decree, making themselves guilty of crimes named in Article 69, part 3, and Article 86, part 2, of the Criminal Code.

Both the incriminated persons behaved in the court as only mean creatures of the tsar could: falsehood, and skill, unscrupulously used, were their weapons. Shipkkov pretends to have invited the parish to collaborate in the confiscation of the Church valuables, but instead of the decree of the Soviet government ordering the confiscation of the Church valuables, read the proclamation of Patriarch Tikhon. Later on he delivered these valuables, but required the mention in the protocol that these valuables were not delivered but confiscated.

Chernikov, also, denied the most evident facts.

The falsehood of these two men provoked disgust in the audience.

The Soviet Government does not want to avenge crimes. It wants only to prevent their repetition. Considering, besides, its strength, in spite of the resistance and the intrigues of the counter-revolutionary parties, the judge found it possible to pronounce a mild verdict, condemning the inculpated only to one year's imprisonment with strict isolation. On application for amnesty, they were released at once.

115
"Unmasked Hypocrites"

(Summary from Moscow *Izvestiia*, No. 142, June 28, 1923)

The alleged letter of "Citizen Belavin" (ex-Patriarch Tikhon) to the

Supreme Tribunal of the Republic is "very significant," and justifies a number of "valuable deductions." That Patriarch Tikhon was counter-revolutionary was known long ago, but now we have it on his own confession. The author emphasizes with particular relish the passage of the letter in which Tikhon is represented to state that he "was brought up in monarchist surroundings" and that "up to his very arrest he was under the influence of anti-Soviet persons." From the letter the author of the article makes the deduction that the Patriarch had been working in the interest of manorial landlords and capitalists abroad, and that his aim had been to restore the old regime in Russia. Thus the "confession" of Tikhon has revealed the "true political meaning" of the campaign led by the capitalists and their henchmen against Soviet Russia, and of their outcries against the alleged "religious persecutions" in Soviet Russia.

The article continues literally:

"And so, although late, Tikhon has repented. He has arrived at this conclusion after a prolonged struggle against the Soviet power, and after he had realized that his entire policy had been a failure, that it not only has not led to victory, but, on the contrary, to contention and schism within the Church. And then he publicly expressed his repentance. In view of this the Soviet power found it possible to comply with Tikhon's request and to release him from prison. The Soviet power has shown magnanimity, and has proved by this act that in its attitude towards Tikhon it was by no means guided by sentiments of vindictiveness, or by a desire to persecute the Church and individual representatives of the clergy, as such. The entire bourgeois press has taken up the defence of Tikhon as of an innocent person unjustly persecuted by the Soviet press. Now, Tikhon himself confesses that he is guilty, and thereby places his gratuitous defenders and apologists in the most silly and ridiculous position. Now, after Tikhon's open confession, it is clear to all and everybody that all the talk about persecution of religion was pure nonsense and impudent calumny, emanating from the enemies of the working classes, and that, in fighting the whiteguard clique of counter-revolutionary clergy, the Soviet power pursued its one and only task: to fortify the position conquered by the workmen-peasant revolution, and nothing else."

116
Attitude of Pro-Soviet Church Authorities

(Summary from Moscow *Izvestiia*, No. 142, June 28, 1923)

Metropolitan Antonin is of the opinion that the Patriarch should now also recognize that the verdict of the recent Church Council was right and just. Krasnitskii thinks that from a legal and formal point of view this repentance does not rehabilitate Tikhon, nor restore him in his rights. From a political point of view the "repentance" is very important as an answer to the "insinuations" of the foreign press concerning Church persecution in Soviet Russia. From a Church point of view Krasnitskii expects that Patriarch Tikhon will now also show his contrition to the Church. If so, it is possible that he will be admitted again as a Church dignitary. Krasnitskii characterizes the Living Church movement as one which has "raised the lower Church strata" and as a struggle between the "believing toilers and the believing owners."

V. N. Lvov, Procurator of the Holy Synod at the time of the Provisional Government, says: "Knowing, as I do, Tikhon's character, I am convinced that he has written his letter sincerely, and that the contents of the letter are true." Lvov also trusts that Tikhon's "evolution" will not stop short at its present stage, but that he will "join the reformist movement."

A. V. Galkin, member of the Presidium of the Supreme Court, by resolution of which the Patriarch was released from prison, says that Tikhon was retained in custody on account of his "never ceasing counter-revolutionary activity." In view of his protests of loyalty he has now been released. "The resolution of the Supreme Court does not, of course, alter anything in the pending criminal case against Tikhon, the hearing of which will commence in due time."

117

Ancient Apostolic Church against Patriarch Tikhon

(Summary from Moscow *Izvestiia*, No. 143, June 29, 1923)

In an interview A. J. Novikov, Director of Affairs of the All-Russian Church Council and Representative of the Union of Congregations of the Ancient Apostolic Church, says: "Knowing Tikhon as a believer, we were convinced that the sentiment of Christian duty would gain the upper hand over his political errors." Novikov emphasizes that the Patriarch was deposed "not for political reasons," but for "crimes of a Church character." The Church Council not only had the right, but was in duty bound to do as it did. In the opinion of the Ancient Apostolic Church, Tikhon should, in addition to his letter to the political authorities, now "give expression to his contrition, in public, before the Orthodox people, and ask forgiveness." "For us there is no Patriarch Tikhon, there is only Citizen Vasilii Belavin."

118
Interview with Patriarch Tikhon

(Summary from Moscow *Pravda* and *Izvestiia*, No. 143, June 29, 1923)

In an interview which a correspondent of the ROSTA (Russian Telegraph Agency) is supposed to have had with Patriarch Tikhon, the latter is supposed to have said as regards his life in prison, that he had been "under no restrictions." The rooms in which he lived in prison were "comfortable." When not engaged in prayer, Tikhon was reading; "the examining magistrate brought me newspapers." "In the foreign press many absurdities were written about me: thus was alleged that I had been tortured in the electric chair. This, of course, is nonsense." In the further course of the interview Tikhon is made to say: "I have entirely adopted the Soviet platform." As regards the activity of Orthodox Russian ecclesiastics abroad, the Partiarch is alleged to have said: "I will request them to stop their counter-revolutionary work as it is not in conformity with their clerical dignity. I hope they will obey, for they still recognize me . . . . well, and if they don't, I will hand them over to the Church Tribunal." The Patriarch does not recognize his deposition by the recent Church Council. "The Council tried me for counter-revolution, which it had no right to do; only the Soviet power can try me for counter-revolution, and it will do so." Further the Patriarch is made to adduce formal grounds why the Church Council could not judge him. Generally speaking, the account emphasizes the Patriarch's negative attitude towards the Church Council and the whole "Living Church." The only resolution of the Council which Tikhon recognizes is the introduction of the Gregorian Calendar.

119
Church Bells for Aviation

(Translation from Moscow *Izvestiia*, No. 143, June 29, 1923)

The branch of the Society of Volunteer Air Fleet (ODVF) at the Lomonossov Institute in Moscow handed to the Presidium of the Society

of Volunteer Air Fleet 4 Church bells from the chapel of the School for
the benefit of aviation.

120
"The Hiss of the Snake"

(Summary from Moscow *Izvestiia*, No. 144, June 30, 1923)

"Calumny and insinuation are the weapon of the weak," Steklov began
his editorial, the "weak" in this case being counter-revolution "beaten in
open fight." Already White-Guard calumny and slander is starting its game
around the release from prison of the ex-Patriarch Tikhon." Steklov has
received an anonymous letter in which a "Black-hundred Man" intimates that
the letter purporting to come from Tikhon was "fabricated by the Bolsheviks
themselves," and secondly, that Tikhon was released "for fear of England,"
Curzon having intervened in favor of the Patriarch, with the result that the
Soviet power had to give in. Steklov would rather pay no attention to the
"gossip of an anonymous idiot," but, seeing that there are "sufficient old
women, nervous and hysterical females who would believe every nonsense,
one must willy-nilly dwell at some length on this matter." Steklov then
mentions newspapers outside of Russia, among them the *Daily Telegraph*
which asserts that Tikhon's repentance was "extorted". He further refers to
"malicious misinterpretation" of the fact that foodstuffs in Moscow have
recently risen in price, and that even the supply has been "temporarily"
reduced. White-Guard "calumny" explains this as a consequence of the
Soviet Government's having given way to the English demands, having
even concluded with Great Britain a secret agreement, according to which
Soviet Russia undertakes to pay the debts of Imperial Russia; the grain
exported from Russia is the first instalment in payment of these debts, and
hence the dearth of foodstuffs in Russia. Steklov admits the dearth, but says
that it has nothing to do with England, being "due to natural causes," and
that the Soviet Government is "taking measures" to stop the further rise of
prices. As to the "web of sticky lie and slander" woven around this affair by
White-Guard spite and rancour, Steklov asserts that "every Soviet citizen who
is in his sound mind knows well that Curzon's onslaught upon us ended in
failure, and that the Soviet Republic has repulsed this attempt on the part
of British imperialism." No agreements whatever, whether secret or otherwise, have been concluded with Britain. These malicious rumors must be
contended with; not only by repressive measures, but by explaining to the
people the "absurdity" of them: all "class-conscious" Soviet citizens must

"spread around them sound views," denouncing the lies of the White-Guardists.

121

Commentary of the U.S. Legation in Riga Concerning the Confession of Patriarch Tikhon

July 1, 1923

The Secretary of State,
Washington.

Sir:

I have the honor to forward a translation of the text of a declaration said to have been signed by Patriarch Tikhon, as published in all the Moscow newspapers of June 27. This declaration admits hostility to the Soviet regime and a number of overt acts directed against it; expresses regret and admits the right of the authorities to bring him to trial; declares the Patriarch has turned his back once for all on all counter-revolutionary organizations and aims, and requests release from confinement. The prayer was granted [see No. 113].

The declaration to which the signature of the Patriarch was reported to have been attached cannot be rejected on purely internal evidence. It has none of the ear-marks of ecclesiastical style, but may have been agreed upon between the prisoner and the legal representative of the Soviet authorities.

The present "Metropolitan" Antonin seems to have found it advisable to dissociate himself from the more active campaign against Patriarch Tikhon, issuing a statement ten days before the publication of the alleged recantation that he and the Church Administration had no interest in the trial of the citizen Vasilii Belavin (ex-Patriarch Tikhon) [see No. 104].

The Moscow Diocesan clergy, however, at the same time passed a series of resolutions fully accepting the social and political programme of the Soviets, and pledged themselves to defend the justice of world-wide social revolution and to assist the Soviet authorities in their domestic policies. Steps were taken at the same time to direct the registration of religious associations, and a commission was appointed to work out a draft of normal regulations of Orthodox associations, or parishes. It would appear thus that the Moscow Diocesan clergy do not desire to accept the regulations of the Commissariat of Justice, which have been communicated to the Department, without offering amendments [see No. 102].

One of the Orthodox bodies that participated in the late ecclesiastical council, the Union of Regeneration of the Church, has issued a rather confused declaration of principles. It accepts, with reservations, the Soviet control of the Church and the principles of the social revolution. It regards the purely secular State as best adapted to assure religious equality and religious freedom; but it warns the Soviet authorities that political and economic power must be balanced by moral authority. While welcoming freedom of religious discussion, it will not submit to political orders directed against religion itself; and it will meet anti-religious propaganda by organizing a missionary corps [see No. 112].

The Communist Soviet authorities have long since realized the folly of their headlong attack on all forms of religion, and they have repeatedly tried to moderate the ardor of the hooligan League of Communist Youth, as the Department has been informed. A further declaration of policy is attached. The Central Soviet of Trade Unions has issued a circular instruction in which atheism is professed as a final goal, but freedom to profess any religious faith and practice any religious cult is safeguarded for the present. Labor unions may not expel or harass members because they are religiously backward, but must exercise tolerance, tact and discretion. At the same time a judicious anti-religious propaganda is commended. It is obvious of course that genuine religious feeling and leadership in a union are incompatible, and this is expressed elsewhere, but not in this instruction [see Nos. 105, 106].

Atheism was proclaimed as an integral part of the Communist creed at the session of the Executive Committee of the Communist International.

The abolition of churches continues to be pressed by local representatives of the Soviets.

A proclamation to the Moslems of the World has been issued in the name of the Soviet Administration of Moslem Affairs, supporting the Soviet authorities in the Anglo-Russian conflict.

I have the honor to be, Sir,
Your obedient servant,
F. W. B. Coleman

122

Additional Instruction Concerning the Implementation of the Decree on the Separation of Church and State

(Translation from Moscow *Izvestiia*, No. 145, July 1, 1923)

In view of all sorts of deviations from the decree concerning Separation of Church and State in the provinces, the Commissariat of Justice, jointly with the Commissariat of Internal Affairs, has issued an instruction to all Provincial Executive Committees, explaining that the decree is a fundamental law. Religious bodies, although classified as private corporations, are not entitled to own property, nor have they the rights of juridical persons. Groups of citizens which have been granted the uses of certain buildings for purposes of religious worship free of charge, shall thereby be held to organize themselves as religious bodies.

Cases of infraction of agreements concerning the closing of churches and places of worship of any religious creed, shall be settled by resolutions of the presidia of Provincial Executive Committees. In closing any churches, the presidia of Provincial Executive Committees shall take into consideration the religious interests of believers, their customs and habits, also statistical data relating to the number of the population using the given church, capacity of churches in the vicinity, etc.

The celebration of religious rites, and the delivery of sermons, so far as they constitute an essential part of Divine service, shall be admitted without first being submitted for approval to the Censor, provided their contents are solely and exclusively of a religious character. Equal freedom is granted for the conduct of prayer meetings, and meetings in connection with the administration of property required for ritual use, and with the maintenance of the church.

The spread and the propaganda of bourgeois-anarchistic and "anti-State" teachings and theories under the guise of religious worship, hostile to the Soviet regime, shall be considered indictable and criminal on general lines.

No religious organization shall have the right to interfere, on the pretence of superiority, with the activity of another religious organization against the will of the latter.

It shall be prohibited to all State institutions to support or favor, by administrative interference, any religious creed to the detriment of another.

In accordance with the agreement concerning the use of a church building free of charge, the respective group of believers shall be liable for the maintenance and the integrity of the national property entrusted to it, and shall also be responsible for the sermons delivered in the given church. Religious central organizations and religious congresses cannot own any ritual property or obtain such property on the basis of agreements, nor can they conclude any agreements or transactions relating to property, or organize compulsory collections of money. Servants of religious cults (priests) shall be subject to taxation on identical lines as all other citizens, including income and property tax. They shall, however, be exempt from payment of the industrial tax.

In view of the municipalization of houses belonging to churches, servants of religious cults shall be given corresponding housing accomodation by the local housing sections, on general lines. They may be ejected from such dwellings only by decree of the Soviet of Commissars. In the event of their tilling the soil with their own hands, servants of religious cults and the members of their families shall be allotted land, or use such lands as may be in their actual possession, on general lines, in accordance with the Code of Land Laws. The decree of the Soviet of Commissars dated January 21, 1921 shall remain in force, and servants of religious cults may hold offices as mentioned in the said decree in all Commissariats, with the exception of the Commissariats of Food, of Justice, of Agriculture, of Education, the Workman-Peasant Inspection, and the Administrative Department of the Commissariat of Internal Affairs: in this connection the exercise of religious rights shall not be held to imply "occupying two situations," if such activity does not take place during hours when attention to official business is required, and if the given person draws no special remuneration, in kind or in money, from the believers for his services.

123

Retirement of Metropolitan Antonin

(Translation from Moscow *Izvestiia,* No. 145, July 1, 1923)

The Supreme Church Council has decided to dispense with the services of the Moscow Metropolitan Antonin. In this connection the Odessa Metropolitan Evdokim, formerly (Orthodox) Archbishop of New York, has been invited to the Supreme Church Council, over which he is to preside.

124

Patriarch Tikhon at the Monastery of Our Lady of the Don

(Summary from Moscow *Izvestiia,* No. 146, June 3, 1923)

On Sunday, July 1, Tikhon conducted Divine service in the Church of the Monastery of Our Lady of the Don. In his sermon he spoke of the "necessity of the Church giving up politics entirely, calling it a grave error on the part of churchmen that they have not refrained from politics before. "Now I am released from prison and have once more received the right to hold Divine service. The task of the Church is to spread the teachings of Christ, the gospel of peace for the whole world, brotherhood, and all-conquering love. This is what the ocean of humanity, stirred up by passions, particularly needs at present. And the Church must attend to this, its principal task." Speaking of the recent Church Council Tikhon insisted that it was unlawful, particularly so its decision concerning the deposition of the patriarch. Speaking on the resolution of the Council, permitting bishops to marry, Tikhon "passed some ironical remarks." In conclusion, he expressed his satisfaction that so large a congregation had gathered for his service. In the Church were present "representatives of several foreign missions and foreign correspondents who took photographs . . . saying that they were intended for foreign illustrated papers." "A young priest, conversant with foreign languages, gave them the necessary explanations." "Tikhon promised to receive the foreign correspondents in audience." The author of the account then proceeds to reproduce some of the comments and remarks overhead in the crowd. Some were of the opinion that Tikhon's step was a "great and irreparable mistake." Fault was also found with Tikhon because in his declaration he had used the new orthography. The copy of the *Izvestiia* containing a fascimile of Tikhon's declaration passed from hand to hand, but still there were people who denied that Tikhon had written it. But the majority of those present considered the declaration a "wise and timely step." "Now there is no more discord between the people and the Church" . . . "You will see, the Soviet authorities will alter entirely their attitude towards the Church as soon as they see that the Church is no longer counter-revolutionary" . . . are sentences supposed to be overheard in the crowd. Of one professor of theology, it was reported that, on reading the declaration of Tikhon, he broke out in tears and said: "All is finished now." The article further emphasizes the Patriarch's hostile attitude towards the Living Church. It is also mentioned that Tikhon intends shortly to address a communication to the believers, in which he will at greater length expound his views already expressed in his declaration to the Supreme Court.

125
Patriarch Tikhon's Open Letter

(Summary from Moscow *Izvestiia*, No. 147, July 4, 1923)

The paper reproduces what purports to be a "Communication" addressed by Patriarch Tikhon to all bishops, clergymen, and believers of the Russian Orthodox Church.

In this document Tikhon is made to point out, first of all, that his deposition by the recent Church Council was illegal. According to canonical rules he had to be summoned thrice before his trial could commence, but such summons never did take place. As regards to accusations of counter-revolution brought against him, the document explains: "I never pretended to be so ardent an adherent of the Soviet power as the Church revivalists now ruling the Supreme Church Soviet represented themselves to be, but neither was I, on the other hand, such an enemy of the Soviet power as they are trying to make me out." If he had levelled any attacks, against the Soviet power, "this was due to my bringing-up" and the general bias prevailing at that Council [Council of 1917]. In the meantime things have changed, and Tikhon had even to apply to the Soviet power for protection of the Russian Orthodox inhabitants of Polish provinces. Already in 1919 he endeavoured to "draw a line between the Church on the one hand, and 'Tsarism' and intervention on the other." Further, when the Council at Sremski Karlovtsi in January, 1921, adopted a resolution in favor of the restoration of the Romanov dynasty, "we considered this resolution out of place." From this can be seen that "I am not such an enemy of the Soviet power and such a counter-revolutionary as the Council was trying to make me out." The document proceeds to deal with the recent Church Council at some length: of the 67 bishops present only 10 or 15 were known to Tikhon. Where were the others? This shows tht they had been unlawfully replaced. Revivalism is called in the "Communication" a "half-truth, lukewarm, liberalizing Christianity." What occupies the revivalists themselves? "Profit and gain, ecclesiastical honors, and the like." Moreover, they admit marriage of bishops, and sanction second marriages of clergymen. The only measure the document approves is the introduction of the Gregorian Calendar. But Tikhon himself is said to have suggested this innovation to the Patriarch of Constantinople in 1919.

As regards Tikhon's attitude towards the Soviet power, the document reads literally as follows: "The crime of which I plead guilty is in reality to be put down to those surroundings which were always goading me, the head of the Orthodox Church, in some way or another, into rebellion against the Soviet power. I now declare emphatically that henceforth all their endeavors will be in vain, for I most deliberately condemn any attempts whatever upon the integrity of the Soviet power, from whatever quarters they may come. Let all monarchists and White-Guard, in the interior as well as abroad, know that I am no enemy of the Soviet power. I have realized the loathsomeness of the lies and slander that are poured out upon the Soviet power by its enemies at home and abroad, which are spread by them throughout the world by word of mouth, as well as in print. They have not even refrained from dragging my person into it; thus the newspaper *Novoie Vremia,* in its issue No. 606 dated (Belgrad) May 5, had a report in which it was asserted that I had been tortured in the CHEKA by the application of electricity. I declare that this is an abominable lie, and the usual slander against the Soviet power.

The God of Peace and Love be with you."

Tikhon

The Monastery of Our Lady of the Don
June 28, 1923

126

The Living Church and Apostolic Church Against Tikhon

(Summary from Moscow *Izvestiia*, No. 147, July 4, 1923)

The revivalists are very active. On June 29 a meeting of revivalist laity took place under the chairmanship of the Metropolitan Antonin, at which a resolution was adopted to the effect that Tikhon's repentance in words was of no use, unless he suited his action to his words by "joining the Soviet, that is the recognized type of Church, sanctioned by the Government." If prior to this he conducts Divine service this will be a "political error," "absence of tact in regard to the Government," also "public adventurism," as well as "civic duplicity and a temptation of public mindedness."

On July 2 the "Living Church" and the "Apostolic Church" central committees held a combined meeting at which it was resolved to form a "united front," refraining from mutual disputes and controversies, and supporting one another by every means against the "politically and ecclesiastically counter-revolutionary" Tikhon movement.

127

A Communist Party Commentary on the Church

(Summary from Moscow *Izvestiia*, No. 147, July 4, 1923, from the article by A. J. Mezhov)

"THE DEAD"

The author undertakes to prove that Church has ever been trying to influence political life and, when necessary, has adapted itself, temporarily, to the political exigencies of the moment. Referring to the literary works of Herzen, to the various French revolutions, to Voltaire and Rousseau, the author first takes up the Catholic Church. In France, the Catholic Church stands at the head of the "bourgeois-landlord reaction;" and the same is the case in Germany, England, America, Italy, and so forth. "Nothing is new under the moon," and now the Orthodox Church in Russia is emulating the example set by the Jesuits. In Russia, of course, the Church cannot apply the same methods as it does in other countries, and so it adapts itself to the new conditions. Not only the "Living Church" is doing this, but even the ex-Patriarch Tikhon now says that the task of the Church is to spread the teachings of Christ concerning peace for the whole world, brotherhood, and all conquering love. The author of the article believes that many of the Church people, more particularly those belonging to the "Living Church," are sincere, but on the whole the note struck is false: "the Church cannot be the tool of freedom and liberty." All these declarations show clearly that their sole intention is to truckle to the Soviet power. This could be seen from the remarks made by one of Tikhon's followers, who hoped the Soviet authorities "would change entirely their attitude towards the Church, if they saw that the Church had ceased to be counter-revolutionary." From the above remark, by the way, the inference could be drawn that the Soviet power persecuted the Church as such. "This has never been the case." "With the Church as such the Soviet State has never contended, nor will it ever do so." But whenever individual representatives of the Church transgressed the laws of the State and supported counter-revolution, the State adopted repressive measures against them, as it did against all other citizens guilty of similar offences. In Church matters the State takes up a neutral position. "But the Communist Party is not neutral. All its views are diametrically opposed to the views and the aims of the Church. The Party will always oppose the influence of the Church (no matter which Church), for that influence . . . bars the road to the emancipation of mankind from the yoke of idols and tyrants, on earth and in heaven, real or imagined. The Church is dead . . . for the vanguard of the world proletariat there can be no neutrality or indifference in the question of religion. The brain and the hearts of the working classes are here at stake; the struggle must be waged, of course, by modern methods, by methods of exhortation, by opposing the results of scientific research to the phantasmagoria of superstition. But this fight must go on — on to ultimate victory."

128
Letter of the Secretary of State, Charles E. Hughes, to Cardinal Mercier Concerning Patriarch Tikhon

July 13, 1923

My dear Cardinal Mercier:

Permit me, in the absence from Washington of the President, to acknowledge the receipt of your letter of June 12, 1923, in reference to Patriarch

Tikhon, and the fear which you entertain that the pronouncement of his deposition by a church council may render more effective such efforts as may be made to bring about his condemnation to death in the Soviet courts.

In reply, my dear Cardinal Mercier, I am happy to say that, according to information which I have recently received, the Patriarch has been released from arrest by the Soviet authorities. Information of a similar tenor was doubtless received by Your Eminence subsequent to the date of your letter now under acknowledgment.

I am, my dear Cardinal Mercier,
Very sincerely yours,
Charles E. Hughes

129
"On the Ecclesiastical Front (1918-1923)"

(A review of the book by P. A. Krasikov, *Izvestiia.* No. 159, July 18, 1923)

This book handles a vital question. The disturbances which shook the Church during the years of revolution have certain social reasons and reflect religious changes in the large masses of believers. Materials concerning the Church are also indispensable to our anti-religious agitators, who have to speak at mass meetings and repulse the efforts of the clergy. The compilation of articles by Krasikov is exactly the stuff for our anti-religious agitators and in general for all interested in Church questions. This book includes all the articles which appeared in the periodical press during the last five years on the subject of the mutual relations between the State and the Church, on the internal struggle between the various religious groups, on the political role of the old Monarchistic Church, on the attitude of the clergy during the famine year, etc. These articles compose a thick volume from which, however, the necessary information can be easily extracted owing to the division of the book into separate chapters.

130
Council of People's Commissars of the U.S.S.R. and the Church Valuables for Re-Evacuation of Refugees from Famine Districts

(Translation from Moscow *Pravda*, No. 162, July 22, 1923)

The Council of People's Commissars of the S.S.S.R. has allotted to the Central Commission for Struggle Against the Consequences of Famine the sum of 2,340,360 rubles out of the funds raised by the sale of Church valuables in order to organize the re-evacuation of refugees from famine districts.

131
Registration of Religious Societies

(Translation from Moscow *Izvestiia*, No. 166, July 26, 1923)

The administrative department of the Moscow Soviet is re-registering all religious societies. The registration proceeds, however, very slowly. Of 500 religious groups which have been previously registered only 20 filed petitions concerning their re-registration.

132
Interview with the Acting President of the Supreme Church Administration, Bishop Georgii Dobronravov, and with Patriarch Tikhon

(Translation from Moscow *Bednota*, No. 1579, July 31, 1923)

THE LIVING CHURCH

The enormous halls of the Holy Trinity Monastery Chapel are gloomy and deserted. Religious pictures are staring from the walls, two or three priests moved about.

I was received by the acting president of the Supreme Church Administration, Bishop Dobronravov, formerly Archpriest and recently consecrated Bishop. He is not a monk, but a married Bishop.

Archbishop Aleksander Vvedenskii has made a tour in the diocese, from which he has just returned (to the South and West). He said that the Tikhonist movement ["Tikhonovchina"] is on the whole blamed for producing perplexity and tending to the destruction of peace and unity in the Church. The speaker also, together with other confreres, has visited the *uyezds* and found that everywhere the actions of Tikhon are considered as incomprehensible and as offending the feelings of the believers, who respect the decision of the Church Council. He said Tikhon was supported only by the "kulaks," rich peasants and merchants, the same "kulaks" who used to sell candles during the Divine services, nothing loath to put their long fingers into the cash boxes. "We, certainly, are not to their taste and our appeal to the toiling masses decidedly does not please them. Our reform movement is based on democratic principles. The "kulaks" of course, are decidedly counter-revolutionaries."

"Our Commission for Struggle against the Consequences of Famine has recently sent lottery tickets to the different places. Of course, wherever such 'kulaks' are at the head of the parish Church Councils, these tickets were not sold but returned for alleged deficiency of financial means in the parishes. We have ordered the expulsion of the Moscow monks as well as the evacuation of the monasteries in the suburbs, because they have nothing to do in the towns. Monasticism, is it not the symbol of labor and prayer? But, what sort of agrigultural occupation is there in the towns? Accustomed to the *dolce far niente* of the monastical life, this, certainly, is not to the taste of the monks.

"As to the question how to struggle against Tikhhon, we have only one possible method—agitation. Archbishop Vvedenskii will begin his lectures about Tikhon next Tuesday, and we are all preaching. The Tikhonist movement has gained ground mainly at Moscow. According to Archbishop Boiarskii who has come from Petrograd, he has there comparatively little support, although the possibility of an outburst in his favor is not excluded. We are in expectation of the imminent arrival of Metropolitan Evdokim, nominated President of the Church Administration in place of Metropolitan Antonin, who was pensioned. It was hard to work with Antonin. On the one hand he was a reformist, on the other hand a monk, and was always going from pillar to post. In addition, his last sermons were too compromising. He had very few followers and even his nearest collaborator and tool, Professor of divinity Bogoliubskii, has abandoned him and gone over to Tikhon.

"We had recently the visit of Nuelson, Bishop of the American Church(!), who told us that America was now extraordinarily interested in the reform movement of our Church. The opening of a theological institute is aimed at in the autumn, in which, in addition to the theological branches, natural and social sciences will be taught, as necessary for any Russian citizen. The American Episcopal Church (!) has promised to furnish part of the necessary financial means. The remainder we expect to be able to collect by holding an 'ecclesiastical week.' [drive]. As a proposed innovation may be mentioned theological instruction corresponding to the indirect American system . . ."

AT PATRIARCH TIKHON'S
(Interview with Patriarch Tikhon)

The Monastery of Our Lady of the Don is one of the most ancient Moscow buildings, encircled by a high wall with turrets and battlements, recalling from a distance an ancient fortress.

Many visitors are waiting in the clean small room provided with ancient furniture, fresh flowers in the windows and on the walls, and crowded with portraits of archbishops. All these visitors are priests come from various districts, deputations of laymen and members of the Living Church. Although early, I had to wait until 15 of my predecessors were received by the Metropolitan [Patriarch]. Crowds of people were still waiting their turn. When introduced to Tikhon, I inquired about his attitude towards the reform Church (Living Church) and the creation of a Church Administration by the New Believers. The Patriarch considers the Living Church as schismatic and will in no case enter into any relation whatever with it. "The Church," he said, "will joyfully accept in its bosom those who repent and acknowledge their fault, but unless they do so, we must consider them as schismatics. The Supreme Church Administration is an usurpation. When I had to go I surrendered to them the administration of the offices and of the affairs until the arrival of the Metropolitan Agafangel. They have usurped the Administration of the Church. I consider all their Church Council decisions, as well as the Church Council itself, decidedly wrong and illegal. According to the decision of the Sixth Ecumenical Church Council, the bishops cannot be married. You know, they have annulled this decision of the Council. The only decision which I approve without reserve is the adoption of the New Style. As regards your inquiries about the leaders of the Living Church, Antonin, Evdokim and Krasnitskii, I can say that I have served together with Antonin, when I was rector of the seminary of Kholm and he was a teacher. It was hard to get on with him. He has a stern character. Besides, they have done away with him, those of the Living Church, dropping him after squeezing him out like a lemon. I have no wish to talk about them, let them say what they want, they cannot stain me. Every day I get news from the provinces relating to the reunion of the Church. The majority of the Moscow Churches have broken off entirely with the Living Church.

"Instead of a synod, we are now organizing a temporary Supreme Church Administration at the Patriarchate. This is an elective organ. I call this administration temporary, because we are compelled to nominate it only for the time being. I shall be the President of it. Two other bishops, one archimandrite, belonging to the monastic clergy, two archpriests, of the white clergy, and laymen will be members of it. Among the latter there will be also workmen. I presume that Archbishop Serafim [of Tver], Metropolitan Tikhon [of Ural] and the administrator of the Moscow Diocese, Bishop Illarion will be members of the council. But in any case this staff must be confirmed by the state authorities. In autumn we will begin with the organization of study in the Moscow Theological Academy, provided of course, there are no objections to it on the part of the Soviet authorities."

In conclusion Tikhon hinted at his trial, which will have to take place, and where he will present himself, and said that he has the intention to convoke an All-Russian Church Council at the beginning of next year. He mentioned besides that the foreign newspapers have much misinformation concerning him, as for instance that he is an American citizen. All these allegations ought, of course, to be considered as nonsense.

133
"Ecclesiastical Disorders: Without Sails or Rudder"
(Vecherniaia Krasnaia Gazeta, July 31, 1923)

The talk of the day in Petrograd circles at present is the "treason" of Archpriest Platonov, the pastor in charge of the St. Andrew's Cathedral, on Vasilevskii Island. Platonov, one of the originators of the Petrograd Church renovation, delivered on July 29th a penitent discourse at the Sunday Service before an audience that overfilled the cathedral. Having related his impressions of his journey through the villages of the Northern District, he pointed out the depression of the village clergy and laymen due to the ecclesiastical disorder, and also to the hostility everywhere to the last Church Conference. Platonov called upon the believers to unite round Tikhon, the only leader of the Orthodox Church, and to reject the Moscow Church Council, also to request the Archbishop of Petrograd, Artemii, to recognize the authority of the ex-Patriarch and thereby to pacify the feud of the parties. It is the opinion of Platonov that now Tikhon will not repeat his former mistakes.

THE WAVERING OF BISHOP ARTEMII

The Archbishop of Petrograd, Artemii, has come to a crossroad. The priest of the Central District, Archbishop Chepurin, upon the insistence of the parishioners, has addressed Artemii a request to permit the usual prayers for Tikhon to be said at the church services. Artemii answered to this in a private letter: "I permit and give my benediction." The eparchial administration was informed of this fact and after a stormy explanation with Boiarskii, the archbishop recanted his "permission and benediction," though that resolution of his had been sent by Chepurin to all the Churches of the Central District.

A SCANDAL AT ST. ISAAKII'S CATHEDRAL

There is a division among the clergy of the Isaakii's Cathedral: the priest Chuev, who has been appointed pastor of the Cathedral, and the keeper of keys Stepanovich, are for the "Living Church," the three remaining priests and the Archdeacon Dmitriev are for Tikhon. On Saturday, at the evening service, Dmitriev publicly prayed for Tikhon, in consequence of which the priest Chuev, being pastor, forbade him to perform church services. The parishioners, having received knowledge of this fact, demanded an explanation from the pastor. Upon the conversation becoming very heated, Chuev had to leave the Cathedral by a back door, accompanied by the shouts of the excited crowd. As a result of this, one half of the parish excommunicates and condemns the other.

IN THE PETROGRAD CATHEDRALS

On Sunday, as the representatives of the Tikhonist movement report, there took place at the Ascension Cathedral the delivery of the church, in accordance to the wish of the parishioners, to its former priests, who have deemed it necessary to perform a complete consecration of the church, after the expulsion of the "Living Churchers." A public confession was arranged, during which the priests who had previously gone over to the "Living Churchers," publicly repented of their misdeeds. At the end of the service, all believers went to communion and this terminated the transmission of the church from one sect to another.

134
"The Priests' Nakedness"
(*Krasnaia Gazeta,* No. 171 (1621), August 1, 1923)

At present the Orthodox Church is a nasty picture to look at. Not long ago the "shepards of Christian souls" of different degrees were running away from Tikhon, like rats from a sinking ship. They started joining the "Living Church" and its branches. Doubtless among the "Living Churchers" and other renovation groups ("Regeneration," "Ancient Apostolic Church") there were and are sincere priests who were nauseated by the deceits of the Church of the monarchy (only imagine the wax dolls of the "undecaying saints"). They fled from the crimes of the Tikhonist movement against the people and from the priests' "White-guard" activities. But there were also those who under cover of the renovation movement tried to hide from the people's wrath, to extinguish the traces of their crimes, or save their income.

The All-Russian Church Congress, that took place this spring, presented a picture of astonishing unanimity in general; in particular, Tikhon was unanimously degraded from being patriarch and was excommunicated from the Church. Not one voice was heard in his defence. Of course, the crimes of the former patriarch were ponderous, but it is as evident, that the Patriarch's adherents were present and did hold their peace. With them as with all other Tikhonists no tendency for deeds of valour was apparent, which might have made them partake of their leader's fate.

Tikhon has repented his crimes against the people, he has denounced his fighting against the Soviet government. The latter has no more reasons for keeping the former patriarch in custody and he has been set free until the day of his law suit.

The Soviet government does not interfere in ecclesiastical matters so long as the Church does not get mixed up with political strife; therefore Tikhon may celebrate Church services as much as he like; fighting on religious ground — that is his own business. Believers are free to choose any branch, any sect — that is their business. But look and see what is going on now: Tikhon celebrates the services and towards Tikhon we see thronging — merchants big and small, speculators and the like income-increasing (profit-making) people. Whether it is because the demons of darkness of the Sukharevskii and Aleksandrovskii markets (i.e. chief markets of the capital) prize very highly Tikhon's canonical tendencies, or because, notwithstanding Tikhon's repentance, they nevertheless see their own in him — it is a fact that only the former patriarch has the greatest success with them.

And now we see unrolled a spectacle which is really delightful: yesterday's "Renovators," "Living Churchers" and the like, having denounced the patriarchal institution — they who excommunicated Tikhon — are now running over from "renovation" to Tikhon like cocks. And what else should it be, if all the income flows towards the former patriarch, if Tikhon stands "outside politics," and if though being "no enemy to the Soviet government" (who now is an "enemy"), he is not carried away by the "social truths" of the revolution. In a word Tikhon is the most befitting shepherd for "nepmen [i:e:. traders and small businessmen during the New Economic Policy]. And as far as most Christian adherents are concerned, their "social truth" is — where the fattest income is. And here we see the Archpriest Platonov (from Vasilevskii Island) coming forth in the cathedral with a "repentance" for his having been carried away by "Living Churchism."

This renovator calls to the orthodox to unite around Tikhon. The archbishop Artemii "blesses and permits" the prayer for Tikhon at the church services, etc. All this is really the priests showing themselves in all their nakedness. It is not possible to go further in deciding one's own convictions: "I serve him who gives an income," "I serve, so, as to receive more income."

"Religion is the opium for the people." So Karl Marx has defined it. Science fights this narcotic, illuminating the brain with the light of knowledge. But at present, in our opinion, this fight against that religious opium is carried on most effectually by the church servitors themselves, who are persons without any convictions and lacking the most simple human conscience.

Formerly every church hid its ulcers, its lies, cheating and corruption under the cover of secrecy and hypocrisy. At present it is difficult, next to impossible to keep facts secret; they must go about naked in the presence of the whole honorable people. But the most horrible hypocrisy has remained. Do you think it is on account of income, that Platonov ran over to the "Living Church?" — Oh, no, he did that inspired by the Holy Ghost — You think he came running back to Tikhon on account of income? — Oh no, he did that by reason of that same "inspiration."

As you see, "inspiration" always wonderfully coincides with "interest."

Such are the servitors of the Church, the merchants of spiritual liquor; they strip themselves without restraint and thereby show what their work is worth. Of course that "work" is advantageous as yet. But is it worth while bobbing one's head against the floors (i.e. praying) in order to increase the income of priests?

135

Disputation Between The Patriarchal Church and
The Reformatory Church

(Translation from Moscow *Bednota*, No. 1581, August 2, 1923)

Three days ago there was a religious disputation in the grand hall of the conservatory, organized by the Supreme Church Administration. The subject of the disputation was: Whom to follow, Patriarch Tikhon, or the Reformatory Church.

The assembly hall was well filled. Not only was the hall of the conservatory brimful, with several thousand people, but all the corridors and staircases and even the courtyards were crowded. The Archbishop of Krutitsk, A. Vvedenskii, one of the important and talented leaders of the Reform Church, reported. Others were invited to speak, including Tikhon's followers, the reformist Serafim, and the administrator of the Moscow diocese, Professor Illarion. But neither of them had come. Vvedenskii was not able to begin his report for a whole hour, the audience requesting the transfer of the disputation to another day when the Tikhon Church could be represented equally. The efforts of the president and of the reporter to convince the public failed, the audience continuing to make a noise, and demanding the return of the entrance fees. The noise ceased only when Archimandrite Eugenii declared that he could not say anything without the permission of Tikhon. This declaration was encountered with cheers lasting for several minutes and an ovation was offered to the Archimandrite by the whole audience, from the pit to the galleries, with the exeception of the first three ranks, occupied by the partisans of the Reform Church. In a speech which followed this declaration of Tikhon's partisan, Vvedenskii mentioned the activity of the tsarist archbishops, Tikhon not excluded, showing them up as the supporters of the monarchical regime and as lacking the spirit of real Christianity. He then talked about the counter-revolutionary activity of the All-Russian Church Council of 1918, presided over by Patriarch Tikhon. Vvedenskii pointed out that the non-counter-revolutionary public did not recognize the reform movement, because of its supposed "surrender" to the Soviet authorities.

"What do you think now of Tikhon?" asked Vvedenskii; "Is he not pro-Soviet to the same extent as we all are? Does he not recognize the Soviet power?" This remark met with exclamations of approval. He continued then to consider the activity of Patriarch Tikhon and his repentance, the insincerity of which was evident, in Vvedenskii's opinion.

The next speaker was a certain Pototskii, who spoke on behalf of Bishop Illarion, and denounced the irregularity of the actions of the reformists.

136
"Church Disputes"

(Translation from Moscow *Rabochaia Moskva*, No. 173,/445/, August 5, 1923)

The dispute: "The Fate of the Church," which was postponed until August 3, passed without the usual noise and clamor of market day at the Sukharëvka. This time Archbishop Vvedenskii succeeded in reporting. He began from the very remotest times, from the first centuries of Christianity.

The speaker then passed to actual Russian life and said: The Church at the time of Nicholas II was a mere servant of the tsar and not of Christ. At the head of the Holy Synod there was a Chief Procurator, a well-to-do official, the Church being thus governed by officials of the Union of the Russian People. [The so-called Black Hundred.] The leaders of the Church, the bishops in monastic orders, members of the Union of the Russian People, mobilized the Church for the strengthening of the autocracy. Upon the assassination of Alexander II, the Church ordered the believers to pray for the prosperity of the imperial family, and one of the bishops declared in the Moscow VEDOMOSTI that the autocracy was a dogma of the Church. The Church was also corrupted by the system of distinctions, which were only given upon approval by the political censorship and control.

Among the great number of bishops and Church dignitaries who joined the Union of the Russian People was Tikhon, then Bishop of Iaroslavl, later Archbishop of Vilna and Metropolitan of Moscow.

After the October days, Tikhon cursed the Bolsheviks. Now he repents. During the famine he declared that relief to the starving was an offense. Of this also he is now repentant. Now they want to make a martyr of him, the repentant sinner. But facts remain facts, and in their evidence the Church Council of 1918 returned a verdict of guilty, depriving him of his dignity, fifteen tsarist bishops condemning him. His Divine services after his release are a sacrilege which cannot be justified by the apostolic regulations, according to which he must be entirely removed from the Church.

The gist of our dissentions with the adherents of Tikhon is, that they consider us pro-Soviet. But Tikhon, is he not pro-Soviet also? It is true, nobody believes in his sincerity — and therefore they follow him. The Tikhonites see in him their political leader in ecclesiastical raiment.

But the Church must once for all do away with the idea of a Church Monarch, and its fundamental organization must be a Church administration with a Church Collegium.

The report of Archbishop Vvedenskii was followed by eager controversies. We must mention here the speech of Zaretskii, a lawyer, who foamed at the mouth in scolding the reformers. It was remarked by the next speaker, a workman named Orlov, that Zaretskii, after nomadizing from one group of the Reform Church to another, had now come back repentant to the "old broken trough." Orlov himself does not believe. Having studied the Spanish Inquisition, he now thoroughly knows those followers of Christ's teaching.

137
"The Clergy and the Soviet Power"

(Translation from Moscow *Pravda*, No. 175, August 5, 1923)

It is well known that religion is always the expression of the life ideal of a social group as a whole. Religious movements nearly always have been the mirrors of definite political movements of the large masses of the people or of single social groups. What is the significance of all these facts after five years of revolution? The large masses of the people have given proofs enough of loyalty to the Soviet government. The Soviet power has rooted itself profoundly, even among the most reactionary classes of our social life. The Union of Soviet Socialist Republics has emphasized this fact still more and given it a more timely significance, and inasmuch as the clergy is connected with large masses of the people, and wants to live with them and at their expense, it is equally attentive to the disposition of these masses. This explains the evolution in the clergy, and reveals its significance.

The question arises whether the older, large Churches include all the religious elements in the populations of our Federation. There are also Baptists, Evangelicals, and a great many other sects and groups. But all these groups are subject to the influence of the masses, insofar as these masses have not yet done away entirely with religious teaching; and they must assimilate themselves to the Soviet structure. And we know that, if there are in our Federation groups hostile to our Soviet regime, these groups belong to those elements which are hostile to the convictions and the interests of our toiling masses, and that they certainly express only the opinion and the interests of a small minority of the population of the U.S.S..R.

138
Registration of Religious Associations

(Translation from Moscow *Izvestiia*, No. 177, August 9, 1923)

In view of applications submitted by provincial executive committees, as well as church organizations, concerning the difficulty of carrying out the registration of religious associations within the time originally stipulated [three months]; the more so since many executive committees also ordered the simultaneous re-registration of religious groups, then greatly complicating the registration; and further in view of the fact that such registration period coincided with the agricultural campaign: the Central Executive Committee has, upon representation of the Commissariat of Justice, decided to extend the term of registration to November 1.

This resolution is the more timely and expedient since the Instruction of April 27 concerning the registration of religious associations was mistakenly interpreted in the provinces to mean that religious groups were to be transformed into associations, with compulsory re-registration. In reality, the Instructions admits the parallel co-existence of groups and religious asociations, so long as such groups have not sufficient members to be transformed into associations (less than 50 members), or so long as they do not want to be transformed. According to the said Instruction, only religious associations are to be re-registered within the stipulated time; the question of re-registration of groups is left entirely to the discretion of the Governorship Executive Committee.

139
"Human Documents:
Liability for Political Offences of Church Hierarchs"
By Metropolitan Antonin

(Translation from Moscow *Izvestiia,* No. 179, August 11, 1923)

In trying to save amid the turmoil of revolutionary movements the pagan monarchist principle and its police-protected Black Hundred organization, the Church Council of 1918 created the Patriarchate. The expressions "by the grace of God" and "tie 'em and gag 'em" remained in circulation, except that they were transferred from the Imperial manifestoes to the Patriarchal encyclicals. That is why the refugee crowd abroad and the White-Guards outside Russia had such extraordinary sympathy for Tikhon. To them he appeared as none other than a twin brother of Nicholas II attired in priestly vestments.

The Council of 1918 opened with the consent of the Provisional Government, but was concluded under Soviet rule. What was the attitude taken by the new Patriarch towards the new political regime? Openly and irreconcilably Tikhon stood up not against the malpractices of one or another revolutionary personage, but against revolution as a whole, against the new principle of power as such, "in all its actual plenitude." He did not recognize its living social truth, and therefore he did not recognize its right to existence. He was hostile to the "moral truth" of the new power and the new political idea.

According to Article 84 of the Apostolic Rules, a clergyman shall be liable to deprivation if he unjustly insults the representative of civic power (the "emperor" or the "prince" — for in those days there were no presidents and commissars). In the year 1751 the Archbishop of Voronezh, Leontii, while passing through Moscow, celebrated a memorial service in the Archangel Cathedral in memory of the Empress Anna Ivanovna, during which he mentioned incidentally the then reigning Empress Elisaveta Petrovna. For this he was deprived of his ecclesiastical rank. His slip of tongue was interpreted as an attempt upon the life of the Empress, the allegation being that he had with malicious intent celebrated a memorial or funeral service over her. Within our memory, Black-Hundred Moscow was wildly clamoring for, and eventually obtained, the deposition of the popular Priest Grigorii Petrov [a clergyman of liberal and reformist, but by no means revolutionary tendencies, some time before the war] for his social and journalistic activity and liberal spirit. His case was not conducted in a regular way. When the case was submitted to me for my opinion, I persued the evidence in the case — some works of fiction by Petrov — and gave a report to the effect that I could find nothing criminal in it. Thereupon, the leaders of the Black-

Hundred movement, the presidents of the "Union of the Russian People," Vladimir, Metropolitan of Moscow, and Bishop Nikon (of the Holy Trinity Monastery), ran with slanders and calumnies to Nicholas II. The latter expressed his displeasure by asking Pobedonostsev [then Chief Procurator of the Holy Synod]: "Is it true that Bishop Antonin has been appointed judge in the case of Grigorii Petrov? What judge can he be if he shares his opinion?" Grigorii Petrov was eventually expelled from holy orders. And none of the bishops raised his voice against the materially and formally unjust verdict of the Synod.

In such a way, while the law of the fist and the garrote was in force, the Black-Hundred people used to get rid of their spiritual opponents, of those who did not agree with them, in a rough and ready fashion without much ceremony, and with supreme disregard of "essence, as well as form." To depose a liberal clergyman was a correct and lawful thing. But when history turned upside down, when the place of Black-Hundred malice was taken by "revolutionary activity," and the clergy who were "inspired with sympathy for the revolution" applied, after the prescription of the Black-Hundred dispensary, a mustard-plaster to the back of the stubborn leader of Black-Hundred Monarchism, the latter raised protests not only by suitable action, but even went so far as to question, as a matter of principle, the competency of the Church Council. His claim was that that Council had no right to try him for counter-revolution, this being solely within the province of the civic power. Why, in the time of Monarchism, did not the "Canonical" Synod entertain any doubts of its competency to try some of the clergy for tendencies that were not even really revolutionary, but simply liberal? And why, under the Soviet regime, are anti-government, genuinely criminal actions committed by clergymen, even of the highest rank, not within the competency of an ecclesiastical court? Do politically criminal offenses not touch to the quick the feelings and the conscience of the Orthodox? If Tikhon in by-gone days recognized the correctness of Petrov's trial, and his deposition by the Synod for revolution, then he also ought to recognize the correctness of the judgment passed on himself under the Soviet regime for counter-revolution. Article 84 of the Apostolic Rules fixes the responsibility of a clergyman in regard to *any given government*: in China — to the heathen government; in Turkey — to the Mohammedan; in Spain — to the Monarchist; in France — to the Republican: and in Russia — to the Soviet government.

When in 1908, on January 26, Nicholas II said to the Chief Procurator of the Synod, Izvolskii: "Inform whom it may concern that Bishop Antonin has to retire from his post," the Synod did not protect me, and did not raise an objection on the grounds of its non-competency. On January 28 the presiding member of the Synod summoned me and told me: "Apply for your discharge not later than by tomorrow, Tuesday; if you don't, you will be dismissed on Wednesday without such application." And on the same day the Procurator Izvolskii told me: "Make haste with your application for retirement, for some members of the Synod (the Bishops Serafim, and Germogen of Saratov) are cognizant of the Emperor's will, and will on their now account raise in the Synod the question of your dismissal." Thus, Bishop Antonin, for revolutionary sentiments, was under the Monarchist regime subjected to sanctions on the part of his ecclesiastical superiors. But after the tables have been turned, under the Soviet regime, Patriarch Tikhon, charged with counter-revolution, is beyond the pale of ecclesiastical jurisdiction.

When Nicholas II, having heard the Procurator Sabler's private report on me after my six years' banishment, said to Sabler on December 22, 1913: "Well, I see that Bishop Antonin is a good man; see that you take him back into service." The holy fathers of the Synod, however, living up to the proverb "The King is merciful, but not the slave," could not forget their animosity, and could find no place to give me. At first they sent me to Ufa. But two days later they remembered that the Monastery of Bereznia, recently founded by the Grand Duchess Elisaveta Feodorovna, was in Ufa, and transferred me in a hurry to the Vladikavkaz diocese. When my health gave way, they made use of some pretext and finished with me: promising me leave to restore my health, they went back on their word, and discharged me. (Of the then judges the Metropolitan Pitirim and Vladimir met with a tragic end; both of them have gone to Kingdom Come; but Tikhon, the Archbishop of Vilna, is now . . . [unfinished sentence]. When, by the grace of the Synod, I somewhat recovered from my sickness, and thought of gaining a livelihood by returning to my service, the members of the Synod who surrounded Tikhon (Arsenii, Kirill and Nikandr, my "friends" who served with me in Petrograd) told me, every one of them: "Oh, thou fool, could anybody give thee some work?"

Thus, according to the language of the old Church, a clergyman cannot be tried for counter-revolution by an ecclesiastical court. But under the Monarchists, not only could a revolutionary clergyman be tried by an ecclesiastical court, but also a fire could be lit on the church floor, and in the name of the holy inquisition he could be roasted on a slow fire for many years. In the language of the Monastery of Our Lady of the Don this is called: "to administer the canonical blessing to the unblessed."

Metropolitan Antonin

140
Proclamation of the Sacred Synod

(Translation from Moscow *Izvestiia,* No. 180, August 12, 1923)

The Sacred Synod has issued the following proclamation, enjoying all believers "to live in peace and goodwill with the Orthodox Church," and decrying the actions of the ex-Patriarch Tikhon, who has led the Church into the road of schism.

Our hearts are filled with grief by the events happening at present in our Holy Orthodox Church. We are in the midst of a turmoil of discord, strife, and a general lack of charity and benevolence. What has happened?

Public opinion and the religious conscience of the believers are charging the ex-Patriarch Tikhon with the two following offenses: first — he does not recognize the new order of things in the political life of the State, nor the Soviet power; secondly, he has caused chaos in all Church affairs, Regarding the first offense, the ex-Patriarch has shown repentance candidly, before all the world: he has recognized the Soviet regime, has confessed that he formerly opposed it, has severed every connection with counter-revolution at home and abroad, and has been set at liberty pending trial in court. He has thus done what we did long ago, and has thereby admitted that we were right when we recognized the Soviet regime.

But his second offense is still on him. While occupying the see of the Patriarch he has, notwithstanding the protests and the warnings of the most prominent hierarchs of the Church, and having lost all his collaborators, continued to manage Church affairs by himself, contrary to the canonical law and the rules of the Church Councils, even of that of the years 1917-1918. As a result of that activity of his, much Christian blood was spilled, many bishops and priests perished, our country was full of weeping and groaning, and even the Church was in jeopardy; now he again sows discord and trouble. Being found guilty by a Council of Bishops many of whom had taken part in his election to the Patriarchate, he has trampled under foot all apostolic rules and laws of the Holy Fathers, in his thirst of power. He has usurped the episcopate on his own authority, declared himself once more Patriarch, and has blasphemously conducted Divine service. He has once more disturbed the peace and quiet of the Church, and the Church is once more a place of strife. All this aggravates his guilt before the Church.

Grieved in our hearts at this, and seeking peace and harmony within the Church, we, your principal bishops and priests, take upon ourselves at this great moment to save God's Church from the turmoil of unrest and human passion. We declare that henceforth, instead of the Supreme Church Soviet, the Sacred Synod of the Orthodox Russian Church stands at the head of Church administration [prior to the revolution it was the Holy Synod or rather: the Most Holy Synod]. We declare that there are no more groups, party divisions, and various Church organizations, but there is One United Holy Council and Apostolic Orthodox Russian Church. We are in contact with the Most Holy Eastern Patriarchs, whose representatives have already offered their official greetings to the President of the Sacred Synod — a recognition that was not accorded the ex-Patriarch after his release from prison. In brotherly union with the Most Holy Eastern Patriarchs, we stand on guard over our Holy Orthodox Church. We stand on the ground of recognition of all necessary innovations in Church life — innovations and reforms long ago contemplated by our best and principal bishops, learned professors and theologians, pre-Council conferences and carried into being by the Church Councils in 1917 and 1923. But with holy fervor, firmly and unswervingly, we observe and will observe to the end of our days, the purity of the teachings of the Orthodox Church, its sacraments, and its dogmas.

Do not therefore be like children in [lack of] wisdom, do not be impressed by high-sounding names and titles: for what they are doing is the will of God. Do not you see that the ex-Patriarch is leading you once more down the path of great grief, sufferings and tears? This path has already been made quite clear in the columns of the press and by impartial public opinion. Stern and relentless judgment awaits the deeds of ex-Patriarch Tikhon.

Beware, therefore: you are treading a dangerous road!

The Proclamation is signed by the following: The President of the Sacred Synod, the Humble Evdokim, Metropolitan of Odessa and Kherson; the Humble Tikhon, Metropolitan of Simbirsk; Veniamin, Metropolitan of Iaroslavl (formerly of Riazan); Petr, Metropolitan of Siberia; Konstantin, Archbishop of Homel; Vitalii, Archbishop of Tula and Epifansk; Artemii, Archbishop of Luga and Petrograd; Sergii, Archbishop of Tomsk; Petr, Archbishop of Voronezh; Aleksii, Archbishop of Smolensk and Dorogobuzh; Georgii, Archbishop of Krasnoiarsk and Enisseisk; Georgii, Bishop of Dmitrovsk; Archpriest Pavel Krasotin, Aleksandr Boiarskii, Dmitrii Adamov, Vladimir Shapovalov, Dmitrii Soloviev, Sergii Kanarskii, Archdeacon Sergii Dobrov, Vladimir Nikolaevich Lvov [formerly the Chief Procurator of the Holy Synod before the revolution and at the time of the Provisional Government]; and the Director of Affairs of the Sacred Synod, A. I. Novikov.

141
"New Developments in the Church Reform Movement"

(Translation from Moscow *Izvestiia,* No. 180, August 12, 1923)

In connection with the activity of ex-Patriarch Tikhon, an All-Russian Congress of plenipotentiaries of the Supreme Church Council was called in Moscow.

With a view to establishing unity within the Church, the Congress considered it imperative to effect a fusion of the two reformist groups: the "Living Church" and the "Union of Congregations of the Ancient Apostolic Church."

This question was submitted to the Supreme Church Council for definite settlement.

In the end the whole reformist movement was amalgamated under the name of the "Russian Orthodox Church." All groups shall be guided in their work solely by the resolutions of the Church Sobor of the Russian Orthodox Church in 1923, and by the acts and measures of the Sacred Synod [the supreme administration organ of the Russian Orthodox Church had its name changed from Supreme Church Council to Sacred Synod.]

The personnel of the Sacred Synod has been increased and some of the more prominent ecclesiastics have been appointed to its anew: the Metropolitan Tikhon of Simbirsk, Archbishop Veniamin of Riazan, Archbishop Vitalii of Tula, Archbishop Artemii of Petrograd, and Bishop Makarii of Penza.

A special commission appointed by the Synod is revising the list of old bishops retired, in order to make use of their services in the matter of re-establishing peace within the Church.

The Greek Synod and the Patriarch of Constantinople are taking up an attitude favorable to the Sacred Synod and the reformist movement.

Official greetings were extended to the President of the Sacred Synod, Metropolitan Evdokim, by the representatives of the Eastern Patriarchs: Prior Iakov on behalf of the Patriarch of Constantinople, and Prior Paul on behalf of the Patriarch of Alexandria.

A Special Commission for Affairs of the Russian Orthodox Church has been organized at the Constantinople Patriarchate. Thus, contact is re-established with the Eastern Orthodox Churches abroad.

With a view to giving the Synod an opportunity of furthering religious life in print, a fortnightly journal *News of the Sacred Synod* is being published.

142
"Open Letter to the Ex-Patriarch Tikhon"

(Translation from Moscow *Izvestiia*, No. 180, August 12, 1923)
[The letter has an editorial footnote: "the original spelling is retained."]

TO THE EX-PATRIARCH

An open letter from the comrades-workers of the Factory "Klara Zetkin," and others.

Citizen Belavin!

Seeing that you were elected Patriarch of all the Russias, it must be thought that you are an educated man. If so, you must know well certain sciences of which we have only heard the name, and that only after the revolution, such as: natural science, chemistry, meteorology, geology, etc. If you have studied these sciences, or are merely acquainted with them, you cannot believe in what we, the children of laborers and peasants were taught namely, that there is a supreme being, God, who rules the world, the universe, who governs and manages all and everything, who sends rain, drought, thunder, storm, harvest, and famines and other horrors, and that we, the people, may compel that being to alter its intentions and to do what we like. We were taught that, if we want rain and there is no rain, we have only to take out into the fields the so-called holy images, to pay the priest a certain amount of money, and the priest will perform certain manipulations and conjuries to make the alleged supreme being comply with our wishes. The rain will come. And so on, and so on. Further, we were taught that if we do not believe in the priests' machinations and conjuries, the supreme being will take revenge upon us, sending us untimely rains, droughts, and bad crops, and committing other criminal horrors of which only the worst enemy, a ferocious robber rather than a supreme, merciful being, would be capable. You as an educated man cannot believe in all these silly and stupid inventions.

Judging by your first repentance before the Soviet power, you ought, if you are honest, to be reasonable and also to summon enough courage to repent before the millions of laborers and peasants deceived by your false teachings, and honestly tell them that "every vegetable has its time" [a Russian proverb]. You ought to tell them that the time of religion is past and that it must go down in history. Instead of regrouping yourselves into Living, New, Ancient, and all sorts of other Churches, you ought to say openly and honestly that all churches are dead and useless. You ought to say so; we repeat, you cannot help saying so, if there is only a trace of honesty and conscience left in you. And if you say so, the People will forgive your crimes, and the blood of those who were killed because of you will no more trouble your conscience. If you maintain silence in reply to this our letter, we will take it that you have nothing with which to refute our words, and that you will continue to take advantage of the ignorance of the masses, dishonestly and with full knowledge, for your own personal gain.

To the above are attached 53 signatures of individual laborers [among them several women], the signature of the plenipotentiary of the "general service section" on behalf of 36 laborers, the signature of the plenipotentiary of the boot-makers' shop, and the signature of the local committee of the transport workers of the Commissariat of Labor, representing 73 persons.

143
Epistle of the Supreme Council of Evangelical Christians to All Communities and All Single Brethren Evangelical Christian Residents in the Union of Socialist Soviet Republics

(Moscow *Izvestiia,* No. 180 (1917), August 12, 1923)

Dear Brethren:

This time we are writing to you for the following reason: in September 1922, the Supreme Council of Evangelical Christians sent an appeal under the heading "A Voice from the East," addressed to all Christians of the world, in which among other things it was said that our brethren should fervently carry on the teachings of Christ on the subject of members of the Church abstaining from taking part in war. Since misunderstandings have arisen among some of our members on the question whether this is applicable to Russia, where the government — the only one in the world — is really fighting for the interests of the working masses: the Supreme Council of Evangelical Christians deems it its duty to explain that the aforementioned appeal referred exclusively to those believers who live outside the boundary lines of Soviet Russia and by reason of their ignorance are still defending the interests of capital.

Concerning the Soviet government, our present attitude towards it must be founded first of all upon the direct indication of God's word, which orders obedience to the existing authority, not from fear, but with a pure conscience (*Romans* 13. 1-5), and secondly, upon the understanding that the Soviet government, which has created a special political organization, finds itself placed in a special position amidst the states of the world and has its special difficulties. Therefore, with regard to the Soviet government we must display ourselves and our zeal by doing our duty in all branches of the government's activity, and must exert all our strength and knowledge in order to keep up and strengthen the Soviet government — which with worldly means tries to accomplish the ideals that have been entrusted by Christ to His Church.

It has come to the knowledge of the union that there have been cases in which some of our brethren, resident in Russia, have propagated refusal of military service, non-payment of taxes, and the like.

Herewith, the Supreme Council of Evangelical Christians categorically condemns such actions and declares that it will not consider such persons as its members.

We believe that a great role is in store for the Soviet government, which has rejected war and calls upon all the peoples to disarm and make peace. Leaning upon the masses of the working people, its vocation is to realize that for which suffering mankind yearns: i.e., the institution of a state of the world in which war at last will be unnecessary and impossible.

The activity of the Soviet government, aiming towards freeing the workers from those who exploit them, towards helping the poor, etc., corresponds to the spirit of the Evangelical Christians — for Christ our teacher, being poor himself, cared for the workers and those who are heavy laden, and has commanded the same to us.

While the attitude of the Evangelical Christians to the workers' and laborers' government of course is sincere and true, our attitude towards all forces that are hostile to the Soviet Republic is by the same token, most inimical.

The All-Russian Union of Evangelical Christians, which numbers up to two million members and followers, considers that the Soviet government is the most vivid expression of the people's will and that the system of government itself, in its idea, is very near to the Russian heart. The greater part of capitalistic and monarchial emigration up to date has not been able to get reconciled with this state of things and goes on fighting against the Soviet government and for their own predominance and their capital, which they will never be able to win back. The Evangelical Christians under the old regime fought for freedom of conscience by the means indicated by Christ, that which the Soviet government is accomplishing by worldly methods.

We exhort all our brethren to work sincerely and with absolute submission in all Soviet military and civil institutions of the republic, and also not to refuse service in the Red Army; to submit to the discipline and all regulations of the Soviet government in the midst of all dangers from the hostile forces, whatever they may be called, that surround the republic.

We have no need of particularly impressing upon the minds of our brethren, the necessity of the most loyal submission to the Soviet government, because God's word itself exhorts us to such submission. (*Romans* 13. 1-5).

Sincere submission to the Soviet government is needful so much the more in view of the fact that it guarantees — according to the decree on the separation of the Church from the State — the spiritual independence of our communities and the exercise of freedom of conscience.

We have the permission to convoke an All-Russian conference and to edit the religious-social periodical, "The Morning Star," etc.

The conference will discuss all questions which have been approached in this epistle and will work out the measures which tend to spread the teachings of the Gospel under the conditions of the Soviet regime.

Presbyter of the Moscow Communion of the Supreme Council of Evangelical Christians: F. Savelev.

Chief Mandatory of the Supreme Council of Evangelical Christians: A. Andreev.

Assistant Chief of the Supreme Council of Evangelical Christians: N. Belevin.

President of the Supreme Council of Evangelical Christians: I. Proganov.

144
"Church Controversies"

(Summary from Moscow *Rabochaia Moskva*, No. 181,/453/, August 17, 1923)

Church disputes are becoming daily occurences. There will be one today in the auditorium of the Polytechnicum, arranged by the Tikhonite Illarion, on the question: The Tikhonites and the Reform Church — What divides them? Tomorrow Vvedenskii will speak again in the conservatory on the question: The Holy Synod and the New Ways of the Church (Tikhon and the Church); the Political Significance of Tikhon's Repentance; the Condemnation of Tikhon by the Church Council, the Re-establishment of the Holy Synod and its Significance; the Role of Monasticism in the Future; Religious Teaching in the Future.

On August 20, in the former theatre of Zimin, Metropolitan Antonin will talk on Church chauvinism; his speech will be directed against Tikhon as well as against the reformers. This speech will include: Revolution in the Ancient Church; Metamorphosis of the Ancient Church; Reason of the Political Repentance of the "Universally Known"; Repentance though not Repenting; Revolution and Reformation; Hopes of the Church.

THE CHURCH IN THE WORKMEN QUARTERS

On August 10, there was a dispute arranged by Vvedenskii on the question: Tikhon's Repentance and the Fate of the Church.

The cash office had rather a good day. The whole speech of Vvedenskii was a continual attack on Tikhon which, however, did not much affect the audience, consisting mostly of workmen. The self-accusatory revelations of Vvedenskii were of high interest and are very precious for the enlightenment and instruction of the masses. They show the rotten condition of Christ's Church, the latent decay in it. Continual and cheerful laughter and applause accompanied these delightful revelations. But the question of Archbishop Vvedenskii as to whom the workmen would follow, Tikhon or the Reformers, provoked a general uproar. They do not want to follow either the one or the other; they worship science, which will, when penetrating the large masses of the toiling people, supplant religion and religious teaching quite naturally, as well as the dark superstitions of the Church. Such disputes are most valuable and desirable for the instruction of the ignorant and the naive. Until late at night, after the dispute was over, mixed groups of believers and non-believers discussed these revelations, which provoked repeated outbursts of laughter.

145
"Another Repentant Priest"

(Translation from Moscow *Rabochaia Moskva,* No. 182,/454/, August 18, 1923)

The President of the Synod, Metropolitan Evdokim, has received a letter from the Old Believer, Archpriest Illarion, now held in the correctional house at Ufa.

Illarion said in part that Tikhon's repentance has opened his eyes, that it was not the Soviet Administration which was to be blamed for the persecution, but, on the contrary, persons like Tikhon, who have necessitated such measures of just punishment.

"Many of us," said he, "thought in our simplicity that we have suffered for our faith; in reality, we suffered only for stubbornness and ignorance. Such you see in your obedient servant, who is rightly punished for his eagerness to serve an unreasonable cause."

146
"Discomfiture"

(Translation from Moscow *Rabochaia Moskva*, No. 182,/454/, August 18, 1923)

Nuns of a church which was liquidated by the [local] Department of the Administration of Liquidation, according to the decision of the Moscow Soviet, presented an appeal to the All-Russian Central Executive Committee. Considering the critical housing situation, and the fact that the church and its premises will be used as boarding houses for workmen, the Central Executive Committee rejected the petition and confirmed the decision concerning the liquidation.

147
"Ecclesiastical Disorders: Under the Power of Tikhon"

(*Krasnaia Gazeta*, No. 174, 255, August 24, 1923)

On Sunday, July 22nd, after the service, a large meeting took place at the Ascension Cathedral under the presidency of the priest Nikitin, on the subject of the contemporary Church. The meeting lasted until 7 p.m. After having listened to the extensive report of the president and the priest Chokoi, who related the history of the Church's strife from May 1922 up to date and described the characteristics of the leaders of the novatory movement, the meeting unanimously voted a resolution denouncing the activity of all novatory groups. It was decided entirely to separate from the Petrograd diocesan administration and from the Supreme Church Administration and as a whole community to recognize the Church with Tikhon as its leader. At the same meeting the resolution was passed, not to recognize as valid the order of the diocesan administration regarding the discharge of the priest Chokoi from the Ascension Cathedral, and to fix next Sunday as a day of public repentance by the whole parish for the intercourse with the "renovating priests" which has been carried on up to now.

TRANSFER OF KRASNITSKII

In consequence of repeated collisions with its parishioners at the Cathedral of Our Lady of Vladimir, the priest Krasnitskii (President of the Committee of the Living Church) by order of the Church Administration has been transferred to the Cathedral of Our Lady of Kazan. This transfer has been occasioned by the last scandal on July 15th, when Krasnitskii could not succeed in reading the resolution of the Supreme Church Administration regarding Tikhon.

AT THE CATHEDRAL OF OUR LADY OF KAZAN

The Cathedral of Our Lady of Kazan is in a desperate financial position, because most of its parishioners have left, refusing to recognize the "Living Church."

148
Commentary of the U.S. Legation in Riga on the Religious Situation in Russia

No. 1233

September 12, 1923

The Secretary of State, Washington

Sir:

Supplementing my despatch No. 1232 of this date, and other despatches communicating current information from the Soviet Russian press in regard to anti-religious propaganda and religious affairs in Russia, I have the honor to forward a number of translations and summaries dealing with the same subjects.

The Supreme (Living Church) Administration has renamed itself the Sacred Synod and has issued a proclamation against Patriarch Tikhon.

This would appear to be an effort on the part of the Living Church to manoeuvre itself into a position of vantage. The calculation is obviously that the Patriarchate was practically forgotten by the masses of the communicants during the more than two centuries between its abolition by

Peter the Great and its revival in 1917, and that the name of the Synod will carry the notion of regularity of succession. It overlooks the immense personal ascendancy of the Patriarch Tikhon, who has acquired the merit of a martyr and the odor of sanctity.

This change is also obviously an invitation to the Soviet authorities to resume the avowed control of religious bodies, and to extend to the Living Church their protection against dissent and schism. The former Chief Procurator of the Most Holy Synod under the Provisional Government is a member of the new Sacred Synod.

Probably the move is too late.

There is further information that the Patriarch is re-shepherding the Orthodox flock, that the Living Church has now lost most of the Petrograd churches, and that its financial resources have been out off by the communicants. Archbishop Krasnitsky [Krasnitskii], having been expelled from his original pulpit at Petrograd, took over the Kazan Cathedral [the Cathedral of Our Lady of Kazan] there, formerly the most popular church in Petrograd. The change seems to have done him little good, for the church is now said to be practically deserted.

An interview had with Patriarch Tikhon is confirmatory of the interview communicated in my despatch No. 1182 of August 29, 1923.

Metropolitan Antonine [Antonin], who has been dropped from the Supreme Church Administration, has published a bitter argument against the refusal of Patriarch Tikhon to submit to the recent Church Council. He [Antonin], has had to submit to discipline more than once; why should Tikhon rebel?

A number of factory hands have availed themselves of the controversy for Atheistic propaganda.

The unsuccessful agitation against Patriarch Tikhon at public meetings, the general defection from the Living Church to Tikhon, and other current information is contained in three enclosures.

The shifting of priests first to the Living Church and then back to Patriarch Tikhon is attributed by the *Krasnaya* [*Krasnaia*] *Gazeta* of Petrograd to mercenary motives only; and this newspaper argues that the priests are themselves doing more to discredit religion than any anti-religious propaganda.

Moscow *Pravda* editorially hints that the time has come for the Evangelical Christian sects to proclaim their political faith; and the "Supreme Council of the Evangelical Christians" obediently publishes a circular letter expressing its pro-Soviet sentiments.

The Moscow *Pravda*, No. 167, July 27, 1923, states that the Presidium of the Baumanovsky [Baumanovskii] Soviet has resolved to put the Baptists out of the houses occupied by them in the Pokrovsky [Pokrovskaia] Street, as it is considered that the premises occupied by them are living quarters and are subject to rational exploitation. The Baptist are given trading premises on payment of the corresponding tariff.

Lenient court action in trials of clergymen seems now to be a settled policy.

The Federation Commissars have appropriated 2,340,360 (gold?) roubles of the fund derived from the sale of Church valuables for the re-evacuation of refugees from famine districts. Four church bells have been handed over to the Volunteer Air Fleet.

A hand-book of anti-religious propaganda is noticed. It has been forwarded to the Department, for such attention as it may deserve, which would appear to be slight.

The registration or re-registration of religious societies seems to be progressing very slowly.

I have the honor to be, Sir,
Your obedient servant,
F. W .B. Coleman

149

Decree of Soviet of People's Commissars of the R.S.F.S.R. Concerning the Sale of Church Property not of a Sacred Character

(Translation from Moscow *Izvestiia*, No. 224, October 3, 1923)

In development of the decree of the All-Russian Central Executive Committee of December 27, 1921, published in the *Compilation of Decrees,* 1922, No. 19, Article 215, the Soviet of People's Commissars of the R.S.F.S.R. resolves:

(1) The Councils of People's Economy of Governorships and Autonomous Republics and Oblasts have the right to sell Church property not of a sacred character (furniture, bells, etc.), which come to the disposal of the local State institutions on account of the liquidation or closing of chapels, monasteries, temples, synagogues, Mohammedan temples, etc., or by other means.

(2) The sums gained from the sale of said property, except expenditures incurred during the sale, are to be handed to the government treasury.

Vice President of the Soviet of People's
Commissars of the R.S.F.S.R.:
A. Rykov
Manager: V. Smolianinov
Secretary: M. Glaser

Moscow, Kremlin
September 19, 1923.

150
"The End of a Church"

(Summary from Moscow *Pravda*, No. 213, September 21, 1923)

A great meeting was held at Petropavlovsk by the railway men of that station, at which almost all of them were present, over 600 men. At that meeting was discussed the question of the church at Petropavlovsk. The workmen saw no use in keeping a church which is not visited by anybody except a few old women. When this question was put up at the meeting, only 15 out of 600 voted against closing the church. The chairman was taken by surprise and said that the decision whether or not to close the church belonged to the Soviet of the Executive Committee and therefore could not be decided at the meeting. It was then decided to ask the Executive Committee to close the church. The next question was, what to do with the church. There were several proposals. The majority were for changing it into a club of the Communist youth. The church with its golden cupola stands on a hill and overlooks the whole settlement. The golden cross on the cupola was hateful to the Communists and it was decided to remove it. Shortly afterwards, by means of a rope, a couple of men reached the cupola and removed the cross and hoisted the red flag instead. Only a few toothless women were crying. Another group at the same time were breaking down the "ikonostas" [the holy partition wall dividing the altar from the congregation] and other church rubbish. The old folk standing outside were expecting God's punishment but nothing came. The church bells were handed over for the needs of airship construction. So the church was changed into a clubhouse, in which several disputes with the clergy were held.

151
Russian Church Property in America

(Translation from Moscow *Izvestiia*, No. 27, October 6, 1923)

The priest I. S. Kedrovskii, who was appointed by the (Living Church Sacred) Synod head of the Russian Orthodox Mission in America, arrived in Moscow on October 4 from the United States.

In an interview with the correspondent of the Russian Telegraph Agency I. S. Kedrovskii gave the following information:

The old leaders of the Orthodox church in America — the Archbishop A. Nemolovskii and the Metropolitan Platon have compromised themselves in the eyes of the believers by their scandalous living and by the dissipation of the Russian people's wealth.

According to the pre-revolution regulations, all Church property was assigned to the bishop. They were able, therefore, to mortgage and to sell to private people a considerable part of the Orthodox church property in America for the total amount of $250,000. These dealings were begun in 1918-1919 with the churches in Cleveland and Gary, and the orphan home in Brooklyn, and were continued up to the present time. Nemolovskii and Platon have sold and mortgaged scores of churches, the sacristy of the cathedral, and money, deposited in the banks by the parishioners, has been spent. At present several churches and St. Tikhon's Monastery are to be sold at public auction.

The one million dollars which was given to the Orthodox clergy in America by the Russian Government out of the sums received from the sale of Alaska, has evidently also been spent.

Where has the money gone? Part of it, of course, has gone into the pockets of the leading priests, who have become wealthy during that time, have become house owners, etc. Part of the money has gone also to political needs. Among the Russian monarchists in America rumors are circulating that the selling out of the church property is being done by order of the monarchist headquarters in Berlin. In America papers has appeared a notice that Archbishop A. Nemolovskii has been appointed head of the Russian monarchist party in America, and that he was thanked for the financial help he had rendered to the monarchist organizations. From the same resources, subsidies are paid to B. Bakhmetev and company, who long ago spent their 187 million dollars.

The Russian parishioners are against the adventures of Platon and Nemolovskii. Only the sudden departure of Nemolovskii to Europe has saved him from an American court. As far as Platon is concerned, I. S. Kedrovskii, on the initiative of parishioners, has started a lawsuit against him for embezzlement of church property, and the court of the first instance has forbidden Platon and the council of the church mission to make any more sales of church property.

The verdict of the jury has to be confirmed by the High Court, which, on the request of the lawyer of I. S. Kedrovskii, has postponed the examination of the case for two months, so that the latter could obtain power of attorney from the Russian Synod for the management of the properties of the Orthodox Church in America.

The value of this property is estimated at $2,500,000, not including 50,000 acres of land in Alaska. I. S. Kedrovskii will remain 5 days in Moscow.

152
A Letter of Rev. E. Walsh, S.J., Director of The Papal
Relief Mission in Russia, to an Officer of the British
Embassy, Moscow

Catholic Relief Mission in Russia

Moscow, November 16, 1923

. . . . But now for the bad news. The addressee came to my office on Thursday November 8th, to tell me that the police had come to the lodgings on Prechistenskii Boulevard during the night and made a thorough search. They left at 2 a.m. without arresting anybody. But about the same time the G.P.U. arested two of the five young men who were preparing for the priesthood under the direction of P. Nicolas. They took all their books, etc., saying "You had better devote your time to studying Communism instead of that Catholic nonsense."

This was all narrated to me by Madame A. who left my office about noon. That night, at 11 p.m. just as the Sisters had finished their night devotions and were preparing to lie down on the floor for their meagre rest, the lodging was invaded by a band of Red soldiers with drawn revolvers, accompanied by six agents of G.P.U., among them a woman. They gathered all the Sisters in one room and kept them there until 5:30 next morning, subjecting all to a most savage interrogation, casting ridicule and scorn on their religious practices and generally terrorizing the community. Easy, isn't it, with a platoon of armed soldiers and a small group of helpless women as victims?

After a night of agony, they brought an automobile and carried off Madame A. and seven or eight Sisters. At the same time, similar searches and arrests were made in the homes of parishioners.

In all, they have arrested 13 persons connected with the Uniate movement.

Next day they arrested the priest P. Nicholas. Being thus without priest, and as the Blessed Sacrament was still in the Tabernacle and in danger of being profaned, the eldest of the Sisters approached the Tabernacle and consumed the Sacred species.

So they are all in Lubyanka [Lubianka] tonight. I do not know what the result will be, but it is my private conviction that they are preparing another great trial like that of last Easter. If they are, the world should be ready to give them the same reception.

In general, I think matters are much worse than when you were here. They have refused all overtures for the release of the Archbishop and the priests. The Archbishop is failing rapidly and I fear death will soon end his sufferings.

I am engaged at present in a serious controversy with the Bolsheviks regarding our Mission and our position is much as yours was last April; — I cannot tell an hour in advance whether we are to go or stay. They have broken their word so often and shown such malice that the Holy See has been obliged to present a mild but definite ultimatum. We should know our destiny within the next four or five days.

The house opposite your Mission is now in our hands but there is a probability of our being put out next Monday, after having spent a huge sum in repairing and equipping it. After signing a solemn contract that there was to be no Commandant or other Soviet Agent living in the house, they have broken their word and are now endeavoring to make me sign an agreement to have one in the house. I have been obliged to refuse, naturally, as we have had enough of spies and informers. In consequence, they have presented a sort of counter-ultimatum, saying "sign or leave the house." Obviously, if they put us out of the house in violation of their written contract, it will mean the end.

All this comes just as the other grave affair takes place. It may be that they are connected and they want to get us out before they begin that trial, if a trial is in preparation.

At any rate, the whole matter is in the hands of the Holy See and I should have definite instructions within three or four days.

With best regards,

Very truly yours,

E. A. W[alsh, S. J.]

153

Report from the U.S. Legation in Riga Concerning Mistreatment of the Catholic Nuns in Moscow

December 7, 1923

The Secretary of State, Washington

Sir:

With reference to repairs and Soviet denials that a number of clergymen and nuns have been arrested in the Soviet Federation, I have the honor to forward a copy of a part of a letter dated November 16, 1923, and received by a member of the staff of the British Legation from Father E. A. Walsh, at Moscow. The addressee is a personal friend of Father Walsh, having recently been assigned to Riga after service in the British Trade Commission at Moscow. Father Walsh is acting Papal Nuncio. (2488, of August 14, 1922)

After referring to the delivery of a letter to a certain address in Moscow, Father Walsh's missive relates that the police made a night search in premises occupied by personnel of the Roman Catholic enterprises at Moscow on November 8, but made no arrests there. About the same time five young men who are preparing for the priesthood were arrested. Their books were taken and they were told they would better study Communism instead of "Catholic nonsense." The following night, it seems, after certain Roman Catholic Sisters had retired to rest, their lodging was invaded by red soldiers with drawn revolvers, and six agents of the State Political Administration, including one woman, doubtless for the event of a bodily search. The Sisters were huddled into one room and kept there until 5:30 a.m., the soldiery casting scorn and ridicule upon their religious faith and cult, and keeping them in constant terror. Eight or nine of the ladies were carried away in an automobile. In all, says Father Walsh, thirteen persons, connected with the Uniate movement, had been arrested when his letter was written. The priest, P. Nicholas, was also arrested. "They are all in Lubianka tonight," adds Father Walsh. He further relates that he had many difficulties, including cares in regard to the premises occupied, and he was uncertain how long he and his assistants would be able to stay.

I have the honor to be, Sir,
Your obedient servant,
F. W. B. Coleman

154
Letter of Archbishop John Baptist Cieplak to Rev. E. Walsh, S.J., Director of the Papal Relief Mission in Russia

Archbshop John Cieplak
118 Fontanka, Petrograd

December 16, 1923

My Reverend Father:

My attorney requests precise information on the charitable activity of the Pontifical Mission in Russia in order to use it in his pleading. If you do not find it inconvenient I shall be obliged to you for sending a short report with some total figures on the number of unfortunates and children whom you have helped; the attorney might derive from it an argument favourable to our cause.

We are very uneasy about our case and the opening of our churches. If you possibly coulld let us know something about the progress of these matters it would please us very much.

Our parishioners are thinking of sending a new delegation to Moscow, what do you think of it?

Please accept, My Father, my deep consideration.

John Cieplak
Archbishop

17. [January] 1. 24 I have received just now your letter of January 11 — Thank you for all that you do for us. The events do not seem to indicate any improvement — pray for us.

1924

155

Letter of Rev. Xavier Klimaszewski to Archbishop John Baptist Cieplak concerning His Experiences in Saratov Diocese

In August 1918 Bishop Kessler, foreseeing hard times and imprisonment (probably he would eventually be shot), went with the chapter to Odessa, a territory free from Bolshevism. He organized a seminary there and at the same time created me Vicar General of the South-Eastern part of the diocese. Reprisals against the Church and clergy started very soon. The Bishop's residence (next to mine) was given by the Bolshevik authorities to juvenile deliquents who, evidently according to instructions received, tried by means of frankly ignominious, indescribable ways to make my life unbearable. Except for one little room my apartment was also taken over by Jewish Communists. During July, 1919, I was imprisoned as a hostage but they set me free after a week.

In January, 1920, my apartment was searched for the fifth time and a protocol was written "that nothing suspicious was found." Nevertheless I was taken to Cheka, supposedly to count the money, but once there I was instantaneously arrested and the keys to my apartment and to the Cathedral were taken from me. Another search was made in my apartment and in the church. This time, however, there were no witnesses. After the boards of the altar steps were torn off, several bombs were planted there and in the apartment dynamite and revolver cartridges. The curate was called in as a witness to testify that bombs and dynamite were stored under my care. A confession was written and handed to me with the advice that if I admitted my guilt and signed the confession about the bombs found I would be sentenced to life imprisonment — if not, I would be shot. To my question concerning the whereabouts of the first protocol stating that nothing suspicious had been found they answered that it had been lost. As I did not feel guilty I did not sign this second confession, considering it but a trick. At the my *curriculum vitae* was taken down on three pages of paper and I was told to sign it. In this case I also refused, demanding the addition of three points: 1. that the first protocol stating that nothing suspicious had

223

been found during the search was lost; 2. that the keys to the Cathedral and apartment were taken after my arrest and that the search during which bombs were found had been made without any witnesses; 3. my signature would be placed on every page of the *curriculum vitae*. For my boldness in stating those points I was put in a completely dark room for several days. Examinations often lasted for whole nights and were accompanied by chicanery, mockery, Russian curses and threats with revolvers. Seeing my obstinacy against signing the *curriculum vitae* the investigators agreed to add the three points I had given. I did sign it, but then came the revenge: I was placed in the worst section of the prison, with the worst felons, after my name had been written on the wall as belonging to the most dangerous of criminals. For the first 3 days I was kept in a room so damp and cold that during the whole time I could not sit down without fear of freezing to death; shaking from fever, I could not say a word. During those 3 days I ran and slapped my arms continuously to stop the blood from freezing in my veins. After 3 days I was taken to the bath under the pretext of disinfection and ordered to exchange my clothes and underclothing for others full of lice. I was then locked in a room where the windows were bare of glass, during a terrible winter when the temperature stayed at 30 C. below. Lice were lifting my underclothing so I took it off and for 2 hours kept hitting the door. I yelled with an inhuman voice as I came nearer to death. After 2 hours I was at last given clean clothes and they locked me in a different single cell [odinochka] together with two other men. The windows there had glass but during the whole winter no heat was provided and the water froze so that for a month I could not wash myself. There was no bed; instead I was given a straw mattress, or rather a bag of bed bugs, which I did not use — a pillow, blanket or chair were out of the question. On the damp asphalt I sat, locked up completely, not let out in the fresh air for over 3 months. I lay down every night expecting to be shot. One night I was led out into the yard to be shot, but instead they took me to the city later on for an examination lasting all night.

Meals were composed of hot water, soup made from water and rotten cabbage, and a pound of bread — every day the same thing. Had it not been for human friendliness and the occasional lunches which were sent I would have starved to death.

The case of the planted bombs became famous and rumors of it reached Moscow, where the authorities after some checking ordered the tribunal to revise their decision. After a detailed examination of the charges, the tribunal set me free and in order to cover up the incident my accusers were arrested and taken to Rostov where they were given good positions.

After my release I wanted to go to my parsonage apartment, but it was already occupied by Jewish Communists. All my belongings as well as the bulk of the diocesan and parochial archives had been taken away by the

Cheka. The situation I found myself in was terrible: I did not have anything except torn clothing and a pair of shoes which were full of holes; I
had neither a penny in my pocket nor a roof over my head and the city was
so overcrowded that I could not even dream of a separate room. For three
weeks I spent my nights at the home of some friends, sleeping in
a passage way and waiting for somebody to ask me to tea or dinner. I had
such a bad attack of rheumatism that walking was difficult even with a stick.
In addition to everything else, cholera and typhoid fever had been raging
in the city so that it was necessary for me to perform many religious services.
Income from religious services (*jura stolae*) was almost non-existent, since
everybody was on the threshhold of poverty. Some good woman made a cape
for me from a dress which she had prepared for her funeral; someone else
furnished a set of underclothing.

Then, three weeks after my release, I left for a German colony in the
province of Samara where the parson had died of typhoid fever. I had only
been there a month when I had to leave because the war with Poland had
started. They wanted to arrest me again and I had to escape. I travelled one
hundred and fifty versts to a small and very poor village with a church, near
Kamyshin, where I stayed in hiding while teaching religion to children. The
search for me continued but with no result. At one time I sought shelter in
a hole and the soldiers walked all around my hiding-place without finding
me. However, they took all the things which I had managed to procure up
to that time. When I returned to Saratov in May, 1921, after the peace
treaty with Poland, the whole Polish colony had already left and I had to
leave also since it was impossible to get not only clothing but even enough
food for sustenance. To the German Catholics left in Saratov, I assigned a
German priest who was receiving from his family in the country all the
produce he needed to live. I authorized Rev. Feryer to take over my post,
and he immediately informed Bishop Kessler of this action.

The position of the clergy was very difficult: many died during epidemics;
several were shot; the majority were imprisoned; and almost without exception they could not live in their parsonages. Some of the German
Catholics emigrated to America or to Germany and others died of hunger
or contagious maladies. Only by administering two or three orphaned
parishes could the pastors make ends meet. Devastation was terrible.

After my return to Poland I accepted, at the proposal of Bishop Ty-
mieniecki, the temporary post of prefect in a Lodz school, and I have remained there till the present. I do not feel too well after all those trials but
I thank God for allowing me to see my country again. People have written
to me from Saratov that after my departure they made five separate searches
in an attempt to arrest me.

May 2, 1924   Rev. Ksawery Klimaszewski
Lodz, at the Church of the Holy Cross

1925

156

Memorandum from the Polish Executive Committee in Belorussia and the Ukraine Concerning Defense of the Catholic Religion in Soviet Russia

No. 2443   Warszawa, May 12, 1925

To His Excellency, Archbishop Cieplak, in Rome
From Polish Executive Committee in Ruthenia

MEMORANDUM

Within the frontiers of today's Soviet Russia, i.e. in the provinces of Kiev, Podolia, and half of Volinia, there was in the year 1915 a Catholic population of 945,000 persons, namely:

Landed gentry	9,670
Working intelligentsia	137,000
Polish workers	140,000
Polish native population	661,630

There were:

Churches	237
Chapels	143
Catholic priests	246

In June 1917, during the Polish Assembly in Kiev attended by 554 delegates from 232 Polish organizations, the Polish Executive Committee in Ruthenia was elected, which as the governing body of the local Polish government was given the tasks of organizing administratively the whole of Ruthenia, developing education, and caring for the numerous Polish population settled in this region for centuries.

The Executive Committee fulfilled [in the Ukraine] these tasks; everywhere provincial, county and rural district Commissioners were elected, and with the cooperation of numerous newly created "Mother Circles" the whole of Ruthenia was covered with a fine network of Polish schools, 1316 in number, employing 2,069 teachers and attended by 85,000 Polish children who studied in their mother tongue and in the Catholic spirit.

The school budget in 1918 amounted to over 18 million rubles in gold supplied from the National Tax levied by the Committee and willingly paid by all Polish classes.

After the occupation of Kiev by Bolshevik forces and the execution (in 1919) of the then Chairman of the Committe, Pereswiat-Soltan, the Polish National Committee was forced to move in 1920, together with the withdrawing Polish Army, to Warsaw — from where it still takes care of Polish education and of the Polish clergy and population in the Ukraine through its Men of Confidence.

After this short presentation of the Committee's activity, we, faithful sons of the Catholic Church, now address Your Excellency in the following matter.

The Treaty of Riga left the Polish people and Catholic clergy in Ruthenia and White Ruthenia [Belorussia] without any protection and threw them on the mercy of hostile elements.

Knowing well the activity of the Soviet Government, its psychology and aims, we assert that present persecutions of the Catholic clergy for counter-revolutionary and national propaganda are only a pretext. Their real motives are different.

a. The policy of the Soviet Government is directed finally toward the destruction of all religious feelings, morality and Christian ethics in the whole population.

b. The Orthodox Church has already been crushed, the Orthodox clergy disorganized, religious spirit destroyed or made a laughing stock, and the Orthodox population, denied any moral or religious ideals, becomes an ever more pliable tool in the hands of the Soviets.

c. The only strong spiritual and moral organization left in Russia is the Catholic Church, which up to now, in spite of terrible reprisals and numerous losses, presents to the Soviets an extremely dangerous moral organization which they want and have to break at any price in order to be able to obtain free access to the large mass of Catholics, still faithful sons of the Church.

In European Russia today there are still over one million two hundred thousand Catholics, and out of this number over 1,150,000 are Poles. Ninety-two per cent of the Catholic priests are of Polish origin.

No wonder that in this battle of extermination against the Catholic Church, the Soviet Government covers up its real aims by acting officially against Polish priests for supposed counter-revolutionism and national propaganda. Thus, its main effort has been concentrated in Ruthenia, where a relatively small area is inhabited even today by over 748,000 Poles, and in White Ruthenia [Belorussia] where under the pretext of upholding White Ruthenian [Belorussia] nationals it also ruthlessly persecutes Polish priests.

Having presented to Your Excellency the real aims of the Soviet Government and the war of extermination to which Catholic priests in Russia are subjected, we must stress with regret that five years of persecution have already caused heavy defections among the clergy and Catholic population of Soviet Russia. The cases of Catholics joining the sect of "shtundists" have become increasingly numerous and at the same time the resistance of the Catholic clergy weakens, their number decreasing alarmingly.

Out of 242 priests in Ruthenia in 1915, only 137 were left in 1922, and now there are but 67.

In the face of horrible reprisals against Polish priests by Soviet Russia and moral and physical cruelty in Cheka prisons, the nerves of those martyrs often cannot hold out. As a result there is an increase in the number of cases of schism, and of forced letters to the Holy Father such as that of Rev. Fedukowicz. After he was twice tortured and hypnotized in prison, Rev. Fedukowicz signed that notorious letter. Later, after he had come back to Zhytomir, he took advantage of the relative freedom to die a martyr's death, like a living torch in the times of Nero, begging for God's forgiveness.

However, similar cases weaken the energy of the rest of the clergy and the letter of Rev. Nanowski of Kaminiets Podolski is an indication of the serious danger to the dignity of the Catholic religion.

Having briefly presented the situation of the clergy in Ruthenia, we take the liberty to send some information with regard to the very important defence of the Catholic religion in Soviet Russia.

It has come to our knowledge that the Curia Apostolica, in the desire to defend the Catholic religion, has entered into negotiations with the Soviet Government.

The Soviets are very anxious to be able to boast officially to the world that they have concluded some sort of a Concordat with the Curia Apostolica. On the other hand Your Excellency knows very well how the Soviets adhere to their treaties.

After all, even though the Treaty of Riga stipulated freedom of religion, education and mother tongue, only one additional piece of national legislation made the Treaty of Riga into a scrap of paper. Thereafter, unscrupulous, barbarian reprisals against Poles and the Catholic clergy were applied.

Since it can be expected that they will apply this document to the agreement with the Curia Apostolica as well, it would be desirable to reserve Canon Laws and the supreme authority for the Holy Father.

Their endeavor to do the same as they did to the Orthodox religion, namely to create self-dependent, autonomous spiritual units, also should be counteracted with all energy. For the Catholic religion it would be deadly, the majesty of the Holy Father would be destroyed and in a very short time these autonomous parishes would be mastered by Communists. One after another they would apostatize from the Church, join the schism of "shtunda," and become centres of ruthless anti-religious propaganda and of various actions against the Catholic Church and the Supreme Spiritual Authorities.

Without anticipating in what form the Curia Apostolica will consider it possible to conclude an agreement with the Soviets, we take the liberty to mention that the power of appointing Bishops or Apostolic Administrators ought to depend only upon the Curia Apostolica. These positions, in view of the fact that Poles form 96 per cent of the Catholics and 92 per cent of the clergy, should be filled, in justice, by Poles of local origin.

Of foreign nationalities we believe the most dangerous would be Lithuanians and after them White Ruthenians and German Catholics.

If, however, on account of the present political situation it were necessary to employ temporarily some non-Polish priests in the highest Church positions in Soviet Russia, then Rev. Bialoholov in White Ruthenia and Rev. Zerr (German) in deep Russia might be nominated. Rev. Zerr is presently staying in the Crimea.

With regard to Polish candidates for the highest Church posts, we take the liberty of proposing for the Ukraine Rev. Prelate Skalski and for his assistant Rev. Naskrecki from Kiev; for the diocese of Podolia, Rev. Jan Swiderski. Lastly, we would propose Rev. Dean Przerebel for the Moskow-St. Petersburg region, or for the diocese of Minsk or Mohylew.

However, since negotiations between the Curia Apostolica and the Soviets might last for a longer period of time, we consider it necessary to give immediate succour to the Catholic priests left in Russia by coming out as soon as possible with an official order from the Vatican forbidding the clergy to sign any act or letter of political or religious character without the knowledge and consent of their Supreme Spiritual Authorities in Metropolis. Excellency:

We place this modest memorandum into your hands. We know that no one else will be able to understand so deeply the terrible distresses inflicted on Catholicism, Christianity and the whole of humanity by the Soviets. We believe firmly that the example of the martyrdom borne personally by Your Excellency will stimulate other priests to persevere at their outposts until the time when the victory of truth, spirit and Christian ethics will come at last. Then the Catholic Church, on today's ruins, cinders and soil so abundantly besprinkled with martyrs' blood, will raise again the Banner of Christ — the Banner of Love, Faith and Forgiveness.
Stamp:

Polish Executive Committee in Ruthenia Presidency Department
Chairman: Jan Lipkowski
Deputy Chairmen: Josefat Andrzejewski
Zygmunt Chojecki

157
Memorandum from the Polish Executive Committee in Belorussia and the Ukraine to the R. C. Archbishop of Mogilev for All Russia, Mgr. J. B. Cieplak, Presented in the Fall of 1925

At the beginning of 1919, after Kiev had been occupied by the Bolsheviks, bloody reprisals were directed primarily against the Poles and the Catholic clergy. In the autumn of 1919 the Chairman of the Polish Executive Committee in Ruthenia, Mr. Pereswiat-Soltan, was shot without trial. In spite of this the Committee functioned in Kiev until the month of June, 1920, but at the time of evacuation it was forced to move to Warsaw, from where it continues its efficacious protection of the Polish population and the clergy left in Ruthenia.

Having presented this short outline of the activities of the Polish Executive Committee in Ruthenia, we wish to complete it with the following statistics based on the appropriate estimation that the number of Catholics in Russia at the present time does not exceed 70% of the number of Catholics registered before the war. The rate of natural increase of the population during the last 12 years has not been taken into consideration.

THE NUMBER OF CATHOLICS IN EUROPEAN RUSSIA IN 1925

Diocese, District, or Province	Catholics in 1925	Church	Chapels	Total Catholics	% of Poles
1. Ruthenia:					
Diocese of Zhitomir	384,700				
Diocese of Kamieniets	325,600	237	143	710,300	98
2. Diocese of Minsk with the district of Petersburg and of Moscow	71,000				
Province of Mogilev	50,200				
Province of Vitebsk	48,600				
Province of Smolensk	12,500	115	155	182,300	94
3. District of Kharkow	13,600				
District of Samara	6,600				
District of Perm	4,250	19	17	24,450	92
4. Diocese of Tiraspol	90,000	40	15	90,000	68
Total in European Russia		411	330	1,007,050	94

On the whole there are today in European Russia more than one million Catholics who as far as their nationality is concerned are divided as follows:

Catholics of Polish nationality ....more than 94%
Catholics of German nationality ....about 4%
Catholics of Italian, French, Russian and other nationalities 2%

The Polish Executive Committee in Ruthenia, knowing Russia and the intentions of the Soviet Government well, ventures to state that the proceedings against the alleged national and anti-revolutionary propaganda are but a pretext for the present persecutions of the Catholic clergy in Russia because the real end of the Soviets is the total abolition of all religious feelings, morals and Christian ideas among the local population. . . .

The Catholic Church remains from the moral and intellectual point of view the only unyielding organization. Even now, in spite of terrible persecutions and numerous victims, it represents to the Soviet Government a great moral power which they are trying to subdue at all costs in order to be able to spread their propaganda freely among the numerous Catholics who until now have remained faithful to the Church and who, by so doing, have given a noble example to the Orthodox population.

Nevertheless, we have to acknowledge with sadness that those five years of ferocious and treacherous persecutions directed by the Soviet Government against the Church and the Polish Catholic population have caused much damage and have weakened the resistance of the Catholic element. The cases of defection among the Catholics and their adhesion to various religious sects, particularly of the "shtundists," become more and more frequent, and the number of priests who remain at their posts diminishes in a frightful way in Ruthenia, where of 245 priests who were there in 1914, only about 70 are left today.

Unfortunately, the defection of a personality as esteemed among the clergy as Rev. Fedukowicz seriously diminished the resistance of certain priests. Letters similar to the one of Rev. F.[edukowicz] have been signed by the following priests: Rev. Chrzczonowicz; Prelate Kruszynski; mitred Rev. Tolstoi; Rev. Nanowski; Rev. Kielus; Rev. Walter; and Rev. Zmigrodzki.

We must also emphasize the fact that a person called Ulanowski, an ex-member of the Communist "Cheka" from the town of Berdichev, declared himself to be a Catholic priest and that the Soviets entrusted him with a parish; it is true that up to now he has few followers, barely two hundred, but nevertheless this fact shows the immense danger which threatens the Church and which might shortly transform it into the so-called "Modern Catholic Church," following the example of "The Modern Orthodox Church" which has already been introduced in Russia by the Soviets.

We take the liberty of mentioning an occurrence in Kiev which took place about a fortnight ago and which shows the means used by the Soviets in their fight against the Catholic population. The Soviet authorities com-

manded the Committee of St. Alexander's Church to sign a commitment to
pay two thousand "chervonets" (about 160,000 liras) per annum as rent
for the church, or else the Soviets would install a cinema in the church.
Since the Catholics population and the clergy are in deep misery and cannot
even collect the funds necessary for urgent repairs on the church, it is certain that they will not be able to pay this enormous sum and that the
church will probably be confiscated by the Soviets as has already taken place
with a whole group of churches in the countryside.

Having thus described the desperate situation of the clergy and the
Catholic population in Russia, the Polish Executive Committee in Ruthenia implores Your Grace to intervene with the Holy See so that it may
come to the aid of these unfortunates by nominating the Bishops or Apostolic Administrators.

We are informed that the Holy See is negotiating with the Soviets who
are anxious to be able to boast to the whole world that they have signed a
kind of "Concordat." However, the way in which the Soviets fulfill treaties
and commitments once they are signed is well known. As proof we can
quote the Treaty of Riga which guaranteed the free use of the mother-
tongue and freedom of conscience and of education. Benefiting from the in-
tercalation of one phrase in the treaty, "conforming to Soviet laws," they
have annulled all the guarantees of the treaty and they are employing
wickedly and unscrupulously the most barbaric reprisals against the Poles
and the Catholic clergy. . . .

After considering the factors discussed above and the statistics which show
that Poles constitute over 94% of all the Catholics in European Russia, the
Polish Executive Committee in Ruthenia, in the name of justice and in the
best interests of the Church and the Catholic population, recommends that
all the religious posts in Russia, especially the posts of Bishops and Apostolic
Administrator, should be occupied by priests of Polish nationality. . . .

On the other hand we know that there are proposed the candidacies of
Rev. Prelate Anthoni Malecki, and Rev. Prelate Dr. Anthoni Okolo-Kulak
for the posts of Bishop or Apostolic Administrator in the districts of Minsk,
Mogilev, Vitebsk, as well as those of Petersburg and Moscow.

If the Holy See has decided to send missionaries to Russia, then from the
point of view of the interests of the Church and of the Catholic population
(of which over 94% is of Polish nationality there should be sent Italian,
French or Slavonic missionaries; such missionaries would be certain of obtaining the sympathy of all the Catholics in Russia, whereas the missionaries
of German nationality would be received with great distrust and would provoke a very understandable discontent.
Excellency:

Since the eleventh century the Poles have been the champions and propaga-
tors of the Catholic Church in Eastern Europe. The attacks of the inumerable

hordes of Mongols and Tartars always fell upon Polish breasts. Similarly in Russia today it is almost exclusively the small number of Polish people and clergy who defend the Catholic religion against the Soviet attacks, which are directed by the most ruthless enemies of Christ.

However, aid has to be supplied to these defenders who are almost worn out by atrocious fights and by the great misery in which they live.

This is why the Polish Executive Committee in Ruthenia takes the liberty of delivering this modest memorandum into the hands of Your Grace with the humble entreaty that it be helped to reach the Holy See.

His Holiness, The Dearest Father, who has shown so much friendliness to Poland and has conquered all Polish hearts, will greatly resent the terrible outrages directed against the Catholic religion, the very bases of Christianity, and the whole of humanity.

In spite of everything, we are convinced that in the near future we shall witness the triumph of the Christian Spirit and of Truth in Russia. And shortly, over today's hecatombs and over this soil impregnated with the blood of true martyrs, the Catholic Church will proudly raise the Banner of Christ, the Banner of Faith, Love and Pardon.

Stamp:

The Polish Executive Committee in Ruthenia

Presidential Department

Chairman of the Committee: John Lipkowski

Deputy Chairman of the Committee and

Chairman of the Society of Extra-Mural

Education in Ruthenia: Jozefat Andrzejewski

Late Chairman of the Committee in Kiev: Sigismund Chojecki

Secretary General: Czeslaw Brzostowski

1926

158
Letter of Archbishop Anastasii to the
Orthodox Metropolitan Evlogii of Paris

Constantinople, April 26, 1926

The Holy Synod and the Council of the Great Church presided over by His Holiness, the Ecumenical Patriarch, Meletius IV, in their meeting from the 11th to the 24th of April, discussed the question of the intended process against the Patriarch of Moscow and made the following resolution:

"To communicate to the representative of the Ecumenical Patriarch in Moscow that not only would the Great Church not allow its representative to take part in the trial, but it would also recommend that the Russian bishops abstain from all participation in the trial because Orthodoxy considers the Patriarch of Moscow and of all Russia a confessor of the faith."

I consider it my duty to communicate the preceding to your Eminence.

Anastasii

APPENDICES

I

Chronology of Soviet Legislation Concerning Religious Bodies: Russian S.F.S.R., 1918-1926

1918

23 January   Decree on the Separation of Church and State. The Code of Laws on the Registration of Births. Marriages and Deaths.
7 December   Decree on Cemeteries and Burials.
22 August   Circular of the People's Commissariat of Education on home chapels.
24 August   Instruction of the People's Commissariat of Justice on the Implementation of the Decree on the Separation of Church and State.
24 August   The Pattern Contract.
5 October   Instruction of the People's Commissariat of Education on the Preservation of the Monuments of Antiquity.

1919

4 January   Decree of the Council of People's Commissars on the Exemption from Military Service on account of Religious Beliefs.
14 Febraury   Decree of the All-Russian Central Executive Committee on the Socialist Land Distribution.
3 January   Circular of the People's Commissariat of Justice on the question of the Separation of Church and State.
3 March   Circular of the People's Commissariat of Education concerning non-admission of the Clergy to educational institutions.
7 May   Circular of the People's Commissariat of Internal Affairs No. 491 concerning the Terms of Registering Births.
19 June   Circular of the People's Commissariat of Internal Affairs No. 644: Administrative Punishments for [Violation of the Order on] Registration of Births, Marriages and Deaths.
14 October   Circular of the People's Commissariat of Internal Affairs No. 386 on the Legal Validity of Certificates of Birth, Marriages and Death of former times.
27 October   Circular of the People's Commissariat of Internal Affairs No. 1190-120 on the Order of Registration.

1920

14 December   Decree of the Council of People's Commissars on the Exemption from Military Service on Account of Religious Beliefs.
20 April   Decree of the Council of People's Commissars on the Conversion of the Holy Trinity and St. Sergius's Lavra [Monastery] into a museum.
25 August   Circular of the People's Commissariat of Justice on the Relics Cult.
30 March   Instruction of the People's Commissariat of Education and the People's Commissariat of Justice on the Inventory and the Preservation of the Monuments of Antiquity and Arts.
13 February   Circular of the People's Commissariat of Internal Affairs No. 155 on Names Given to Children, etc.
9 December   Circular of the People's Commissariat of Internal Affairs No. 359: the Scope of Relation and Relation in Law.

235

1921

13 June   Decree of the All-Russian Central Executive Committee on the Prohibition of Teaching [religion], on the Freedom of Preaching, on the Use of the
Edifices of the Temples.
27 September   Decree of the All-Russian Central Executive Committee on Disappearance, Change of Name, Legal Declaration as Dead, etc.
27 December   Decree of the All-Russian Central Executive Committee on the Distribution of Church Valuables.
11 January   The Circular of the People's Commissariat of Internal Affairs No. 8
     Relating to the Order of Determining the marriageable age in cases of doubt.
23 April   The Circular of the People's Commissariat of Education Relating to the
Prohibition of Teaching the So-Called "Law of God."
14 June   The Circular of the People's Commissariat of Internal Affairs No.
305 Relating to the Issuance of Certificates of Birth, Marriage and Death.
15 August   The Circular of the People's Commissariat of Agriculture and
Commissariat of Internal Affairs, the People's Commissariat of Agriculture and
the Workers-Peasants' Inspection on Various Subjects.
5 October   The Appeal of the People's Commissariat of Agriculture to the
Sectarians, Concerning the Colonization of lands.

1922

———————   The Code of Laws on Labor. The Rest Days.
———————   The Criminal Code. The Violation of the Rules on the Separation of
Church and State.
12 June   The Decree of the All-Russian Central Executive Committee Con-
cerning the Order of Convocation of the Congresses of Associations.
August   3   The Decree of the All-Russian Central Executive Committee Con-
cerning Private Non-Profit Societies.
August   10   The Instruction of the All-Russian Central Executive Committee on
the Registration of Societies.
August   10   The Instruction of the All-Russian Central Executive Committee on
the Procedure of Convening Congresses.
October   31   The Statute on the Governorship Executive Committees.
January   9   The Circular of the People's Commissariat of Internal Affairs No. 17
on the Governership Registers.
February   8   The Circular of the People's Commissariat of Internal Affairs No. 54
on Illiteracy in Connection with the Registration of Births, Marriages and Deaths.
February 15   The Circular of the People's Commissariat of Justice on the Decision
of Experts.
March   1   The Circular of the People's Commissariat of International Affairs
No. 25 on Diverse Citizenships of Spouses.
April   13   The Order of the Revolutionary-Military Council of the Republic on
the Red Oath.
April   27   The Circular of the People's Commissariat of Justice on the Responsi-
bility for Robbery and Theft of Church Property.
May   22   The Instruction of the People's Commissariat of Internal Affairs
Concerning Funerals.
June   17   The Circular of the People's Commissariat of Internal Affairs and
the People's Commissariat of Agriculture No. 202 on Cemeteries and Funerals.
August   11   The Circular of the People's Commissariat of Internal Affairs No.
54: the Family Name of the Child, Born Out of Wedlock.
August   The Circular of the People's Commissariat of Internal Affairs No. 265 on
the Non-Registering One's Religion with the Office of Registering Births, Marriages and Deaths.
September 13   The Sanitation Rules of the People's Commissariat of Health Regarding the Laying Out of Cemeteries, Crematories and the Burial of the Deceased.

1923

July   7   The Civil Procedural Code. Divorces. The Exemption from Military Service.

April   19   The Decree of the All-Russian Central Executive Committee on the Procedure of Annuling Agreements and the Closing of Churches.

April   19   The Decree of the Council of People's Commissars on the Special Means of the Main Administration of the Museums.

July   30   The Decree of the All-Russian Central Executive Committee on the Days of Rest According to the New Style.

September 19   The Decree of the Council of People's Commissars on the Procedure of Realization [Sale] of Church Valuables.

November 12   The Decree of the Central Executive Committee of the U.S.S.R. on the Collection of Rent.

January   3   The Instruction of the People's Commissariat of Internal Affairs on Administration Banishment.

January   16   The Circular of the People's Commissariat of Labor on the Holding of Several Employments.

January   26   The Circular of the People's Commissariat of Justice on the Procedure of Implementation of Decisions Concerning the Adoption of a Child.

February   23   The Circular of the People's Commissariat of Agriculture Concerning the Use of Land by the Ministers of Cult [Religious].

March   19   The Circular of the People's Commissariat of the Workers and Peasants' Inspection Concerning the Icons.

June   9   The Circular of the All-Union Central Council of the Trade Unions Concerning Anti-Religious Propaganda.

March   31   The Circular of the People's Commissariat of Internal Affairs No. 103 Concerning the Prohibition of Renting or Leasing the Churches.

April   27   The Instruction of the People's Commissariat of Justice and the People's Commissariat of Internal Affairs on the Order of Registration of Societies.

July   6   The Circular of the People's Commissariat of Justice on the Procedure of Contracting Marriages Abroad.

June   19   The Instruction of the People's Commissariat of Justice and the People's Commissariat of Internal Affairs on the Question of the Separation of Church and State.

————————   The Circular of the People's Commissariat of Internal Affairs on the Evaluation of the Objects of Cult in Gold Currency.

August   31   The Circular of the People's Commissariat of Justice and The People's Commissariat of Labor Concerning the Collection [of Fines] According to the Orders of the Courts.

September 3   The Circular of the People's Commissariat of Finances No. 102 Concerning the Taxes on the Construction of the Edifices of Cult.

September 5   The Circular of the People's Commissariat of Justice No. 115 concerning the Land Lease Payments on the [Land] under the Edifices of Cult.

September 20   The Circular of the People's Commissariat of Justice No. 190 on the Order of Closing the Edifices of Cult in the Factories.

October   24   The Circular of the People's Commissariat of Health No. 249 on the Sanitation Rules for Ministers of Cult.

October   29   The Circular of the People's Commissariat of Justice and the People's Commissariat of Labor on the Definition of the Term 'Lessee.'

November 16   The Circular of the People's Commissariat of Internal Affairs No. 294 on the Order of Payment of Fees for Birth, Marriage and Death Certificates for [Use] Abroad.

November 19   The Circular of the People's Commissariat of Internal Affairs No. 379 on the Land Lease Payments for the [Land] under the Edifices.

December 3   The Circular of the People's Commissariat of Labor on the Special Days of Rest.

December   8   The Circular of the People's Commissariat of Justice No. 254 on the Public Honoring of Persons Who Are Summoned to Court.

Dcember   15   The Circular of the People's Commissariat of Justice No. 258 concerning the Apartment Rent, the Tuition Fees, etc., of ministers of Cult.

December   20   The Circular of the State Insurance [Agency] No. 24 the Tariff Circular Concerning Insurance on Church Edifices.

December   22   The Instruction of the People's Commissariat of Internal Affairs and the People's Commissariat of Education No. 461 on the Order of Teaching Children Out of School.

1924

January   7   The Decree of the All-Russian Central Executive Committee and the Council of People's Commissars on the Transfer and Utilization of the Monuments of Antiquity.

January   9   The Instruction of the All-Russian Central Executive Committee on Eviction.

January   9   The Decree on Eviction.

March   27   The Decree of the All-Russian Central Executive Committee on the Village Marshalls.

May   9   The Amendments by the All-Russian Central Executive Committee on the Criminal Code for the Autonomous Republics.

May   9   The Decree of the Central Executive Committee of the U.S.S.R. on Societies.

May   29   The Decree of the Central Executive Committee and the Council of the People's Commissars of the U.S.S.R. on the Land Lease.

June   3   Resolutions of the XIII-th Congress of the Russian Communist Party (Bolsheviks) on the Question of Anti-Religious Propaganda.

July   7   The Instruction of the All-Russian Central Executive Committee concerning the Preservation of the Monuments of Antiquity.

July   14   The Decree of the All-Russian Central Executive Committee and the Council of People's Commissars of the U.S.S.R. on the Right to Change Given Names and Family Names.

July   25   The Decree on Stamps [Stamp Duty].

August   11   The Statute of the Administrative Departments of the Governorship Executive Committees.

August   22   The Decree of the All-Russian Central Executive Committee on Agricultural Co-operatives.

August   29   The Decree of the Central Executive Committee and the Council of People's Commissars of the U.S.S.R. concerning the Self-Taxation of Citizens.

September 26   The Decree of the Central Executive Committee and the Council of People's Commissars of the U.S.S.R. Concerning the Local Taxation [Stamp Duty] in Connection with the Change of Name.

October   16   The Decree of the All-Russian Central Executive Commitee on Changes in the Code on the Registration of Births, Marriages and Deaths.

October   16   The Statute of the Uyezd Executive Committees.

October   16   The Statute of the Volost' Executive Committees.

October   16   The Statute of the Village Soviets.

December   15   The Decree of the All-Russian Central Executive Committee and the Council of People's Commissars on Labor Co-operatives [Artels].

January   19   The Circular of the People's Commissariat of Finance No. 497 on the Reduction of Fees on Building Permits.

February   16   The Circular of the People's Commissariat of Internal Affairs No. 68 on Information About the Mother of a Child during Registration of Births, Marriages and Deaths.

February   16   The Decree of the Central Executive Committee of the U.S.S.R. on the Special Financial Means of the General Administration of the Museums.

February   26   The Circular of the People's Commissariat of Finance on the Question Who Should Be Classified as a Servant of the Cult.

March   7   The Circular of the People's Commissariat of Finance No. 779 on Suspension of Collections of Supplementary Rents.

March   13   The Decree of the Council of the People's Commissars on the Rent for Premises Occupied by Institutions.

January   19   The Circular of the People's Commissariat of Finance on the Reduction of Taxes on Edifices to ¼ of one per cent.

March   13   The Circular of the People's Commissariat of Justice and of the People's Commissariat of Finance 655 and 656 on Compulsory governmental insurance on edifices of the cult.

April   1   The Circular of the People's Commissariat of Education and of the People's Commissariat of Internal Affairs on the Order of Instruction [and Education] outside of the Schools.

April   7   The Circular of the People's Commissariat of Internal Affairs No. 149 on the Registration of Births, Marriages and Deaths and on Immunity to Punishment of Ministers of Cults.

April   23   The Circular of the People's Commissariat of Justice and of the People's Commissariat of Internal Affairs on the Prohibition of Confiscating Church Buildings *De Facto* Until the Case is passed upon by the All-Russian Central Executive Committee.

June   7   The Circular of the People's Commissariat of Justice and of the People's Commissariat of Internal Affairs on Church Wardens.

June   18   The Circular of the People's Commissariat of Internal Affairs No. 259 on Bringing the Registration of Births, Marriages and Deaths into Order.

June   21   The Circular of the People's Commissariat of Justice and of the People's Commissariat of Internal Affairs No. 64 on Marriages in the Occupied Territories.

July   30   The Circular of the Supreme Court No. 27 on the Time of Receiving Certificates concerning Military Service.

August   20   The Instruction of the People's Commissariat of Justice and the People's Commissariat of Internal Affairs Concerning the Tranfers of [Ownership] of the Old Believers' Churches.

August   21   The Instruction of the People's Commissariat of Internal Affairs Concerning Apartment Rent.

August   23   The Circular of the People's Commissariat of Internal Affairs Concerning Church Houses. [Houses Belonging to Churches].

September   5   The Instruction of the People's Commissariat of Internal Affairs Concerning the Procedure in Changes of Names.

September   5   The Circular of the People's Commissariat of Justice No. 136 Concerning the Establishment of the Norms of Alimony.

September   6   The Circular No. 137 on the Procedure of the Receiving an Adopted Son into a [Farmer's Family].

September   19   The Circular of the People's Commissariat of Internal Affairs No. 402 Concerning the Stamp-Duty on documents Issued by the Bureau of Registration of Births, Marriages and Deaths.

September   13   The Instruction of the People's Commissariat of Justice and the People's Commissariat of Internal Affairs Concerning the Procedure of the Transfers of Churches to the Old Believers.

October   16   The Circular of the People's Commissariat of Health Concerning the Illnesses Which Constitute Valid Ground for the Right to [possess] Additional Housing Facilities.

October   18   The Circular of the People's Commissariat of Justice and the People's Commissariat of Finance Concerning the Struggle Against Taxation Without [Proper] Authorization.

November   17   The Circular of the People's Commissariat of Justice on the Protection of Minors [Adolescents].

December   3   The Circular of the People's Commissariat of Finance on the Procedure of Taxing Locally the Buildings of the Cult.

December   18   The Circular of the People's Commissariat of Justice and the People's Commissariat of Labor Concerning the Collection of Alimony by Order of the Court.

August   19-21   The Circular of the All-Russian Central Executive Committee on Cult Affairs (Secret).

September   5   The Decree of the Central Executive Committee and the Council of People's Commissars of the USSR on the Procedure of Voluntary Collections [of Money].

September 29   Decree of the All Russian Central Executive Committee and the Council of Peoples Commissars Concerning Additional Housing Facilities.

1925

January   16   The Instruction of the Central Executive Committee and the Council of People's Commissars of the US.S.R. Concerning Re-Election to City and Village Soviets.

January   26   The Circular of the All Russian Central Executive Committee on the Regulation of Trade in Private Businesses During Local Holidays.

February   9   The Decree of the All Russian Central Executive Committee and the Council of People's Commissars on Special Days of Rest.

March   30   The Decree of the All Russian Central Executive Committee and the Council of People's Commissars on the Change of Article 19 of the Code on Registration of Births, Marriages and Deaths.

April   7   The Decree of the Council of People's Commissars on Appropriations for the General Administration of Museums of 60 per cent of the realized [sold] State Funds of Museum Significance.

May   8   The Decree of the All Russian Central Executive Committee on a Uniform Farm Tax.

June   1   The Decree of the All Russian Central Executive Committee and the Council of People's Commissars on Apartment Rent.

July   17   The Decree of the Central Executive Committee and the Council of People's Commissars of the USSR on the Abolition of Office Fees.

August   24   The Decree of the All Russian Executive Committee on the Procedure of Using Insurance [Benefits] for the [Loss of Property] Caused by Fire in the Edifices of the Cult.

September 18   The Law on Obligatory Military Service.

October   13   The Instruction of the All Russian Central Executive Committee on Re-Elections to City and Village Soviets.

October   29   The Statutes on the Income Tax.

November 30   The Decree of the All Russian Central Executive Committee and the Council of People's Commissars on Nationalized and Municipalized Properties.

January   2   The Circular of the People's Commissariat of Finance on Privileges in Connections with the Taxation of Church Edifices and the Servants of the Cult.

January   7   The Circular of the People's Commissariat of Finance No. 484 on the Procedure of Apportioning Local Taxes on Church Edifices.

January   9   The Instruction of the People's Commissariat of Internal Affairs No. 18 on the Procedure of Registration of Births, Marriages and Deaths in Village Soviets.

January   14   The Circular of the People's Commissariat of Finance of the USSR No. 329 [on the Question] What Should be Considered the Principle Occupation.

January   21   The Circular of the People's Commissariat of Justice on Voluntary Collections [of Money].

February   12   The Circular of the People's Commissariat of Internal Affairs No. 73 on the Procedure of Issuing Permits for the Celebration of Religious Rites.

February   26   The Circular of the People's Commissariat of Internal Affairs No. 122 on the Procedure of Restoration of Records.

February 26 The Circular of the People's Commissariat of Internal Affairs No. 123 on the Procedure of Permitting Early Marriages.

May 15 The Circular of the People's Commissariat of Internal Affairs No. 265 on the Procedure of Registration of Births and Deaths.

June 13 The Circular of the People's Commissariat of Internal Affairs and the People's Commissariat of Health No. 328/128 on Medical Certificates.

June 20 The Circular of the People's Commissariat of Internal Affairs and the People's Commissariat of Justice No. 389/154 on the Procedure of Changing the Name During Marriages.

June 30 The Circular of the People's Commissariat of Internal Affairs No. 365 on the Corrections in the Column "Marital Status" and on Oktiabrinas. [Communist 'Baptism' in connection with October Revolution].

July 7 The Circular of the People's Commissariat of Justice No. 188 Concerning the Struggle Against Evading Military Service.

July 13 The Circular of the People's Commissariat of Internal Affairs and the People's Commissariat of Health No. 328 on the Issuance of Medical Certificates About Deaths and in Connection With Marriages.

July 25 The Instruction of the People's Commissariat of Justice No. 155, the People's Commissariat of Internal Affairs No. 402 and the People's Commissariat of Finance No. 20 on Church Houses.

August 19 The Circular of the People's Commissariat of Internal Affairs No. 444 on the Procedure of Changing the Name.

September 14 The Circular of the People's Commissariat of Internal Affairs on the Village Cemeteries.

November 4 The Circular of the People's Commissariat of Finance on the State Income Tax.

November 5 The Instruction of the People's Commissariat of Justice and the People's Commissariat of Health on the Procedure of Issuance of Medical Certificates.

November 12 The Circular of the People's Commissariat of Internal Affairs No. 595 on the Question of Separation of Church and State.

December 17 The Circular of the People's Commissariat of Internal Affairs No. 668 on the Burial of Dead Bodies by Militia.

December 24 The Circular of the People's Commissariat of Internal Affairs No. 686 on the Deposition [Safe-Keeping] of the Acts of Registering Births, Marriages and Deaths in the Archives.

December 25 The Circular of the People's Commissariat of Internal Affairs No. 687 Concerning Notations in Military Documents.

(*Cf. for guidance Gidulianov, P.V., Otdelenie tserkvi ot gosudarastva v SSSR; Polnyi sbornik dekretov, vedomstvennykh resporiazhenii i opredelenii Verkhsuda RSFSR, i drugikh Sovetskikh Sotsialisticheskikh Respublik: USSR, BSSR, ZSFSR, Uzbekskoi i Turkmenskoi [Separation of Church and State in the USSR; A Complete Collection of the Decrees, Departmental Orders and Decisions of the Supreme Court of the Russian S.F.S.R. and the Order Soviet Socialist Republics the Ukranian S.S.S., the Byelorussian S.S.R., the Transcaucasian S.F.S.R., the Uzbek [S.S.R.] and the Turkmen [S.S.R.],* 3-d edit., Krasikov, P.A., ed., Moscow, Iuridicheskoe Izdatel'stvo N.K.Iu. R.S.F.S.R., 1926, pp. 677-686, and *passim.*)

II
Chronology of Soviet Legislation Concerning Religious Bodies: Moslem Republics, 1920-1925

AZERBAIJAN
1920

June 30 Decree on the Preservation of the Monuments of Antiquity.

1922

July   21   Decree on the Observation of Friday.
October   4   Decree of the Council of People's Commissars on Private Non-Profit Societies.
October   4   The Instruction of the Council of People's Commissars on the Registration of Private Societies.

1923

September   8   The Civil Code.
December   20   Decree on Administrative Deportations.
August   1   Decree on the Obeservation of Shakhsei-vakhsei.

ABKHAZIA

1921

October   11   The Circular of the People's Commisariat of Internal Affairs Concerning the Registration of Births, Marriages and Deaths.

1923

February   15   The Circular of the People's Commissariat of Internal Affairs Concerning Confiscations.
February   16   The Circular of the People's Commissariat of Internal Affairs Concerning the Procedure of Transferring [the Ownership of] the Temples.
February   21   Decree of the Central Executive Committee on Private Non-Profit Societies.
March   2   The Order of the People's Commissariat of Internal Affairs on the Obligatory Registration of Births, Marriagges and Deaths.
March   2   The Order of the People's Commissariat of Internal Affairs on the Registration of the Clergy.

1925

January   1   Decree of the Central Executive Committee Concerning the Preservation of the Monuments of Antiquity.

UZBEKISTAN
The Turkestan Autonomous Soviet Socialist Republic

1921

January   10   Decree on the Observation of Friday.
May   22   Decree on the Preservation of the Monuments of Antiquity.
July   31   Decree on the same subject.

1922

June   20   Decree of the Central Executive Committee on the Restoration of the Wakfs [property which had been given to Moslem religious institutions].
December   23   Decree of the Central Executive Committee: "The Statutes on the Courts of Kazis."

1923

January   30   The Circular of the People's Commissariat of Justice Concerning the Courts of the Kazis and Beys' [Jurisdiction] over Divorces.
February   14   The Statute of the Educational Religious Society "Makhkamei-Shariah."
January   6   Decree on the Courts of the Beys in Ferghana.

1924

November   27   Decree of the Central Executive Committee of the Uzbek Soviet Socialist Republic on the Preservation of [legal] Force of the Local Laws [based on the Moslem Religious Law].

(Cf. also Gidulianov, P.V., Otdelenie tserkvi ot gosudarstva v SSSR; Polnyi sbornik dekretov, vedomstvennykh rasporiazhenii i opredelenii Verkhsuda RSFSR, i drugikh Sovetskikh Sotisialisticheskikh Respublik: USSR, BSSR, ZSFSR, Uzbekskoi i Turkmenskoi [Separation of Church and State in the USSR; A Complete Collection of the Decrees, Departmental Orders and Decisions of the Supreme Court of the Russian S.F.S.R. and the Other Soviet Socialist Republics: the Ukrainian S.S.R., the Byelorussian S.S.R., the Transcaucasian S.F.S.R., the Uzbek [S.S.R.] and the Turkmen [S.S.R.],] 3-d edit., Krasikov, P.A., ed., Moscow, Iuridicheskoe Izdatel'stvo N.K.Iu. R.S.F.S.R., 1926, 685-686; 6, 61, 62, 64, 113, 116, 177, 178, 271, 273, 278, 304, 375, 396, 399, 516, 517, 536.)

III

Biographical Notes on Some Orthodox and Roman Catholic Prelates Referred to in the Present Collection of Documents

METROPOLITAN VLADIMIR

Metropolitan Vladimir (Vasilii Nikiforovich Bogoiavlenskii) was born on January 1, 1848, at Malye-Morshki, governorship of Tambov, in the family of a priest. In 1874, he graduated from the Kiev Theological Academy, and became a teacher of the Tambov Theological Seminary. In 1882, he was ordained; and in 1886, after his wife and child had died, he took monastic vows. In 1888, he was consecrated Bishop of Staraia Russa; in 1891, he was appointed Bishop of Samara. In 1892, he became Archbishop of Kartalia and Kakhetia, Exarch of Georgia; and in 1898, he was appointed Metropolitan of Moscow and Kolomna. In 1912, he was transferred to the See of Petersburg and Ladoga, and in 1915, to that of Kiev and Halich. During the Bolshevik capture of Kiev, he was murdered on January 25, 1918.
[Cf. Polskii, M., Protopresbyter, comp., *Novye mucheniki rossiiskie; pervoe sobranie materialov [The New Martyrs of Russia; The First Collection of Materials]*, Jordanville, N.Y., Holy Trinity Monastery, 1949, 10-24].

PATRIARCH TIKHON

Patriarch Tikhon (Vasilii Ivanovich Belavin) was born in the family of an Orthodox Priest at Toporets, Governorship of Pskov, on January 19, 1865. Between 1878 and 1883 he attended the Pskov Seminary, and in 1888 he graduated from the St. Petersburg Theological Academy. He was a teacher at the Pskov Seminary, then Inspector and Rector at the Khelm Seminary. In 1891, he took monastic vows, and was ordained. In 1898, he was consecrated Bishop of the Aleutian Islands and Alaska. Later he was Archbishop of Iaroslavl, and of Vilna, and Metropolitan of Moscow. On November 5, 1917, he was elected Patriarch of Moscow. He anathemized the Soviet government on January 19, 1918; but, arrested in the fall of 1922, he was compelled to sign a declaration in which he renounced his 'counter-revolutionary tendencies' and proclaimed himself 'no enemy to the Soviets.' He was released on June 26, 1923, and used his freedom to combat the 'Living Church.' He died in Moscow on March 25, 1925.
[Cf. Andreev, I.M., *Kratkii obzor istorii Russkoi Tserkvi ot revoliutsii do nashikh dnei [An Outline of Russian Church History from the Revolution to Our Day]*, Jordanville, N.Y., Holy Trinity Monastery, 1953, 16-27, 37-47.]

JOHN BAPTIST CIEPLAK

John Baptist Cieplak was born of a mining family on August 17, 1857, in Dombrova Gornicza in Poland. He studied in Kielce gymnasium, 1868-1873; then he entered the theological seminary, and later the Theological Academy in St. Petersburg. In 1901 he received the doctorate in theology. In 1908 he was appointed titular bishop of Evarien and suffragan bishop of Mohilev in Russia. He displayed great zeal in his work among the Roman Catholics in the Russian empire. On August 6, 1914, after the resignation of Archbishop Vincent Kuczynski, Cieplak was appointed administrator of the archdiocese of Mohilev.

When Archbishop Edward Ropp was nominated ordinary of Mohilev in 1917, Bishop Cieplak was his assistant, struggling heroically for the freedom of the Roman Catholic Church in Russia. On April 29, 1919, the Metropolitan Ropp was imprisoned by the Bolsheviks in Moscow. On November 17, 1919, Archbishop Ropp was exiled to Poland and exchanged for a Communist called Radek (Sobelson). Archbishop Cieplak then became the leader of all the Roman Catholics in Russia. Among them were Russians, Ukranians, Belorussians (White Ruthenians) Lithuanians, Poles, Armenians, Germans, Latvians, Estonians, etc., etc. In April of 1920, Archbishop Cieplak was arrested in St. Petersburg, released after two weeks and again arrested in May, 1922. (Monsignor Constantin Budkiewicz was his assistant in church affairs. Cieplak was also assisted by Fr. Abrikosov and Exarch Fedorov, both native Russians.) The Archbishop was summoned to Moscow from St. Petersburg and ordered to appear in March, 1923, before the Supreme Tribunal at Moscow. Later, on March 10, he was arrested with other Catholic priests. The trial began on March 21, and on March 25, 1923, he was condemned to death, together with Mgr. Constantine Budkiewicz. The Archbishop, however, was saved by many protests from different parts of the world, and released from the Butyrka prison. For a time, he had stayed also in the infamous Muscovite prison at Lubianka. Banished from Russia, he arrived in Poland on April 21, 1924. Then, in May, he went to Rome to report on the status of the Catholic Church in Soviet Russia. He visited the U.S.A. in November, 1925. Here he learned that he had been appointed Archbishop of Vilna, Poland, by the Holy See. But before he could return to Poland, he died on February 17, 1926, in Passaic, N. J. Cieplak was a truly holy man, and a great Catholic bishop. (See F. Domanski, *John Baptist Cieplak*, Chicago, 1954.)

LEONIDAS FEDOROV

Exarch Leonidas Fedorov of the Russian Catholic Rite was ordained in Bulgaria in 1911. He returned to Russia and was exiled to Siberia by the tsarist government because of his missionary work among the Russian Orthodox. He was made the exarch by Archbishop John B. Cieplak in 1921, for the Russian Catholics of the Byzantine Rite. He was imprisoned by the Bolsheviks on March 25, 1923, and died a prisoner in Viatka, March 7, 1935.
(See P. Mailleux, "The Catholic in Russia and Exarch Fedorov," *Religion in Russia: A Collection of Essays Read at the Cambridge Summer School of Russian Studies*, ed. George Bennigsen. London, 1940).

METROPOLITAN EVLOGII

Metropolitan Evlogii (Vasilii Georgievkii) was born on April 23, 1868, in the Governorship of Tula. In 1892, he graduated from the Moscow Theological Academy. In 1893, he made Head Master of Efremov Ecclesiastical School; he moved to the Seminary in Tula in 1894, took monastic vows, and was ordained in 1895. Then he was Inspector of the Vladimir Seminary and Rector of the Khelm Seminary. In

1902, he was consecrated Bishop of Lublin. In 1905 he was transferred to the See of Kholm, and in 1914 to that of Volinia. He was a member of the First and the Second State Dumas in 1905 and 1907. He was a prisoner of the Bolsheviks in 1919. In 1920, while in exile, he was appointed by Patriarch Tikhon Head of all the Russian Churches in Western Europe. In 1912 he was made Archbishop, and in 1922, he was was raised to the rank of Metropolitan. In 1922, he separated himself from other Russian Bishops in exile; in 1927, he joined Metropolitan Sergii's declaration concerning the cooperation with the Soviet authorities. In 1931, he recognized the jurisdiction of the Patriarch of Constantinople, but, in 1945, he returned to the jurisdiction of the Patriarch of Moscow. He died on August 8, 1945. Cf. "The Metropolitan Evlogios," *The Christian East*, London, The Anglican and Eastern Church Association, Vol. III, No. 4 (December 1922), p. 151; and Andreev, I.M., *Kratkii obzor istorii Russkoi Tserkvi ot revoliutsii do nashikh dnei* [*An Outline of Russian Church History from the Revolution to Our Day*], Jordanville, N.Y., Holy Trinity Monastery, 1953, 139-150.

METROPOLITAN NIKOLAI OF KRUTITSK

The present Metropolitan of Krutitsk, the Vicar of the Patriarch of Moscow, Nikolai, is the most important bishop in the Russian Orthodox Church since 1945. He controls all the political affairs of the Moscow Patriarchate. His role during the Bolshevik persecution of the Church is rather mysterious.

Metropolitan Nikolai comes from the old Polish-Belorussian gentry living in Lithuania. His family name is Boris Iarushevich (Jaruszewicz). He was born on January 13, 1892. He was educated in St. Petersburg, where his father taught religion at the Kseninskii Institute. Boris Iarushevich studied Physics and Mathematics at St. Petersburg University, and in 1910 he started his theological studies at the Theological Academy, where he excelled in Canon Law. On October 23, 1914, he became a monk, taking the monastic name Nikolai, but was never a regular member of a monastic community. He was a military chaplain in 1915-1916. In 1917 he wrote his Master's thesis, and in 1918 he was a senior priest (canon) of the Cathedral of Sts. Peter and Paul in St. Petersburg. In 919 Nikolai was archimandrite.

During the period of severe persecution of religion, he was made on March 25, 1922, Archbishop of Peterhof, vicar of the St. Petersburg metropolitan. At that time he was thirty years of age. In 1922 he was arrested and exiled, but in 1924 he was permitted to return to St. Petersburg (Leningrad). He joined the party of the clergy which collaborated with the Soviet authorities on the basis of "coexistence". After the invasion of Eastern Poland by the Russians in the fall of 1939, Archbishop Nikolai went there in order to subordinate the Polish Autocephalic Orthodox bishops to the Moscow Russian Patriarchate. He knew how to crush the opposition among the clergy of the Polish Autocephalic Orthodox Church. In 1941 he was made metropolitan of Kiev and Halich. On November 2, 1942, he was appointed a member of the Extraordinary State Commission for Establishing and Investigating the Crimes of the German-Fascist Invaders and their Accomplices. He is the most active prelate in political affairs for the Patriarchate. He is a diplomat and demagogue of the Bolshevik type, a propagandist of the Russian Communist "peace" policy. (See *Zhurnal Moskovskoi Patriarkhii*, No. 4 (1952), pp. 9-21, No. 12 (1954), pp. 18-21; Vassilii Alexeev, *Russian Orthodox Bishops in the Soviet Union, 1941-1953* (New York, 1954), p. 105; N. Grigorev, "Metropolitan Nikolai Krutitsky," *Bulletin of the Inst. for the Study of the USSR*, vol. III (1956), May, pp. 34-39.

METROPOLITAN ANTONII

Metropolitan Antonii (Aleksei Khrapovitskii) was born in the old noble family at Vatagino, Governorship of Novgorod, on March 17, 1863. He graduated from the 5th St. Petersburg Gymnasium, and the St. Petersburg Theological Academy

(1885). On May 18, he took monastic vows, and on September 30, 1885, he was ordained. He was Deputy Inspector of St. Petersburg Academy, teacher of the Khelm Seminary, teacher of St. Petersburg Academy, Rector of St. Petersburg Seminary, Rector of the Moscow and of Kazan Theological Academies. In 1897, he was consecrated Bishop of Cheboksary, and in 1900 he became Bishop of Ufa. In 1902, he was transferred to Zhytomir, Volinia; and, in 1913, to Kharkov. In 1917, he became Metropolitan of Kharkov, and then of Kiev. He was the Head of the Supreme Church Administration on the territory of the White Army, and then in exile, in Yugoslavia. He died on August 10, 1936, at Sremski Karlovtsi, Yugoslavia.

Cf. Andreev, I. M., *Kratkii obzor istorii Russkoi Tserkvi ot revoliutsii do nashikh dnei* [*An Outline of Russian Church History from the Revolution to Our Day*], Jordanville, N.Y., Holy Trinity Monastery, 1953, 105-108.

METROPOLITAN PETR

Metropolitan Pëtr (Pëtr Fedorovich Polianskii) was born in the governorship of Voronezh, in 1863. He received his education in the Voronezh Seminary and the Moscow Theological Academy from which he graduated in 1892, receiving the degree of Master of Theology soon afterwards when his dissertation was completed. He was soon appointed Executive Secretary, and then Member of the Committee on Education of the Holy Synod. In 1917-1918, he took active part in the work of the All Russian Orthodox Church Sobor, and became a close collaborator of Patriarch Tikhon. In 1920, he took monastic vows, and on April 25 he was consecrated bishop, as the Vicar of the Patriarch; later he was granted the rank of Metropolitan of Krutitsk after the death of Patriarch Tikhon, Metropolitan Petr became *Locum Tenens* of the Patriarchal See of Moscow. He opposed the Renovators' movement, and refused to issue a declaration on the cooperation with the Soviet government. On December 10, 1925, Metropolitan Pëtr was arrested, and late in the fall of 1926 exiled to Tobolsk (West Siberia), and then to Khe, on the Ob. He refused to support Metropolitan Sergii in his surrender to the Bolsheviks, and remained in exile until his death in December 1936.

Cf. Polskii, M., *Novye mucheniki*, 135-143.

METROPOLITAN AGAFANGEL

Mteropolitan Agafangel (Aleksandr Lavrentevich Preobrazhenskii) was born on September 24, 1854, in the governorship of Tula. He received his education in Theological Seminary and the Moscow Theological Academy. He was a teacher, and after having taken monastic vows, inspector and rector of the seminary. On September 10, 1889, he was consecrated bishop, serving at first as a Suffragan Bishop, and after 1893, as the Ruling Bishop of Tobolsk; later was Archbishop of Riga, then of Iaroslavi. In 1918 he was raised to the rank of metropolitan. In May 1922, Patriarch Tikhon appointed Metropolitan Agafangel his successor. Metropolitan Agafangel was prevented from taking his office, and in August he was arrested. Soon he was exiled to Narym Territory (now Tomsk region). After some time he was released, and returned to Iaroslavl. He opposed the Declaration on cooperation with the Soviet government published by Metropolitan Sergii; and as a consequence, the Diocese of Iaroslavl separated itself in 1928 from the Church headed by Metropolitan Sergii. Metropolitan Agafanfel died in October 1928.

Cf. Polskii, M., *Novye mucheniki*, 144-147.

METROPOLITAN ARSENII

Metropolitan Arsenii (Avksentii Stadnitskii) was born in Kishinev on January 22, 1862, of Polish background, graduated from the local seminary, and then was a teacher in his native governorship. In 1881, he entered the Kiev Thelogical Academy,

graduated from it with honors, and successfully defended his Master's thesis. In 1897 he was appointed inspector, and then rector, of the Moscow Theological Academy, and in 1899, he became the Vicar of the Metropolitan of Moscow. In 1904 he sucessfully defended his Doctoral dissertation in the field of Church history, and in 1907 became a member of the State Council. Appointed Archbishop of Novgorod in 1910, he remained in that See also after the revolution. In 1917, he was raised to the rank of Metropolitan. He was a *Lucum Tenens* of the Patriarchal See of Moscow. Several times he was arrested and sent to exile (concentration camps). He died in exile in Tashkent, in February 1936.
Cf. Polskii, M., *Novye Mucheniki*, 148-149.

PATRIARCH SERGII

Patriarch Sergii (Ivan Nikolaevich Stargorodskii) was born in the family of an Orthodox Priest at Arzamas, Governorship of Nizhnii Novgorod, on January 11, 1867. He graduated from the Arzamas Church School, the Seminary of Nizhni Novgorod, and the St. Petersburg Theological Academy (in 1890). In 1895, he received the degree of Master of Theology. Having taken monastic vows, he was a missionary in Japan, a teacher in the St. Petersburg Academy, Inspector of the Moscow Seminary, Pastor of the Russian Embassy Church at Athens, then Inspector and Rector of St. Petersburg Academy. In 1901, he was consecrated Bishop of Iamburg [Jahmburg], and, in 1905, became Archbishop of Vyborg [Viipuri] and Finland. In 1918, he became Metropolitan of Nizhni Novgorod. He supported the Renovators' Supreme Church Administration in 1922, but repented and returned to the Patriarchal Church in 1924. He became *Locum Tenens* of the Patriarchal See of Moscow on December 10, 1925. On July 29, 1927, he signed a declaration of cooperation with the Soviet government. In 1942, he edited the propaganda book *The Truth About Religion in Russia*. On September 8, 1943, he was elected Patriarch of Moscow. He died on May 15, 1944..
Cf. Andreev, I. M., *Kratkii obzor istorii Russkoi Tserkvi*, 72-77.

METROPOLITAN ALEKSANDR VVENDENSKII

Metropolitan Aleksandr Ivanovich Vvedenskii was born in 1888. He graduated from the St. Petersburg University and the St. Petersburg Theological Academy. In 1914 he was ordained. He took active part in the 'Living Church' movement, and advocated cooperation with the Soviet government. He was consecrated Bishop without having taken monastic vows. In 1924, he became the Metropolitan of the Synodal (Renovated) Church.
Cf. "Vvedenskii, Aleksandrf Ivanovich," *Bol'shaia Sovetskaia Entsiklopediia* [*The Large Soviet Encyclopaedia*], I-st edit., Shmidt, O.Iu., ed., Moscow, Slovarno-Entsiklopedicheskoe Izdatel'stvo "Bol'shaia Sovetskaia Entsiklopediia," vol. 26, p. 114.

IV

List of Orthodox Bishops Imprisoned and Exiled by the Bolsheviks

Metropolitan Agafangel, of Iaroslavl — exiled to Narym Territory (now Tomsk region).
Metropolitan Kirill, of Kazan — exiled to Ust-Kuloma.
Metropolitan Mikhail, Exarch of Kiev — exiled to Tashkent.
Metropolitan Arsenii, of Novgorod — exiled to Bokhara.
Metropolitan Sergii, of Vladimir — in 1925 released from the Vladimir prison and exiled to Nizhnii Novgorod (now Gorkii).

Metropolitan Serafim (Chichagov) — imprisoned in the Butyrka prison in Moscow.

Archbishop Nikandr, of Krutitsk — exiled to Bokhara.

Archbishop Grigorii, of Ekaterinburg (Sverdlovsk) — imprisoned in the Vladimir prison.

Archbishop Illarion, formerly the Administrator of the Moscow Diocese — exiled to Solovki.

Bishop Feodor — imprisoned in the Butyrka prison in Moscow.

Bishop Gurii — imprisoned in the Butyrka prison in Moscow.

Bishop Nikolai, of Zvenigorod — imprisoned in the Butyrka prison in Moscow.

Bishop Valerian, of Smolensk — imprisoned in the Butyrka prison.

Bishop Platon, of Bogorodsk — imprisoned in the Butyrka prison.

Bishop Feodosii, of Kolomna — imprisoned in the Butyrka prison.

Bishop Grigorii, of Petropavlovsk (Kòzyrev) — imprisoned in the Butyrka prison in Moscow.

Bishop Manuil, of Lemeshevek, temporarily in charge of the Petrograd Diocese — imprisoned in the Petrograd prison.

Bishop Serafim, of Kolpino, — imprisoned in the Petrograd prison.

Bishop Veniamin, of Lubin — imprisoned in the Vladimir prison.

Bishop Damaskin, the Suffragan Bishop of the Chernikov Diocese — imprisoned in the Odesa prison.

Bishop Gervasii, of Rybinsk — imprisoned in the Iaroslavl prison.

Bishop Nikodim (Krotkov) of Tavria — exiled to Tashkent.

Bishop Arsenii, of Taganrog — exiled to Solovki.

Bishop Mitrofan (Schherbakov) — exiled to Solovki.

Bishop Gavriil, of Ostashkovo — exiled to Solovki.

Bishop Sofronii, of Novonikolaevsk — exiled to Solovki.

Bishop Kiprian, of Semipalatinsk — exiled to Solovki.

Bishop Ioakim, of Simbirsk (Ulianovsk) — exiled to Solovki.

Bishop Ignatii, of Belëvsk (Sadkovskii) — exiled to Solovki.

Bishop Pëtr (Sokolov), the Suffragan Bishop of Simbirsk (Ulianovsk) — exiled to Solovki.

Bishop Pamfil — exiled to Iarensk, (Vologda governorship.)

Bishop Serafim (Ostroumov) of Orel — returned from Velikii Ustiug.

Bishop Nifont, of Tsaritsyn (Stalingrad) — exiled to Velikii Ustiug.

Bishop Afanasii, of Kovrovsk — exiled to Ust-Kuloma.

Bishop Avvakum — exiled to Ust-Sysolsk.

Bishop Nikolai, of Peterhof — exiled to Ust-Sysolsk.

Bishop Vasilii, of Kineshma — exiled to Ust-Kuloma.

Bishop Feofil, of Novyi Torzhok — exiled to Vizinga.

Bishop Serafim, of Dmitrievsk — exiled to Vizinga.

Bishop Vasilii (Bagdashevskii), of Kanev — died at Izhma.

Bishop Dmitrii (Vebitskii), of Belaia Tserkov — exiled to Izhma.

Bishop Lev, of Tagil — exiled to Kazalinsk.

Bishop Pavel, the Suffragan Bishop of the Viatka Diocese — exiled to Kazalinsk.

Bishop Pavel (Borisovskii), of Viatka — exiled to Narym territory (now Tomsk region.

Bishop Viktor, the Suffragan Bishop of the Viatka diocese — exiled to Narym territory (now Tomsk region).

Bishop Antonii, of Arkhangelsk — exiled to Narym territory.

Bishop Kornilii, of Viazniki — exiled to Narym territory.

Bishop Ioanikii, of Staraia Russa — exiled to Narym territory.

Bishop Aristarkh, of Orenburg (Chkalov) — exiled to Narym territory.

Bishop Stefan (Bekh), of Izhevsk — exiled to Narym territory.

Bishop Dosifei (Protopopov), of Saratov — exiled to Narym territory.

Bishop Evfimii, of Olonets — exiled to Narym territory.

Bishop Dorofei (See unknown) — exiled to Narym territory.

Bishop Evsevii, of Eisk — exiled to Yakutsk region.

Bishop Aleksei (Simanskii), of Iamburg — exiled to Semipalatinsk.
Bishop Sergii (Lavrov), of Sukhum — exiled to Tashkent.
Bishop Andrei (Ukhtomskii), of Ufa — exiled to Tashkent.
Bishop Innokentii, of Ladoga — exiled to Ura-Tiube.
Bishop Damian, of Pereiaslavl — exiled to Nedzhenken.
Bishop Daniil (Troitskii), of Bolkhovo — exiled to Nedzhenken.
Bishop Pëtr (Zverev), of Staritsa — exiled to Perovsk.
Bishop Anatolii (Grisiuk), of Samara — exiled to Turkestan.
Bishop Pavel, of Buzuluk — exiled to Turkestan.

Cf. Valentinov, A.A., ed., *Chernaia Kniga ("Shturm nebes"); Sbornik dokumental-'nykh dannykh, Kharakterizuiushchikh bor'bu sovetskoi kommunisticheskoi vlasti protiv vsiakoi religii, protiv vsekh ispovedanii i tserkvei* [The Black Book ("The Storming of the Heavens"); A Collection of Documentary Data, Characterizing the Struggle of the Soviet Communist Government Against All Religion, Against All Confessions and Churches], Paris, Izdanie Russkago Natsional'nago Studencheskago ob"edineniia, 1925, 257-259.

V

List of the Desecrated Relics of Saints

February 12, 1919 St. Avraamii, the Martyr, Vladimir
February 13, 1919 Prince Andrei, Vladimir
February 17, 1919 Prince Gavriil, Iurevskolskii
February 20, 1919 Reverend Daniel the Monk, Pereiaslavl
February 10, 1919 Pëtr and Fevroniia, Murom
February 10, 1919 Bishop Ioann, Suzdal
February 7, 1919 Prince Konstantin and his
  Children: Mikhail and Fedor,
  and his mother Irina.
February 10, 1919 Bishop Ioann, Suzdal
February 12, 1919 Evfimii of Suzdal, Suzdal
February 3, 1919 Mitrofanii, Bishop of Voronezh - Voronezh
January 28, 1919 Tikhon of Zadonsk, Zadonsk
April 11, 1919 Sergii Radonezhskii, Sergiev-Posad
March 17, 1919 Savva of Zvenigorod, Zvenigorod.
April 3, 1919 Prince Mstislav the Bold, Novgorod
April 3, 1919 Gavriil the Martyr, Moscow
January 3, 1919 Prince Vladimir, Novgorod
April 3, 1919 Anna, the wife of Iaroslav, Novgorod
April 3, 1919 Ioann of Novgorod, Novgorod
April 3, 1919 Kirill of Novoozero, Beloozersk
February 1, 1919 Iakov of Borovichi, Governorship of Novgorod
February 27, 1919 Vsevold - Gavriil, Governorship of Pskov
February 21, 1919 Evfimii, Ignatii and Akakii, the Martyrs, of Athos, Balashov
February 29, 1919 Pitirim of Tambov, Tambov
May 18, 1919 Prince Mikhail of Tver, Tver
February 15, 1919 Efrem of Novyi Torg, Torzhok
February 11, 1919 Evfrosiniia of Suzdal, Suzdal
February 5, 1919 Iulianii of Novyi Torg, Torzhok
  Ostashkov
February 25, 1919 Nil Stolbenskii of Stolobenskii or Stolobnyi Island, Lake Seliger,
February 2, 1919 Makarii of Kaliazin, Kaliazin
February 9, 1919 Prince Konstantin, Governorship of Iaroslavl

February 15, 1919 Prince Georgii, Vladimir
February 17, 1919 Feodosii of Totma, Totma, Governorship of Vologda
March   6,   1919 Prokopii of Ustiansk, District of Belsk
March   6,   1919 Evstafii, Antonii and Ioann, Saints, of Vilno.
April   3,   1919 Bishop Nikita, Novgorod
April   3,   1919 Prince Fedor, Novgorod
May   25,   1919 Arsenii the Thaumaturgus, Tver
April   9,   1919 Prince Feodor, Governorship of Iaroslavl
April   9,   1919 Prince David, Iaroslavl
Cf. Valentinov, A.A., ed., *Chernaia Kniga,* 259-260.

VI

STATISTICS OF THE ROMAN CATHOLIC CHURCH IN RUSSIA, 1922.

	Dioceses	Deaneries	Parishes	Branch Parishes	Chapels	Oratories	Faithful
1.	Mohilev	17	99	24	198	13	233,964
2.	Kamieniets	10	100	11	68	20	319,721
3.	Zhytomir	9	82	27	116	4	350,059
4.	Minsk	7	38	18	79	1	200,000
5.	Tiraspol	12	113	39	41		355,275
6.	Vladivostok	1	3	1	4		
7.	Vic. Apost. of Siberia	4	13	21	24	20	101,140
8.	Armenian R. C. rite	4	56		3		37,252
	Total	64	504	141	533	58	1,597,411

(See *Sacrum Poloniae Millenium,* vol. II (1955, Roma), p. 524).

VII

FUNDS OF THE ROMAN CATHOLIC CHURCH CONFISCADED BY THE RUSSIAN GOVERNMENT ON AUGUST 25, 1917.

1. Sustaining Fund of the Empire	4,984,673	rubles	
Interest	202,349	"	
2. Sustaining Fund of the Kingdom	353,087	"	
Interest	13,720	"	
3. Foundations:			
a. Permanent Investments	1,522,672	"	
a. Interest	60,107	"	
b. Temporary Investments	202,125	"	
b. Interest	7,994	"	
4. Building Capital	375,300	"	
Interest	14,380	"	
5. Saratov Funds	38,615	"	24 kopecks
Interest	1,497	"	35 "
6. Houses' Value	3,640,400	"	
Total	11,381,009	rubles	59 kopecks

See A. Petrani, *Kolegium duchowne w Petersburgu* [Department of Ecclesiastical Affairs] Lubin, 1950, pp. 119-124.

VII

MEASUREMENTS

a) The value of the Russian Ruble.

Year	Ruble		Dollar	Cents
1852	Gold	1	0	79
	Silver	1	0	75
1893	Gold	1	0	77
	Silver	1	0	49
1899	Gold	1	0	51
	Silver	1	0	51
1916	Gold	1	0	51.45
1919	Gold	1	0	51.46
1921	Gold	1	0	51.46
1923	Gold	1	0	51.46
1924	Gold	1	0	51.46

(See *The World Almanac*. New York, 1893-1925.)

b) Measurements

Verst — 3,500 feet.
Desiatina — 2¾ acres.
Pood — 40 Russian pounds.

c) The Russian Calendar

Pre-1700 Calendar: from the Creation of the World, September 1, 5509.
Julian Calendar, introduced by Peter the Great, January 1, 1700:

In the 18th century, it was 11 days behind the Gregorian calendar.
In the 19th century, it was 12 days behind the Gregorian calendar.
In the 20th century, it was 13 days behind the Gregorian calendar.

The Soviet government decreed February 1, 1918 to be February 14, 1918, thus eliminating the discrepancy between the calendar used in Russia and the calendar used in the western world.

IX

A List of Abbreviations Used in the Present Work

Bolsheviks, from *bol-shinstvo* — majority Russian Social-Democratic Labor Party faction led by Lenin.

Cheka (Ch.K.) — Chrezvychainaia Komissiia po bor'be s kontr-revoliutsiei spekuliatsiei i prestupleniiami po dolzhnosti — The Extraordinary Commission for the Struggle against Counter-Revolution, Speculation and Office Crimes, the first designation of the Soviet secret political police.

Gorkom, Gorodskoi Komitet, City Committee of the Communist Party.

Gorsovet, Gorodskoi Sovet, City Soviet.

G.P.U., Gosudarstvennoe Politicheskoe Upravlenie, The State Political Administration, one of the designations of the Soviet secret police.

Goskhran, Gosudarstvennoe Khranilishche, State Valuables Safe Deposit.

Gosplan, Gosudarstvennyi Komitet po Planirovaniiu, The State Planning Committee.

Menshevik, from *men'shinstvo*, minority, Russian Social-Democratic Labor Party faction led by anti-Leninists.

Mestkom, Mestnyi Komitet, the Local Committee of a Trade Union.

N.E.P. — Novaia Ekonomicheskaia Politika — New Economic Policy.

N.K.V.D. — Narodnyi Komissariat Vnutrennikh Del — People's Commissariat of Internal Affairs, one of the designations of the Soviet secret police.

R.S.F.S.R. — Rossiiskaia Sotsialisticheskaia Federativnaia Sovetskaia Respublika, Russian Socialistic Federal Soviet Republic; later: Rossiiskaia Sovetskaia Federativnaia Sotsialisticheskaia Respublika, Russian Soviet Federative Socialist Republic.

Sel'sovet, Sel'skii Sovet, Village Soviet.

Sovnarkom, Sovet Narodnykh Komissarov, the Council of People's Commissars.

V.C.I.K. (or V.Ts.I.K.), Vserossiiskii Tsentral'nyi Ispolnitel'nyi Komitet, The All-Russian Central Executive Committee.

V.C.U. (or V.Ts.U.), Vysshee Tserkovnoe Upravlenie, The Supreme Church Administration, The Higher Ecclesiastical Administration.

X

A Selective
Bibliography

I. DOCUMENTS AND OTHER PRIMARY SOURCES

A collection of Reports on Bolshevism in Russia, London, His Majesty's Stationery Office, 1919.

Acta Apostolicae Sedis, Rome, Vatican Press, XIII (1921), XV (1923), XVI (1924).

Aleksiĭ, Patriarch of Russia, *Slova, rechi, poslaniia, obrashcheniia, stat'i; 1948—1954* [Sermons, Speeches, Messages, Addresses, Articles; 1948—1954], v. I - II, Moscow, Izdatel'stvo Moskovskoĭ Patriarkhii, 1954.

Alfavitnyĭ ukazatel' k Zhurnalam Vremennago Pravitel'stva za aprel' 1917 goda [Index to the Journals of the Provisional Government for April 1917], Petrograd, Gosudarstvennaia tipografiia, 1917.

A Selection of Papers Dealing with the Relations Between His Majesty's Government and the Soviet Government, 1921 — 1927, London, His Majesty's Stationery Office, 1927.

Barron, J. B., and Waddams, H. W., *Communism and the Churches; A Documentation,* New York, Morehouse-Gorham Company, 1950.

Bolshevik Propaganda. Hearings before a Subcommittee of the Committee on the Judiciary, U.S. Senate, Sixty-fifth Congress, Third Session, February 11, 1919, to March 10, 1919. Washington, D.C., Government Printing Office, 1919.

Bunyan, James, and Fisher, Harold H., *The Bolshevik Revolution, 1917—1918; Documents and Materials,* Stanford, Stanford University Press, 1934.

Certain Legislation Respecting Religion in Force in the Union of Soviet Socialist Republics, London, His Majesty's Stationery Office, 1930.

Communist Takeover and Occupation of Armenia; Special Report No. 5 of the Select Committee on Communist Aggression; House of Representatives; Eighty-Third Congress; Second Session; Under authority of H. Res. 346 and H. Res. 438, Washington, United States Government Printing Office, 1955.

Communist Takeover and Occupation of Byelorussia; Special Report No. 9 of the Select Committee on Communist Aggression; House of Representatives; Eighty-Third Congress; Second Session; Under authority of H. Res. 346 and H. Res. 438, Washington, United States Government Printing Office, 1955.

Communist Takeover and Occupation of Georgia; Special Report No. 6 of the Select Committee on Communist Aggression; House of Representatives; Eighty-Third Congress; Second Session; Under authority of H. Res. 346 and H. Res. 438, Washington, United States Government Printing Office, 1955.

Communist Takeover and Occupation of Ukraine; Special Report No. 4 of the Select Committee on Communist Aggression; House of Representatives; Eighty-Third Congress; Second Session; Under authority of H. Res. 346 and House Res. 438, Washington, United States Government Printing Office, 1955.

Degras, Jane, *Calendar of Soviet Documents on Foreign Policy, 1917—1941,* London, Royal Institute of International Affairs, 1948.

—————, (ed.), *Soviet Documents on Foreign Policy,* London, Oxford University Press, 1951.

Deianiia soveshchaniia glav i predstavitelei avtokefal'nykh pravoslavnykh tserkvei (8 - 18 iiulia 1948 g.) [Acts of the Conference of Heads and Representatives of the Autocephalous Orthodox Churches, July 8 - 18, 1948], v. I-II, Moscow, Izdanie Moskovskoi Patriarkhii, 1948.

Deianiia Vtorogo Vsezarubezhnogo Sobora Russkoi Pravoslavnoi Tserkvi zagranitsei s uchastiem predstavitelei klira i mirian sostoiavshegosia 1 - 11 (14 - 24) avgusta 1938 goda v Sremskikh Karlovtsakh v Iugoslavii [Acts of the Second All Emigree Sobor of the Russian Orthodox Church Abroad With the Participation of the Representatives of the Clergy and Laity, Which Took Place between August 14 and 24, 1938, at Sremski Karlovtsi, Yugoslavia], Belgrad, Tipografiia "Merkur," 1939.

Diiannia Soboru Hreko-Katolyts'koï Tserkvy u L'vovi, 8 -10 Bereznia, 1946 [Acts of the Sobor of the Catholic Church of the Byzantine Rite at Lvov, March 8 - 10, 1946], Lvov, Vydannia Prezydiï Soboru, 1946.

Diiannia Vseukraïns'koho Pravoslavnoho Tserkovnoho Soboru v m. Kyevi 14-30 zhovtnia n. s. 1921 r. [Acts of the All-Ukrainian Orthodox Church Sobor in Kiev, October 14 - 30, 1921], [2d edit.], Frankfurt am Main - Darmstadt, C. Winter, 1946.

Documents inédits; "L'Église Orthodoxe Panukrainienne," créée en 1921 à Kiev (Orientalia Christiana No. 3), Rome, Pontificio Istituto Orientale, June 1923.

Documents Officiels emane de la Secretairerie d'état du Saint-Siege au sujet de la persecution des Catholiques en Pologne et en Russie et de la rupture des relations avec le gouvernement Russe, Zürich, Imprimerie F. Schulthess, 1878.

Dvenadtsatyĭ Sezd Rossiĭskoĭ Kommunisticheskoĭ Partii (Bolshevikov); Stenograficheskiĭ otchet [The Twelfth Congress of the Russian Communist Party (Bolsheviks); A Shorthand Report], Moscow, Izdatel'stvo "Krasnaia Nov'," 1923.

Elenchus Cleri et Ecclesiarum Archidioeceseos Mohiloviensis in Russia in Diem 1 Januarii 1926, Warsaw, 1926.

Elenchus Omnium Ecclesiarum et Universi Cleri Archdioeceseos Mohiloviensis et Dioec. Minscensis pro Anno Domini 1904 Conscriptus, n.p., n.p., n.d..

Eudin, Xenia J., and Fisher, Harold H., *Soviet Russia and the West, 1920 - 1927; A Documentary Survey*, Stanford, Stanford University Press, 1957.

Gessen, V.I., ed., *Arkhiv russkoi revoliutsii* [Archives of the Russian Revolution], v. I - XXXII, Berlin, "Slowo-" Verlag, 1922 - 1927.

Gidulianov, P. V., *Otdelenie tserkvi ot gosudarstva v SSSR; Polnyĭ sbornik dekretov, vedomstvennykh rasporiazheniĭ i opredeleniĭ Verkhsuda RSFSR, i drugikh Sovetskikh Sotsialisticheskikh Respublik: USSR, BSSR, ZSFSR, Uzbekskoĭ i Turkmenskoĭ* [Separation of Church and State in the USSR; A Complete Collection of the Decrees, Departmental Orders and Decisions of the Supreme Court of the Russian S.F.S.R. and the Other Soviet Socialist Republics: the Ukrainian S.S.R., the Belorussian S.S.R., the Transcaucasian S.F.S.R., the Uzbek (S.S.R.) and the Turkmen (S.S.R.)] 3d edit., Krasikov, P. A., ed., Moscow, Iuridicheskoe Izdatel'stvo N.K.Iu. R.S.F.S.R., 1926.

Glówny Urząd Statystyczny Rzeczypospolitej Polskiej, *Pierwszy powszechny spis Rzeczypospolitej Polskiej z dnia 30 Września 1921 roku* [The General Office of Statistics of the Polish Republic, The First General Census of the Polish Republic of September 30, 1921], Warsaw, Glowny Urzad Statystyczny, 1927, v. XXI.

Hansard, *Parliamentary Debates*, Fifth Series, vol. 53 (1923).

_____, *Parliamentary Debates*, Fifth Series, vol. 161 (1923).

_____, *Parliamentary Debates*, Fifth Series, vol. 162 (1923).

La Legislation soviétique contre la réligion, Orientalia Christiana, Vol. V-1 (October, 1925), Rome, Pontifical Oriental Institute, 1925.

L'Église georgienne et la Russie: Une lettre du catholicos Léonid au Patriarche Tykhon." *Echos d'Orient*, 1932, VII-IX.

Makowski, Julian, *Umowy Miedzynarodowe Polski, 1919—1934* [International Agreements of Poland, 1919—1934], Warsaw, Drukarnia Wl. Lazarskiego, 1935.

Meisel, James H., and Kozera, Edward S., ed., *Materials for the Study of the Soviet System; State and Party Constitutions, Laws, Decrees, Decisions and Official Statements of the Leaders in Translation*, 2d ed., Ann Arbor, Mich., The George Wahr Publishing Company, 1953.

Ministerstvo Iustitsii SSSR, *Osnovy Sovetskogo gosudarstva i prava* [The Ministry of Justice of the USSR, The Foundations of the Soviet State and Law], Moscow, Iuridicheskoe Izdatel'stvo, 1947.

Narodnyĭ Komissariat Iustitsii, *Alfavitno-predmetnyĭ ukazatel' za ianvar' 1922 g. k dekretam, postanovleniiam, rasporiazheniiam i prikazam* [The People's Commissariat of Justice, The Subject Index for January 1922 to the Decrees, Decisions, Instructions and Orders], Moscow, Izdanie Narodnogo Komissariata Iustitsii, 1922.

_____, *Materialy Narodnogo Komissariata Iustitsii* [Materials of the People's Commissariat of Justice], Moscow, Izdanie Narodnogo Komissariata Iustitsii, 1918-1922, Vypusk I, II, III, IV, V, VI, VII, VIII, X, XI, XII, XIII, XV.

Nardonyĭ Komissariat po Delam Natsional' nosteĭ, *Otchët Narodnogo Komissariata po delam natsional'nosteĭ za 1921 god* [The People's Commissariat for the Affairs of Nationalities, Report of the People's Commissariat for the Affairs of Nationalities for 1921], Moscow, Narodnyĭ Komissariat po delam natsional'nosteĭ, 1922.

_____, *Politika Sovetskoĭ vlasti po natsional'nomu voprosu za tri goda 1917 - 1920* [Soviet Nationality Policy for Three Years 1917 - 1920], Moscow, Gosudarstvennoe Izdatel'stvo, 1920.

Nardonyĭ Komissariat po Inostrannym Delam, *Genuezskaia Konferentsiia, Materialy i dokumenty* [The People's Commissariat of Foreign Affairs, The Genoa Conference; Materials and Documents], Moscow, Narodnyĭ Komissariat po inostrannym delam, 1922.

_____, *Mezhdunarodnaia politika R.S.F.S.R. v. 1922 g.* [Foreign Policy of the R.S.F.S.R. in 1922], Moscow, Narodnyĭ Komissariat po inostrannym delam, 1923.

_____, *Rosja Sowiecka a Polska* [Soviet Russia and Poland], Moscow, Narodnyĭ Komissariat po inostrannym delam, 1921.

_____, *Sovetskaia Rossiia i Pol'sha* [Soviet Russia and Poland], Moscow, Narodnyĭ Komissariat po inostrannym delam, 1921.

Notes Exchanged on the Russian-Polish Situation by the United States, France, and Poland, No. 155, New York, American Association for International Conciliation, 1920.

Opisanie dokumentov Arkhiva zapadnorusskikh Uniatskikh mitropolitov, 1701-1839 [A Description of Documents in the Archives of the West Russian Uniate Metropolitans, 1701-1839], 2 vols., St. Petersburg, Sinodal'naia Tipografiia, 1907.

"O postanovke antireligioznoĭ propagandy i agitatsii" ["On the Methods and System of the Anti-Religious Propaganda and Agitation"], *Dvenadtsatyĭ Sezd Rossii Kommunisticheskaĭ partii (bol'shevikov); Stenograficheskiĭ otchët; 17-25 aprelia 1923 g.* [The Twelfth Congress of the Russian Communist Party (Bolsheviks); A Shorthand Report; April 17-25, 1923], Moscow, Izdatel'stvo "Krasnaia Nov'," 1923.

People's Commissariat of Justice, *The First Code of Laws of the Russian Socialistic Federal Soviet Republic*, Petrograd, People's Commissariat of Justice, 1919.

Polish-Soviet Relations, 1918-1943; Official Documents, Washington, Polish Embassy, 1943.

Poslannia Vseukraïns'koĭ Pravoslavnoĭ Tserkovnoĭ Rady do Ioho Blazhenstva Tsarhorods'koho Patriarkha Vasyliia III, z 13 liutoho 1926 r. [Message of the All-Ukrainian Orthodox Church Council to His Holiness Basil III, Patriarch of Constantinople, of February 13, 1926], Munich, P. Belej, 1955.

Protokol Velykykh Mykil's'kykh Zboriv Vseukraïns'koĭ Pravoslavnoĭ Tserkovnoĭ Rady 11-13 travnia 1927 roku [Minutes of the St. Nicholas Assembly of the All-Ukranian Orthodox Church Council, May 11-13, 1927], Munich, P. Belej, 1954.

Protokoly deviatogo Sezda RKP(b) [Minutes of the Ninth Congress of the Russian Communist Party (Bolsheviks)], Moscow, Partiĭnoe Izdatel'stvo, 1934.

Recueil des documents diplomatiques relatifs aus relations entre la Russie et la Pologne, 1918-1920, Moscow, Commissariat du Peuple pour les affaires etrangeres, 1920.

Rocznik politiczny i gospodarczy, 1937 [The Year-Book of Politics and Economy, 1937], Warsaw, Polska Agencja Telegraficzna, 1937.

R.S.F.S.R., *Sbornik dekretov i postanovlenii soiuza kommun Severnoĭ Oblasti* [A Collection of Decrees and Decisions of the Union of the Communes of the Northern Region], Vypusk I, Petrograd, 1919.

Sed'moĭ sezd Rossiĭskoĭ Kommunisticheskoĭ partii; Stenograficheskiĭ otchët [The Seventh Congress of the Russian Communist Party; A Shorthand Report], Moscow, Gosudarstvennoe Izdatel'stvo, 1923.

Sprawozdanie stenograficzne z 17 posiedzenia Senatu Rzeczypospolitej z dn. 27 Marca, 1923 r. [A Shorthand Report of the 17th Session of the Senate of the Polish Republic, of March 27, 1923], Warsaw, 1923, vol. XVII.

Sprawozdanie stenograficzne z 32 posiedzenia Sejmu Rzeczypospolitej z dn. 12 kwietna, 1923 r. [A Shorthand Report of the 32d Session of the Diet of the Polish Republic, of April 12, 1923], Warsaw, 1923, vol. XXXII.

Sprawozdanie z Działalności Komisji Likwidacyjnej do Spraw Królestwa za Czas od 15-go Marca do 1-go Sierpnia 1917 r. [A Report of the Activity of the Liquidation Commission With Regard to the Affairs of the Kingdom (of Poland) for the Period Between March 15th and August 1st, 1917], Petrograd, Drukarnia Społeczna, 1917.

Stenograficheskiĭ Otchët Vtorogo Vsesoiuznogo Sezda Soiuza Voinstvuiushchikh Bezhozhnikov [Shorthand Report of the Second All-Union Congress of the Union of the Militant Godless], Moscow, 1930.

Sviashchennyĭ sobor pravoslavnoĭ Rossiĭskoĭ tserkvi; Deianiia [Holy Sobor of the Orthodox Russian Church; Acts], v. I-IX, Petrograd, 1918.

Svod sakonov Rossiĭskoi Imperii dopolnennyĭ po prodolzheniiam 1906, 1908, 1909 i 1910 gg. i pozdneĭshimi uzakoneniiami 1911 i 1912 gg. [The Code of Laws of the Russian Empire Supplemented by Additions of 1906, 1908, 1909 and 1910, and the Latest Legislation of 1911 and 1912], v. I-IV (each volume in 4 parts), 2d ed., Dobrovolskiĭ, A.A., ed., St. Petersburg, [Izd.] I.I. Zubkov pod firmoiu "Zakonovedenie," 1913-1914.

Trinadtsatyĭ Sezd Rossiĭskoĭ Kommunisticheskoĭ Partii (Bolshevikov); Stenograficheskiĭ otchët; 23-31 maia 1924 g. [The Thirteenth Congress of the Russian Communist Party (Bolsheviks); A Shorthand Report; May 23-31, 1924], Moscow, Izdatel'stvo "Krasnaia Nov'," 1924.

Tsentral'noe statisticheskoe upravlenie, *Biulleten' tsentral'nogo statisticheskogo upravleniia* [Central Statistics Administration, Bulletin of the Central Statistics Administration], No. 77 (August 25, 1923), Moscow, Tsentral'noe statisticheskoe upravlenie, 1923.

_____, *Statisticheskii spravochnik SSSR za 1928* [Statistical Reference-Book on the USSR for 1928], Moscow, Statisticheskoe Izdatel'stvo, 1929.

U. S. Department of State, *Papers Relating to the Foreign Relations of the United States, 1923*, Vol. II, Washington, Government Printing Office, 1938.

Verwaltungsbericht der Militarverwaltung Bialystok-Grodno für die Zeit 10 Oktober 1916 bis 1 April 1917, No. 22, Druckerei der Militarverwaltung Bialystok-Grodno, [n.d.]

Vossoedinenie Ukrainy s Rossieiu; dokumenty i materialy v trekh tomakh [Re-Unification of Ukraine with Russia; Documents and Materials in Three Volumes], 3 vols., Moscow, Izdatel'stvo Akademii Nauk SSSR, 1954.

BOOKS AND PAMPHLETS

Alexeev, Wassilij, *Russian Orthodox Bishops in the Soviet Union, 1941-1953,* New York, 1954.

Algermissen, Konrad, *Die Gottlosenbewegung der Gegenwart und ihre "Uberwindung,* v.I-II, Hannover, J. Giesel, 1933.

Almedingen, Martha E., *The Catholic Church in Russia Today,* New York, Kenedy, 1923.

Amman, Albert M., *Abriss der Ostslawischen Kirchengeschichte,* Vienna, Thomas Morus Presse, 1950.

Amosov, N. K., *Khristianstvo, ego proiskhozhdenie i politicheskaia rol'* [Christianity, its Origin and Political Role], Moscow, Voennoe Izdatel'stvo Ministerstva Oborony Soiuza SSR, 1955.

Anderson, Paul B., *People, Church and State in Modern Russia,* New York, The Macmillan Company, 1944.

Andreev, I. M., *Kratkiĭ obzor istorii russkoĭ tserkvi ot revoliutsii do nashikh dneĭ* [An Outline of Russian Church History from the Revolution to Our Day], Jordanville, N.Y., Holy Trinity Monastery, 1952.

————, *Pravoslavno-Khristianskaia apologetika; kratkoe konspektivnoe izlozhenie kursa lektsiĭ, chitannykh v sv. Troitskoĭ Dukhovnoĭ Seminarii v 1952-53 uchebnom godu* [Orthodox Christian Apologetics; A Summary of Lectures Held at the Holy Trinity Theological Seminary in the Academic Year 1952-53], Jordanville, N.Y., Holy Trinty Monastery, 1953.

————, *Żametki o katakombnoĭ tserkvi v SSSR* [Notes on the Underground Church in the USSR], n.p., n.p., 1947.

Arsenev, Nikolaĭ S., *Pravoslavie, Katolichestvo i Protestantism* [Orthodoxy, Catholicism and Protestantism], Paris, YMCA Press, 1948.

————, *La Sainte Moscou,* Paris, Cerf, 1948.

Arturov, O. A., *Vatikan i ego politika* [The Vatican and Its Policy], Moscow, Izdatel'stvo "Pravda," 1947.

Barinov, G. P., *Osnovnye voprosy konstitutsii SSSR* [The Basic Questions of the USSR Constitutional Law], Moscow, Gosudarstvennoe Uchebno-pedagogicheskoe Izdatel'stvo, 1948.

Baskin, M. P., *Materializm i religiia* [Materialism and Religion], Moscow, Gosudarstvennoe Izdatel'stvo Politicheskoĭ Literatury, 1955.

Bennigsen, George, (ed), *Religion in Russia; A Collection of Essays Read at the Cambridge Summer School of Russian Studies, 1939,* London, Burnes, Oates, and Washbourne, Let., 1940.

Berdyaev, N., *Christianity and Class War,* New York, Sheed and Ward, 1933.

————, *The Origin of the Russian Communism,* New York, Charles Scribner's Sons, 1937.

————, "The Religion of Communism," *Vital Realities,* New York, Macmillan and Co., 1932.

————,"Russian Religious Psychology and Communistic Atheism," *Vital Realities,* New York, Macmillan and Co., 1932.

————, "Russia, Religion and Revolution," *Living Age,* October, 1931.

————, *Wahrheit und Lüge des Kommunismus,* Darmstadt, 1953.

Desson, Paul, *De la séparation de l'église et de l'état et de ses conséquences relativement aux libertés religieuses,* 5th edit., Paris, Retaux-Bray, n.d.

Biriukov, D. A., *Nauka i religiia v psikhicheskoĭ deiatel'nosti cheloveka* [Science and Religion in Man's Psychic Activity], Moscow, Izdatel'stvo "Znanie," 1956.

Bochenski, J. M., "Die Religion," *Auspolitik und Żeitgeschichte,* Beilage zur Wochenzeitung *Das Parlament,* October 9, 1957, Bonn.

——————, Der sowietrussische dialektische Materialismus (Diamat). Bern, 1950.

Briem, Efraim, Kommunismus und Religion in der Sowjetunion, Basel, Verlag Friedrich Reinhardt A. G., 1954.

Buchanan, George, My Mission to Russia and Other Diplomatic Memories, 2 vols., Boston, Little, Brown and Company, 1923.

Bukharin, Nikolaï, Finance Capital in Papal Robes, New York, Friends of the Soviet Union, 1930.

——————, Historical Materialism; A System of Sociology, New York, International Publishers, 1925.

——————, and Preobrazhenskiĭ, E. A., The ABC of Communism, Translated by Eden and Cedar Paul, London, The Communist Party of Great Britain, 1922.

Bulatov, Ivan, Imperialism and the Church Prepare War Against the U.S.S.R., Moscow, Tsentral'noe Izdatel'stvo, 1931.

Bunyan, James, Intervention, Civil War, and Communism in Russia; April-December 1918; Documents and Materials, Baltimore, The Johns Hopkins Press, 1936.

——————, and Fisher, H.H., (eds.), The Bolshevik Revolution; 1917-1918; Documents and Materials, Stanford, Calif., Stanford University Press, 1934.

Capuccio, L., Russia regno dell' anticristo, Milano, 1933.

Carr, Edward H., The Bolshevik Revolution, 1917-1923, 3 vols., London, Macmillan Company, 1950-1953.

——————, German-Soviet Relations between the Two World Wars, 1919-1939, Baltimore, Johns Hopkins Press, 1951.

Chamberlin, W. H., The Russian Revolution, 1917-1920, 2 vols., New York, Macmillan and Co., 1935.

Chekhovskyĭ, V., Za tserkvu, Khrystovu hromadu, proty tsarstva t'my [In Defense of the Church, the Christian Community, Against the Kingdom of Darkness], 2d ed., Frankfurt am Main, UNRRA, 1947.

Cianfarra, Camille M., The Vatican and the Kremlin, New York, E. P. Dutton and Company, 1950.

Clark, Colin, A Critique of Russian Statistics, London, Macmillan and Company, Ltd., 1939.

Cumming, C. K., and Pettit, W. W., Russian-American Relations; March, 1917-March, 1920, New York, Harcourt, Brace, and Howe, 1920.

Curtiss, John Shelton, Church and State in Russia; The Last Years of the Empire, 1900-1917, New York, Columbia University Press, 1940.

——————, The Russian Church and the Soviet State, 1917-1950, Boston, Little, Brown and Company, 1953.

Dadeshkeliani, I., The Autocephaly of the Orthodox Church of Georgia, London, 1922.

D'Arcy, Martin, Communism and Christianity; An Examination of the Christian and Communist Philosophies in Their Views of Human Life and Happiness, Aylesbur, G.B., Penguin Books, Ltd., 1956.

Dark, Sidney, and Essex, R. S., The War Against God, New York, The Abingdon Press, 1939.

Demidov, V. M., Rec., Iz bezdny k Bogu (Puti vozrozhdeniia russkago naroda); Sbornik stateĭ [From the Abyss to God (The Ways of Regeneration of the Russian People); A Collection of Articles], Jordanville, Russian Monastery, 1942.

Denkin A. I. Gen. Ocherki Russkoi Smuty: Krushenie vlasti i armii. bor'ba generala Kornilova, [Outline of the Russian Smuta: Catastrophy of the Government and the Army; General Kornilov's Struggle], 3 vols., Paris, 1921/22.

D'Herbigny, Michel, L'Aspect religieux de Moscou en Octobre 1925, Rome, Pontifical Oriental Institute, 1926.

_____, *Militant Atheism,* London, 1933.

Domanski, Francis, *The Great Apostle of Russia, Servant of God, Archbishop Cieplak,* Chicago, n.p., 1954.

Doroshenko, Dmytro I., *Die ukrainische autocephale Kirche,* Orient und Occident, Heft 14, Leipzig, 1933.

Dyboski, Roman, *Poland in World Civilization,* New York, J.M. Barrett, 1950.

Emeliakh, L., *Proiskhozhdenie Khristianskikh tainstv* [Origin of the Christian Sacraments], Moscow, Izdatel'stvo "Znanie," 1956.

Emhardt, William Shauncey, *Religion in Soviet Russia* together with an *Essay on the Living Church by Sergius Troitsky,* London, Morehouse Publishing Company, 1929.

Enisherlov, M., Ed., *Voinstvuiushchee Bezbozhie v SSSR za 15 let (1917-1932); Sbornik* [The Militant Godlessness in the USSR for 15 years (1917-1932); A Symposium], Moscow, 1932.

Fedotoff, G. P., *The Russian Church since the Revolution,* London, S.P.C.K., and New York Macmillan, 1928.

Fischer, Louis, *The Soviets in World Affairs; A History of the Relations between the Soviet Union and the Rest of the World, 1917-1929,* 2 vols., Princeton University Press, 1951.

Fisher, Harold H., *The Famine in Soviet Russia, 1919-1923; The Operations of American Relief Administration,* Stanford, Stanford University Press, 1935.

Florynsky, Michael, *The End of the Russian Empire,* New Haven, Yale University Press, 1931.

Francis, David R., *Russian from the American Embassy; April 1, 1916 - November, 1918,* New York, Charles Scribners' Sons, 1921.

Fulop-Miller, R., *The Mind and the Face of Bolshevism,* New York, Alfred Knopf, 1928.

Glan, Ia., *Antireligioznaia literatura za 12 let (1917-1929)* [Anti-Religious Literature for Twelve Years (1917-1929)], Moscow, 1930.

_____, *Antireligioznaia literatura posleoktiabr'skogo perioda, 1929-1930* [Post-Revolutionary Anti-Religious Literature, 1929-1930], Moscow, 1930.

_____, *Antireligioznaia literatura pooktiabr'skogo perioda, 1930 (iiul') - 1932 (noiabr')* [Anti-Religious Literature of the Post-Revolutionary Period, 1930 (July) - 1932 (November)], Moscow, 1933.

Grabski, Stanislaw, *The Polish-Soviet Frontier,* New York, Polish Information Center, n.d.

Gsovski, Vladimir, *Church and State behind the Iron Curtain,* New York, Mid-European Studies Center, 1955.

_____, *Soviet Civil Law,* Ann Arbor, University of Michigan Press, 1948.

Gurian, Waldemar, *Bolshevism; An Introduction to Soviet Communism,* Notre Dame, University of Notre Dame Press, 1952.

Hecker, J. F., *Religion and Communism,* London, Chapman and Hall, 1933; and New York, Wiley, 1934.

_____, *Religion under the Soviets,* New York, Vanguard Press, 1927.

Heyer, Friedrich, *Die Orthodoxe Kirche in der Ukraine von 1917 bis 1945,* Köln-Braunsfeld, Rudolf Müller, 1953.

Iaroslavskii, Emelian, *Na antireligioznom fronte* [On the Anti-Religious Front], Moscow, Izdatel'stvo "Krasnaia Nov'," 1924.

_____, *Protiv natsionalizma, protiv religii; Sbornik statei* [Against Nationalism, Against Religion; Articles], Moscow, OGIZ - "Moskovskii Rabochii," 1931.

_____, Protiv religii i tserkvi [Against Religion and the Church], vol. I-V, Moscow, OGIZ - Gosudarstvennoe Antireligioznoe Izdatel'stvo, 1932-1935.

_____, Religion in the U.S.S.R., 2d edit., London, Modern Books, 1932.

_____, RKP i religiia [Russian Communist Party and Religion], Moscow, 1925.

Ibrahimov, Gali, Kak vesti antireligioznuiu propagandu sredi tatarok i bashkirok [How to Conduct Anti-Religious Propaganda among the Tartar and Bashkir Women], Moscow, Gosudarstvennoe Izdatel'stvo, 1928.

Ihnatiuk, D., Ukraïns'ka avtokefal'na tserkva i Soiuz Vyzvolennia Ukraïny [The Ukrainian Autocephalous Church and the Union for the Liberation of Ukraine], Kharkov-Kiev, Derzhavne Vydavnytstvo Ukraïny, 1930.

Ivanov, V. N., Osnovnye prava i obiazannosti grazhdan SSSR [Basic Rights and Duties of the USSR Citizens], Moscow, Gosudarstvennoe Izdatel'stvo Iuridicheskoĭ Literatury, 1953.

Kalinin, Michael I., O kommunisticheskom vospitanii; Izbrannye stat'i i rechi [Communist Education; Selected Articles and Speeches], 3d edit., Moscow, Izdatel'stvo TK VLKSM "Molodaia Gvardiia," 1949.

Kasiak, I. Ž historyi Pravaslaunaĭ Tsarkvy Belaruskaha narodu [History of the Belorussian Orthodox Church], New York, Vydan'ne Belaruskaĭ Tsentral'naĭ Rady, 1956.

Kerenskii, A. F., The Crucifixion of Liberty, New York, Day Co., 1934.

Kessler, Joseph Aloysius, Geschichte der Diözese Tyraspol, Dickinson, Verlag von Rev. Georg Aberle, 1930.

Klostermann, R. A., Probleme der Ostkirche; Untersuchungen zum Wesen und zur Geschichte der Griechisch—Orthodoen Kirche, Goteborg, Wettergren und Kerbers Forlag, 1955.

Kokh, Hans, Teoriia III Rymu v istoriï vidnovlenoho Moskovs'koho Patriiarkhatu (1917-1952) [The Theory of the Third Rome in the History of the Restored Patriarchate of Moscow (1917-1952),] Munich, Tserkovno-Arkheografichna Komisiia Vizytatora dlia Ukraïntsiv u Zakhidniï Evropi, 1953.

Kologrivof, Ivan, Essai sur la saintete en Russie, Bruges, Beyaert, 1953.

Komu sluzhat tserkovniki i sektanty; Sbornik stateĭ [Whom Churchmen and Sectarians Serve; A Collection of Articles], Iaroslavl, Iaroslavskoe oblastnoe izdatel'stvo, 1938.

Konstantinov, F. V., Istoricheskiĭ materializm [Historical Materialism], 2d edit., Moscow, Gosudarstvennoe Izdatel'stvo Politicheskoĭ Literatury, 1954.

Krasikov, P., Na tserkovnom fronte (1918-1923) [On the Ecclesiastical Front (1918-1923)], Moscow, Gosudarstvennoe Izdatel'stvo, 1923.

_____, Sovetskaia vlast' i tserkov' [Soviet Regime and the Church], Moscow, Gosudarstvennoe Izdatel'stvo, 1920.

Krylenko, N. V., Sudebnye rechi, 1922-1930 [Court Speeches, 1922-1930], Moscow, Gosularstvennoe Iuridicheskoe Izdatel'stvo, 1931.

Krylev, I., Pochemu my boremsia protiv religii? [Why Do We Fight against Religion?], Moscow, OGIZ, 1940.

Kulakov, V. V., Konstitutsiia SSSR i obrazovanie sezdov sovetov v skhemakh [The Constitution of the USSR and the Formation of the Congresses of Soviets; With Charts] 4th edit., Moscow, Gosudarstvennoe Izdatel'stvo, 1925.

Kulski, W. W., The Soviet Regime; Communism in Practice, Syracuse, Syracuse University Press, 1954.

Kurdiumov, M., Tserkov' i novaia Rossiia [The Church and the New Russia], Paris, [Impr. de Navarre], 1933.

Lama, Friedrich, Papst und Kurie in ihrer Politik nach dem Weltkrieg, Illertissen, Martinusbuchhandlung, 1925.

Lawton, Lancelot, *The Russian Revolution, 1917-1926*, London, The Macmillan Company, 1927.

[Lenin, V.I.], *Lenin on Religion*, London, n.d.; New York, International Publishers, 1932.

————, *The Letters of Lenin*, Translated and edited by Elizabeth Hill, and Doris Mudie, New York, Harcourt, Brace, and Company, 1937.

————, *O religii* [On Religion], Moscow, Gosudarstvennoe Politicheskoe Izdatel'stvo, 1955.

Lukachevskii, A. T., (ed.), *Antireligioznyĭ uchebnik* [Anti-Religious Textbook], Moscow, OGIZ, 1933.

Lupalo, I. G., *Nauka protiv religii* [Science against Religion], Moscow, Gosudarstvennoe Izdatel'stvo Tekhniko-Teoreticheskoĭ Literatury, 1953.

McCabe, Joseph, *Russia and the Roman Church*, London, Watts and Company, 1941.

McCullagh, Francis, *The Bolshevik Persecution of Christianity*, New York, E. P. Dutton and Company, 1924.

————, *Przesladowanie Chrzescijanstwa przez bolszewizm rosyjski* (translation by K. Illakowicz of the English edition, as above). Krakow, Wyd. Księży Jezuitów, 1924.

Mackiewicz, S., *Russian Minds in Fetters*, London, Allen and Unwin, 1932.

Maliszewski, Edward, *Bialoruś w cyfrach i faktach* [Belorussia in Figures and Facts], Piotrkow, Wiadomości Polskie, 1918.

————, *Polacy i Polskość na Litwie i Rusi* [The Poles and the Polish National Spirit in Lithuania and Ruthenia], 2d ed., Warsaw, Wł Lazarski, 1916.

Manning, Clarence, *Ukraine under the Soviets*, New York, Bookman Associates, 1953.

Meldin, William K., *Moscow and East Rome; A Political Study of the Relations of Church and State in Muscovite Russia*, Geneva, Librairie E. Droz, 1952.

Melgunov, S. P., *Krasnyĭ terror v Rossii, 1918-1923*, [The Red Terror in Russia, 1918-1923], 2d edit., Berlin, n.p., 1924.

Middlendorp, Wilhelm, *Kreuz und Sowjetstern; zum Geisteskampf der Gegenwart*, Zürich, 1952.

Mikhnevich, D. I., ed., *V pomoshch' nauchno-ateisticheskoĭ propagande; Rekomendatel'nyĭ ukazatel' literatury* [Aid to Scientific Atheistic Propaganda; List of Recommended Literature], 2d ed., Moscow, [Publichnaia Biblioteka,], 1955.

Milyukov, Paul N., *Istoriia vtoroĭ Russukoĭ revoliutsii* [A History of the Second Russian Revolution], v. I-III, Sofia, Rossiĭsko-Bolgarskoe Knigoizdatel'stvo, 1921-1924.

————, *Outlines of Russian Culture; Part I: Religion and the Church*, Philadelphia, University of Pennsylvania Press, 1942.

Moulens, Joseph, *Mon Ambassade en Russie Sovietique, 1917-1919*, Paris, Librairie Plon, 1933, vol. I.

Niebuhr, R., *Moral Man and Immoral Christianity*, New York, Scribners' Sons, 1932.

Nikodim [Milash,], *Bishop, Pravoslavno Tserkveno pravo; po opshtim tsrkvenopravnym izvorima i posebnym zakonskym naredbama* [Orthodox Church Law; According to the General Sources of Ecclesiastical Law and Supplementary Legal Provisions], 3d., Beograd, Izdavachka Kn'izharnitsa G. Kona, 1926.

Nikolaev, K. N., *Vostochnyĭ obriad* [The Oriental Rite], Paris, Y. M. C. A. Press, 1950.

Okolo-Kulak, Anthony, *Kościoł w Rosji Dawniej, obecnie, i w przyszłości* [The Church in Russia, Past, Present and Future], Cracow, Wydawnictwo Księzy Jezuitów, 1928.

Oldenbourg, S., (ed.), *Le coup d'état bolcheviste*, Paris, 1929.

Park, Alexander G., *Bolshevism in Turkestan, 1917-1927*. New York, Columbia University Press, 1957.

Pavelkin, P., *Religioznye sueveriia i ikh vred* [Religious Superstitions and their Danger], Moscow, Gosudarstvennoe Izdatel'stvo Politicheskoĭ Literatury, 1952.

Pawlowski, Stanislaw, *Ludność rzymsko-katolicka w Polsko-Ruskiej Cześci Galicji* [The Roman-Catholic Population in the Polish-Russian Part of Galicia], Prace geograficzne [Works on Geography], Zeszyt III, Lvov, Ksiąznica Polska, 1919.

Perovsky, E. I., *Ateisticheskoe vospitanie deteĭ v shkole i sem'e* [The Atheistic Education of Children in the School and in the Family], Moscow, Izdatel'stvo "Znanie," 1955.

Petrani, Aleksy, *Kolegium Duchowne w Petersburgu* [The Ecclesiastical College at Petersburg], Lublin, Catholic University of Lublin, 1950.

Plekhanov, G. V., *Fundamental Problems of Marxism*, New York, International Publishers, 1929.

Polskiĭ, M., Protopresbyteros, *Kanonicheskoe polozhenie vyssheĭ tserkovnoĭ vlasti v SSSR i zagranitseĭ* [Canonical Status of the Supreme Church Authority in the USSR and Abroad], n.p., Holy Trinity Monastery, 1948.

————, *Novye mucheniki rossiĭskie; pervoe sobranie materialov* [The First Collection of Materials Pertaining to the New Russian Martyrs], Jordanville, N.Y., 1949.

Prokof'ev, V.I., *Ateizm russkikh revoliutsionnykh demokratov* [Atheism of Russian Revolutionary Democrats], 2d ed., Moscow, Gosudarstvennoe Izdatel'stvo Politicheskoĭ Literatury, 1955.

————, *Velikie russkie mysliteli v bor'be protiv idealizma i religii* [The Great Russian Thinkers in the Struggle against Idealism and Religion], Moscow, 1952.

Raevskiĭ, S., *Ukrainskaia avtokefal'naia tserkov'* [The Ukrainian Autocephalous Church], New York, Tipografiia Iova Pochaevskago v sv. Troitskom Monastyre, 1948.

Rauch, George von, *A History of Soviet Russia*, trans. by P. and A. Jacobsohn, New York, Frederick A. Praeger, 1957.

Reyburn, Hugh Y., *The Story of the Russian Church*, London, Andrew Melrose, Ltd., 1924.

Robinson, G. T., *Rural Russia under the Old Regime*, New York, Longmans, Green, and Company, 1932.

Romer, Eugene, *Spis ludności na terenach administratowanych przez zarząd cywilny ziem wschodnich (Grudzień, 1919)* [A Census of Population on the Territories Administered by the Civil Administration of Eastern Lands (December, 1919)], Prace geograficzne [Works of Geography], Zeszyt VII, Lwow, Ksiąznica Polska, 1920.

Ropp, Edward de, *Elenchus cleri et ecclesiarum archidioeceseos Mohiloviensis in Russia in diem 5 Decembris 1931 auctoritate et mandato Ex.mi, Ill.mi ac Rev.mi Domini Eduardi De Ropp Dei Miseratione et S. Sedis Ap. gratia Archiepiscopi Metrop. Mohiloviensis continuatus et editus, 1932*, Warsaw, 1932.

Rutkowski, Francis, *Arcybiskup Jan Cieplak (1857-1926); Szkic biograficzny* [Archbishop John Cieplak (1857-1926); A Biographical Sketch], Warsaw, Archdiocesan Press, 1934.

Saint Denis, Andre, *Pie XI contre les idoles*, Paris, Librairie Plon, 1939.

Schwartz, Salomon M., *The Jews in the Soviet Union*, Syracuse, The Syracuse University Press, 1951.

Schweigl, Joseph, S.J., *Die Hierarchien der getrennten Orthodoxie in Sowjetrussland; I: Ihr gegenseitiges Verhaltniss (Orientalia Christiana, V. XIII-1, No. 46)*, Rome, Pontificum Institutum Orientalium Studiorum, June 1928.

Schweigel, P. J., *Moskau gegen den Vatikan*, Augsburg, Haas und Grabherr, 1930.

Sheinman, M. M., *Bog i kapital* [God and Capital], Leningrad, 1926.

————, Vatikan mezhdu dvumia mirovymi voĭnami [The Vatican between the Two World Wars], Moscow, Izdatel'stvo Akademii Nauk SSSR, 1948.

Shibaev, V. P., *Etnicheskiĭ sostav naseleniia evropeĭskoĭ chasti Soiuza SSR* [Ethnic Composition of the Population of the European Part of the Union of SSR], Leningrad, Izdatel'stvo Akademii Nauk SSSR, 1930.

Shmurlo, E., *Le Saint-Siege et l'Orient Orthodoxe Russie, 1609-1654,* Prague, Orbis, 1928.

Shob, D., *Lenin,* New York, Doubleday and Company, 1948.

Shorichev, L. F., *Voprosy strategii i taktiki v trudakh I.V. Stalina perioda 1921-1925 godov* [Problems of Strategy and Tactics in the Writings of J. V. Stalin in the Period between 1921 and 1925], Moscow, Izdatel'stvo "Pravda," 1950.

Shuster, George N., *Religion behind the Iron Curtain,* New York, The Macmillan Company, 1954.

Smirnov, N. A., *Ocherki istorii izucheniia islama v SSSR* [An Outline History of Studies in Islam in the USSR], Moscow, Izdatel'stvo Akademii Nauk SSSR, 1954.

Spinka, Matthew, *Christianity Confronts Communism,* London, The Religious Book Club, 1938.

————, *The Church and the Russian Revolution,* New York, The Macmillan Company, 1927.

Spridovich, A. I., *Istoriia Bolshevizma v Rossii ot vozniknoveniia do zakhvata vlasti, 1883-1903-1917* [A History of Bolshevism in Russia from Its Inception Until Its Rise to Power, 1883-1903-1917], Paris, Franco-Russian Press, 1922.

Spuler, Bertold, *Die Gegenwartlage der Ostkirchen in ihrer völkischen und staatlichen Umwelt,* Wiesbaden, Metopen, 1948.

Stalin, Joseph, *Sbornik stateĭ* [A Collection of Articles], Moscow, Gosudarstvennoe Izdatel'stvo, 1920.

Stepanov, I., *The Problems and Methods of Anti-Religious Propaganda,* Moscow, Gospolitprosvet, 1923.

Stepun, F., *The Russian Soul and Revolution,* New York, Scribner and Sons, 1935.

Stepun, F., *Das Antlitz Russlands und das Gesicht der Revolution,* Bern, n.p., 1934.

Sultan-Galiev, M., *Metody antireligioznoĭ propagandy sredi musul'man* [Methods of Anti-Religious Propaganda among the Moslems], Moscow, 1922.

Sznuirson, Josef Icchak, *Di Jesurim fun Lubavicher Rebin in Soviet Rusland* [The Tortures of a Rabbi from Lubavich in Soviet Russia], Riga, 1930.

Timasheff, Nicholas S., *Religion in Soviet Russia, 1917-1942,* New York, Sheed and Ward, 1942.

————, *The Great Retreat; The Growth and Decline of Communism in Russia,* New York, E. P. Dutton and Company, Inc., 1946.

Titlinov, B., *Tserkov' vo vremia revoliutsii* [The Church During the Revolution], Petrograd, 1924.

Tobias, Robert, *Communist-Christian Encounter in East Europe,* Indianapolis, School of Religion Press, 1956.

Tokarzewski, Marjan, *Przyczynek do historji meczeństwa rzymsko—katolickiego w diecezjach kamienieckiej i Luck-Żytomierskiej (1863-1930 r.)* [Some Data on the History of the Roman-Catholic Martyrology in the Dioceses of Kamenets and of Lutsk and Zhitomir (1863-1930)], Luck, Drukarnia Kurji Biskupiej, 1931.

Torma, A., - Perlitz, H., *The Church in Estonia - The Fate of Religion and Church under Soviet Rule in Estonia, 1940-41,* New York, World Association of Estonians, 1944.

Trakiskis, A., *The Situation of the Church and Religious Practices in Occupied Lithuania;* Pt. I: *Under Soviet Occupation, 1940-41,* New York, Lithuanian Bulletin, 1944.

Trostsky, Leon, *The History of the Russian Revolution*, 3 vols., New York, Simon and Schuster, 1932; one-volume edition: London, Gollauch, 1934.

_____, *My Life*, New York, Charles Scribner's Sons, 1930.

Troitskiĭ, S., *Razmezhevanie ili raskol* [A Separation — or The Schism], Paris, YMCA Press, 1932.

Tyszkiewicz, S., *Sovetskoe Bezbozhie i papstvo* [The Soviet Godlessness and the Papacy], Rome, n.p., 1950.

Uïbo, A., *Iz istorii bor'by nauki protiv religii* [From the History of the Struggle of Science Against Religion], Moscow, Izdatel'stvo "Znanie," 1956.

Umiastowski, R., *Russia and the Polish Republic, 1918-1941*, London, Aquafondata, 1944.

Vaks, Bor., *Ot Oktiabria do Genui; Mezhdunarodnye otnosheniia R.S.F.S.R.; Spravochnik* [From October to Genoa; Foreign Relations of the R.S.F.S.R.; A Guide], Moscow, Izdatel'stvo Narodnogo Komissariata po inostrannym delam, 1922.

Valentinov, A. A., *The Assault of Heaven; A Collection of Facts and Documents Relating to the Persecution of Religion and Church in Russia Based Mainly upon Official Sources*, Berlin, Max Mattisson, Ltd., 1924.

_____, *Chernaia kniga ("Shturm nebes"); Sbornik dokumental'nykh dannykh, kharakterizuiushchikh bor'bu sovetskoĭ kommunisticheskoĭ vlasti protiv vsiakoĭ religii, protiv vsekh ispovedaniĭ i tserkveĭ* [The Black Book ("The Storming of the Heavens"); A Collection of Documentary Data, Characterizing the Struggle of the Soviet Communist Government Against All Religion, Against All Confessions and Churches], Paris, Izdanie Russkago Natsional'nago Studencheskago Obedineniia, 1925.

Vries, Wilhelm de, S.P., *Christentum in der Sowjetunion*, Heidelberg - Waibstadt, Kempert Verlag, 1950.

Il Cristianesimo nell'Unione Sovietica. Roma, La Civiltà Cattolica, 1948.

Vvedenskiĭ, A. I., *Tserkov' i gosudarstvo, 1918-1922* [Church and State, 1918-1922], Moscow, Mospoligraf, 1923.

Walsh, Edmund A., *Total Empire; The Roots and Progress of World Communism*, Milwaukee, The Bruce Publishing Company, 1951.

_____, *Why Pope Pius XI Asked Prayers for Russia on March 19, 1930; A Review of the Facts in the Case Together With Proofs of the International Program of the Soviet Government*, New York, The Catholic Near East Welfare Association, 1930.

_____, *The Fall of the Russian Empire*. Boston, Little, Brown & Co., 1927.

_____, *The Last Stand, An Interpretation of the Soviet Five Year Plan*. Boston, The Atlantic Monthly Press, 1933.

Wasilewski, Jan, *Arcybiskupi i administratorowie archidiecezji Mohylowskiej* [Archbishops and Administrators of the Archdiocese of Mogilev], Pinsk, 1930.

Wasilewski, Leon, *Kresy Wschodnie; Litwa i Bialorus; Podlasie i Chełmszczyzna; Galicya Wschodnia; Ukraina* [East Territories; Lithuania and Byelorussia; Podliashia and Khelm Region; East Galicia; Ukraine], Warsaw, Towarzystwo Wydawnicze, 1917.

Webb, Sidney and Beatrice, *Soviet Communism; A New Civilization?*, 2 vols. London, Longmans, Green, and Company, 1936.

Weiant, Edmund Taylor, *Sources of Modern Mass Atheism in Russia*, [Basel], n.p., [1950].

Zaïtsev, Kirill, Rev., *Pravoslavnaia tserkov' v Sovetskoĭ Rossii; Chast' pervaia: Vremia Patriarkha Tikhona; Nezavisimaia tserkov' v bezbozhnom gosudarstve* [Orthodox Church in Soviet Russia; Part One: The Times of Patriarch Tikhon; An Independent Church in An Atheistic State], Shanghai, Tipografiia "Zaria," 1947.

Yearbook of the American Jewish Committee. New York, 1920-1927.

ARTICLES

Akselrod, L. (Ortodoks), "Karl Marks i religiia" ["Karl Marx and Religion"], *Protiv idealizma; Kritika nekotorykh idealisticheskikh techenii filosofskoĭ mysli; Sbornik stateĭ* [Against Idealism; A Critique of Some Idealist Currents Of Philosophical Thought; A Symposium], 3d ed., Moscow, OGIZ, 1933, 64-74.

Brentano, H., "Zur Geschichte des Katholizismus in Russland," *Die Kultur,* IV (Vienna, 1906), 385-410.

Cabagi, Vasan Giray, "Sovetskiĭ Soiuz i islam" ["The Soviet Union and Islam"], *Vestnik Instituta po izucheniiu istorii i kul'tury SSSR* [Journal of the Institute for the Study of the History and Culture of the USSR], Munich, Buchdruckerei EINHEIT, 1954, No. 3(10), 42-55.

Chemko, J., "Pokhozhdeniia mitropolita Andreia grafa Sheptitskogo v Amerike" ["Adventures of Metropolitan Andres Cout Sheptitskii in America"], *Revoliutsiia i tserkov'* [Revolution and the Church], Nos. 1-3 (1922), 60.

"Demokratizatsiia Vatikana" ["The Democratization of the Vatican"], *Revoliutsiia i tserkov' [Revolution and the Church],* Nos. 3-5 (1919), 60.

Edlinskiĭ, Gr., "Uniia s Rimom i mitropolit graf Sheptitskii" ["The Union with Rome and Metropolitan Count Szeptycki"], *Revoliutsiia i tserkov'* [Revolution and the Church], Nos. 1-3 (1924), 108-109.

Elkin, A. S., "Iaroslav Galan - strastnyĭ borets protiv Vatikana" ["Iaroslav Galan As A Passionate Fighter Against the Vatican"], *Voprosy istorii religii i ateizma; Sbornik stateĭ* [Problems of the History of Religion and Atheism; A Symposium], Moscow, Izdatel'stvo Akademii Nauk SSSR, 1954, II, 245-275.

"Epizody pol'skoĭ voĭny" ["Episodes from the Polish War"], *Revoliutsiia i tserkov'* [Revolution and the Church], Nos. 9-12 (1920), 54-55.

Faizulin, G., "O poslednem svobodnom mufti Idel'-Urala" ["The Last Free Mufti of Idel-Ural"], *Vestnik instituta po izucheniiu istorii i kul'tury SSSR* [Journal of the Institute for the Study of the History and Culture of the USSR], Munich, Buchdruckerei EINHEIT, 1951, No. 1, 103.

——————, "The Persecution of the National-Religious Traditions of the Moslems in the USSR." *Caucasian Review,* No. 3 (1956), 69-76.

George, Andre, "Le proces de Mgr. Cieplak en Russie," *Correspondent,* CCLXXXXV (Paris, 1924), 532-536.

Gorev, Mikhail, "Vskrytie moshcheĭ Tikhona Zadonskogo i Mitrofana Voronezhskogo" ["The Opening of the Relics of Tikhon of Zadonsk and of Mitrophan of Voronezh"], *Revoliutsiia i tserkov'* [Revolution and the Church], No. 2 (1919), 9-23.

Grigorev, N., "Metropolitan Nikolaĭ Krutitsky," *Bulletin of the Institute for the Study of the USSR,* III (1956), May, 34-39.

Hanski, Pierre, "La tragedie de l'église Russe," *Etudes,* CLXXII (1922), 295-312.

Hermogen, *Archbishop,* "Vatikan i krestovye pokhody" ["The Vatican and the Crusades"], *Zhurnal Moskovskoĭ Patriarkhii* [Journal of the Moscow Patriarchate], (March, 1953), 58-64.

Iaroslavskii, Emelian, "Antireligioznaia propaganda v sovremennykh usloviiakh" ["Anti-Religious Propaganda Under the Present Conditions"], *Bolshevik,* Moscow, Izdatel'stvo "Pravada." 1937, No. 4.

——————, and Shvabe, M., "Antireligioznaia propaganda" ["Anti-Religious Propaganda"], *Bol'shaia Sovetskaia Entsiklopediia* [The Large Soviet Encyclopedia], 1st ed., Shmidt, O.Iu., ed., Moscow, Aktsionernoe Obshchestvo "Sovetskaia Entsiklopediia," 1926, III, 59-68.

Iuzufoglu, A., "Razgrom pravoslavnykh tserkveĭ i mecheteĭ v Sibiri" ["The Destruction of Orthodox Churches and Mosques in Siberia"], *Vestnik instituta po izucheniiu istorii i kul'tury SSSR* [Journal of the Institute for the Study of the History and Culture of the USSR], Munich, Buchdruckerei EINHEIT, 1954, No. 2(9), 110-113.

Ivanov, A., "Znachenie krestovykh pokhodov v razvitii vzaimootnoshenii mezhdu Pravolslavnym Vostokom i Katolicheskim Zapadom" ["Hhe Significance of Crusades in the Development of Mutual Relations between the Orthodox East and the Catholic West"], *Zhurnal Moskovskoĭ Patriarkhii* [Journal of the Moscow Patriarchate], February 1954, 39-46.

Karewicz, F., Archbishop, "Z dziejów pracy unijnej w Rosji" [From the Acts of the Unification Work in Russia"], *Kościół katolicki w Rosji; Materiały do jego historji i organizacji* [The Catholic Church in Russia; Materials on Her History and Organization], Warsaw, Secretariat of the Archbishop of Mogilev, 1932, 43-57.

Kirimal, E., "Kirimda Sovietlerin din siiaseti" ["Soviet Religious Policy in the Crimea"], *Dergi*, No.1 (1955), 55-67.

—————, "Polozhenie musul'manskoĭ religii v Krymu" ["The Moslem Religion in the Crimea"], *Vestnik instituta po izucheniiu istorii i kul'tury SSSR* [Journal of the Institute for the Study of the History and Culture of the USSR], Munich, Buchdruckerei EINHEIT, 1955, No. 2, 55-67.

Kishkovskii, A., "Marxism and Religion," *Bulletin of the Institute for the Study of the USSR*, III, No. 4 (April 1956), 21-29.

Kocharian, S., "Religion and Communism," *Caucasian Review*, No. 2 (1956), 64-73.

Kolpiński, Diodor, "Początki katolicyzmu wschodniego obrządku w Rosji" ["The Beginnings of Catholicism of the Eastern Rite in Russia"], *Kościół Katolicki w Rosji; Materiały do jego historji i organizacji* [The Catholic Church in Russia; Materials on Her History and Organization], Warsaw, Secretariat of the Archbishop of Mogilev, 1932.

Komorovskii, "Kul'turnye dostizheniia poliakov RSFSR," ["Cultural Achievements of the Poles in the RSFSR"], *Zhizn' natsional'nosteĭ* [The Life of Nationalities], January 1923, 232-233.

Kremer, Dr., "Vatikan i sovetskoe pravitel'stvo" ["The Vatican and the Soviet Government"], *Revoliutsiia i tserkov'* [Revolution and the Church), Nos. 1-2 (1924), 9-13.

Krushel, S., and Koreĭskiĭ, Iu., "Razgrom pravoslavnykh khramov v SSSR; Snesennye i zakrytye khramy v Khar'kove; Likvidatsiia tserkveĭ v Moskovskoĭ i Riazanskoĭ oblastiakh" ["The Destruction of the Orthodox Churches in the USSR; Churches Destroyed and Closed in Kharkov; The Destruction of Churches in Moscow and Riazan Regions"], *Vestnik instituta po izucheniiu istorii i kul'tury SSSR* [Journal of the Institute for the Study of the History and Culture of the USSR], Munich, Buchdruckerei EINHEIT, 1954, No. 4, 110-111.

Kulikowski, C., "Kościoły katolickie w Rosji w latach 1772-1922" ["Roman Catholic Churches in Russia, 1772-1922"], *Sacrum Poloniae Millenium*, v. II (1955), Rome; (Map and Statistics), p. 524.

Lenin, Vladimir I., "A. M. Gor'komu" ["To A. M. Gorky"], *Sochineniia* [Works], 4th edit., Moscow, Gosudarstvennoe Izdatel'stvo Politicheskoĭ Literatury, 1950, XXXV, 89-91. (Nov. 1913).

—————, "A. M. Gor'komu" ["To A. M. Gorky"], *Sochineniia* [Works], 4th edit. Moscow, Gosudarstvennoe Izdatel'stvo Politicheskoĭ Literatury, 1950, XXXV, 92-94. (Dec. 1913).

—————, "Dukhovenstvo i politika" ["The Clergy and Politics"], *Sochineniia* [Works], 4th ed., Moscow, OGIZ - Gosularstvennoe Izdatel'stvo Politicheskoĭ Literatury, 1948, XVIII, 283-284.

—————, "Dukhovenstvo na vyborakh i vybory s dukhovenstvom" ["The Clergy on Elections and Elections with Clergy"] *Sochineniia* [Works], 4th ed., Moscow, OGIZ - Gosudarstvennoe Izdatel'stvo Politicheskoĭ Literatury, 1948, XVIII, 313-315.

—————, "Klassy i partii v ikh otnoshenii k religii i tserkvi" ["Class and Parties in their Attitude to Religion and the Church"], *Sochineniia* [Works], 4th ed., Moscow, OGIZ - Gosudarstvennoe Izdatel'stvo Politicheskoĭ Literatury, 1947, XV, 382-390.

—————, "Liberaly i klerikaly" ["The Liberals and the Clericals"], *Sochineniia* [Works], 4th ed., Moscow, OGIZ - Gosudarstvennoe Izdatel'stvo Politicheskoĭ Literatury, 1948, XVIII, 204-205.

Lenin, Vladimir I., "Ob otnoshenii rabocheĭ partii k religii" ["Attitude of the Workers' Party toward Religion"], *Sochineniia* [Works], 4th ed., Moscow, OGIZ - Gosudarstvennoe Izdatel'stvo Politicheskoĭ Literatury, 1947, XV, 371 - 381.

—————, "O znachenii voinstvuiushchego materializma" ["The Significance of Militant Materialism"], *Sochineniia* [Works], 4th ed., Moscow, Gosudarstvennoe Izdatel'stvo Politicheskoĭ Literatury, 1950, XXXIII, 201-210.

—————, "Sotsializm i religiia" ["Socialism and Religion"], *Sochineniia* [Works], 4th ed., Moscow OGIZ - Gosudarstvennoe Izdatel'stvo Politicheskoĭ Literatury, 1947, X, 65-69.

—————, "Zadachi soiuzov molodëzhi; Rech' na III Vserossiĭskom Sezde Rossiĭskogo Kommunisticheskogo Soiuza Molodëzhi 2 oktiabria, 1920" ["The Tasks of the Youth Associations; An Address to the Third All Russian Congress of the Russian Young Communist League, October 2d, 1920"], *Sochineniia* [Works], 4th ed., Moscow, Gosudarstvennoe Izdatel'stvo Politicheskoĭ Literatury, 1950, XXXI, 258-275.

Lototskyi, Alexander, "Kościół rosyjski na drodze do rewolucji" [Russian Church on the Road to Revolution"], *Przegląd Współczesny* [The Contemporary Review], [Warsaw], 1938, No. 2.

—————, "Tserkovna sprava na Ukraïni" ["The Church Affairs in Ukraine"], *Literaturno-naukovyĭ visnyk* [Journal of Literature and Science], Lvov, Naukove Tovarystvo im. Shevchenka, 1923, V.

Lototskyi, Alexander, "Zagadnienie religijne v Z.S.S.R." ["The Religious Problem in the U.S.S.R."] *Przegląd Współczesny* [The Contemporary Review], [Warsaw], May 1932, No. 121.

Loster, Antoni, "Towarzystwa św. Wincentego a Paulo w Rosji" ["The Society of St. Vincent de Paul in Russia"], *Kościół Katolicki w Rosji; Materiały do jego historji i organizacji* [The Catholic Church in Russia; Materials on Her History and Organization], Warsaw, Secretariat of the Archbishop of Mogiley, 1932, 87-104.

Margolin, Iuliĭ, "Kak bylo likvidirovano sionistskoe dvizhenie v Sovetskoĭ Rossii" ["The Suppression of the Zionist Movement in Soviet Russia"], *Vestnik instituta po izucheniiu istorii i kul'tury SSSR* [Journal of the Institute for the Study of the History and Culture of the USSR], Munich, Buchdruckerei EINHEIT, 1934, No. 6, 90-111.

Mengli-Girai, G., Svoboda, P., and Galenkin, K. "Razrushenie i zakrytie khramov v SSSR" ["The Destruction and Closing of Churches in the USSR"], *Vestnik instituta po izucheniiu istorii i kul'tury SSSR* [Journal of the Institute for the Study of the History and Culture of the USSR], Munich, Buchdruckerei EINHEIT, 1945, No. 3, 104-107.

Meysztowicz, Walerian, "L'église Catholique," *Pologne*, 1919-1939, I (1946), 335-362.

—————, "Kościoly Katolickie ob. lac. na obszarach Rosji (1772-1914)" ["Catholic Churches of the Latin Rite on the Territory of Russia (1772-1914)"], *Sacrum Poloniae Millenium*, Rome, II (1955), 467-497.

Mikhaïlov, Andre, "Les origines anticatholiques du Bolchevisme," *Etudes,* CC (1929), 14-43.

Nikanov, V., "Rol' pravoslavnoĭ tserkvi v osvoboditel'noĭ voĭne ukrainskogo naroda" ["Rôle of the Orthodox Church in the Liberation War of the Ukrainian People"], *Zhurnal Moskovskoĭ Partiarkhii* [Journal of the Moscow Patriarchate], [Moscow], December 1953, 3-41.

Oleshchuk, F. N., "Voprosy ateisticheskoĭ propagandy v rabote V. I. Lenina 'O znachenii voinstvuiushchego materializma'" ["Problems of Atheistic Propaganda in V. I. Lenin's Work 'The Significance of Militant Materialism'"], *Voprosy istorii religii i ateizma; Sbornik stateĭ* [Problems of the History of Religion and Atheism; A Symposium], Moscow, Izdatel'stvo Akademii Nauk SSSR, 1954, II, 29-44.

Olino, A., "Likvidatsiia tserkveĭ v Irkutskoĭ oblasti" ["The Destruction of Churches in Irkutsk Region"], *Vestnik instituta po izucheniiu istorii i kul'tury SSSR* [Journal of the Institute for the Study of the History and Culture of the USSR], Munich, Buchdruckerei EINHEIT, 1956, No. 2, 111-114.

Olsr, Giuseppe, "Storia Religiosa," *Enciclopedia Cattolica*, X (1953), 1464-1466.

Orlovskiĭ, E., "Natsional'nyĭ vopros v Pol'she" ["The Nationality Problem in Poland"], *Zhizn' natsional'nosteĭ* [*The Life of Nationalities*], (1923, 139-146.

"Petlura and the Vatican," *Soviet Russia*, III (1920), 214-215.

Pipes, Richard E., "Russian Moslems Before and After the Revolution," in Gurian, Waldemar, ed., *Soviet Imperialism; Its Origins and Tactics*, [*A Symposium*], Notre Dame, Ind., University of Notre Dame Press, [1953], 75-90.

Ploskiewicz, Walery "Władza biskupów Rz.-katolichich w świetle prawodawstwa b. Imperjum Rosyjskiego" ["The Authority of the Roman-Catholic Bishops in the Light of Legislation of the Former Russian Empire"], *Kościół Katolicki w Rosji; Materiały do jego historji i organizacji* [The Catholic Church in Russia; Materials on Her History and Organization], Warsaw, Secretariat of the Archbishop of Mogilev, 1932, 71-79.

P., "Polonja na Dalekim Wschodzie" ["Polonia in the Far East"], *Przegląd powszechny* [The General Review], CLIX (1923), 281-284.

Poppe, N., "The Destruction of Buddhism in the USSR," *Bulletin of the Institute for the Study of the USSR*, III, No. 7 (July 1956), 14-20.

_____, "Polozhenie buddistskoĭ tserkvi v SSSR" [Buddhism in the USSR"], *Vestnik instituta po izucheniiu istorii i kul'tury SSSR* [Journal of the Institute for the Study of the History and Culture of the USSR], Munich, Buchdruckerei EINHEIT, 1954, No.5, 35-46.

"Prikhvostni pol'skikh panov" ["The Hangers-On of the Polish Lords"], *Revoliutsiia i tserkov'* [Revolution and the Church], Nos. 6-8 (1920), 102.

Saaruni, G., "Bor'ba Armianskoi tserkvi protiv bol'shevizma" ["The Struggle of the Armenian Church against Bolshevism"], *Vestnik Instituta po izucheniiu istorii i kul'tury SSSR* [Journal of the Institute for the Study of the History and Culture of the USSR], Munich, Buchdruckerei EINHEIT, 1951, No. 3.

Schmemann, Alexander, "The Church in Soviet Russia," *Proceeding of the Conference of the Institute for the Study of the History and Culture of the USSR*, New York - Munich, Münchener Buchgewerbehaus, G.m.b.H., March 20-22, 1953.

S. K., "Ukraińska prawosławna autokiefalna cerkiew," [The Ukrainian Orthodox Autocephalous Church"], *Sprawy Narodowościowe* [Nationalities' Affairs], I (1927), 63-64.

"Sovetskaia politika v religioznom voprose" ["Soviet Policy on Religious Question"], *Revoliutsiia i tserkov'* (Revolution and the Church], No. 1 (1919), 1-5.

Timasheff, N. S., "The Church in the Soviet Union," *The Russian Review*, I (1941), 20-30.

_____, "Gosudarstvo i tserkov' " ["The State and the Church"], *Pravo Sovetskoĭ Rossii* [The Law of Soviet Russia], Prague, 1925, I.

_____, "Religion in Russia, 1941 - 1950," in Gurian, Waldemar, ed., *The Soviet Union: Background, Ideology, Reality; A symposium*, Notre Dame, Ind., University of Notre Dame Press, 1951, 153-194.

Troitzky, S. "Pochemu zakryvaiutsia tserkvi v Rossii" ["Why the Churches in Russia Are Being Closed?"], *Put'* [The Way], Paris, Izdanie Religiozno-Filosofskoĭ Akademii, 1930, No. 23.

Urban, Jan, "Prace Jezuitów w Rosji" ["The Work of the Jesuits in Russia"], *Kościół Katolicki w Rosji; Materiały do jego historji i organizacji* [The Catholic Church in Russia; Materials on Her History and Organization], Warsaw, Secretariat of the Archbishop of Mogilev, 1932, 11-23.

Volkonsky, P. M., "Obrazovanie russkoĭ katolicheskoĭ tserkvi v Rossii" ["The Formation of the Russian Catholic Church in Russia"], *Katolicheskiĭ vestnik* [The Catholic Messenger], XI (Harbin, 1941), 154-159.

Walsh, Edmund A., "The Church in Contemporary Russia," *The Catholic Church in Contemporary Europe, 1919 - 1931,* New York, P. J. Kenedy and Sons, 1932, 212-292.

PERIODICALS

Antireligioznik [The Anti-Religious], Moscow, The Union of the Militant Godless, 1922.

Ateist [The Atheist], Moscow, 1921-1923.

Bezbozhnik [The Godless], Moscow, The Union of the Militant Godless, 1922-1926.

Bezvirnyk [The Godless], Kiev, 1922-1926.

Bol'shevik [The Boleshevik], Moscow, Central Committee of the Communist Party of the Soviet Union, 1924-1926.

Dziennik Petrogradzki [The Petrograd Daily], Petrograd, 1917.

Izvestiia, Moscow, 1919-1926.

Kommunist [The Communist] (Also *Komunar* [The Communist], Kharkov, and Kiev, Central Committee of the Communist Party (Bolsheviks) of Ukraine, 1919-1926.

Kurjer Polski [The Polish Courier], Warsaw, 1917-1923.

Kurjer Warszawski [The Warsaw Courier], Warsaw, 1917-1926.

Naród i państwo [The Nation and the State], Warsaw, 1918-1926.

New York Times, The, 1917-1926.

Osservatore Romano, Rome, 1917-1926.

Polska [Poland], Warsaw, 1918-1926.

Pravda [The Truth], Moscow, Central Committee of the Communist Party of the Soviet Union, 1917-1926.

Vestnik Vremennago Pravitel'stva [The Messenger of the Provisional Government], Petrograd, 1917.

Vidrodzhennia [The Revival], Kiev - Kamienets, The Ministry of Confessions, 1918-1920.

Visti, [The News], Kharkov - Kiev, 1918-1926.

Zhizn'natsional'nosteĭ [The Life of Nationalities], Moscow, 1918-1926.

Zhurnal Moskovskoĭ Patriarkhii [Journal of the Moscow Patriarchate], Moscow, 1918-1925.

INDEX